The U.S. Army
in the West,
1870–1880

THE U.S. ARMY IN THE WEST,

1870–1880

UNIFORMS, WEAPONS, AND EQUIPMENT

Douglas C. McChristian

Foreword by John P. Langellier

University of Oklahoma Press
Norman and London

On the facing page:
Seventh Cavalry soldiers, ca. 1875,
wearing cap insignia in manner that was
typical prior to general order of 1877.
Musician at left is wearing double trou-
sers stripes. (Little Bighorn Battlefield
National Monument)

Library of Congress Cataloging-in-Publication Data

McChristian, Douglas C.
    The U.S. Army in the west, 1870–1880 : uniforms, weapons, and
equipment / by Douglas C. McChristian.
      p. cm.
    Includes bibliographical references and index.
    ISBN 0-8061-2705-8
    1. United States. Army. Infantry—Equipment. 2. United States. Army. Infantry—
Uniforms. 3. West (U.S.)—History—1860–1890.
    I. Title.
    UD373.M33 1995
    356'.186'097309034—dc20   94-48216
                                                        CIP

Text design by Cathy Carney Imboden. Text typeface is Bembo.

The paper in this book meets the guidelines for permanence and durability of the Committee on
Production Guidelines for Book Longevity of the Council on Library Resources, Inc.♾

1 2 3 4 5 6 7 8 9 10

To Don Rickey

CONTENTS

ILLUSTRATIONS

Illustrations are from private collections unless otherwise indicated.

FOREWORD

By John P. Langellier

DURING THE LAST SEVERAL DECADES of the 1800s the subject of clothing and equipment was discussed among many officers and some enlisted personnel in the U.S. Army. Not only did the officials in the Ordnance Department and Quartermaster Corps, who were responsible for design, procurement, fabrication, and distribution of firearms, accoutrements, uniforms, and the like, have much to say on the matter, but so, too, did the rank and file who were issued these items.

Because of this widespread interest among American soldiers in the late nineteenth century, considerable information has survived for present-day researchers. Beginning in the 1950s, several individuals took advantage of the availability of such data; over the years they have produced a series of articles for the Company of Military Historians' journal, *Military Collector and Historian*.[1] Starting in the 1960s, the Arizona Historical Society offered several small but well-illustrated monographs, such as Sidney Brinckerhoff's work on military headgear in the Southwest followed later by his other monographs on metal uniform insignia and footgear.[2] In addition, Gordon Chappell's *Brass Spikes and Horsehair Plumes* and *Search for the Well Dressed Soldier* were published by Arizona, and the Wyoming Archives, Museums, and Historical Department released Chappell's summer helmet monograph.[3]

These works set the tone for good scholarship, excellent documentation, and useful pictorial material that was carried on in *They Continually Wear the Blue,* two catalogs from the Smithsonian Institution on their military headdress collections, and the fine treatment of chevrons for the Smithsonian by William Emerson.[4] In addition, a series of works on holsters and other accoutrements was released in more recent times and several reprints of regulations related to the uniform from 1847 through 1902 were produced by Jacques Noel Jacobsen's Manor Publishing.[5]

Despite the appearance of these works on limited subjects, no overview emerged treating the period between the end of the Civil War and the beginning of the Spanish American War. An ambitious multi-volume series by the Company of Military Historians ended its coverage with the period shortly after the Civil War and lacked notes.[6] Additionally, many of the illustrations were artists' conceptions rather than historical or modern photographs of specimens. Many of these same limitations are found in Randy Steffen's publications, which, although of considerable merit, relied solely upon the author's artwork.[7] While Steffen's drawings were of high quality, they often depicted material incorrectly, as did the text. In the latter instance Steffen relied heavily on general orders and regulations, which were frequently ignored or modified when it came to actual issuance of gear. Moreover, Steffen provided no notes.

Against this background, Douglas McChristian, a longtime student of the post–Civil War U.S. Army in the West, has assembled an impressive array of information—not only written documentation but also surviving specimens and photographic evidence from the nineteenth century. Of equal importance, he has been careful to cite his sources so that serious students can weigh his findings against their own research. The result of long years of labor in archives, museums, and private collections, this book is a must for curators, historians, and others who are interested in a concise, well-written, and professional synthesis of many elements of material culture for the U.S. Army during the mid-1860s through the early 1880s. The author builds upon previous publications while adding new information and insights. In so doing, McChristian has offered a worthy model for others who wish to continue the exploration of this topic.

PREFACE

THE DECADE OF THE 1870S was a pivotal era in the evolution of American military equipage. Several important boards were convened during those years to evaluate and recommend matériel best suited to accomplishing the army's then-current and projected missions. These resulted in major changes to clothing, arms, and other equipment.

This span of years also witnessed the last major operations against the Indians throughout the West. The unconventional nature and demands of Indian campaigning, as well as the extremes of environment peculiar to the trans-Mississippi, proved to be key factors influencing military clothing and accoutrements. Despite the realities of western service, however, the army as an organization was extremely conservative in such matters. This philosophy was manifested in the army's tendency to model its equipage and tactics after those of European powers. Thus, the progression of the army's material culture must be examined within the context of both the frontier experience and its self-perceptions at the time.

That this process continued during the following decade cannot be denied, though it decreased in scale and intensity. In fact, few items introduced after 1880 were of completely new design. The majority simply were refinements or modifications of similar articles having their origins in the previous decade.

Wherever it has been possible to do so, the equipage has been evaluated through the experiences of those best qualified to do so, the officers and soldiers themselves. I have attempted to employ as many firsthand narrative sources as possible, many of which are published here for the first time. These contemporary perspectives breathe life into what would otherwise be a sterile and overly technical presentation.

The parameters of this study are limited to identifying and codifying changes in the items used by the regular infantry and cavalry operating within the geographical confines of the trans-Mississippi region. Admittedly, nearly all the army's branches served in the West, but the infantry and the cavalry composed the primary garrisons of virtually all frontier posts in the interior. As combat arms, they were the ones who actively campaigned against the Plains Indians. Accordingly, these organizations were most influential in effecting changes to the various classes of equipage.

I have made no attempt to deal with horse equipments in this volume. Others, notably the late Randy Steffen, have published sound, comprehensive works on this subject, and I see no need to attempt any improvement on those efforts here.

The myriad changes witnessed in army equipage after the Civil War were of such overwhelming complexity and proportions that they have seemingly defied comprehensive analysis by historians. Over the years, numerous articles and monographs have addressed, in fragmented fashion, particular items and classes of material that appeared between the Civil War and the Spanish-American War. Today many, if not most, of these scholarly treatises are out of print, and many are difficult to locate.

This book consolidates into a cohesive presentation much of the essential information found in those sources. At the same time, I have supplemented this information with data resulting from my own research and have addressed some items in detail here for the first time, particularly infantry equipment. I owe much to the pioneer researchers in this field, the likes of James S. Hutchins, Gordon Chappell, Sidney Brinckerhoff, and others who truly broke the ground with their authoritative essays.

Many people have contributed to the preparation of this book. Heading the list are my respected colleagues Paul L. Hedren and Jerome A. Greene, who offered me encouragement and support to undertake this work. Jerry also generously allowed me to examine and photograph specimens in his own extensive military collection and offered many valuable suggestions for improving the manuscript.

The staffs of several institutions graciously assisted with my research over a number of years. Donald E. Kloster of the Armed Forces History Division, Smithsonian Institution, retrieved specimens, shared his knowledge, and provided key photographs. Mark Santiago and Jay Van Orden of the Arizona Historical Society facilitated the use of that institution's collections and arranged for original photography.

Others who helped in a variety of ways were the staff at the National Archives, Washington, D.C.; Michael J. McAfee, curator of the West Point Museum; Museum Director Terry Van Meter and his assistant Bill McKale of the U.S. Cavalry Museum, Fort Riley, Kansas; Stuart G. Vogt and William E. Meuse, both formerly curators at Springfield Armory National Historic Site; and Curator Elaine Harmon, former Curator Judy Hitzeman, and Historian Mary L. Williams at Fort Davis National Historic Site. Michael J. Winey, photographic archivist at the U.S. Army Military History Institute, was particularly helpful, as was Curator Kitty Deernose at Little Bighorn Battlefield National Monument. Ann Marie Baker of the Adams County Museum, Deadwood, South Dakota, generously made specimens available to me to photograph. Stephen Allie, director of the Frontier Army Museum at Fort Leavenworth, Luther Hanson at the U.S. Army Quartermaster Museum, Tom Tankersley at Yellowstone National Park, Lory Morrow and Becca Kohl at the Montana Historical Society, Venice Beske at the Wyoming State Library, Thomas A. Lindmier at the State of Wyoming Historic Sites Division, Historian James Ogden at Chickamauga-Chattanooga National Military Park, and Don McTernan at Springfield Armory National Historic Site all assisted me in obtaining photographs from their respective collections.

I cannot thank enough the many enthusiastic individuals, across the nation, who willingly opened their collections to me and shared their knowledge. I owe much to Dwight Clark, who went beyond the call in providing information and photographs of objects in his collection. I am equally indebted to Dennis L. Gahagen, who provided similar assistance and generously contributed his fine photographic essay on the 1870 St. Louis Board cartridge boxes. My special thanks go to Michael Ward for making me a guest in his home and giving me unrestricted access to his premier collection. Historian Jack McDermott allowed me to plumb his exhaustive files of historical material relating to the Indian wars.

Others who assisted me were J. Edward Green III, Glen Swanson, who provided copies of images unobtainable elsewhere, James "Putt" Thompson, Kurt Cox, Jason Pitsch, Tom Wilder, Dr. Sherry Smith, Don Troiani, Charles E. Luxmore, John A. Doerner, Roye D. Lindsay, and B. William Henry, Jr. I wish to acknowledge especially Hayes Otoupalik, collector, dealer, and peerless authority on militaria, who kindly placed his extensive photo files at my disposal. My sincere thanks to one and all.

I am grateful to artist and collector Ralph Heinz for sharing his *Allen Creek*, used as the jacket art.

I am particularly indebted to a select group of historians and subject-matter experts. All gave unselfishly of their time to critically review the manuscript and to provide insightful, constructive comments. Among these are Dr. John P. Langellier, historian and a foremost scholar on army uniforms; historians Douglas D. Scott and Don Rickey; Dick Harmon, an authority on antique firearms; and Bill Phillips, longtime student of army accoutrements.

I would be remiss if I failed to acknowledge William K. Emerson and Michael J. Winey, who served as the University of Oklahoma Press's official reviewers. They devoted much time and effort to submit thoughtful, objective comments for improving the final manuscript; they will recognize the result of many of their comments in the published work.

Finally, I owe my greatest debt to Mary, my wife and friend. She assisted me, tolerated my obsession, and made many sacrifices so that I might complete this project.

DOUGLAS C. MCCHRISTIAN

Hardin, Montana

THE U.S. ARMY
IN THE WEST,
1870–1880

INTRODUCTION

WRITING FROM THE HEADQUARTERS of the Thirteenth Infantry in 1875, Colonel Philip Regis De Trobriand observed, "It is a remarkable fact, that the whole story of modern accoutrements can be summed up as a long and obstinate fight between the military governments and authorities, which will persist in loading the soldiers, and the soldiers who will still more obstinately persist in unloading themselves."[1] His statement captured the essence of the army's struggle to develop equipage for its far-flung forces during the Indian campaigns. The army struggled within its own bureaucracy to provide what it deemed best for its troops, whereas the soldiers themselves, seeking more practical solutions, exercised their initiative by obtaining what the army either overlooked or refused to issue.

For thirty years following the Civil War the U.S. Army was preoccupied, philosophically at least, with preparing itself for the next conventional war. Yet, few real preparations were made for that contingency in view of the prevailing isolationist doctrine then dominating the nation's foreign affairs. Suffering from conflicting identities, the army viewed itself as a conventional military force, improving its professionalism through education in the military sciences and emulating the great European powers. In reality, though, the army found itself employed as a frontier constabulary pitted against the highly unconventional Plains Indians.

After four years of the bloodiest fighting ever seen on this continent, the people and Congress were tired of war and everything relating to the military. Congress, in traditional peacetime stance, was opposed to a large military establishment, an attitude manifested in the niggardly appropriations for the army. National attention was focused on expanding industrialism, reconstructing the South, exploiting the West, and in the process, fulfilling the national quest of Manifest Destiny. With literally tons of matériel left over from the war, there was little interest or support for expending funds on new supplies for the army.

Although the Quartermaster General's Office had predicted that the war surplus would outfit the army for many years to come, it failed to take into account that much of the clothing was stored in inadequate warehouses scattered throughout the East. Moths and mildew ravaged the available matériel faster than it could be issued to the troops. To make matters worse, this clothing was adapted largely to the environmental conditions found in the East. Even at that, it consisted of only the basic necessities. There were few specialty items, and seasonal uniforms were hardly conceived of, much less issued.

In addition, the individual equipments that had seen the Union Army through the war were constructed largely of leather, with a few items, such as haversacks and knapsacks, being made of a combination of leather and canvas. Their basic design was little advanced over what the army had been issuing for decades. These were heavy, cumbersome accoutrements designed for conventional warfare on eastern battlefields and specifically for use with percussion-primed weapons. However, the technological advances made during the war led to the invention of breech-loading weapons using metallic cartridges. Shortly after the end of the war, some of these designs were adopted by the army, with little or no forethought as to how the new arms would affect related equipments. The soldier soon found himself with a variety of accoutrements that were incompatible with his weapons.

By the 1870s, opinion divided between what the rank-and-file frontier soldier needed to accomplish the job and what the army staff branches thought he needed. This philosophy manifested itself, for instance, in the Ordnance Department's penchant for burdening the soldier with European-style equipments and was paralleled by the adoption of long-range single-shot arms. Moreover, the Quartermaster General's staff persistently designed uniforms aimed more at satisfying parade-ground splendor than at providing for practicality in the trans-Mississippi West.

Central to this conflict was the army's organizational structure at the time, which proved to be as much a hindrance to the process as was the high command's reluctance to accept new ideas. Through a quirk in the War Department's organization, the commanding general of the army was responsible for the discipline and military control of the army line branches—infantry, cavalry, and artillery. He answered directly to the president and thus was given the advantage of being able to wield considerable power over army affairs.

Conversely, the chiefs of the various staff bureaus were under the control of the secretary of war, who was responsible for political, fiscal, and administrative affairs. Thus, the Ordnance and Quartermaster departments, charged with supplying the army's material needs, fell under the purview of the secretary. When the bureau chiefs had strong ideas regarding equipage, or were otherwise motivated to approve certain items, they had only to convince the secretary and find the necessary funding to implement their ideas. In those instances, the army line had little control over the activities of the staff branches; thus its influence on the development of arms, clothing, and equipments used by the troops was limited.

Nevertheless, attempts were occasionally made to bridge this gulf by the appointment of ad hoc boards composed of line officers. These boards were charged with reviewing and offering recommendations on the various items of current issue, along with samples submitted from both government shops and civilian inventors. In many instances, the officers serving on the boards lacked the requisite frontier service. These boards more often than not tended to rely on conventional military doctrine, to the soldier's detriment.

This situation may be attributed, at least in part, to an attitude prevailing among some individuals in the officer corps who felt that Indian campaigning hardly qualified as real warfare. By comparison with the recent rebellion, the sporadic and short-lived campaigns against the western Indians were perceived as hardly more than a nuisance, at least to the uninitiated. Those older officers who had served through the Civil War often viewed them as anticlimactic, thankless, and more often than not, an unwelcome interruption in the routine of garrison life. Although the Indian wars provided some degree of experience for the younger officers commissioned after the war, few saw them as contributing significantly to the military expertise needed for the next conventional conflict. From the bottom to the top of the army's chain of command, the Indian campaigns were viewed as isolated events of fleeting duration, with each incident viewed as being the last. As so aptly expressed by historian Robert M. Utley, "The frontier not only failed as a training ground for orthodox wars, it positively unfitted the Army for orthodox wars."[2] Just as this had been true in 1861, it was even more painfully evident when the nation went to war with Spain in 1898.

The army's service on the western frontier did have a positive, long-term influence on the soldier's clothing and equipment. Certainly, the army had experienced the environment of the trans-Mississippi before the Civil War, but this rather limited exposure had little impact on the development of equipage because of the relatively small numbers of troops stationed on the frontier. Accoutrements remained unchanged, whereas developments in specialized clothing primarily were unofficial adaptations to local conditions. But this changed by the 1870s, when the bulk of the army's manpower was shifted to the West. The number of posts increased with the expansion of the railroads, mail routes, and settlement and with the establishment of Indian reservations. Soon troops were scattered from the Mississippi to the Pacific coast and from the Canadian border to the Rio Grande.

Service on the windswept high plains and the torrid southwestern deserts exposed soldiers to temperatures varying from summer highs of 120 degrees to winter extremes of 60 degrees below zero. The entire spectrum could be experienced within a single year at some stations. In certain parts of the West it was not unusual to experience a 50-degree temperature fluctuation within a twenty-four-hour period. Added to this were wind, rain, snow, and everything in between. Although the army staff had its ideas as to what constituted the proper equipage of the "modern" soldier, the rank-and-file regular nevertheless adapted quite readily to the special requirements imposed by the frontier. Above all, he was highly selective in using only those articles of army issue that suited his needs. Beyond those, he ingeniously altered items or simply fabricated essential gear not supplied by the army.

In the end, the army's frontier experience significantly influenced the evolution of American military equipments and clothing. The Indian wars in the West and the resourcefulness of the American soldier proved a unique combination to fuel this progression. At the same time, the industrial revolution produced great technological advances in the manufacture of clothing and ordnance of all kinds. Many of the developments of this era set army precedents that lasted well into the twentieth century. Although additional items were developed before the curtain closed on the Indian wars, most of the equipage used by the army as it sailed for Cuba in 1898 either had been adopted in the 1870s or had evolved in modified form from those items. In hindsight, the decade of the 1870s marked a turning point in the army's equipage. These changes would characterize it as a uniquely American force for decades to come.

A Problem of Morale

The War Surplus, 1865–1871

WITHIN JUST FOUR YEARS after the shelling of Fort Sumter, the Union army had swelled to more than one million blue-clad men. Supplying this immense force with its many necessities was a task of unprecedented magnitude. It was a job Quartermaster General Montgomery C. Meigs accomplished with phenomenal success (fig. 1). By 1865, government warehouses throughout the North literally bulged with supplies amassed during the conflict. With the end of the war and the consequent reduction of the army to a peacetime force of fifty-six thousand men, most supply contracts were canceled forthwith.

Meigs was compelled to change priorities quickly. During the war years his department had endeavored to establish a network of manufacturers who could provide the clothing and equipment necessary to conduct the war. Now, however, Meigs turned his attention to preserving this enormous surplus for future use. He perceived the Quartermaster Department's postwar mission primarily as one of warehousing and preservation, rather than the development of supply sources. Designing new clothing for the army was yet beyond his comprehension. Both Meigs and the war-weary Congress felt that the surplus was adequate for supplying the regular army for many years to come. Justifiably proud of the military supply system he had engineered, Meigs considered the clothing to be more than adequate, both in quality and in quantity, for the soldiers who would now be chasing Indians in the Far West.

General Meigs was quickly disillusioned. No sooner had the regular army replaced the volunteer troops on the frontier than complaints were voiced about the mediocre quality of the uniform items when exposed to the rigors of western service. No doubt these shortcomings would have revealed themselves sooner or later, but the end of the contract system negated any legal recourse the army might have had.

The problems stemmed from several sources. Contractors were at times unable to meet the government specifications either for lack of standard materials and dyes or because of time constraints in meeting their obligations. Some government inspectors, pressured by the exigencies of wartime production, overlooked flaws in materials and workmanship, thereby passing contract goods that would never have been accepted during peacetime. Taking advantage of these circumstances, some unscrupulous contractors intentionally defrauded the government by taking production shortcuts and utilizing inferior materials. Whatever deficiencies this clothing may have had went largely unnoticed because

On the facing page:

1. Brigadier General Montgomery C. Meigs, who served as the quartermaster general of the army from May 15, 1861, until his retirement on February 6, 1882. During his tenure, the army witnessed the enormous logistical challenges of the Civil War and most of the western Indian campaigns. (National Archives) either soldiers did not wear it for long periods of time (for any number of reasons) or their complaints went unheard amid the din of war. Much of this contract-manufactured matériel was placed in storage, where it lay until several years later, and only then were the flaws discovered.[1]

Unfortunately for the regulars, these shoddy, ill-fitting goods were shipped to frontier posts where soldiers had no choice but to accept them. One of the chief complaints heard from company officers was the lack of consistency in the color of the uniforms. Even in a single company formation, the variety of shades of blue could be astonishing. In a letter to the *Army and Navy Journal,* one soldier vividly expressed his discontent with the wartime clothing: "The old uniform manufactured during the war is certainly—to use a mild expression, a 'sham.' Scarcely any two garments are the same color, especially coats, pants, and blouses. In a lot of a hundred pairs of pants there are often found all shades from a deep to a pale muddy blue, while the uniform coats and blouses range from gray-green to black."[2]

Another scam used by contractors was to label the garments improperly as being sizes larger than they actually were. In this way they could get by with using less material, which proved significant when making several thousand pieces. If the inspectors were not vigilant, or perhaps were corrupt themselves, the error would go undetected until a soldier attempted to wear the clothing. Colonel Innis N. Palmer, commanding Fort Laramie, Wyoming Territory, in 1867, vigorously protested that the clothing received there ran about two sizes smaller than marked. Consequently, most of the items were so small that they would not fit anyone in the garrison.[3] Another officer lamented, "The miserable tissues furnished the army call very loudly for some substitute."[4]

These inferior goods were as costly as they were a nuisance to the rank and file. The soldier was allowed a fixed number of each item (caps, blouses, trousers, and the like) for each year of his enlistment. The monetary value of the individual articles was established by a general order, annually, the total for each year forming the soldier's uniform allowance. When he drew less than his yearly allowance, the credit was added to that of the following year. Exceeding his allowance, the soldier was charged the balance due against his final pay at discharge.[5] Depending on how judiciously he managed this allowance, the soldier might come out with a net profit, or loss, at the end of his enlistment. Needless to say, a great many soldiers who served during the late 1860s wound up owing the government because the wretched clothing either wore out rapidly or simply fell to pieces, forcing them to draw more than their allowance covered.

Additionally, much of the clothing simply did not fit. One curmudgeon in the ranks scoffed, "No Government clothing . . . was ever known to fit properly a man of natural or undeformed proportions."[6] In every company one man, usually someone with prior experience as a tailor in civilian life, was assigned to alter the clothing of his comrades, for a fee. Since the costs of altering clothing came from the soldier's own pocket, this arrangement was grossly unfair. Although some soldiers, particularly the noncommissioned officers, preferred to have their uniforms specially tailored, most of the men considered the company tailors to be no more than a necessary evil. Choosing to have a uniform tailored to a perfect fit was one thing, but hackles were raised throughout the army when the men were forced to spend their own meager pay simply to get the clothes to fit at all.

Reacting to these complaints, Surgeon General Joseph K. Barnes was prompted to investigate the situation from a hygienic perspective. In August 1867 he issued a directive requesting all post surgeons to give their opinions about the quality and suitability of the issue clothing at their respective stations. Early the following year, Alfred A. Woodhull, an officer who was destined to become one of the army's most ardent champions for medical reform, compiled the submissions in a published report. In his opening remarks, Assistant Surgeon Woodhull wrote:

> Assuming that no change in the kind or quality of clothing now prescribed is attainable, the most general complaint is its quality. The same article appears to vary in character at different posts, but each is condemned by some one or another, and the more important by nearly all. Equally prominent is the shameful carelessness in the cut and make. It has even been suggested that the original standards have been lost, so far do the articles issued depart from the wants of the men. All who allude to it regard it as a serious hygienic defect that the men cannot be reasonably comfortable, until the clothing provided by the government is re-made or substituted by other at their personal (and often great) expense . . . it is condemned by nearly every one.[7]

Despite official recognition of the problem, and the anticipation that something would be done to correct it, nothing happened.

The clothing worn by the frontier regulars during the latter years of the decade was, with few exceptions, drawn from the surplus stock. The garments not only were of dubious quality but also were poorly adapted to western conditions. In the West, extremes in weather were more pronounced, topography was harsher, and the demands of military service were generally greater than in the East, with the men performing much rough outdoors work in the West. The amount of physical labor led soldiers to refer to themselves as "armed laborers" and was also the origin of the soldier slang term "government workhouse," meaning a fort.[8] The Quartermaster Department expected the men to make do with clothing that had been at least acceptable during the war. But, few officials in Washington were familiar with living in regions where the mercury soared to well over one hundred degrees in the summer, then plummeted to perhaps fifty degrees below zero during the winter.

The standard uniform coat for infantry soldiers was a dark-blue woolen, single-breasted frock that had been adopted in 1857. Reflective of civilian styles of the mid-nineteenth century, it was rather snugly fitted in the body and had long skirts (fig. 2). The unhemmed skirt, according to regulations, was to extend "one-half the distance from the top of the hip to the bend of the knee."[9] The coat had nine brass general-service buttons down the front, with the collar and cuffs trimmed with welts of sky-blue cloth. Actually, the cuffs were separately applied, with the piping let into the seam thus formed.

Both field and band musicians wore coats decorated with worsted lace "herringbone" across the chest area. These facings, termed "blind buttonholes," extended outward from each button, the lengths increasing progressively to the middle of the chest, then narrowing toward the waist (fig. 3). The outer ends of the herringbones were framed by a border of like material. Although some units had worn the uniform coat exclusively during the war, as was prescribed by regulations, most of the regulars in the West found it too heavy and hot with its padded chest, high collar, and long skirts. Woodhull reported:

2. Noncommissioned officers of the Eigh-teenth U.S. Infantry, ca. 1866, wearing the uniform frock adopted in 1857. They display a mixture of regulation and private-purchase forage caps. All are armed with the Springfield rifled musket. (Fort Laramie National Historic Site, National Park Service)

On the facing page:
3. Infantry musician, ca. 1866. Cavalry musicians wore similar "herringbone" braid on their jackets. (Smithsonian Institution)

The present tight-fitting, wadded uniform coat receives estimates varying with the location, but for use through all seasons objection is found by almost every reporter. . . . The primary, radical and insuperable objection to the coat is the tightness of its fit, which involves an almost unvarying amount of clothing throughout the year and renders excessive muscular action almost impracticable. . . . Notorious experience had illustrated the impossibility of fatigue or campaign duty in such a costume.[10]

Consequently, the frock usually was reserved as a full-dress coat to be worn for parades and guard duty. When used for this purpose, the coat was adorned with two detachable brass epaulets, or "scales," as they were known. These were made in three patterns, one for privates and corporals, another with larger crescents for sergeants, and a third with roundheaded rivets on the scallops for regimental and general staff noncoms (fig. 4). Serving no practical function, they were heartily disliked by the soldiers, who had to keep them polished to a high luster. The scales were attached to the uniform by thin brass straps, or springs, on the undersides; the straps passed through flat brass staples, sewn

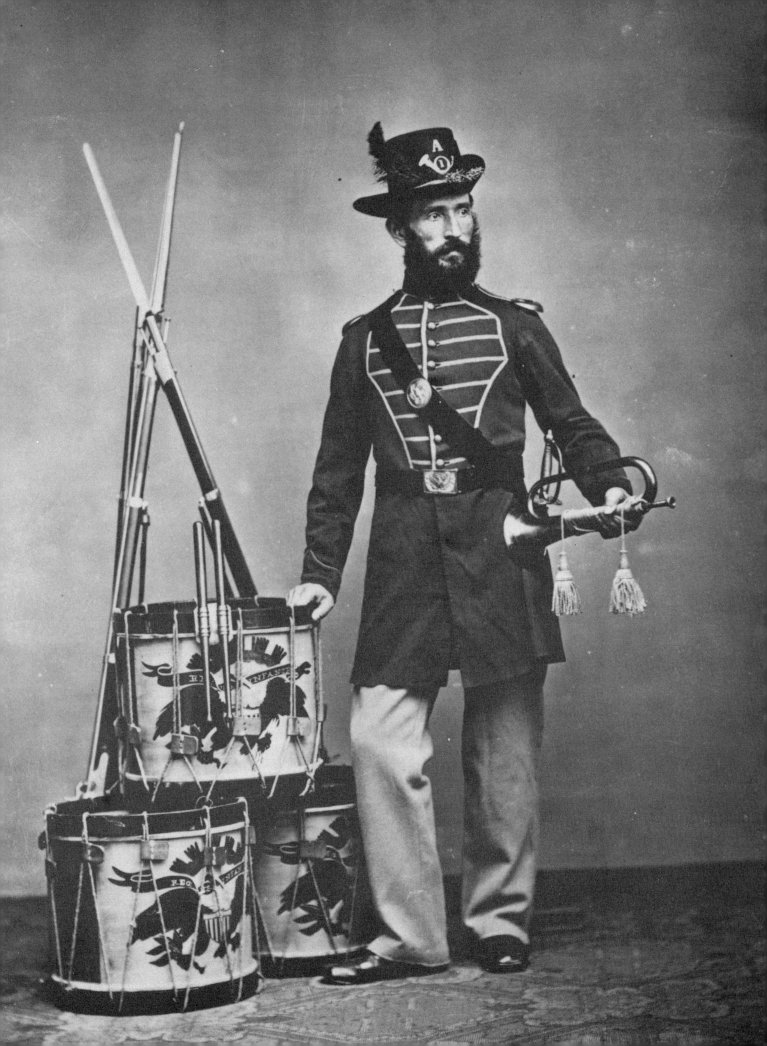

4. Members of the Thirty-sixth Infantry's regimental noncommissioned staff wearing full-dress uniform, including distinctive shoulder scales, swords, and sword belts with sashes. (Fort Laramie National Historic Site, National Park Service)

above each shoulder seam. The end of the strap next to the neck was held down by a small turnkey stitched to the coat.

Commissioned personnel of all branches wore a pattern of frock coat similar to the enlisted version. Officers, however, were obligated to purchase their own clothing from private vendors; therefore, most of these frocks were made of exceptionally fine quality dark-blue broadcloth. The moderately high stand-up collar sometimes was lined with black velvet. The uniforms for captains and lieutenants were single-breasted with nine eagle buttons, whereas those for all higher grades were double-breasted. The uniforms of majors and colonels were distinguished by having seven buttons, evenly spaced, in each row. All these uniforms were similar in that the 2½-inch cuffs were turned up and fastened by three small eagle buttons along the under seam. At the rear of the waist seam were two large eagle buttons above the folds of the skirts. Concealed within these folds were bag pockets on each side, the lower ends of the openings also being trimmed with one button each.

Officers' buttons, incidentally, were somewhat larger in size and generally were of finer quality and detail than those of enlisted men. Besides being gilt-plated, they bore the branch letter, either *I* or *C*, within the shield on the eagle's breast.[11]

Cavalrymen were issued a uniform jacket of European influence, similar jackets being worn by both the British and the French cavalry in the mid-nineteenth century (fig. 5). The jacket was intended to serve for both dress and field. Although widely known today as a "shell jacket," it was actually a longer version of a true shell, which reached only to the waist. The American pattern was made longer both front and rear to fit over the hips so as not to ride up above the trousers, as the traditional shell jacket was inclined to do. The cavalry jacket was made of dark-blue wool uniform cloth with twelve cuff-size brass eagle buttons in a single row down the front to maintain the jacket's close fit. Yellow worsted lace extended around the top and bottom of the collar, down the front closure, and around the waist. Each cuff had an inverted "V" of the same lace. On both sides of the standing collar were two blind buttonholes of lace, each terminating with a small eagle button. The two curved back seams were also covered with yellow lace, and at each lower end was a small stuffed-cloth belt supporter intended to help carry the considerable weight of the saber and belt, revolver, and ammunition. These supporters also prevented the untidy appearance caused when the tail of the jacket rode up over the belt. However, it was not uncommon for soldiers to remove these useless appendages, sometimes known in soldier slang as "bounty jumpers," either because they ripped off under the weight of the belt or because they were uncomfortable to the soldier while sleeping on the ground in the field.[12]

The regulations called for a body lining of white flannel, but most examples have a mixed tan-and-white woolen fabric. Less frequently, others are seen with a lining of plaid cotton material, sometimes called "hickory." Sleeves were lined with natural muslin. A large inside pocket usually was let into the lining over the left breast.

Beginning in 1858 the infantry had been authorized to wear a hat similar to that adopted for the mounted units three years earlier. Made of black felt, it had a 6¼-inch high, flat-topped crown reminiscent of the hats worn by the nation's Puritan founders (fig. 6). The left side of the brim was to be worn hooked up by a stamped-brass eagle insignia. In mounted units the regulations called for the right side to be folded up, ostensibly so that it would not interfere with use of the saber. Some infantry officers, however, complained that executing the "carry" and the "right shoulder" in the manual of arms caused the men to either tilt their heads to one side or to have their hats disarranged by their rifles. To

5. Third Cavalrymen wearing regulation uniform jackets and 1855-pattern saber belts. Note the shorter collars on the jackets of the men standing. These may have been modified for greater comfort or may represent the so-called St. Louis Depot pattern, which was made with only one, rather than two, blind buttonholes. (Wyoming State Archives & Historical Department)

avoid the problem, it became common in some infantry units to hook up the right side instead of the left.[13]

In addition to the eagle insignia worn by both infantry and cavalry, distinctive branch insignia were authorized to be worn on the front of the hat. Infantrymen wore a stamped-brass bugle, or "looped hunting horn" inspired by the French *votigeurs*, with the regimental number frequently placed within the bend and with the company letter above (fig. 7). Enlisted cavalrymen sported crossed sabers, blades up, with both the unit number and the company letter placed above the sabers (fig. 8).[14] The insignia were attached by means of brass wire loops soldered to the backs. Leather keys were used to fasten the devices yet permit their removal for polishing. However, the insignia were all made of such thin brass that one officer rated them little better than pasteboard and hardly worth the effort to put on the hat.[15] These trimmings were topped off with a tasseled worsted hat cord, yellow for cavalry and blue for infantry.

"The condemnation of the hat . . . is all but universal," Woodhull noted. The problems included "its size and great weight and want of ventilation."[16] Beyond that, it looked decidedly unmilitary on the heads of most men. One soldier described it as "the most ugly, uncomfortable, and unsoldierly covering that a malignant mind could have devised for the heads of suffering humanity."[17] It also was annoyingly vulnerable to prairie winds. The most solemn and precise guard mounting could be completely shattered when an inopportune gust whirled through the formation, sending hats tumbling across the parade ground. In the Department of the Platte, noted for it strong winds, Brigadier General C. C. Augur unilaterally resolved the problem by issuing orders permitting the forage cap to be worn with the dress coat at all of the posts under his command.[18] Possibly, other commanders took similar action. Most soldiers favored the forage cap as everyday headgear, though the cap issued by the Quartermaster Department was often ill-fitting and of mediocre quality.[19] It was made of dark-blue wool broadcloth with a thin, tarred-leather visor (fig. 9). On the front of the cap, above the visor, was a leather chin strap (similarly coated), which was adjusted with a brass slide and which was fastened at either end by a small regulation eagle button. The high crown, cut longer in back and lined with brown or black glazed cotton, was unstiffened so that it flopped forward. A circular piece of pasteboard covered with cloth formed the top. Woodhull wrote:

The objections to the cap are, the difficulty of cleansing with soap and water, owing to the pasteboard it contains, the interference of the oblique visor with vision, its want of grip, for the northern stations in winter its want of warmth, the deficient protection it affords the face and neck against sun and rain in any climate, and especially, the absence of ventilation and the transmission of solar heat by its resting directly upon the top of the head—an evil that is aggravated by its color.[20]

6. Pattern 1858 uniform dress hat for cavalry. (Hayes Otoupalik Collection)

On the facing page:
7. Infantryman wearing the regulation full-dress uniform, including hat with prescribed trimmings. (Smithsonian Institution)

There was little consistency in the manner of wearing the insignia on the forage cap. Some units wore only the company letter on the front of the cap, according to regulations, though this often proved impractical because the crowns of many of the contract caps fell so far forward that the letter could not be seen. Photographic evidence suggests that many soldiers wore the branch insignia atop the crown and that others displayed the branch device along with letter and number. Still others used no insignia at all. The most that can be said is that no particular arrangement predominated.

The most common outer garment worn by frontier soldiers of all branches was the sack coat, adopted in 1858 solely as a fatigue jacket. However, it was much easier and cheaper to manufacture than the uniform coat. The sack coat proved extremely popular with troops during the Civil War because of its simplicity and comfort. Reflective of the common workingman's clothing of the period, it was made of dark-blue flannel with four large eagle buttons down the front (fig. 10). The body was cut full and was authorized in both lined and unlined versions. Both styles had a large pocket inside the left breast. Like most of the contract clothing, the coats varied in the lining, but a common lining was the brown-and-white checked cotton material also seen in cavalry jackets. Schuylkill Arsenal, the government's own clothing factory, employed a lining of rather heavy, brownish-colored flannel. The sleeves also were lined with muslin. According to army regulations, the lined version was intended only for recruits. Although the reasoning behind this is unclear, the statement has led to a generally accepted belief that the unlined sack coat was the most common form. However, this is not borne out in annual inventories published by the Quartermaster General's Department or in records of issues shipped to posts in the late 1860s.[21] The two types appear to have been made and issued in nearly equal quantities. Considering that virtually all subsequent patterns of blouses adopted by the army during the period were made in both lined and unlined versions, as a small concession to varying climates, it seems entirely reasonable to assume that the sack coat was no exception.

On the frontier the regulars wore the sack coat almost exclusively for all duties, except dress occasions. The blouse was a more comfortable and practical

Above:

8. Typical officer's dress hat of the 1860s, complete with embroidered insignia, cords, and plume. (Hayes Otoupalik Collection)

Below:

9. Regulation-issue 1858-pattern forage cap worn by enlisted men of all branches for general garrison duties and preferred by some for field service. (Hayes Otoupalik Collection)

On the facing page:

10. Soldiers at Fort Sumner, New Mexico, wearing 1858-pattern sack coats. (Courtesy Museum of New Mexico, Neg. No. 28537)

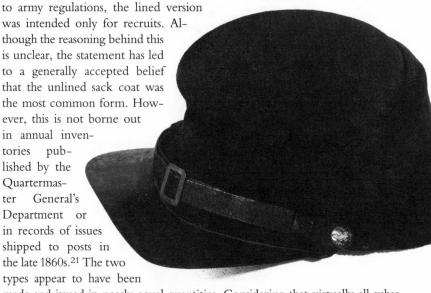

garment than either the dress coat or the cavalry jacket. Its only real flaw, besides a rather slouchy appearance, was the loosely woven material, which permitted dust and grime to accumulate in the fibers. Consequently, soldiers had to have the blouses (and trousers, for that matter) washed frequently to keep them clean, whereas closely woven cloth would have allowed brush-cleaning rather than washing. Repeated abuse in the washtubs soon took its toll by shortening the life of the garments.[22]

For field duty, commissioned officers frequently discarded their impractical frocks in favor of either issue-grade or commercially produced versions of the sack coat (fig. 11). The privately purchased sacks often were longer than the issue style, sometimes reaching nearly to the knee, but still having only four eagle buttons. Occasionally they were trimmed around the collar and the front opening with black mohair braid.[23]

According to regulations, cavalry officers were permitted to wear "a plain dark blue cloth jacket, with one or two rows of buttons down the front, according to rank," for stable duty.[24] Not surprisingly, many officers used these jackets, or something similar, for field service. No doubt, some of these garments were nothing more than cut-down dress frocks. In some instances, according to photographic evidence, officers adopted the enlisted mounted uniform jacket, with the standing collar either reduced in height or replaced entirely with a falling collar.[25]

Officer rank was indicated by straps of branch-colored wool bordered by gilt worn on each shoulder next to the seam. Within the border of each strap was a device denoting the particular rank. A spread eagle identified a colonel, whereas a lieutenant colonel had silver leaves at each end of the strap. Majors had gold leaves, captains two bars at each end, and first lieutenants a single bar at each end. The straps of a second lieutenant were simply left plain.

Chevrons for noncommissioned officers were made of separate one-half-inch stripes of worsted lace for company grades and silk for staff sergeants; the stripes were sewn on dark-blue wool backing to match the uniform. Sky blue denoted infantry; chevrons for cavalry were yellow. They were to be worn points down above the elbows on both sleeves of the dress coat and the overcoat. The sack coat was omitted from chevron regulations because it was intended to be used only for fatigue. In practice, however, this point of the regulations universally was ignored, since the sack was the everyday uniform throughout the army.

Corporals wore two bars, sergeants three, and orderly or first sergeants three with a diamond cradled in the angle. Each regimental headquarters had one quartermaster sergeant, identified by three bars with a tie of three straight bars, and a sergeant major, designated by three bars surmounted by an arc of three stripes.

For each five-year period of service, veterans wore branch-colored half-chevrons diagonally on both sleeves of the dress coat just above the points of the cuff trim. Those who had served during a recognized war were authorized to wear, in lieu of the peacetime chevron, a special red stripe three-quarters of an inch wide, with a one-half-inch wide overlay of the appropriate branch color.

Army trousers, Pattern 1861, were made of heavy sky-blue wool kersey, with pockets and waistband lining of unbleached drill (fig. 12).[26] Plain two-piece pressed-tin buttons were used for the waist fastening, suspenders, and fly. The legs were cut rather full and nearly straight, those for infantry being made plain and those for cavalry having a reinforcement (or saddle piece) in the seat and legs (fig. 13).[27] The bottoms of the outer seams were left open, and hemmed, for

On the facing page:
11. Officers of the Seventh Cavalry, Camp Sandy Forsyth, near Fort Dodge, Kansas, November 1868. These officers exhibit an assortment of uniforms typically worn for field service. (Glen Swanson Collection)

about three-quarters of an inch to permit the cuff to spread over the shoe or a boot. Army trousers had two front pockets let into the side seams, plus a watch pocket in the waistband seam, but frog-mouth pockets with square-cut flaps also were common (fig. 14). The latter style provided better access but also less security for the contents. At the rear center of the waistband was a vent with a small hand-sewn grommet on each side for a cord lace to provide some degree of adjustment (fig. 15). The men growled frequently about the poor fit of the trousers, especially the disproportionate sizes of waists and legs. All too

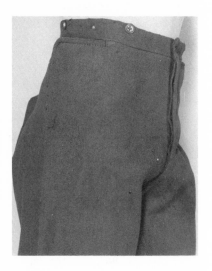

Above left:

12. *Front view of Pattern 1861 dismounted trousers for enlisted men. Note the side-seam pockets and watch pocket. (West Point Museum Collections)*

Above center:

13. *Rear view of 1861-pattern mounted trousers showing the distinctive reinforcement, or "saddle piece." (West Point Museum Collections)*

Above right:

14. *Pattern 1861 mounted trousers made of sky-blue kersey with frog-mouth pockets. (West Point Museum Collections)*

Left:

15. *Rear view of Pattern 1861 dismounted trousers, showing typical construction details and vent at the waist for adjustment. (West Point Museum Collections)*

often, when one part fit, the other did not. "When I tried them on," lamented one newly recruited soldier, "I could have turned around in every article."[28]

Noncommissioned officers were distinguished by stripes of worsted lace in the respective branch color on the outer seams of the legs. These extended full length from the waistband to the cuff. Corporals had ½-inch stripes; the stripes for sergeants of all grades were 1½ inches wide. The stripes were issued separately from the trousers and had to be sewn on by hand.

Under his uniform the soldier wore a pullover shirt of either white or gray flannel.[29] Flannel was used because of "its conduction of heat and its superior absorption of moisture," but it had a "tendency to cause undue perspiration, difficulty of washing and the liability of all woolen goods to convey septic disease."[30] Since these shirts remained in stock and were issued until the mid-1870s, they will be described in more detail in the following chapter.

During the war a coarse-knit shirt also was procured and issued to soldiers. Just what these may have looked like has not been determined, but it is assumed they were similar in cut to the other shirts. Although far fewer of these shirts were purchased than the other two types, they were nevertheless on hand in significant numbers through the end of the decade.[31]

In addition to shirts, soldiers were issued long flannel drawers, which were common to workingmen throughout society of the period. Judging from an official photograph published in 1875, these had a rather narrow waistband, perhaps two inches wide, fastened with two buttons.[32] Their main fault was that they came in only one weight of flannel, which was too heavy for summer and not heavy enough for winter temperatures at the northern posts. "The system of proportioning the clothing to the actual temperature," quipped Woodhull, "is practised by every community except the military."[33]

To alleviate some of their discomfort, soldiers frequently indulged "in various modifications, improvements and otherwise."[34] The most common of these alterations was to cut off the legs of the drawers above the knees. Some soldiers, desperate to find relief from the stifling heat, opted to simply dispense with underwear altogether. But the rough kersey trousers, especially when saturated with perspiration, usually chafed even the most hardy man into submitting to his drawers. Some medical officers recommended that drawers be provided in as many as three weights for various climates and conditions, but such enlightened reforms would not materialize for several more decades.[35]

Shoes, officially known as bootees, and boots were rather crude in form, with distinctive lefts and rights not appearing until the beginning of the Civil War. Many of those produced by contractors during the war were, in fact, only barely distinguishable. Boots, having tops about fourteen inches tall, were to be reserved for cavalry, whereas shoes with leather laces were issued to foot troops. The uppers of both styles of footgear were made with the dressed side turned outward and were dyed black. The soles either were stitched to the uppers or were fastened by machine-set wooden pegs. Neither of these methods held up very well under harsh frontier conditions. In fact, the overall quality of most of these shoes left a great deal to be desired because wartime contractors frequently used inferior materials, such as thin, split leather for uppers and composition materials or even pressed paper for soles.[36] Even when shoes and boots were made correctly, the soldier was obliged to soak them in water and then wear them until they were dry in order to get any sort of reasonable fit.[37]

For cold weather, the army augmented the soldier's clothing with a knee-length greatcoat of thick, sky-blue kersey. A cape, extending to the elbow on the infantry version and to the wrist on cavalry coats, plus body lining of burlap, buckram, or dark-blue flannel, provided additional insulation for the torso. The sleeves were lined with heavy muslin and were provided with deep functional cuffs that could be turned down over the hands as a poor substitute for mittens (fig. 16).

On the western plains, where winter temperatures frequently plunged below zero, soldiers learned to put on all the clothing possible and still be able to move. Those who had to be outdoors in inclement weather usually wore several layers of underwear and shirts, two pairs of trousers, and one or two blouses, plus the overcoat.[38]

Since the regulation overcoat provided so little protection from the elements, troops stationed in northern latitudes sometimes procured their own fur coats, made of either buffalo hide or bearskin.[39] Woodhull observed:

> There are some posts where the cold is represented by twenty-five degrees below zero, and lower, in the winter. Active operations then are practically impossible but a certain amount of guard and police duty must always be performed regardless of weather. At such posts it is strenuously urged that there be provided for the use of the guard and a few others outer garments of buffalo-robe sufficient to entirely envelop the wearers. . . . [O]ur men do wear them in many places, but what is here recommended is that they be furnished at such posts by the supreme authority.[40]

Officers also wore a calf-length caped overcoat, known as a "cloak coat," made of dark-blue melton. It had a wide falling collar and a long wool-lined cape extending to the wrists. The double-breasted front was closed by four black silk-cord loops and frog buttons spaced evenly from the neck to the waist. Each button was surrounded by a 2¼-inch knot of black braid. The coat contained two outside pockets with vertical openings, placed just above the hip. To facilitate riding, the back of the coat was slit up from the hem 15 to 17 inches. This opening could be closed for dismounted wear by a series of buttons and buttonholes within a concealed fly. The edges of the collar, cape, pocket openings, cuffs, and slit, as well as the front and lower borders of the coat itself, were trimmed with flat black silk braid ½ inch wide. Both the body of the coat and that of the cape were lined with wool fabric. The officer's rank was indicated by knots of silk braid on both cuffs, one strand for a first lieutenant and up to five for a colonel. The sleeves for second lieutenants were plain.

16. *Infantryman wearing the dismounted overcoat, ca. 1866.* (Smithsonian Institution)

Regulations made an exception for officers engaged in active field service. Under these circumstances, officers were allowed to wear the enlisted man's mounted overcoat, thus preserving their more expensive coats for garrison duty.[41]

During the 1860s overshoes made of tanned buffalo hide with rawhide soles were made available by special requisition. Apparently, they were first added to the supply table in 1862 and were intended for issue to the posts in the Northwest, where frigid winters were always experienced.[42] Hardly higher than the bootees themselves, they were intended to keep the feet warm rather than dry. Since the army failed to provide appropriate footgear for wet snow, many soldiers elected to purchase civilian boots, or to draw cavalry boots, to wear in snow and mud. Still others bought commercial arctic overshoes or had to improvise their own winter footgear.[43] Eighteenth Infantryman William Murphy, stationed on the Bozeman Trail in northern Wyoming during the winter of 1866–67, recalled: "Burlap sacks were at a premium and saved our lives. We wrapped them around our shoes to keep from freezing, for there were no overshoes or rubbers to be had at the fort."[44]

It comes as no surprise that the army failed to make any provision for special winter headgear. No one, except the soldiers themselves, seemed to question this as being a serious oversight for troops operating on the western plains. Despite almost universal complaints from posts throughout the plains, virtually no action was taken to alleviate the soldier's suffering.[45] Some men resorted to using the overcoat cape as a hood, tying it about the neck to hold it in place, but this had the disadvantage of depriving the body of that extra insulation.[46]

In lieu of any issue item, the men often bought their own fur or woolen caps, or they adapted an earflap to the regulation forage cap. Such items were sanctioned officially at some posts, such as Fort Laramie, Wyoming Territory, where orders were issued authorizing the men to wear earflaps, heavy gloves, and mufflers on guard and fatigue duties.[47] The earflap contrivance, resembling a havelock, consisted of either animal fur or a "piece of wadded cloth, to be attached, by means of three buttonholes on the upper edge, to the buttons on the sides of the cap and to an extra button sewed on the middle seam behind, and tied beneath the chin by tapes attached near the lower front corner."[48] The lappet was made long enough so that the overcoat collar could be turned up over it to form a fairly effective shield against biting winter winds.

Woodhull estimated that, on average, approximately one-eighth of the men stationed at the Dakota posts suffered frostbitten hands or feet.[49] The soldier was faced with only two choices when it came to protecting his hands. Either he could turn down the overcoat cuffs, a poor measure of protection against the bitter elements, or he could buy his own mittens. (A few men made their own mittens of fur, but this was the exception.) The commercially made mittens generally were of two basic styles, one having the index finger separated and the other with thumb only. Occasionally, examples will be seen with all five fingers. A deep gauntlet, flared to admit the coat sleeve, was a distinctive feature common to all the various types of these mittens. Buffalo hide, fur side outermost, except for the palm area, was perhaps the most common material used in constructing the mittens, although other types of fur, such as bear and seal skin, also were utilized. The hands usually were lined in either wool or sheepskin, and the cuffs were insulated with wool, corduroy, or wadded cotton. A combination of high-level apathy and the conservative Meigs delayed the general issuance of such gloves to the enlisted men for several more years.

When the troops were in the field, they were allowed considerable freedom to wear whatever best suited their needs, so long as they had the basic items necessary for survival and combat. Whereas the army presented a fairly uniform appearance in garrison, in the field it was the very antithesis of military pomp. For years, conditions on the plains had dictated the use of broad-brimmed hats for campaigning.[50] Most soldiers during the late 1860s wore the sack coat and regulation trousers, but in hot weather some men preferred muslin shirts rather than the standard flannel issue. Although blouses nearly always were worn in garrison, except for strenuous physical labor, the men were at liberty to remove them while on campaign and scouting duty. They carried blouses, to be sure, because daytime temperatures might approach one hundred degrees, then plummet to the thirties before dawn. On the northern plains a soldier on guard or picket duty would be chilled to the bone by morning, even during the summer. Additionally, marching orders usually prescribed that only one blanket be carried during summer marches, making the blouse an essential garment to men living entirely in the outdoors.

During the immediate postwar years, infantry and cavalry accoutrements remained basically unchanged from those used during the Civil War (fig. 17). The rank-and-file infantryman wore a black bridle-leather waist belt measuring slightly less than two inches in width. It was coupled by an oval, lead-filled brass plate bearing the letters "U.S." on the face. On the reverse was a hook that

17. *Infantry soldier outfitted for the field with equipments prescribed by regulations during and immediately after the Civil War. Included is the onerous and seldom-used double-bag knapsack.* (Smithsonian Institution)

mated to a series of holes in the belt to adjust the size. The free end of the belt was provided with a sheet-brass clasp, open on the front, with ears that hooked over the edges of the overlaid belt to keep the two aligned.

The bayonet in its leather scabbard was worn on the belt at the left hip. The weapon itself had an eighteen-inch blade, triangular in cross section, with a three-inch long socket fitting the muzzle of the rifle. A mortise in the socket allowed it to pass over the front sight base, with a rotating lock ring holding it firmly on the piece. The bayonet was carried in a sheath of black bridle leather with brass ferrule and tip. The frog on the Pattern 1862 scabbard was made of a separate piece of leather cut on a curve, folded back upon itself to form the belt loop, and riveted to a collar surrounding the sheath.[51]

Although great quantities of these scabbards were left over from the war, an ordnance board meeting early in 1868 specified that steel scabbards were to be procured on all new contracts.[52] The steel tubular scabbard, patented by J. E. Emerson in 1862, was purchased in large numbers by the army during the war.[53] The steel scabbards were light, inexpensive, and much more durable than leather ones.

The foot soldier carried forty rounds of .58-caliber musket ammunition in a large leather cartridge box measuring approximately 7 inches wide by 5½ inches deep by 1½ inches. Of necessity, the box had to be well constructed of heavy leather with tin compartments inside to contain the paper cartridges. This design prevented the rather fragile ammunition from being damaged by the motions of marching and the effects of weather. The Pattern 1855 cartridge box was made with two flaps, an outer one covering the entire front of the box and a short, stiff inner one to preclude cartridges from jolting out in combat when the outer flap was left unbuttoned. The outer flap usually was fitted with an oval brass "U.S." plate similar to that worn on the waist belt. A variation of this box introduced in 1864 differed only in that the flap was embossed with "U.S." enclosed by an oval border. Inside the box were two tin containers, each containing two paper-wrapped packets of musket cartridges. Sewn to the front of the box, under the flap, was a tool pouch containing the worm, wiper, and combination screwdriver. The 1855-pattern cartridge box was extremely heavy, even without the ammunition, and was cumbersome to use in combat.

The box was suspended from the shoulder by a wide sling, usually made of bridle leather, less frequently of buff leather. On the sling was a circular lead-backed brass plate, bearing an eagle coat of arms. Two iron wire loops protruded from the lead fill. These were inserted through slits in the sling and keyed with leather strips at a point over the soldier's breast. The sling had the disadvantage of constricting both the clothing and the soldier's breathing; therefore, by the war's end many soldiers had discarded it in favor of wearing the box on the waist belt (fig. 18). There was, however, a resurgence of the use of the sling by 1870. This may have resulted from the greater use of cartridge belts for actual field duty and, at the same time, increased emphasis on proper soldierly appearance on the parade ground in the postwar regular army.[54]

The adoption of the Springfield breechloader prompted the trial issue of a number of cartridge boxes, representing no less than nine different patterns submitted by various inventors. In addition to these, the Ordnance Department provided very limited numbers of looped cartridge belts designed by Colonel William B. Hazen (two patterns) and Colonel P. V. Hagner. Another belt, from an unidentified source, consisted merely of several percussion cap pouches arranged along the length of a standard waist belt. This belt may have been the army's first pocket cartridge belt, a practical concept that would take root early in the twentieth century. This particular effort to identify a new method for carrying small-arms ammunition was short-lived, however. By the early spring of 1872 virtually all of these experimental boxes and belts had been recalled.[55]

18. Infantry accoutrements: 1855-pattern cartridge box (left); buff-leather waist belt with 1856-pattern plate, cap pouch, and bayonet with scabbard (center, top); wartime production bridle-leather belt with accoutrements (center, middle); cartridge box tins (center, bottom); and Pattern 1864 cartridge box with embossed "U.S." on the cover (right). (Hayes Otoupalik Collection)

On dress parade infantry sergeants of all grades, as well as staff noncoms, carried a light, straight sword, with brass hilt and guard, that had been introduced in 1840. Useless in combat, the NCO (noncommissioned officer) sword was a carryover from the eighteenth-century European custom of providing swords as symbols of authority for sergeants. Musicians carried a similar but shorter sword, to allow for the shorter stature of most boy musicians; these swords lacked the kidney-shaped guard. In both cases the swords served simply as dress-parade ornaments, but just the same they would remain a part of the regulation equipage for years to come.

The sword was suspended from a wide leather shoulder belt and hung at the wearer's left side. The scabbards issued through the Civil War were made of black leather with brass throat and tip. However, the 1868 Ordnance Board recommended that "no more leather sword or bayonet scabbards [should] be purchased; but, should any be required, that they be made of steel," in accordance with patterns that had been "in service on trial."[56] In other words, the leather scabbards were to be used up; henceforth the regulation pattern would be of steel, lightweight yet considerably more durable. At the same time, the board adopted a sliding belt frog of black bridle leather. The frog provided a less cumbersome way to carry the sword and remained in use as long as the sword itself.[57]

In place of the standard-issue waist belt, sergeants and musicians wore a special belt made of black bridle or buff leather (fig. 19). This belt took the Pattern 1851 plate bearing an eagle surrounded by a separately applied German-silver wreath. When the sword sling was worn, the waist belt was placed over it to secure the sword to the body. Beneath this belt, for dress occasions, sergeants wore a red worsted sash (fig. 20). In actual practice, however, the sword slings

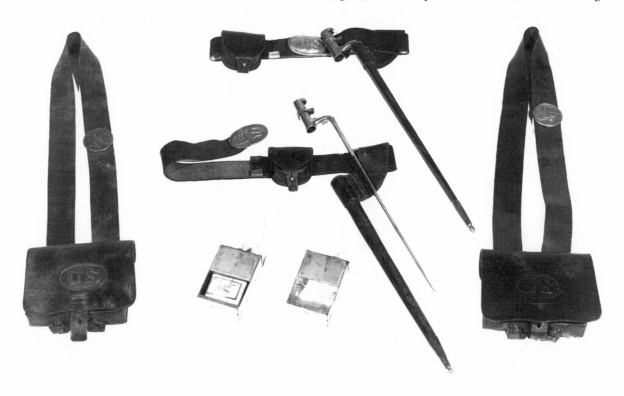

were all but nonexistent among the postwar regulars. A survey of Ordnance Department records suggests that most sergeants and musicians wore the prescribed noncommissioned officer's waist belt but either used the sliding belt frog for their swords or dispensed with wearing the sword altogether.[58]

Cavalrymen carried all their accoutrements on a saber belt made either of buff or of bridle leather. Judging by the extant examples, one does not appear to have been more common than the other, although ordnance specifications adopted in 1861 prescribed black buff leather.[59] Presumably the bridle-leather belts were manufactured later in the Civil War as the supply of buff leather failed to keep pace with the army's needs. This belt, slightly less than two inches wide, was fitted with two straps for slinging the saber and a support strap passing over the right shoulder. It was coupled with the 1851-pattern eagle belt plate.

Another belt that found its way into the hands of cavalry on the frontier was the Mann's pattern. This belt, which also employed the standard eagle plate, was originally a component of the accoutrement set patented in 1863 and 1864 by William D. Mann of Detroit, Michigan. Although Mann failed in his endeavors to win a large government contract for his equipment, he arranged to have some rather large quantities issued without charge for field trials. The Mann's Patent saber belt, made of black bridle leather and measuring slightly less than two inches wide, incorporated two hourglass-shaped fittings of sheet brass for the saber slings. Both of these slides held a large D-ring top and bottom for the support strap and slings, respectively, and were affixed to the belt with a copper rivet through the center. Few, if any, of the special cartridge boxes were shipped to the western frontier, but material evidence from various military sites indicates that some of the belts were issued to troops, probably because they would function as well as the regulation belt. The belt was intended to be used with the Stuart saber sling, which consisted of a large brass belt hook with two leather straps attached. Thus, the sling could be hooked to the front D-ring. However, the regulation separate straps could be used with the Mann belt.[60]

The cavalry trooper wore on his belt a revolver holster (righthand, butt forward), a percussion cap pouch, a pistol cartridge pouch containing packets of combustible cartridges, and a leather box for carbine cartridges. The demands of the war had forced the Union army to contract for a wide variety of carbines to arm its cavalry. Responding to this situation, established American arms manufacturers and independent inventors had a heyday vying for a piece of the market. Since there was no standard caliber, however, this mixture of carbines complicated the supply of both ammunition and individual equipment. The army purchased no less than half a dozen different patterns of carbine cartridge boxes during the war years. By the war's end one carbine, the Spencer repeater, reigned over all others, and it was this pattern that was issued almost exclusively to the postwar regular army. Although limited numbers of the patented Blakeslee

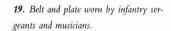

19. Belt and plate worn by infantry sergeants and musicians.

quick-loading box, holding either six or ten tubes each of Spencer metallic cartridges (seven to the tube), were produced, these shoulder-slung carriers saw little if any use on the western frontier. Just why they did not is uncertain, but it may have been because a relatively small number were on hand or because the conservative army of that day thought that placing repeating arms in the hands of soldiers was a needless waste of ammunition. Such a cartridge box could only add to the problem, despite its obvious advantages on the plains.

The box that became standard issue, then, was a traditional pattern of black leather with a full flap. It held a wood block drilled for twenty rounds of ammunition. Like the infantry box, it had belt loops on the reverse and a tool pocket sewn to the front. By the time the trooper, generally a small man to begin with, placed his cap pouch, holster, and two cartridge boxes on his belt, with the saber slung to the left side, he had fully twelve pounds of equipment around his waist alone (fig. 21).

To prevent his losing the carbine while mounted, the trooper was issued a 2½-inch-wide bridle-leather sling with a large iron snap hook. The carbine was attached to this snap hook by a ring mounted on its left side. The sling itself was worn over the left shoulder so that the carbine dangled at the right hip. This arrangement, though an obvious safety hazard to the mounted soldier, ensured that he could neither drop his weapon nor become separated from it should his horse be shot.

Shortly before the end of the Civil War the army began to consider seriously the adoption of a standard breech-loading rifle using a metallic cartridge. The success of the self-contained rimfire cartridge in the Spencer arms and its advantages of durability, resistance to moisture, and rapidity of fire greatly impressed the Ordnance Department. The great volunteer Union army had only begun to be mustered out when a board of officers met to inspect various patent weapons and to recommend one or more for trial. With the war just ended and with more than one million rifled muskets on hand, economy dictated that a system be devised for converting these arms into breechloaders. As a result, five thousand muskets were changed to breechloaders on a design submitted by Erskine S. Allin, the master armorer at Springfield Armory. The Model 1865 Springfield rifle utilized most of the parts of the musket, except that a tip-up breech system was adapted to the original barrel (figs. 22 and 23). It was chambered for a huge .58-caliber rimfire cartridge, which was nothing more than a metallic version of the old musket round.

The first of these arms, of which a total of only five thousand were produced, were ready for shipment by March 1866.[61] Although some extremely limited numbers of the Model 1865 were shipped to frontier garrisons, it never saw any significant use in the West.[62] The underpowered cartridge, combined with a fragile and needlessly complex extractor, condemned this rifle from the outset.

With the dismal performance of the .58 rimfire, coupled with the design weaknesses in the Allin-conversion rifle, the army began pursuing the development of a more effective cartridge and a more reliable long arm for the infantry. The 1866 "Board on Breechloading Arms" favored an experimental .45-caliber round loaded with seventy grains of powder. Ordnance tests proved the superior accuracy and power of this cartridge. Such proof notwithstanding, Chief of Ordnance Alexander B. Dyer (fig. 24) recommended a .50-caliber cartridge

On the facing page:
20. *Infantry sergeant wearing full-dress uniform, ca. 1866. (Smithsonian Institution)*

Above:
21. *Cavalryman wearing the regulation full-dress uniform, ca. 1866, and armed with the Spencer carbine. Note that for field service the brass scales would have been removed and the hat would have been replaced by the forage cap or a slouch hat. (Smithsonian Institution)*

because the .45/70, in his opinion, was "entirely too long for general service."[63] Oddly enough, this very cartridge was adopted officially just a few years later and remained the standard for another twenty years.

The overriding consideration, in the wake of the wide variety of arms used during the Civil War, seems to have been achieving consistency in bore diameter. In his endorsement on the subject, Commanding General of the Army Ulysses S. Grant wrote, "The superiority of the .45-caliber in accuracy, range, and penetration seems to have been placed beyond doubt, but a uniformity of caliber being so desireable and there being such a large number of caliber .50 on hand, it would not be advisable to adopt this caliber [.45]."[64]

Above:

22. *Model 1865 Springfield rifle.* (Fuller Collection, Chickamauga-Chattanooga National Military Park)

Inset:

23. *Breech detail of Model 1865 Springfield rifle.* (Fuller Collection, Chickamauga-Chattanooga National Military Park)

Grant betrayed a surprising lack of basic knowledge about munitions and about the arms then in the government inventory. There were indeed many arms on hand in .50-caliber, but they were by no means chambered for the same cartridge, nor could they be modified. For instance, the Model 1865 Spencer repeating carbine, in general use by the cavalry at that time, was chambered for the .56/50 rimfire cartridge. Although the bore was .50-caliber, the short and relatively weak action of the Spencer design made it impossible to rechamber these carbines for the .50/70 cartridge. Beginning late in 1867, the breechloading percussion Sharps carbine was modified to .50/70, but its .52-caliber barrel had to be relined with a rifled tube to accept the smaller-diameter bullet.[65] Both rifles and carbines just as easily could have been reduced to .45-caliber, but the underlying reason may have been the way the decision appeared on paper to a penny-pinching Congress. Whatever the motive, the .50/70 cartridge became standard for the infantry and for that portion of the cavalry armed with the Sharps conversion carbines (fig. 25).

Soon thereafter the secretary of war ordered Springfield Armory to convert an additional twenty-five thousand muskets into breechloaders. The Model 1866, also designed by Allin, still utilized most of the original rifled-musket parts but incorporated an improved breech system with a more positive extractor. The caliber was reduced by boring out the .58-caliber barrel to accept a rifled .50-caliber liner tube, which was then brazed in place.

Initial issues of the Model 1866 rifle began in the spring of 1867. By the end of June, the Fourth, Twenty-second, Thirtieth, and Thirty-eighth regiments were armed entirely with it, and a reissue to the Thirty-sixth was nearly complete. Companies D and K of the Eighteenth also received the new Allin rifles. Significantly, all of the units that initially received the new arms were posted on the central and northern plains, the scenes of most of the hostile Indian activity at the time.[66]

25. *(Top to bottom) Sharps carbine converted to fire the .50/70 cartridge; Model 1860 Spencer carbine, caliber .56/56; and Model 1865 Spencer carbine, caliber .56/50. (Hayes Otoupalik Collection)*

Fortunately for a detachment of Twenty-seventh Infantrymen, the new breechloaders reached the isolated posts along the Bozeman Trail in Wyoming and Montana territories just weeks before the celebrated Wagon Box and Hayfield fights. The army's successes in these actions were directly attributable to the Springfield "needle gun," as it was dubbed by soldiers because of its long firing pin.[67]

Meanwhile, the remainder of the infantry was armed with an assortment of both percussion and metallic-cartridge weapons. The Third Infantry, for instance, was armed entirely with seven-shot Spencer rifles, whereas the Thirty-seventh, stationed at posts in Kansas, Colorado, and New Mexico, had the strong and reliable .52 Sharps percussion rifle. Except for the Twelfth Infantry and two companies of the Twenty-first Regiment, both of which retained the experimental Model 1865 Springfield, the rest of the infantry was still armed with the old rifled muskets for a time. However, this situation soon changed when the National Armory increased its production of the second-model Allin conversion.[68]

At the end of the decade the Ordnance Department began issuing an improved version of the Allin-Springfield rifle. The Model 1868, also chambered for the .50/70 cartridge, incorporated an entirely new barrel and receiver, which was a marked improvement over the makeshift arrangement used in the previous model. This new rifle also was fitted with a long-range rear sight, making better use of the superior capabilities of the .50/70 cartridge. The barrel was shortened by four inches, and the overall weight of the weapon was reduced by about one pound, resulting in a rifle with better handling characteristics.

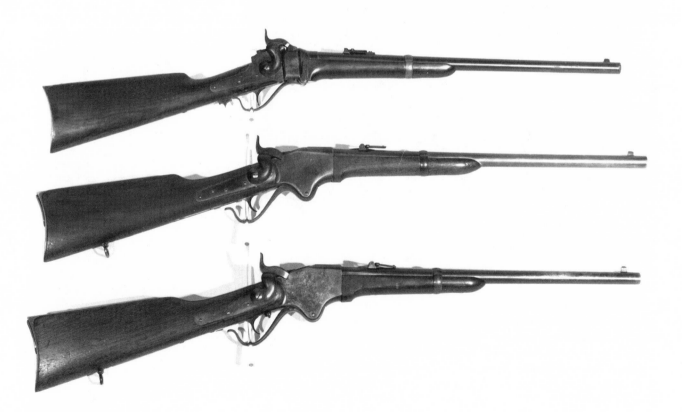

Mass production of the Model 1868 got under way in 1869, but the regular infantry continued to use both old and new models for a few more years. Ordnance records disclose that Model 1866 rifles were used almost exclusively by line companies until the fall of 1870. Even then, the Fifth Infantry was the only unit to receive a complete issue of the new Model 1868, with significant numbers also going to the Seventh. Once the new model was available in large numbers, however, the transition proceeded at a fast pace. Virtually all of the Model 1866 rifles had been turned in by line companies by the end of the first quarter of 1871.[69]

The issue of a long arm for the cavalry was less easily resolved. The seven-shot Spencer, chambered for the .56/50 rimfire cartridge, had an effective range of less than two hundred yards. On wooded eastern battlefields this limitation had been of little consequence. But after the war, when as yet the Ordnance Department had little appreciation for distances on the Great Plains, the rate of fire, reliability, and metallic ammunition of the Spencer made it the logical choice for primary issue to the regulars taking station in the West. By mid-1867, all cavalry units, except the First and Fifth regiments, which still retained the .52-caliber percussion Sharps, were armed with Spencers, but within another two years the suitability of the Spencer was being challenged.[70]

> The cavalry have been supplied with Spencer carbines, or with Sharp's [sic] carbines altered to receive the musket metallic cartridges caliber .50. About 30,000 of these arms have been altered. The Spencer carbine at the end of the war was generally regarded with favor, and as being the best arm that had been in service, and it continues to be regarded as a superior arm by the cavalry. The altered Sharp's carbine gives great satisfaction, and is preferred by some of the cavalry regiments to the Spencer. In some respects—particularly in the ammunition, which is the same as the breech-loading musket ammunition—it is decidedly superior to the Spencer carbine.[71]

Despite its advantages as a repeater, the Spencer's days were numbered. In 1867 the army, in its eagerness to consolidate to a single more-powerful caliber, contracted with the Sharps Arms Company to convert some 31,098 Sharps carbines Models 1859, 1863, and 1865 to chamber the new .50/70 cartridge.[72] During the early 1870s, the trend was to replace the Spencers with the more powerful converted Sharps carbines.

The revolution in firearms technology generated by the development of the centerfire cartridge and the ability to mass-produce metallic ammunition profoundly affected tactics and accoutrements. Crude though it was, the Model 1866 Springfield rifle dramatically increased the individual soldier's firepower from an average of three shots per minute, at best, with the musket to thirteen using the breechloader. Moreover, it was accurate at distances exceeding six hundred yards. The old school of tactics was outmoded almost overnight. Whereas General Silas Casey's system of rifle and light-infantry tactics was founded on close-order formations to produce effective volumes of fire, the breechloader made this as obsolete as it was foolhardy, considering that the enemy would be similarly armed. Units formed en masse could be devastated by the concentrated fire of an enemy using breechloaders.

Concurrent with the advent of the .50/70 Springfield, Lieutenant Colonel Emory Upton devised an improved system of tactics he had begun work on during the war and had afterward adapted to the breech-loading rifle. Upton, a brilliant military scholar and aggressive field commander who would command the U.S. Military Academy from 1870 to 1875, anticipated the new conditions imposed by the breechloader. He seized the opportunity to develop these into revised tactics applicable to the entire army. Upton included the more easily maneuvered closed formations, principally for parade purposes, but he relied heavily on open deployments, or skirmish formation, for combat.[73]

The entire system was based on sets of four men, each set maintaining its integrity yet working in concert with the others. This permitted deployments from either column or line to be made with greater speed and in less space than formerly, thus allowing troops to close upon the enemy without requiring a broad frontal formation. By relying on rapid deployments from column, Upton's system enabled troops to approach enemy formations quicker and without exposing themselves to as much enemy fire.

Upton also placed greater responsibility on the individual soldier to use his rifle effectively against specific targets, rather than on enemy concentrations, and to take advantage of cover afforded by the terrain. Movement and fire discipline were controlled at all times by the officers and noncoms. Although not particularly intended for Indian fighting, Upton's concept was somewhat better adapted to it than were previous systems, especially regarding the movement of troops over broken terrain. Interestingly, all infantry tactics used by the U.S. Army since that time have been influenced by Upton's system.

The breechloader also necessitated a new means for carrying ammunition, but the transition was slow in coming. The increased rate of fire meant that a soldier had to carry more ammunition in such a way that it would be readily accessible yet not too uncomfortable to carry. This initiated a long struggle between the Ordnance Department and the common soldier. On the one hand was the reality that so long as the immense war surplus remained on hand, there would be little chance of convincing Congress that new accoutrements were needed. Weighed against this was the demand for equipment that would permit the soldier to realize the potential firepower of the new weapons.

The only immediate concession made to the breechloader was to remove the tin compartments from the infantry cartridge box. Three principal methods were devised for adapting the 1855-pattern box for metallic ammunition, though a number of other designs were submitted by private inventors. One called for placing two of the twenty-round pasteboard cartons, one atop the other, in the leather box. When the soldier expended the cartridges in the upper one, he switched cartons, placing the empty one in the bottom and the full one on top. However reasonable this may have sounded in theory, the procedure was difficult to perform, especially under fire, since the only way to extract the lower carton was by inverting the cartridge box and shaking it out. The packaging of cartridges in five-round packets, eight to a carton, was done for a limited time, and this may have alleviated the problem. Another alternative was to use wooden blocks drilled for twenty rounds each in place of the cartons, which did nothing to correct the fundamental problem.[74]

The Ordnance Department altered some of the musket boxes by lining the interior and the inner flap with sheepskin (fig. 26). This allowed the cartridges to be carried loose in the box, making it easier to extract them than by either of the other two methods.[75] The numbers of these boxes actually produced must have been relatively small, since ordnance records for 1870, the only known records in which these boxes appear, indicate that they were issued to only a few companies of the Twenty-second Infantry.[76] Since no evidence has been found regarding conversions of cavalry cartridge boxes, it is assumed that they simply were used as issued.

Many foot soldiers preferred to carry their cartridge boxes on the waist belt rather than using the shoulder sling. The combined weight of the blanket roll, haversack, and canteen, plus ammunition, on the shoulders could be sheer torture for the soldier, not to mention making him top-heavy. By wearing the box on his belt and positioning it at the small of his back, the soldier was at once able to rid himself of the sling and to improve his mobility. In action, he could slide the box around to his right side or even to the front to make loading his weapon easier and faster. Although this helped to bring the weight closer to the human center of gravity, it also had the disadvantage of concentrating the weight of forty cartridges on the man's abdomen. Neither method seems to have been predominant, although ordnance records suggest that wearing the box on the waist belt was more popular during the late 1860s than it was by 1870–71.[77] Perhaps wearing the shoulder belt proved to be the lesser of two evils. Using their own ingenuity, some soldiers equalized their load by wearing two boxes on the waist belt, one on each side.[78] Little did they know that such an arrangement would be officially adopted just a few years hence.

Even though the leather cartridge box often was used on campaign, soldiers were quick to adopt the looped belts worn by civilian frontiersmen armed with metallic cartridge weapons. Known variously as thimble, fringed, prairie, or scouting belts, these were found among troops on the frontier as early as 1867.[79] The men fabricated them by sewing forty to fifty leather or canvas loops on an issue waist belt or other piece of "appropriated" leather. Despite the obvious merits and popularity of the thimble belt, it would still be a number of years before the army would officially transform the concept into a regulation-issue belt.

Cavalrymen in the field were afforded the comparative luxury of packing their essentials on their saddles. Although exact arrangements of gear varied from one unit to the next, the general method was to roll and strap the overcoat and poncho on the pommel; the blanket, shelter half, and a change of underclothing formed the cantle pack. The saddlebags in use since 1859 were simply too small to contain more than the spare horseshoes, horse grooming tools, and on occasion, extra ammunition. Therefore, the trooper, like his doughboy counterpart, was forced to carry his rations in a haversack, which was slung over the saddle. His canteen was likewise tied to one of the cantle rings.[80]

The army intended that the foot soldier's kit be carried in a knapsack, but this item was never very popular during the Civil War, and it found even fewer advocates among the frontier regulars. The Civil War–pattern knapsack, still standard issue nearly a decade later, was made of black painted canvas in the form of two bags approximately twelve inches square.[81] These two bags were connected along their top edges by a gusset and had their openings to the inside.

26. *Rifled musket cartridge box as altered for use with the .50/70 Springfield breechloader. The tins have been replaced with sheepskin lining to prevent the cartridges from rattling about.*

The pack was closed along the bottoms of the two bags by three narrow leather straps and buckles. Black leather shoulder straps about two inches wide were sewn to the back of the knapsack. On the top gusset were two straps for holding the rolled blanket. In the 1860s, before footlockers were officially sanctioned, knapsacks were used mostly to store the soldier's extra clothing in barracks. Other than at muster-day inspections, they rarely were seen packed up in marching order.

For serious campaigning, most soldiers preferred the blanket roll, which had become so popular on both sides during the war. Never recognized officially, the roll had been resorted to by foot soldiers as a less irksome way to carry their bedding and incidentals. It was made by simply rolling up a blanket, lengthwise, with a change of underwear and socks inside. The ends of the roll were brought together and tied with a cord or leather strap, thus forming a horseshoe, or "scarf," as it was sometimes known, that could be worn over one shoulder, usually the left. Admittedly, the roll was hot and cumbersome and hindered breathing, but the men could pack it up quickly, and it was more comfortable to wear than the onerous knapsack. In the West, where marching distances often were staggering, the blanket roll was the infantry's undisputed choice.[82]

The canteen issued universally to all branches had been standard since 1858 (fig. 27). It was made of two pieces of pressed tin, soldered together to form an oblate spheroid body having a capacity of three pints. Spaced equidistant around the canteen's seam were three sling loops, also of tinned iron. The sling itself was made of a single piece of white cotton drill folded double and stitched along both edges. At the top was a pewter spout with a cork stopper attached to one of the sling loops by a length of iron jack chain. A two-piece fitted cover was made of either brownish-gray blanket cloth or sky-blue kersey. Some, though less frequently, were covered with dark-blue wool. The earliest examples of the Pattern 1858 canteen were smooth sided, but in 1861 a second style appeared that had a series of concentric rings, or corrugations, pressed into each side to make the canteen more resistent to denting.[83] Both styles were produced in enormous quantities by various contractors.

The soldier carried two or three days' rations of hard bread (hardtack), bacon or salt pork, and coffee in his haversack. This was simply a small bag about twelve inches square made of either drill or canvas, with a nonadjustable sling of the same material sewn to the upper corners. A single leather strap fastened the flap closed. The exterior of the entire bag, as well as the sling, was waterproofed with black paint, which invariably flaked off in service. An uncoated liner buttoned inside so that it could be removed for washing, though few soldiers bothered to do so. Regulations prescribed that infantrymen were to wear the

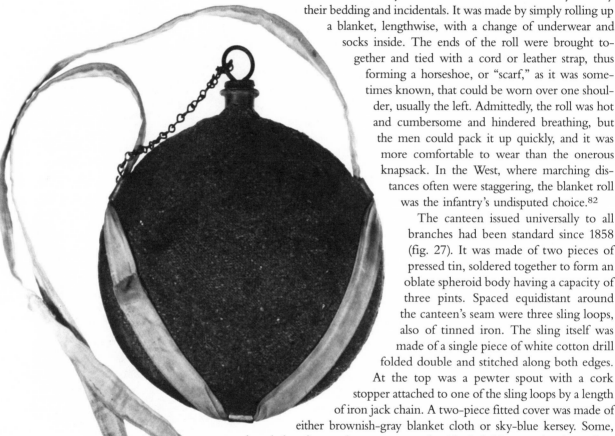

27. 1858-pattern canteen.

haversack, with the canteen over it, on the left side in order to leave the cartridge box unobstructed.[84] Cavalry troopers were given the discretion to either wear the haversack while mounted or attach it to the saddle, the most common method being simply to loop the sling over the cantle roll, with the bag suspended on the near side of the horse.

The appropriations acts of 1869 and 1870 further reduced the size of the army by nearly one-half, leaving it at a strength of only thirty-thousand enlisted men. This thin blue line was charged with manning over two hundred military posts, many of them located in remote areas of the West. At the same time, Congress maintained its stance not to resupply the army until the war surplus was consumed, a policy fully endorsed by General Meigs. Thus, during the late 1860s, Congress saw no need to appropriate funds for new clothing, nor did Meigs in fact request any, because of the huge quantities then on hand at the various supply depots. Theoretically, the stockpiles on hand should have been sufficient to maintain the recently reduced army for many years to come. However, the predictions failed to take into account serious problems that belied the inventory reports.

Perhaps the greatest cause for concern was the lack of proper long-term storage facilities. For the most part, the warehouses rented or hastily built during the war years had been viewed as temporary solutions to immediate problems, with little if any thought being given to postwar needs. All of the major depots lay in cities east of the Mississippi, with dozens of storehouses located among the various western frontier posts. Among the former were makeshift buildings that were not well adapted to their purpose. Nevertheless, they continued in service after the war's end for lack of anything better. The fort storehouses, constructed by unskilled soldier labor and of locally available materials, provided storage for the matériel but scant protection from the elements. Consequently, large quantities of clothing were ruined by water leakage and mildew, along with insect and rodent damage. At Jeffersonville Depot, Indiana, alone during 1869, an inspection disclosed that fourteen million dollars' worth of government property was inadequately stored. General Meigs thus took immediate action to consolidate his overextended supply network into four principal clothing depots, located at New York City, Washington, D.C., Jeffersonville, and Philadelphia. Schuylkill Arsenal, at Philadelphia, was the only one meeting the army's standards at that time. All of the other locations were relinquished and the goods shipped to one of these four permanent facilities.[85]

Clothing was originally packaged either in large, tightly compacted bales wrapped with painted canvas or in boxes lined with moisture-resistant petroleum paper. Despite these measures, Meigs discovered that much of the clothing sent to the field late in the war had been injured or destroyed because the containers had been damaged by rough handling and poor storage. Moths, against which the army had no defense, found their way into even the tightest of containers, ravaging the woolen clothing to such a degree that it was unfit for use. Labor and materials for packing and repacking these stores, plus warehouse rent, civilian employee salaries, and fire protection, consumed much of the Quartermaster Department's meager postwar budget. Although the proceeds from auctions of salvageable clothing partially offset these costs, such sales only depleted the stockpiles of clothing needed by the army.[86]

In the midst of this difficult situation, Congress stipulated on July 12, 1870, that appropriated funds had to be expended for their stated purpose. In other words, the officers responsible for managing the money could not shift an excess balance from one account to cover a deficit in another. Although this was done in an effort to induce economy and improve accountability in the army, it deprived the army staff of the financial flexibility enjoyed previously.[87]

Further compounding the problem was the army's consumption of clothing at a rate faster than had been anticipated. By the end of 1869, quantities of major items such as sack coats, caps, trousers, and overcoats had diminished by over 40 percent from their numbers just two years earlier.[88] The acceleration stemmed from two principal causes. One of these was the latent discovery that unscrupulous wartime contractors had defrauded the government by marking the garments with sizes larger than they really were. In this way the manufacturers realized additional profit through the savings in cloth. Venting the frustration felt by soldiers throughout the army, Private Mack McKinney, Tenth Cavalry, decried the quality and size shortages of trousers in this bit of doggerel, which appeared in the February 5, 1870, issue of the *Army and Navy Journal*:

ODE TO A PAIR OF TIGHT BREECHES

Written maliciously and with direct animosity against No. 1's and a sparsity of cloth, and directed personally against those unmentionables, but preceded with a sigh!

> Ah, life is short, and so art thou,
> But yet I'll wear thee;
> I'll storm thee, Breech', I'll do it now;
> I'll get thee on, but Mars tell how
> Unless I tear thee?
>
> What nimble fingers stitched thy seams,
> That seem still shrinking?
> What jaunty shearess cut that seat,
> That needs extension near two feet
> Or more, I'm thinking?
>
> What Shylock gave his bond due sealed
> To fitting make thee
> To warriors limbs in camp or field?
> Appropriate fact, "Thoul't never yield
> An inch"—De'il take thee!
>
> Shades of old hats and carpet rags,
> Grasp my propellers;
> Ghosts of old coats and gunny bags,
> Of all the human garb the tags (including mummies),
> Ye're here, poor fellows.

The other cause behind the army's depletion of clothing, and one that particularly irritated Meigs, was that soldiers, according to Meigs, drew clothing in sizes larger than what they actually wore. Their purpose in doing so was to have the company tailors rework the garments for a custom fit. Defending his position, Meigs wrote: "The stock manufactured during the war and on hand at its close was divided in proper proportions among the four sizes used, so that there was never any difficulty in clothing a brigade. . . . But since the Army has been distributed into small garrisons, with leisure to indulge individual taste, the universal demand for large sizes and rejection of small sizes of clothing have resulted as noted."[89]

Although this did occur in some instances, the practice was not as prevalent as Meigs wanted to believe. One reason the men asked for larger sizes was that they were already wise to the sizing discrepancies and, therefore, took the only practical alternative available to them. Then too, because the average sizes were in the greatest demand, they were the first to be consumed. Meigs failed to recognize that without a means to replenish the static supply, the popular sizes gradually would be exhausted. When that happened, soldiers resorted to drawing the larger garments to be sized down by the tailors.[90]

By 1871 the depleted condition of the army's clothing stockpile was so acute that only small-size garments were available at most of the depots. For a period of months the Clothing Branch was compelled to issue yard goods along with the uniforms so that the garments could be enlarged by the company tailors. Late that fiscal year Congress finally awakened to the crisis and passed an emergency appropriation for clothing.

The pride of the nation just a few short years before, the army was now humiliated by the government's lack of concern for its basic welfare. Surgeon Woodhull recognized the importance of the uniform to the army's morale. He wrote, "When our soldiers are marked and proud men we shall have a better army."[91] In the decade to come the army and Congress finally would join forces to attempt to rectify the problem.

Distinctive and Honorable Dress for the Soldier, 1872–1873

The dawn of a new decade witnessed renewed agitation throughout army circles for an improved uniform. Officers and enlisted men clamored in unison for new clothing of better quality and more modern style. Heard among the complaints were charges that the clothing not only fit poorly but also was shoddy and old-fashioned-looking when compared with that worn by the armies of European nations, notably Great Britain, Germany, and France. Officers who had been in service for some years remembered the Woodhull report and questioned why its recommendations had never been followed.

During the deliberations over the new uniform, a few outspoken individuals, latecomers to the service for the most part, had the audacity to suggest that the army adopt gray uniforms, which were cooler and less conspicuous on the battlefield. Woodhull, in fact, had addressed this very issue from a purely scientific viewpoint by observing that after black, dark blue absorbed more solar heat than any other color. Gray, he determined by actual test, absorbed six to eight degrees less.[1] But, these would-be reformers neglected one important factor. To men who had just spent four years fighting a gray-clad enemy to preserve the Union, even the suggestion of adopting this color was an insult bordering on treason. In the public mind as well, blue had come to symbolize the federal army. Responding to this suggestion, General Montgomery C. Meigs retorted: "The uniform in which the people of the country fought the battles and made the campaigns of the war is endeared to them by the recollection of many a hard-fought field and many a bivouac. It is simple, inexpensive, serviceable, and military. . . . The dark blue coat and blouse, the light blue trousers, form a uniform unsurpassed in any service for actual duty in the field."[2]

In spite of Meigs's objections to the adoption of a new uniform for the army, the adjutant general issued orders on July 3, 1871, for a board of officers to be convened for the purpose of revising the army's regulations, including those pertaining to the uniform.[3] After nearly a year of deliberations, the board completed its task and submitted its recommendations to the secretary of war. After the requisite reviews and approvals, the new uniform regulations were published as general orders on July 27, 1872.[4]

Although still based on the now-traditional dark-blue and sky-blue color scheme, the new-pattern clothing authorized for the army was a dramatic change from the uniform issued during the 1860s. The designs borrowed heavily from those being worn in Europe at the time. In several instances they were the manifestations of suggestions contained in the 1868 Woodhull report. Generally speaking, the clothing was made of higher-quality material than were previous uniforms, and the workmanship was better, since most of the items for enlisted men were being manufactured at government facilities.

The description of the new uniform first reached the army through the pages of the *Army and Navy Journal,* where it was hailed as the long-awaited farewell to the old Civil War outfit. The army's jubilation at the good news was short-lived, however. Whereas Meigs had intended to supply the entire army with the new clothing by December 1872, the program faltered for lack of funding. The congressional appropriation had been based on the assumption that much of the surplus stock of yard goods would be utilized in making the new clothing.[5] However, there had been so many complaints about the poor quality of the fabrics that new specifications had been adopted. But, Meigs claimed, the additional cost of these improved materials had depleted the available funds before all of the troops could be outfitted in the new uniform. Although the Quartermaster Department had large stocks of material on hand to use for the new clothing, a major change such as this required much additional labor, not to mention the funds needed to purchase new trimmings and to contract for quantities of some items.[6]

Consequently, production of the new uniform came to an abrupt halt several months into the fiscal year. Nothing more could be done until July 1, 1873, when a new appropriation would be authorized. In the meantime, the army had to be content with a mixture of both old and new clothing, a transitional limbo that would last longer than anyone anticipated. In October 1873 Meigs proudly announced: "Nearly all the troops have now received the new uniform. The old pattern clothing stored in the Philadelphia depot has . . . been sold at public auction. . . . [T]he surplus of such clothing distributed at military posts throughout the country is being reported for sale as fast as the new uniform takes its place."[7]

It had been a long time in the making, but the army finally had its new uniform. After being bombarded with complaints for so long, the head of the Clothing Branch at the Philadelphia Depot, Captain John F. Rodgers, was understandably defensive in his announcement of the recent uniform change: "It is, in quality, appearance, and workmanship, vastly superior to the old. None but good cloth has been used, and the prices paid for making it have been sufficient to insure good work. The patterns are all better than those formerly used, and if the Army complains, the Quartermaster's Department need feel no remorse."[8]

With the distribution of the 1872-pattern uniform, the Quartermaster Department began divesting itself of the now-obsolete Civil War clothing. Enormous quantities of goods were sold at public auctions in Philadelphia during 1873, the proceeds amounting to over a half-million dollars. Orders were issued for post quartermasters to follow suit as soon as they had received sufficient stocks of the new uniform to meet their needs.[9] In a decision that the army would live to regret, the depot at Jeffersonville, Indiana, was directed to defer its sales until the following year, perhaps in the event that some emergency should arise. Little did it know that Congress would discover this cache and force the army to issue the old clothing. Meanwhile the department busied itself at turning out enough new-pattern uniforms to supply the army for the next twelve months.

Thus, by mid-1874 the transition to the 1872 uniform was largely complete insofar as the garrison dress was concerned. For this purpose, the soldiers were attired much as the regulations intended. But in the field, where the men were permitted to dress pretty much as they pleased, the situation was entirely different. Soldiers commonly used their older clothing for field service and rough work around the posts, thereby conserving their new, more expensive clothing for more formal military activities. The Quartermaster Department, in fact, encouraged this practice by fixing the prices for certain articles of the "old pattern" at the levels established in 1871 as an inducement for the men to use up surplus stocks.[10]

OFFICERS' UNIFORMS

It should be noted that officers were not authorized a clothing allowance, as were enlisted men, and therefore were responsible for purchasing their own uniforms. Although the various items are found described in the 1872 regulations, none were produced at the government facilities or by contract. Virtually all officers' items were made by commercial firms, according to sealed samples and specifications provided by the Quartermaster Department. Therefore, minor differences and variations existed among extant specimens produced by different firms. Some companies even listed various grades of some items, such as shoulder straps, dress coats, and belts, and offered a wide variety of custom embellishments to suit an officer's individual budget or taste. Most of these firms published illustrated catalogs for their customers' convenience, and most operated retail outlets in the respective home-office cities.

Headgear

Dress Helmet Emulating several Old World nations, the U.S. Army adopted a black felt helmet for its mounted troops. Although this style of helmet may have had Germanic origins, soldiers in Russia and Great Britain also wore similar decorative headgear during the mid-nineteenth century. The very successful Prussian armies of the era popularized this style of headgear, especially for cavalry and other mounted troops. Although the army specifications officially placed the origin of the helmet's style "in antique Greek sculpture," one of the senior members of the 1872 Uniform Board later stated that the selection had been based on a British pattern issued to the English Horseguards.[11] In fact, the shape of the helmet, with its nearly vertical front visor and long, squared cape, was more suggestive of the British helmet than the Prussian style.

An extract from the specifications describes the helmet for cavalry officers:

Pattern as shown in accompanying cuts numbered 8, 9, and 10; heavy body of [black] fur bound with fine patent leather; measurements about as indicated on cuts [i.e., front 11½ inches from visor edge to plume socket; rear 11 inches from edge of visor to plume socket]; patent leather chin strap ⅝ of an inch wide with gilt slide; patent-leather visor strap folded ⅜ on an inch wide, double stitched, connecting chin-strap buttons; goat skin sweat-leather.[12]

The front of the helmet bore a large gilt eagle representing the arms of the United States (fig. 28). On the eagle's breast was a Union shield bearing the number of the regiment in silver three-fourths of an inch high. Arching over the eagle between its spread wing tips was a scroll bearing the national motto in relief lettering. Atop the helmet was a plume socket and base plate having four

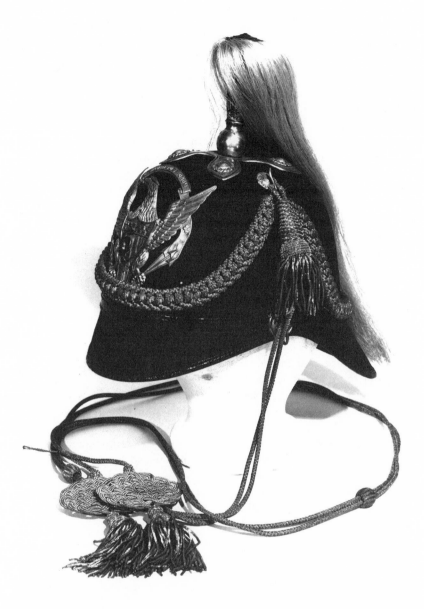

28. Cavalry officers' helmet, 1872.
(Hayes Otoupalik Collection)

miter-shaped feet, all in gilt. The plume itself was made of yellow horsehair and was about twenty inches long.

A small gilt scroll and ring was located on each side of the helmet, about midway between the gauze metal ventilator and the plume socket plate. These were for attaching the braided bands draped fore and aft on the visors. The chin strap was affixed at each end by a gilt metal button bearing crossed sabers in relief. These were seven-eighths of an inch in diameter with beveled edges. The cords and bands were described as follows:

> Gold thread cord, 2½ lines; the bands loop plaited and fastened to rings and scrolls at sides and festooned on front and back of helmet; the front festoon falls to the upper edge of visor and the rear one to a corresponding depth behind; the loop plaiting is about ¾ of an inch wide; at left ring and scroll a pendant tassel of sixty or seventy fringes where the cords are fastened; gilt

cords about 5 feet 8 inches long with two netted slides of about ¾ inch diameter; flat braided ornament 2¾ inches in diameter and tassels on each end of cord.[13]

Additional features never documented in detail were noted on the helmet owned by First Lieutenant William W. Cooke, Seventh U.S. Cavalry, killed at the Battle of the Little Bighorn. The specimen bore no maker's markings but appeared to conform in all respects to the style produced by the Horstmann Brothers firm of Philadelphia. Other than the visors, which were lined in fine green leather, the helmet shell was unlined. There was, however, an unusual type of combination sweat leather and head liner. The sweat portion itself was 1¾ inches wide. Extending from this sweat, and cut from the same piece of lightweight black leather, were six broad "fingers" 2½ inches in length, each punctured with a ⅛-inch hole near its tip. The fingers were laced together at the top with a common black cotton, brass-tipped shoe string, thus forming an adjustable liner.

Dress Cap   The dress cap for officers of infantry was a stiff shako having a felt shell covered on the outside with indigo-blue cloth and lined on the inside with brown glazed cotton drawn with a string at the top (fig. 29). The exterior was decorated with a strand of gold-lace braid ⅛ inch wide around the top and base, these being joined by a piece placed vertically on each side and at the back. (One example had 3/16-inch-wide braid.) The cap was made 3½ inches high in front, rising to 6½ inches high at the rear, giving it a rakish flair. A Horstmann-made example had a brown leather sweat 1¾ inches deep, whereas a specimen manufactured by the Boston firm Bent & Bush had a narrower, 1½-inch sweat of black leather.

The black varnished leather visor of the officers' cap was unbound and was about 1⅜ inches deep at the center with gently rounded corners. The slide on the black patent-leather chin strap was gilt, as were the officers' side buttons bearing the branch letter on the shield. Whereas the enlisted cap had a stamped metal ventilator in the top, the officers' pattern was supposed to have had a small brass one with a revolving fan. The vent most commonly used was made of gauze mesh.[14]

On the front of the officers' cap was a gold embroidered "Arms of the United States" eagle insignia surmounted by thirteen silver stars. Below this, also in gold metal embroidery, was the infantry bugle branch device with the regimental number in silver placed within the loop. Mounted atop the cap was a plume of white cock feathers secured in a gilt holder. The plume holder passed through a small metal-lined opening near the top front edge of the cap, the tip of the holder fitting into a leather socket inside.

Forage Cap   The lower-crowned chasseur-pattern cap had proven to be very popular during the Civil War. Officers on the frontier and elsewhere wore it widely after the war. Despite Surgeon Woodhull's criticisms of the forage cap, the style itself generally was well liked by the army, so well in fact that his objections largely were disregarded by the 1872 Uniform Board. The army preferred to continue its use, perhaps because the French-style cap had become so venerated by the war.

The body of the cap was made of lightweight indigo-dyed woolen cloth, with a band about 1¼ inches deep. The total height of the cap was about

3 inches in front and about 6 inches in the rear, with a crown diameter of about 5 inches. A black patent-leather chin strap ⅜ inch wide, adjustable by a small gilt slide, was attached by a small officers' button at each end of the visor. Visors varied somewhat from one cap to another, though the regulations called for them to be made of black patent leather with an unbound edge.

Although no particular material was specified for the crown piece, both pasteboard and leather were used. The lining was to be of silk, but the material actually used, as well as its color, varied from one cap to another. Japanned leather or goatskin was specified for the sweat leather. Many examples exhibited a cross-hatched design on the sweat that was distinctive of the hatters' trade in this era.

Campaign Hat The only consideration the 1872 Uniform Board gave to special campaign clothing was a new broad-brimmed fatigue hat to be issued to both officers and enlisted men for field service. Except for its color, this black felt hat was nearly identical to the "Andrews hat," which had been specially procured for Colonel Timothy P. Andrews's Voltigeur Regiment during the Mexican War. The five hundred original pearl-gray hats failed to reach the troops before the end of the war and were placed in storage. They were rediscovered in 1851, and the entire stock was issued to the Second U.S. Dragoons serving in Texas.[15] Thus, the 1872 hat became the first general-issue headgear specifically designed for protection against the elements encountered on the western frontier. Previously, the troops either had used the old 1858-pattern hat or had purchased civilian hats for use in the field.

The 1872 folding campaign hat was a strange-looking affair at best (fig. 30). The wide brim was cut in a peculiar oval or "lens" shape and was fitted with

Below left:
29. *Infantry officers' dress cap, 1872.* (Hayes Otoupalik Collection)

Below right:
30. *1872-pattern campaign hat worn by Captain Frederick W. Benteen.* (Glen Swanson Collection)

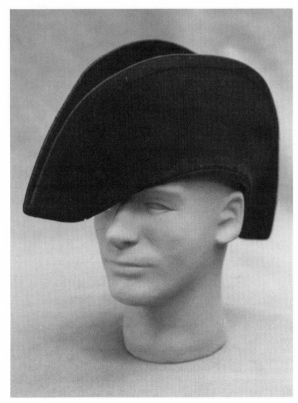

hooks and eyes so that it could be worn extended, to shed sun and rain, or fastened up like a *chapeau bras*. The crown was 5½ inches high, creased down the middle, and the brim measured 5 inches wide at the sides, narrowing to 3¾ inches where the hooks and eyes were attached. It measured 4½ inches front and rear. Around the base of the crown was a 1-inch-wide ribbon of black ribbed silk tied off in a standard hatter's bow on the left side. Black silk binding, 1 inch wide, covered the edge of the brim.

The hat was made of blended fur felt, but rather than being "light colored," as the Woodhull report had recommended, it was black. Since the original Andrews hat had been light gray, and Woodhull had been so adamant about adopting a heat-reflecting hue, it is difficult to understand why the board ignored this important feature. Likewise, there was no provision for ventilating the hat's crown.[16]

Cap Badges   The insignia worn by officers on their forage caps was described as follows: "For officers of Infantry: A gold embroidered bugle, on dark blue cloth ground, with number of the regiment in silver within the bend. For officers of Cavalry: Two gold embroidered sabers, crossed, edges upward, on dark blue cloth ground, with the number of the regiment in silver in the upper angle."[17] The insignia was centered on the front of the cap above the band and sewn in place by means of its oval cloth backing. On some custom-made caps, the embroidery was stitched on the material of the cap itself before assembly.

Coats, Blouses, and Trousers

Dress Coat   The 1872-pattern full-dress coat for line officers was a double-breasted frock of fine-quality dark-blue broadcloth (figs. 31, 32, and 33). The coats for majors, lieutenant colonels, and colonels had nine large eagle buttons in each row, those for lieutenants and captains seven. The buttons for officers were gilt finished, bearing the branch letter within the shield, an *I* for infantry and a *C* for cavalry.

The coat had a standing collar with rounded upper corners measuring from 1 to not more than 2 inches high. Specimens examined averaged about 1⅛ to 1¼ inches and were lined with black velvet in most instances. The collar hooked at the bottom.

The skirt was split and overlapped in the rear with a pocket concealed in the folds on each side. Two large eagle buttons were placed at the top of the tails on the waist seam, and another pair appeared at the bottom of the skirts.

The cuffs, about three inches deep, were made of the same material as the coat and were closed with three small gilt eagle buttons. Those for lieutenants and captains bore two double stripes, or blind buttonholes, of one-fourth-inch gold lace. Each of these extended the depth of the cuff and terminated with a small eagle button. The coats for majors and colonels were distinguished by three double stripes on each cuff.[18]

Most of these coats had lining made of black sateen, padded and quilted in the chest area. There were, at the pleasure of the owner, one or two inside breast pockets. At the waist was an inner belt of broadcloth about 2¼ inches wide with two pair of hooks and eyes for cinching the midriff. Sleeves usually were lined with white cotton sateen having blue or black pinstripes.

Undress Blouse   For daily duty wear, officers were authorized a single-breasted sack coat with falling collar (fig. 34). Like the dress coat, it utilized the

issue-pattern officers' eagle buttons, five on the front opening and three on each cuff. The outer shell was made of dark-blue wool serge, and the lining usually was made of black or dark-green cotton sateen or "Italian cloth." One specimen examined had a lining of light-blue flannel.

The most distinctive feature of this new blouse was the decorative ¼-inch black worsted braid extending in herringbones from each button and buttonhole and terminating in trifoliates. The sleeves were adorned with galloons of like braid extending from the cuff seams, about 2½ inches above the openings, to the elbows. Black woven braid, ½ inch wide, bordered the edges of the collar, the front opening, the two back seams (terminating in trifoliates at the shoulders), and the skirt bottom. The skirt itself was slashed on either side.

Overcoat   Commissioned officers below the rank of brigadier general received a new-pattern overcoat. Whereas they previously had worn the French-pattern "cloak coat," the 1872 regulations provided for a more practical garment. In overall appearance the new coat was not unlike the mounted enlisted men's overcoat, except that it was made of dark-blue melton.

The front of the coat, double-breasted, closed with two rows of large eagle buttons bearing the branch letter. A detachable cape, buttoning only at the neck, reached to the fingertips with the arm extended. It had a stand-and-fall collar. The skirt of the mounted version extended to the midpoint of the calf, whereas the dismounted coat fell three inches below the knee.

In addition to shoulder straps, the wearer's rank was denoted by knots of flat black silk braid, one-eighth of an inch wide. The braid was placed on each sleeve above the cuff, except for second lieutenants' uniforms, whose sleeves were plain. A first lieutenant was identified by a single line of braid, surmounted by a single knot. Captains, majors, lieutenant colonels, and colonels had two, three, four, and five lines, respectively, with a single knot near the elbow.

As a concession to conditions in the West, regulations provided, "On the frontier and campaign, officers may wear the soldier's overcoat, with insignia of rank on the sleeve."[19] However, it is doubtful many officers bothered to abide by the latter rule.

Trousers   The 1872 uniform regulations prescribed distinctive changes in the trousers for regimental officers. Whereas they had previously been made of dark-blue cloth, usually woolen serge, the 1872-pattern trousers were of the same sky-blue shade as those worn by enlisted men. The quality of the cloth was usually a finer grade of broadcloth, not the common kersey. However, officers could purchase regulation yard goods for making their own uniforms and sometimes took advantage of this option to have wives or company tailors produce field outfits for them. Officers' trousers also incorporated cotton lining in the waist, a cloth adjustment belt with buckle in the rear, and sometimes a hip pocket, though many specimens have no pockets.

The color of the new trousers created no noticeable stir among the army's brass, but the newly authorized stripes brought an immediate reaction. Whereas the old trousers had a narrow welt of branch-colored cloth sewn into the outer seams of the legs, the 1872-pattern had 1½-inch-wide stripes. This departure from what had been a long tradition in the army was almost more than some older officers could swallow. "Why couldn't the new pants be half red and half blue," wrote one embittered artillery officer, "instead of *only* an inch and a half stripe?" He went on to suggest that since there would be little difference between the stripes for officers and those for sergeants, the sergeants might sew theirs on the *inseams* for easier identification.[20] Like the noncoms, infantry officers wore stripes of dark blue, whereas cavalry officers wore yellow.

Insignia On each shoulder of the dress coat, an officer wore a "Russian-pattern" knot, about 6¾ inches long, designating his rank. These shoulder knots were made of double rows of intertwined gold braid with a large oval-shaped outer end measuring about 2¾ inches by 3¾ inches wide (fig. 35). Within the loop of this end was a padded center section covered with branch-colored facing cloth upon which both the insignia of rank and the regimental number were embroidered in silver wire. Since second lieutenants had no insignia at this time, their knots bore only the unit number. First lieutenants were designated by one bar, captains by two bars, majors by gold leaves, lieutenant colonels by silver leaves, and colonels by a silver eagle with spread wings. Under the knot was a metal hinge, which was slipped under a sheet brass staple sewn near the shoulder seam, thus attaching the knot to the uniform. The end keyed over a standing brass wire staple mounted to a kidney-shaped base plate sewn near the base of the collar. A small officers' eagle button adorned the small end of the knot. For blouses, officers wore shoulder straps of branch color—yellow for cavalry, light blue for infantry—framed with gold bullion one-quarter to three-eighths of an inch wide (fig. 36). The straps bore the respective rank devices described for dress knots, one device at each end. They were worn centered over the midpoint of the shoulder and parallel to the sleeve seams of the blouse. Shoulder straps of the 1870s did not differ materially from those sold during the Civil War.

35. *Dress shoulder knots worn by First Lieutenant Thomas W. Custer, Seventh U.S. Cavalry.* (Little Bighorn Battlefield National Monument)

Footwear Army regulations prescribed only that officers wear shoes of black leather, at least ankle high.[21] This broad guideline granted the officers wide latitude in their footwear. Photographic evidence reveals that officers wore almost anything that pleased them. In garrison many officers wore commercially manufactured high-top brogans, simply for practicality and comfort, regardless of branch affiliation. Off duty, some individuals sported high-topped gaiters with elastic in the sides rather than laces.

Cavalry officers frequently wore top boots ranging in height from midcalf to the knee, in both field and garrison situations. The shorter Wellington boots, worn under the trousers legs, were also popular for both mounted and foot officers. On campaign, some officers preferred to wear shoes with canvas leggings rather than the hot, cumbersome leather boots. To preserve their more expensive boots, officers frequently purchased the enlisted men's pattern for field wear.[22]

ENLISTED MEN'S UNIFORMS

Headgear

Dress Helmet for Cavalry As produced by various contractors, the enlisted dress helmet had a body made of heavy, black, pressed-fur felt, unlined but edged with thin patent leather (fig. 37). Around the front was a visor strap of black enameled leather stitched to the helmet along its upper and lower edges. This was held in place by a stamped-brass button bearing crossed sabers located at each end of the strap. Over this was an adjustable black leather chin strap, ⅝ inch wide, bearing an open-frame brass slide.[23] The 2½-inch-wide sweatband was made variously of goatskin or sheepskin.

The helmet was ornamented with a large stamped-brass eagle bearing a

36. Shoulder straps, worn on the undress blouse and denoting the ranks of officers. (Little Bighorn Battlefield National Monument)

LIEUTENANT-GENERAL.

MAJOR-GENERAL.

BRIGADIER-GENERAL.

COLONEL.

LIEUTENANT-COLONEL, OR MAJOR.

CAPTAIN.

FIRST LIEUTENANT

SECOND LIEUTENANT.

Union shield on its breast and surmounted by a scroll or facsimile ribbon bearing the motto "E Pluribus Unum." Unlike the officers' helmet, the enlisted men's helmet did not have a regimental number affixed to the plate. Atop the helmet was a brass socket holding a pale-yellow horsehair plume about fourteen inches in length that draped over the sides and rear of the helmet. This socket was attached to a base plate having four miter-shaped feet contoured to the helmet's dome and affixed to it by small decorative brass buttons.[24] There was also a small ventilator on either side of the crown; the Horstmann Company used one of gauze screen, whereas the other contractor, Bent & Bush, used a pinwheel design of stamped brass.[25]

Suspended by brass scrolls, one on either side of the helmet, was a triple-braided yellow worsted band, festooned front and rear. The ends of this band were coupled at the left side by a small tassel. They passed through the tassel and continued in the form of double worsted cords approximately 5 feet 8 inches in length. At the outer end of each cord was a flat woven aiguillette about 2½ inches in diameter from which another tassel was suspended. When the helmet was worn, these cords draped to the left shoulder, where they were held together by a braided slide. There, they were separated and passed to the front and rear of the neck, then were crossed under the right shoulder strap of the uniform coat and were rejoined by a slide under the right arm. Together, they were brought across the chest where they were suspended by a small loop from the button on the left shoulder strap.[26]

Dress Cap Although French prestige waned after the Germans defeated France in the Franco-Prussian War of 1870–71, France nevertheless continued to serve as a strong influence for the uniform styles adopted by the United States. The 1872 dress cap for foot troops, quite similar to what the Woodhull report had recommended, was a stiff felt shako covered with dark-blue woolen cloth (fig. 38). A distinctly French design, it rose vertically in the front approximately 3½ inches, and the top sloped upward, making it 5½ inches high at the rear. The body of the infantry model was distinguished by a braid of sky-blue worsted, ³⁄₁₆ inch wide, around its sides just below the top. A like braid was stitched around the base of the cap just above the edge. Additionally, there were three vertical pieces, one down the rear center and one slanting front to rear down each side. The visor, made of heavy enameled black leather, was worn straight and horizontal across the forehead. The specifications failed to stipulate whether or not it was to be bound, so both bound and raw-edged visors were made, according to manufacturer.[27] Likewise, there are variations in the dimensions of the visors, since no measurements were given in the specifications. The visor on an extant J. H. Wilson contract specimen measures only 1¼ inches deep at the center.

37. Enlisted man's dress helmet, 1872, worn by Private William Williams, Seventh U.S. Cavalry. (Little Bighorn Battlefield National Monument)

Left:

38. *Pattern 1872 infantry dress cap worn by enlisted men.*

Right:

39. *Forage cap for all enlisted men, 1872.*

The cap was provided with a two-piece chin strap of lightweight enameled leather ⅝ inch wide, the pieces joined by a brass slide on the left side. The two outer ends of the strap were affixed to the cap body, just behind the visor, by cuff-size eagle buttons. Finishing the inside was a sweatband, 1½ to 2 inches wide, made of Belgium leather. Most, if not all, regular army specimens were marked "U.S.Q.M.D." inside the sweat on the right side of the cap.[28]

Centered in the top of the cap was a small japanned ventilator, ⅝ inch in diameter, intended to release body heat radiating from the soldier's head. The manufacturer's label, made of paper and shaped to conform with the shape of the top, was glued on the inside surface.

The infantry dress cap was trimmed with a pear-shaped white woolen pompon, mounted upon a stamped-brass half-sphere at the front center of the cap. Also on the front of the cap was a miniature version of the stamped-brass eagle used on the cavalry helmet, worn with the wing tips just below the top of the cap. This insignia measured 1½ inches across the wing tips. Below this was the new smaller-size horn insignia authorized for the infantry in 1872.

Forage Cap The old "bummer" cap was replaced by a smart-appearing chasseur-pattern forage cap of dark-blue woolen broadcloth, which first saw issue early in 1873 (fig. 39).[29] This piece of headgear was worn universally by all branches of the army. Although its use usually was confined to the garrison for everyday wear, a few soldiers wore it for field service. Compared with the high crown of the 1858 cap, the crown of the 1872 version was only about 2¾ inches high in front, the top rising about an inch from front to back, making for a forty-five-degree angle.[30] At the rear, the crown rose approximately 5 inches above the band, which was 1¼ inches wide. The top of the cap was circular, about 4¾ to 5 inches in diameter, and was formed upon a thick piece of tarred pasteboard.

The forage cap had a stiff, unbound patent-leather visor and a narrow two-piece chin strap of enameled leather coupled with a small stamped-brass slide.

The black enameled-leather chin strap, ½ inch wide, was held in place by two small eagle buttons, one at either side just behind the ends of the visor. The sweat was identical to that in the dress cap, except that the name of the manufacturer and the contract date were usually imprinted in silver lettering on the right side. The sweats in both types of caps, as well as in dress helmets, nearly always had a fine crosshatch design embossed over the surface.

The interior of the cap was lined with brownish-colored glazed muslin loosely stitched to the 1¼-inch-wide band of leather used as a stiffener between the sweat and the outer shell of the cap. This liner was gathered at the top by a piece of string.

Campaign Hat　The enlisted hat (fig. 40) was virtually identical to that for officers, with one exception. In place of the edge binding, the enlisted version had two rows of stitching, one-quarter inch apart, around the outer edge of the brim. These were intended to add a degree of stiffness to the brim but had little effect in doing so.[31]

The old worsted hat cord, of which hundreds of thousands remained in stock, was retained as an issue item, even though not included specifically in the revised regulations. It is interesting to note that hat cords were included in the unit price of the first contracts awarded to P. Herst of Philadelphia on October 19, 1872.[32] Apparently, Colonel L. C. Easton, commanding the Philadelphia depot, later realized that the army still had an enormous stock of cords on hand, whereupon he omitted them from the last two contracts.

Whether or not soldiers wore the cords was left to the discretion of unit commanders or to individual soldiers' preference. Beyond its purely ornamental value, the cord served no practical purpose. Hat cords were never particularly popular, and in the 1870s those men who drew them soon lost or discarded them.

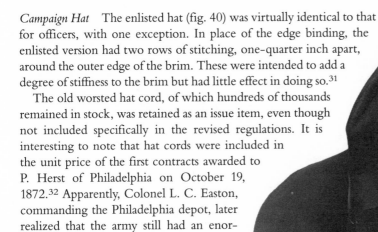

40. *Folding campaign hat, 1872. Universally despised, this hat nevertheless saw considerable use in the major campaigns of the 1870s. (Hayes Otoupalik Collection)*

Insignia　The bugle and the crossed sabers remained the respective branch insignia for infantry and cavalry; however, the sizes of both ornaments were reduced by about one-half. The new bugle measured 2 inches wide, whereas the crossed sabers were 2¾ inches wide (fig. 41).

The designs for bugles and crossed sabers were also more refined than the old 1851 insignia. The branch devices for enlisted men were made of thin stamped brass with attachment wires soldered on the reverse. The letters and numbers, issued separately, measured one-half inch high and were made in similar fashion, with fine wire loops on the backs for fastening them to the cap. Although the regulations did not provide for wearing branch insignia on the campaign hat, photographic evidence indicates that, in rare instances, some individuals did so.

The regulations were ambiguous concerning just how the insignia were to be worn on the forage cap. The statement that "the badge of corps or letter of company" was to be worn on the cap caused no little confusion in the ranks, as

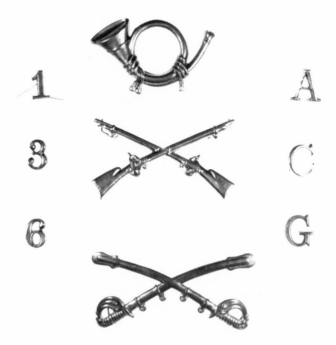

41. Cap insignia for enlisted men: 1872 infantry bugle (top); 1875 infantry crossed rifles (center); cavalry crossed sabers (bottom). Examples of numbers and letters are on each side.

On the facing page:

42. Unidentified Seventh Cavalry private, ca. 1873. His cap exhibits the short-lived regulation manner of wearing branch insignia with the company letter only. This soldier's 1872 cap, four-button sack coat, and 1855 saber belt reflect the mixture of old- and new-pattern equipage so typical at the time. He also appears to have the old Stuart saber hanger and a new 1872 saber knot. (B. William Henry, Jr., Collection)

evidenced in period photographs.[33] Awakening to this omission, army headquarters promulgated General Orders No. 67 on June 25, 1873, which specified that both the bugle and the company letter were to be worn. However, this still did not resolve the problem entirely because there were no explicit instructions as to where the letter was to be placed. Presumably, it was to be affixed within the bend of the bugle device for infantry, as for officers, and cradled in the upper angle of the crossed sabers.[34] However, the regulations also were construed to mean that only the company letter or only the branch device was to be worn on the cap (fig. 42). This heralded the beginning of several years of confusion over the proper manner for wearing cap insignia, an issue that will be discussed in greater detail in a subsequent chapter.

Cap Cover   A waterproof cover had been provided for the 1858 forage cap, but this item must have been overlooked by the officers who recommended the new uniform. In 1874 the omission was noted when it was reported that all of the old covers in storage had undergone chemical change and were no longer fit for issue.[35] This report may have been true, or the situation may have been created to procure covers of the proper shape to fit the lower-crowned 1872 forage cap.

There were no specifications published for the cap cover, but one extant specimen was made of shiny-black lacquered linen, patterned in the same general shape as the body of the forage cap. However, it was made of only three pieces, a top and two sides, without a band. It was hand stitched throughout, with a narrow welt around the top and a buttonhole on each side corresponding to the chin strap buttons on the cap. The lower edge of the cover was bound with black hatter's ribbon, or braid, one-half inch wide.

These covers proved unpopular with the troops, probably because a forage cap, with or without a cover, was poor protection from the rain. The cap fit the head so closely that water ran down the sides of the head and the back of the

neck. The campaign hat was a much better choice for inclement weather. By 1877 so few of the covers were being drawn that they were discontinued as an issue item.[36]

Coats, Blouses and Trousers

Dress Coat   Surgeon Woodhull had spared no ammunition in bombarding the old 1857 uniform coat. His opinion survey had pointed up its many faults, particularly the tight fit and odd proportions. Moreover, it was "insufferable in the warmer months" due to its "bungling collar" and "excessive weight." Woodhull advocated the abolishment of the dress coat altogether, calling it "the joint-heir of metallic armor and of a martinet genius" exemplified in the British and Prussian armies.[37] In its place he recommended a looser-fitting garment that could be used for both dress and fatigue, but the 1872 Uniform Board ignored Woodhull's opinion by once again adopting a formal dress coat for the rank and file. Although the new coat was a distinct departure from the old one, its reliance on contemporary European style was obvious. If sheer appearance counted for anything, the U.S. Army had made its "fashion statement" of the era.

The body of the coat was made of twilled dark-blue wool flannel with a rather tight-fitting waist (basque-style) and a skirt reaching to the midpoint of the hips, though the pattern for foot troops was made 2¾ inches longer than the mounted version (fig. 43). It was single-breasted, with nine standard eagle buttons spaced evenly between the neck and waist. The standing collar was cut 1¼ to 1½ inches high and was faced with finer-grade cloth corresponding to the branch of service—yellow for cavalry and sky blue for infantry. These panels extended back about 4 inches from the front opening, which hooked up square with two black japanned hooks and eyes. The regimental number of stamped brass, ½ inch high, the same as for cap insignia, was worn in the center of each panel.

Let into each shoulder seam was a tapered strap extending nearly to the collar, its free end fastened down with a cuff-size eagle button. On each cuff was a cloth facing, scalloped along its outer edge, with three small buttons. In addition to these facings, a branch-colored piping extended around the upper and lower edges of the collar and down the edge of the front opening.

Cavalry coats, in addition to being somewhat shorter for the mounted man, were distinguished by the piping around the bottom edge of the skirt (coats for dismounted men were raw-edged) and by slashes on each side of the skirt to permit more freedom of movement (fig. 44).[38] Whereas the coat for infantry and other dismounted troops was adorned on the rear with two scalloped facings about 8½ inches long, extending down from the waist and sewn into pleats on either side of the vent, the mounted version had a more elaborate, three-pronged facing on the back of the skirt.

Features that were to prove dysfunctional were the two belt supporters let into the waist seam on either side at about the position of the elbow. These were intended to help support the weight of the saber or the waist belt, but also, and more practically, they ensured that the belts would be worn uniformly at the proper level. These straps, piped in branch color as well, each buttoned to the coat body with a small eagle button.

Both models were lined in the sleeves and body with off-white drill and were padded in the chest area. On the inside of the left breast was a vertically opening

pocket. Black Italian cloth, a lightweight, closely woven cotton material, was used to line the skirts from the waist down.

Fatigue Blouse   The new-pattern blouse was nearly identical to the one Surgeon Woodhull had recommended several years earlier, though the pattern had been refined by Inspector Frank S. Johnson of the Philadelphia Depot.[39] Known as the "Swiss Blouse," it was a loose-fitting dark-blue woolen jacket with a falling collar and a skirt extending to the hips (fig. 45). Like the dress coat, it had a row of nine large eagle buttons down the front closure.

The most radical feature of the new blouse was its pleated front, something that raised eyebrows immediately among the rank and file. On either side were four pleats measuring about 1¼ inches wide. These extended from the yoke all the way to the bottom of the skirt. A belted section, 1¾ inches wide, was laid over the pleats at the waist to gather them and provide a space where the belt would be positioned uniformly. The grizzled veterans who looked askance at their fashionable new pleats probably did not comprehend, or appreciate, the hygienic principles the Quartermaster Department had so thoughtfully designed into this garment. As Woodhull had explained it back in 1868: "By being made sufficiently loose to wear beneath it, if necessary, three woolen shirts and a waist-coat it will be adequate, with proper outer clothing in inclement weather. . . . By reducing undergarments, it will be no more oppressive at the hottest posts than any possible clothing must be."[40] The soldier, therefore, had increased latitude in layering his undergarments, a principle ignored for the most part until it was revived by the U.S. Army during World War II. Woodhull further claimed that the pleats allowed the wearer greater freedom of movement and unconstricted breathing during marches and physical labor. Yet, they would lie flat and neat for garrison duties.

Although a convincing argument may have been made for pleating the chest area, it is doubtful that many soldiers saw the necessity for pleating the skirts too. The pleats gave the blouse an undeniably "frilly" look (fig. 46). Conveniently concealed within the pleats were three bag pockets, one in the left breast and two in the skirts, the latter being especially handy when the belt and other equipments hindered access to the pants pockets. These pockets were made of brown glazed cotton.

The 1872 blouse was made in both lined and unlined versions, with the collar, yoke, and cuffs trimmed with branch-colored worsted braid approximately ⅛ inch in diameter. The braid on the cuff was stitched on in an inverted "V" design about 4 inches deep, the ends extending around the sleeve about 1½ inches above the opening. The cuffs, incidentally, had neither slashes nor buttons.

Trousers   The trousers for enlisted men still were to be made of the familiar sky-blue kersey, but the pattern was altered from the style issued since 1861. The waistband, secured with two pressed-tin buttons, was widened to 3½ inches in the front, tapering toward the rear. Apparently, the old method of waist adjustment

45. Fatigue blouse, 1872. (Smithsonian Institution)

was to be retained, that is, by means of a vent cut into the waistband and a cord passing through sewn grommets, one on either side of this vent.

The newly designed trousers were to have two front pockets only, with curved top openings to make them more accessible. The first orders for 1872-pattern trousers were sent to Schuylkill Arsenal in June of that year. However, Secretary of War William W. Belknap was alarmed when he became aware of the increased cost for making pants of this style. Consequently, he overruled the uniform board by ordering that the old pattern, with side-seam pockets and a narrower waistband, be continued. Therefore, only minor numbers of the new-pattern trousers were manufactured and distributed for trial among troops on the eastern seaboard; none reached troops in the West.[41]

Although the legs of the new trousers were not to be cut as full as their predecessor's, they remained straight-cut. Those for mounted men were to be made with an additional layer of kersey on the seat and the inside of the legs. The saddle piece extended the life of the trousers and, perhaps more important, provided extra padding between the rider and his saddle, thus reducing the frequency of saddle sores.

During the 1876 Sioux Campaign, according to Lieutenant Edward S. Godfrey, many Seventh Cavalrymen lined the seats and legs of their trousers with white canvas from the knees up (fig. 47).[42] Godfrey's comment has often been applied generally to the frontier cavalry; however, it should be kept in mind that this action may have been a response to a particular set of circumstances existing at that time and place. The fact that the men lined their trousers before they left Fort Abraham Lincoln may suggest that this was not a field expedient. It is unlikely that so much canvas would have been available for such purposes after the expedition departed for Montana. Rather, the Seventh Cavalry's modified pants may have been a reflection of the size shortages in 1861-pattern mounted trousers. Godfrey's statement that "many, perhaps most" of the men used canvas lining suggests that at least half of the soldiers resorted to this, implying at the same time that the rest wore regulation mounted trousers.

Indeed, soldiers may have used canvas for saddle pieces simply because it wore better than the kersey reinforcement. A pair of canvas-lined Pattern 1876 trousers examined evidenced no stitching from a previous saddle piece, thus indicating this pair originally was the dismounted version. The saddle piece on this specimen extended from the seat to the cuffs, similar to the regulation pattern.

As a concession to the soldiers' longtime practice of having the company tailors remake their trousers to achieve a better fit, the Quartermaster Department began issuing "unmade" trousers in 1872. One-third of the total of each requisition were to be sent out in kit form, with the component pieces precut to a given size. Bundled inside each roll were buttons, lining, and pocket material, along with needles and thread. Those soldiers who wanted to do so could draw the unmade articles and have a tailor make them up for a custom fit. These kits proved to be so popular with the troops that the practice eventually was extended to include blouses as well.

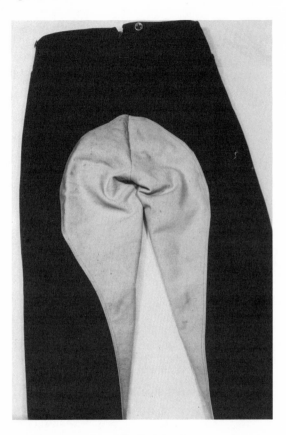

On the facing page:

46. Two unidentified soldiers of Company B, 6th U.S. Infantry, ca. 1873. The private wears his pleated fatigue blouse in the as-issued fashion, whereas the sergeant reflects a marked contrast, with the pleats on his blouse stitched down. Both men wear the 1872 bugle and company letter on their caps. Many "doughboys" in the 1870s preferred to wear boots rather than high-top brogans.

Above:

47. A pair of 1876-pattern trousers with canvas saddle piece.

Noncommissioned officers wore stripes of facing cloth down the outer leg seams of their trousers, ½ inch wide for corporals and 1 inch for all sergeants of the line. The upper ends of the stripes were sewn into the waistband seam and lay centered down the outer leg seams to the cuffs. Although the width for corporals' stripes remained unchanged in the 1872 regulations, sergeants' stripes were narrower than before, the 1½-inch stripes being reserved exclusively for officers.

The trouser stripes not only were ornamental but also served a functional purpose to further distinguish the noncoms, particularly in the field, where blouses might not be worn. Stripes for infantrymen were dark blue; those for cavalry were yellow. Contrary to common belief, trumpeters at this time were not authorized to wear the double stripes so often associated with their function. Such stripes were not made official until 1883.[43]

The most common style of button used on army trousers during the 1870s was a plain-faced, two-piece, pressed-tin button left over from the war surplus. It measured ¹¹⁄₁₆ inch in diameter, with four holes. This larger size was used for waistbands and suspenders, whereas a smaller ⁹⁄₁₆-inch button of the same style was used on the fly.

A second type of pressed-metal button is known to have been in use during the period. This button was made both of white metal and of brass with an iron back and had a rather wide, flat flange imprinted with a cross-hatched design. It had the same measurements and hole arrangement as the earlier pressed-tin variety. Although its application to trousers has not been confirmed, examples of the stippled button have been excavated on the Little Bighorn Battlefield, a benchmark site dated precisely to June 25–26, 1876.[44] Such evidence suggests that the stippled pressed-metal button may have been used on the Pattern 1861 trousers manufactured in the 1870s.

MUSICIANS' UNIFORMS

The army clearly distinguished between field and band musicians. Field musicians, two per foot company, were drummers, fife players, and buglers who were members of the company and provided daily tactical calls on marches and campaigns. In garrison they were detailed to the guard to sound the scheduled calls regulating post activities. At forts or cantonments where no band was present, they assembled to provide music for retreat parade and guard mount.

For dress occasions field musicians invariably wore the regulation coat with double "herringbones," or loops, of worsted braid extending outward from each button on the torso. The fatigue blouse and trousers, as well as the headgear, were the same as those authorized for privates.[45]

The uniforms worn by regimental band members were another matter. Regulations permitted the regimental commander to embellish them according to his own whim, the cost to be borne by the regimental fund. Given this latitude, the colonels frequently took a personal hand in designing a distinctive uniform, based on the regulation one. Some bands wore the regulation musician's coat, whereas others opted for the standard line-issue version. Many bands applied extra rows of buttons to the chest for a triple-breasted effect. Commercial shoulder knots, fringed epaulets, and breast cords frequently were purchased to add considerable flair to the bandsmen. Another fairly common departure from regulations was the commercially made waist belts sported by some bands. These usually were made of white webbing or of fine bag leather with colored decorative stitching. The 1851-pattern eagle belt plate was popular with many bands, though various specially designed commercial plates were used as well.

Judging by period photographs, it was not unusual for bandsmen to have special trouser stripes. Among the infantry bands, wide dark-blue stripes were quite popular, and in at least the First and Fifth infantry regiments, bandsmen wore single wide stripes of white facing cloth. Presumably this was done not only to distinguish them when in fatigue uniform but also to complement the white pompon on the shako. Other bands preferred double one-half-inch stripes—dark blue for infantry, yellow for cavalry. Some cavalry musicians further embellished these by adding dark-blue cloth between the stripes (frontispiece).

Infantry and cavalry bands usually wore the basic headgear of their respective branches; however, some of the infantry units added braided cords and feather plumes to their shakos. Over the years nearly every regimental band took on a unique appearance and became a source of esprit de corps for the entire unit.

CHEVRONS

Noncommissioned officers received new chevrons based on a design conceived and later patented by Frank S. Johnson, an employee at Schuylkill Arsenal.[46] These chevrons, though neater in appearance, were clearly a concession to more economical manufacture. Rather than being made with separate stripes of silk or worsted, as were the patterns in use since the 1850s, the 1872 chevrons were made on a single piece of wool "facing cloth" corresponding to the branch color. The stripes were delineated by lines of black silk chain-stitching, spaced one-half inch apart.

The insignia for the various grades were not changed from those in use previously (fig. 48). Corporals were distinguished by two stripes, sergeants by three stripes, and first sergeants by three stripes and a lozenge, or diamond, cradled in the angle of the chevron. Each regimental headquarters was assigned a quartermaster sergeant, who wore three stripes with a tie of three bars, and a sergeant major (senior in the regiment and assistant to the adjutant), whose chevrons had three stripes with an arc of three stripes.

Additionally, principal musicians, a grade peculiar to infantry bands, were recognized by a special chevron with three stripes surmounted by a bugle.[47] (Before 1872 the two principal musicians authorized for each band usually wore the chevrons of a duty sergeant.) The new chevrons were issued in pairs and were intended to be worn with the bells of the bugles facing forward. However, photographic evidence suggests that in practice some musicians wore them backward.

The cavalry also received two new noncommissioned grades, chief trumpeter and saddler sergeant, which were also attached to the regimental headquarters staff. Although both of these grades had been recognized informally during and after the Civil War, they had been authorized no special insignia.[48] The chief trumpeter, who was responsible for the training, appearance, and scheduling of the company trumpeters, was authorized a chevron of three stripes with a single arc enclosing a bugle like that on the principal musician's chevron. The regiment's master saddler was now distinguished by a sergeant's chevron having a saddler's round knife in the angle.

The special devices of all the 1872-pattern chevrons, such as diamonds, trumpets, and so forth, were cut out in silhouette on a field of dark-blue flannel. The device itself was formed by backing the cutout with a piece of branch-colored facing material.

The regulations remained silent regarding drum majors, or chief musicians, as bandleaders were variously called. No particular chevron was prescribed, since the entire matter of their uniforms was left to the discretion of regimental commanders.[49] Most bandleaders were enlisted from among professionals in civilian life because of their special qualifications, and they were paid accordingly from the regimental fund or by donations. In essence, they performed the duties of first sergeant for the band, with the principal musicians being equivalent to duty sergeants. In some regiments a principal musician served as the bandleader, and the other noncoms wore the chevrons of duty sergeants. A survey of historical photographs indicates that when the chief musician was designated, he wore either the chevrons of a sergeant major or none at all. In some units a fur busby and baton, and perhaps certain elements of an officer's uniform, served as badges of his office while on parade.

Those men who had seen prior service were authorized to wear half-chevrons on both sleeves of their dress coats. Each service chevron indicated a prior enlistment of either three or five years.[50] The first chevron was posi-

48. Chevrons for noncommissioned officers, 1872.

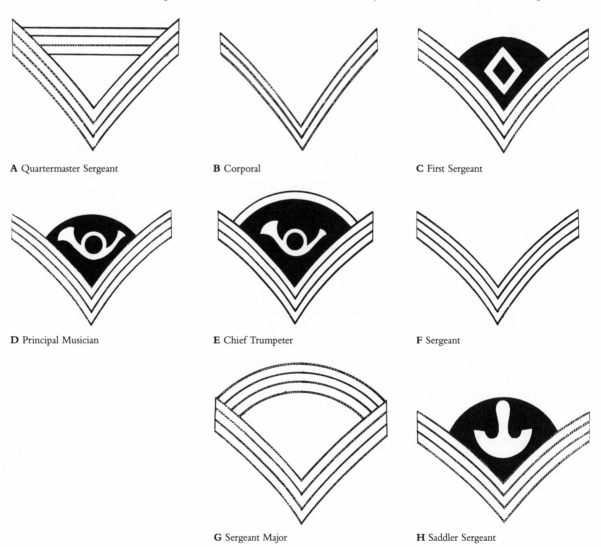

A Quartermaster Sergeant

B Corporal

C First Sergeant

D Principal Musician

E Chief Trumpeter

F Sergeant

G Sergeant Major

H Saddler Sergeant

tioned one-half inch above the front corner of the cuff facing, with the chevron for each successive enlistment being placed above and one-fourth inch apart.

The chevron for peacetime service was made of either blue or yellow facing cloth, one-half inch wide, to match the other uniform trimmings. If the soldier had served in a declared war at any time during an enlistment, he wore a distinctive chevron with red edges, made by overlaying a standard sky-blue or yellow stripe on a red one three-fourths inch wide. The exception to this was the chevron for artillery service during wartime, which was to be red edged with white. With so many Civil War veterans in the ranks at this time, the question soon arose as to what color should be worn when such service had been in branches other than the one in which the soldier currently was assigned. On September 15, 1873, the adjutant general rendered a decision that veterans were to wear chevrons of the color corresponding to their branches of prior service. Consequently, soldiers who had served formerly in several different branches might have a veritable rainbow on each sleeve (fig. 49).[51]

UNDERCLOTHING

Shirts

Sweeping changes notwithstanding, ample quantities of shirts, drawers, and stockings remained on hand from the war surplus. Their suitability may have been questionable, but the board saw no reason to adopt new patterns, especially when the prospects for a large appropriation were slim at best. So, for the time being anyway, the army was to be outfitted with the same styles of underclothing it had worn for more than a decade.

A question arises as to why the army chose to provide the troops with woolen shirts rather than something more comfortable. The U.S. Army of the mid-nineteenth century was not yet ready to concede that men serving in different parts of the country might need different types and weights of clothing to suit the particular climate. Wool, as any outdoorsman knows, absorbs moisture yet maintains body warmth in cold temperatures. A soldier could always wear more shirts, following the more modern principle of layering, to increase his comfort level in really cold temperatures. It must be remembered that soldiers spent much of their time in the outdoors day and night, year round. Almost everywhere in the West, even during summer, nighttime temperatures could be uncomfortably cool. The army did not go to the expense of providing more than one basic weight of clothing because it felt that having the men a little too warm was better than exposing them to illness and frostbite during the winter.

Army-issue flannel shirts came in two colors, white and "bluish gray." The latter was singled out by Surgeon Woodhull as being made of very coarse material that irritated the soldier's skin "in the most excrutiating [sic] manner," particularly in hot climates. The shirt was worn next to the skin, since cotton flannel undershirts were not adopted by the army until the mid-1880s. In his 1868 report Woodhull questioned the necessity of issuing both types of shirts, when "three separate grades [of one or the other] and many sizes" would be more practical.[52]

The patterns of these two shirts were identical, having a short pointed collar

49. *Service stripes on dress coat worn by First Sergeant Joseph W. Hunting, Company E, Fifth U.S. Infantry. The lower stripe is of pre-1872 vintage and is yellow edged with red, denoting Hunting's Civil War service with the Second Massachusetts Cavalry. The upper, for his enlistment with Company B, Thirty-seventh U.S. Infantry, is the peacetime stripe prescribed by the 1872 regulations.*

with one four-hole tin button at the neck. The opening, with slightly overlapping sides, extended to about the bottom of the wearer's sternum. The sleeves were cut on a straight taper with a distinct drop off the shoulder. They were of one-piece body construction, with either false or separately attached cuffs.[53] Each cuff bore a small pressed-tin button.

Many soldiers preferred to buy nonregulation shirts wherever they could find them. One officer said his men bought "cassimere shirts for winter, and percale shirts for summer."[54] Generally speaking, the summer shirts were plain white, without collars, though ones having pinstripes of blue or red also were fairly common. The shield-front, or "fireman's," shirt of lightweight wool or wool flannel was another popular item purchased widely among both officers and enlisted men.[55]

In keeping with the propriety of the times, the shirt was not intended to be worn as an outer garment in polite company (fig. 50). Rather, it was to be covered by the coat or blouse.[56] The soldier's shirt, after all, was considered to be an undergarment. In Victorian society a man, soldier or not, would have been considered uncouth indeed to appear in his shirt sleeves around the garrison, especially where he might be observed by ladies. Exceptions to this custom were permitted when soldiers were engaged at physical labor or were in the field in hot weather.

50. *Soldier modeling white flannel shirt and canton drawers of the styles issued during the Civil War.* (U.S. Army Quartermaster Museum, courtesy Smithsonian Institution)

Drawers

The canton flannel drawers were of the same basic pattern as those issued previously, with a fairly narrow, straight band fastened with two buttons. These were usually four-hole buttons made of bone or white porcelain commonly available on the commercial market. The fly was formed simply by the cut, the left side overlapping the right. Like the trousers, the waist on the drawers was extremely high by modern standards, extending all the way to the navel. Surgeon Woodhull implied either that the drawers issued during the war had no ankle adjustment or that some patterns may have had buttons to keep them from riding up on the leg. But, the drawers shown in Quartermaster Department photographs of 1875 clearly show the ankles with an opening to the front of each and with cloth tapes for tying them. One authority has surmised that this feature was added sometime after 1868 and that it was this altered pattern that was photographed and labeled as the "old pattern."[57]

Soldiers complained bitterly about the old-pattern drawers, especially their cut. Speaking on behalf of his men, an officer pointed out that the legs were "too small and the waist too large"; another criticized them as being "of such bad shape that they rip and tear, especially about the crotch, before they are otherwise worn out. Consequently, when the smallest men require Nos. 3 & 4, Nos. 1 & 2 are useless."[58] The Clothing Branch took heed of these comments, and within the next few years the army would get more comfortably fitting drawers.

Stockings

For some unexplained reason, the uniform board initially overlooked the subject of stockings, despite the fact that Woodhull had roundly condemned them four years earlier. At that time he had characterized them as being "miserable in texture" and too short, citing the example of a soldier who lost both legs to severe frostbite.[59] His views on the woolen socks were shared almost unanimously by the rank and file.

The ink was hardly dry on the new regulations when General Meigs's attention was called to the oversight concerning stockings. Major James D. Bingham, head of the Clothing Branch, reported on September 30, 1872, that action had been taken to make samples on which standards for better-quality socks would be based.[60] Unfortunately, little is known about the appearance of these stockings, but it may be that the specifications published in 1876 for socks of "pure, brown, woolen yarn" were, in fact, the same as those effected in 1872.[61]

In any event, the troops still were not satisfied with their socks, be they the Civil War leftovers or the new style. Lieutenant Colonel George A. Woodward called them "the poorest articles issued to troops." He added: "A great many of the men do not wear them at all, preferring to buy a better article of dealers. Thirty days is about their maximum duration in garrison. On campaigns they will not last over ten days. They are very uncomfortable to march in owing to the lumpy character of the seams."[62]

Winter and Other Specialized Clothing

Kersey Overcoats

The uniform board elected to simplify the matter of supplying overcoats, and in the same stroke improve uniformity throughout the service, by stipulating that foot troops were to wear the 1861-pattern mounted coat with the wrist-length cape and stand-and-fall collar (fig. 51).[63] This double-breasted coat, made of standard sky-blue kersey, had two rows of six large eagle buttons down the front and a small iron wire hook and eye at the neck. The cape, sewn permanently at the base of the wide collar, was closed with twelve cuff-size eagle buttons. The coat itself extended to the wearer's knees and was lined in the torso with either drab-colored burlap or dark-blue flannel blouse material. The sleeves, lined in heavy cotton drill, had turned-up cuffs about 4½ inches deep. At the waist on the rear of the coat was a tapered belt about 1¾ inches wide, the ends of which overlapped in the middle and fastened with two eagle buttons. The skirt was vented in the rear seam with an opening about 18 inches deep. (This vent was only about 12 inches deep on the foot model.) Although this coat, along with suitable layering of other garments underneath, was adequate for average winter conditions in the East, it was woefully unsuited for the high plains.

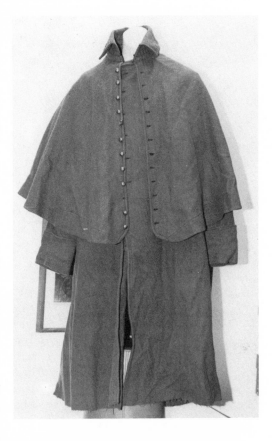

51. Civil War 1861-pattern mounted overcoat authorized for all branches in 1872. (Smithsonian Institution)

Overcoat, Blanket-Lined

Attempting to make up for the shortcomings of the standard overcoat, the quartermaster general, in 1871, experimented with adding a lining of army blanket material in some of the mounted overcoats (fig. 52). This practice actually had been initiated by enlisted men of the Seventh Cavalry (and perhaps others) at least as early as 1868, during the winter campaign launched against the

Cheyennes. First Sergeant John Ryan remembered: "[The men lined] their overcoats with woolen blankets, while others made leggings from pieces of condemned government canvas. . . . By lining the skirt of the coat they were made very comfortable as far down as the knees, and then the leggings in addition to the long cavalry boots, kept the men pretty warm."[64]

A surviving example of the Quartermaster Department's version, in the Smithsonian Institution, is lined with extremely heavy, coarse, brownish-colored blanket exhibiting the black end-stripes of the bedding blanket.[65] Initially, condemned blankets from the war surplus were used for this purpose. When the supply of these was exhausted, the Clothing Branch substituted gray shirting flannel. This material soon was pointed out as being too light in weight for the purpose, and authority was given to use new blankets from the stocks on hand.[66]

With typical conservatism, the quartermaster general issued these special coats only to those frontier posts lying north of forty-two degrees latitude, or just above the line of the new transcontinental railroad.[67] No doubt the troops at posts like Fort Bridger, Wyoming Territory, which was situated at forty-one degrees, were distressed to learn that General Meigs had arbitrarily excluded them from receiving the modified overcoats. He would have been hard pressed, in fact, to convince a soldier on the plains of Kansas or eastern Colorado of the rationality of his decision. Although the blanket-lined overcoat was an improvement in cold-weather gear, it clearly fell short of the mark.

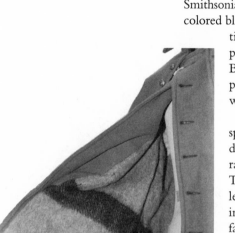

52. *Blanket lining of the 1871 modified overcoat.* (Smithsonian Institution)

Overcoat, Double-Caped

When the 1872 Uniform Board specified that all troops would henceforth wear the mounted overcoat, they failed to take into consideration the number of such coats on hand. Not only were there too few to supply the army at large, but there were barely enough available to meet the needs of the cavalry and light artillery, both of whom used the mounted overcoat. To compound the situation, the available appropriation was so small that Meigs could not consider manufacturing new ones.

Nevertheless, his innovative staff responded to the overcoat shortage with a solution that stands as a tribute to their pragmatism. In his annual report, Major James D. Bingham proudly stated: "To prevent loss to the Government, and with a view to utilizing the large supply of great-coats (foot) on hand, the Quartermaster-General recommended the issue of these overcoats after attaching to them mounted capes. . . . [T]hese great-coats have since been issued with double capes, and the result thus far shown that this arrangement has been of benefit to the Government, as well as to the enlisted men of the Army."[68] Thus, long capes were made up and attached to the old infantry coats for the cost of labor alone (fig. 53). The most cost-effective solution was simply to leave the short cape intact and attach the long one beneath, because taking time to rip off the short cape would have added to the cost.

As soon as the sample of the double-caped overcoat was ready, Meigs took it to Secretary of War Belknap for his examination. Although the sample coat did not comply with the letter of the regulations, it answered the purpose. Moreover, the two capes were even warmer and would save the old coats from being wasted, all of which appealed to the secretary. The altered coat was adopted officially for all branches of the service on June 25, 1873.[69] Even though Captain John F. Rodgers at the Philadelphia Depot (fig. 54) enthusiastically proclaimed the double-caped overcoat to be "an admirable garment" that would "give great satisfaction to the Army," its appearance readily invited soldier witticism.[70] Ex-private Charles Parker later recalled: "These [overcoats] were of blue shoddy, the one I drew had a standing collar and, I think, four small capes, three anyhow. It reminded me of the old-time London cabby as featured in some of Dicken's [sic] works."[71] The double capes obviously made a lasting impression on Private Parker.

So, throughout the mid-1870s the enlisted men of the army were issued a mixture of regulation mounted overcoats, mounted coats with blanket lining, and altered double-caped overcoats. Not until the end of the decade would a standard coat be adopted, and because a soldier received only one for his entire enlistment, several more years would pass before everyone finally wore the same pattern.

Fur Overcoats, Caps, and Mittens

The Quartermaster Department still failed to realize, or at least acknowledge, that winter conditions in many areas of the West were drastically different from those east of the Mississippi. Troops serving on the plains often had to endure blizzards and temperatures far below the zero mark. The regulation clothing

Left:

53. Double-caped overcoat, 1873. Proclaimed to be "an admirable garment" by the Quartermaster Department, it was a stopgap measure to comply with the spirit of the new uniform regulations. (Adams County Museum, Deadwood, South Dakota)

Right:

54. Captain John F. Rodgers, military storekeeper at the Quartermaster Department's Philadelphia Depot, 1862–94. Rodgers is credited with several clothing innovations, including the double-caped overcoat and the introduction of the dark-blue woolen army shirt. (Massachusetts Commandery, Military Order of the Loyal Legion and U.S. Army Military History Institute)

simply was not heavy enough to protect the men from exposure for garrison duty, much less field service. At Fort Laramie, Wyoming Territory, the commanding officer took pity on his men by allowing them to wear fur or cloth ear lappets, fur gauntlets, and mufflers on the post and to add fur caps and leggings for field duty.[72]

Until 1871 the soldier had two choices for protecting his hands: he could either turn down the overcoat cuffs or buy his own mittens or fur gauntlets. In that year the army finally authorized the issue of two pairs of gray knitted-wool mittens to each man annually.[73] These had a rather long, straight-cut wrist with separated thumb and index finger. An officer at Fort Seward, Dakota Territory, denounced the mittens as an utter failure that kept "the hands of the men clean but serve[d] no other purpose."[74] Observing how Indians dressed for winter, many officers pleaded for at least limited issues of buffalo coats, fur caps, and fur gauntlet gloves. As usual, the army's machinery was slow to react to purely human needs, so soldiers were forced to buy or make their own special winter clothing to avoid serious frostbite or even death from the elements.

White Gloves

White dress gloves had formed a part of the enlisted dress uniform for many years, but it was not until the major overhaul of 1872 that they were made a part of the soldier's allowance.[75] Before this, the men had to purchase them from the sutlers.

Made of a cotton-wool blend called "Berlin," the gloves had three welts about 3½ inches long on the back of the hand extending from a point between each finger (fig. 55). A ¼-inch hem was stitched around the opening of each glove. Army-issue gloves can be distinguished by the gores sewn between the fingers to provide a better fit and by the strip of ¼-inch-wide elastic sewn to the underside of the wrist.[76]

Stable Frocks and Overalls

During the requisite morning and evening stable duty, it was impossible for a cavalryman to groom his mount without becoming covered with loose hair and dust. Therefore, it was essential that the soldier be provided with overalls to cover, or substitute for, his uniform. A two-piece outfit made of seven-ounce white cotton duck was worn over the shirt and, in cold weather, even the blouse.

The frock was a simple, unlined coat reaching to the knees (fig. 56). It had a short rollover collar and was closed with three pressed-tin buttons spaced equidistant from the neck to the waist. Seeing no need for improvement in this most utilitarian of army garments, the uniform board recommended that the current pattern remain in service.

Overalls for mounted men were first authorized with the 1872 regulations (fig. 57). Before this only the engineers had bottoms, actually a one-piece coverall, for their work clothes. However, the advantages of allowing the cavalry trooper to wear trousers that matched his frock were obvious, so the old engineer overalls were dispensed with in favor of a special new two-piece outfit. The new trousers were added to the stable clothing allowance for cavalry and light artillery.

Even though the stable frocks and overalls were never intended to be worn beyond the corrals, many soldiers in the desert Southwest were quick to see the

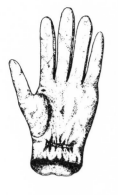

Left:

55. *White Berlin gloves, as worn by enlisted men on all dress occasions and guard duty.*

Right:

56. *Stable frock as worn by cavalrymen throughout the 1860s and 1870s.* (Smithsonian Institution)

advantages of such clothing for field service.[77] Besides being lighter in weight and cooler, this clothing did not collect dust and perspiration as did wool. But, it was more visible, at least for a while. Active campaigning soon took care of this as "dust, soot, rain, and grime . . . made their impression upon the canvas suits which each had donned" in General George Crook's command during the 1873 Apache campaign.[78]

The overalls remained unchanged for the remainder of the decade, and in fact the century, but the stable frock underwent minor design alterations in 1879. The later version had a standing collar about two inches high, an improvement made to keep dust and hay from going down the neck opening. The frock also was shortened to hip length, much like the regular fatigue blouse.

FOOTGEAR

Shoes and Boots

An effort to provide the soldier with new and better footwear was initiated even before the board met to consider a new uniform. Like so many other items on hand since the war, the supply of shoes and boots had dwindled to the point that some men had trouble getting a proper fit. Other clothing could at least be altered to fit, but footgear posed a more difficult problem. There had also been complaints for many years that the quality of the shoes and boots had diminished with the wartime contract system. Although some manufacturers apparently supplied good-quality products, others defrauded the government by using

57. White duck overalls.

inferior materials. More pointed criticism came from troops serving in Arizona and other southwestern territories, where it was found that the rocky terrain utterly destroyed their footgear in a relatively short time. The constant abrasion of sandy soil and sharp rocks cut the sole stitching and literally ground off the heels. Always defensive of his department, Meigs quickly countered that soldiers were neglecting "to guard the soles with iron nails [hobnails], a precaution taken by every Alpine tourist before he ventures among the rocks."[79] Meigs failed to acknowledge that the soldier, as usual, would have to make up for this deficiency at his own expense.

Responding to the size shortage, the Quartermaster Department contracted for a supply of both boots and shoes during 1871. As an experiment, a portion of these were made with patented brass "French screws," which were threaded, for attaching the soles (fig. 58), whereas the remainder had either wood-pegged or sewn soles. Meigs concluded that the shoes and boots with the brass-screwed soles would be "better suited to the hard work and various soils to which they [were] exposed in Army use."[80] Since no other changes were noted, it may be assumed that these items conformed otherwise to the Civil War patterns.

The response to the brass-screwed footgear was so positive that a special board of officers was convened in the spring of 1872 to consider these and other improvements. On May 2 the secretary of war approved the procurement and issue of two thousand pairs of shoes and three thousand pairs of boots for an extensive field trial. Later that same year the new patterns were adopted for general issue.[81]

In addition to the improvements made in attaching the soles, the 1872-pattern boots and brogans were made on lasts that more closely resembled the natural contours of the average foot. The shoes were not markedly different in outward appearance, retaining the basic two-piece construction, upper and top, with an internal counter stitched in place (fig. 59). The top reached about to the ankle bone; the heel was broad and about one inch high. The dressed side of the leather, dyed black, was turned outermost, to have the smooth side next to the foot. The coarser texture of the dressed side was also easier to maintain. Like the old-pattern "bootees," the new ones had four sets of holes and were issued with oiled-leather laces. Woven-cotton laces with brass or copper tips were available on the commercial market and were preferred by some soldiers, though these were not as durable for field duty.

The cavalry boots, on the other hand, were made somewhat taller, one of the complaints having been that the old boots were too short to accommodate the pants leg. Most soldiers wore the trousers over the boots. However, this caused the trousers legs to ride up unless instep straps were worn, which rarely was done. The 1872-pattern boots measured fifteen inches high in front, sloping in a gentle curve to fourteen inches at the side seams. The rear portion of the leg was straight cut at this same height. More important than the shape of the top was the less noticeable increase in its circumference, which allowed ample room for the trousers to be tucked inside.

The manner of sewing on the pull straps also was changed so that half of each strap was on the outside of the top. This end then passed through a slot where it was joined with the opposite end and stitched to the inside of the leg below in two parallel lines. This reduced the bulk inside the boot top so that it would not chafe the wearer's leg.

The new regulations also recognized, finally, that cavalry troopers needed shoes in addition to boots.[82] Hot and heavy to trudge around in while dismounted, boots were not well suited to the routine fatigue details that occupied most of a soldier's time.

These patterns of boots and shoes remained standard only until 1876, when

58. Pair of 1872-pattern army shoes with brass-screwed soles. (Smithsonian Institution)

59. Army-issue boots and shoes: old-pattern shoes (first row), 1872 boots (second row), 1872 shoes (third row), and old-style boots (fourth row). (U.S. Army Quartermaster Museum, courtesy Smithsonian Institution)

60. *Old-pattern buffalo overshoes (above) and the taller Pattern 1873 overshoes (below).* (U.S. Army Quartermaster Museum, courtesy Smithsonian Institution)

modified versions were adopted. Their use, however, continued for some years beyond that, until leftover stocks were consumed.

Buffalo Overshoes

The 1872 regulations made no immediate provision for changing the style of the buffalo overshoes in use since the early 1860s. But, on June 6, 1873, an improved model was adopted that corrected the shortcomings of the earlier pattern. Whereas the old ones were low cut, only about as high as the brogan itself, and had only one fastening strap, the 1873-pattern overshoes came over the ankle and had two straps (fig. 60). As Third Infantryman Charles Parker described them, "Uppers made of softly tanned buffalo hide, hairy side in, the soles made of rawhide, these were very clumsy but were very comfortable on dry snow, but useless for a mounted man, as the stirrup would not accommodate them."[83]

The overshoes worked well in extremely cold, dry conditions, but they were inefficient and even dangerous to the feet when wet. Although daytime temperatures in many areas of the West could be above freezing, temperatures could plummet far below freezing during the night. A man with soggy buffalo overshoes could very well have frozen feet by morning. Within the next few years the army would reconsider the concept of using animal skins for winter footgear.

To Contrive Means for Carrying Clothing and Rations, 1870–1872

THE CIVIL WAR PRESENTED unparalleled opportunities for testing military hardware, affording a heyday for inventors hoping to profit by securing government contracts. The war inspired a plethora of military equipage inventions, among them numerous knapsacks and attendant support systems, weapons, and an almost infinite variety of cartridge boxes. Some of these patented designs proved worthy enough to be ordered, at least in limited quantities, by the army. But, the exigencies of the war prevented thoughtful consideration as to how well suited the designs were to the army's long-term needs. Thus, by war's end the army found itself with a hodgepodge of equipments and weapons.

In the immediate aftermath of the war, the regular army was concerned more with dismantling the volunteer forces, implementing Reconstruction, and reorganizing itself than it was about evaluating its hardware. It was not until early in 1868 that an ordnance board was convened to examine the army's personal equipments, thus initiating a process of trial and error that was to continue over the next dozen years. Although this first assemblage did not make the sweeping changes that were to be witnessed later on, it did effect a few minor changes (outlined in chapter I) and laid the groundwork for future considerations.

An interdisciplinary board composed of officers from the three combat arms met at Fort Leavenworth to review Upton's system of tactics in the summer of 1869. They had hardly begun when revised orders arrived from army headquarters in the fall directing the board to also investigate the whole subject of arms and accoutrements. The army's hierarchy had decided, at last, that the time had come to reevaluate equipage in the light of the general adoption of breech-loading arms, though the Allin-Springfield system for foot troops was still a tenuous standard.

It was certainly no secret that the army had been dissatisfied with the double-bag knapsack for a long time. Among its problems were that it "was not stiff enough in the sides to preserve its form, and the material too flimsy for the knapsack to keep its shape; and . . . the shoulder straps were put on too near together in the shoulders, making it hang back from them, and throwing the weight . . . upon the small of the back, while they pulled back the arms."[1] Apparently, the old knapsacks had been issued originally with a light wooden frame to make the main bag rigid, but most soldiers discarded these immediately. To make the knapsack hug the shoulders more closely, the men resorted to one of two remedies. The first was to loop the shoulder straps over a stick passed laterally through the blanket roll straps; the other was to simply pass the blanket roll straps under the shoulder slings before buckling on the roll.[2] Despite these field expedients, the basic shortcoming of the knapsack was in the design itself, not to mention the soldier's inherent aversion to knapsacks.

Recognizing this, the army began experimenting with alternative patterns as early as 1866.[3] When the board originally formed to evaluate army tactics, but handed the additional responsibility for examining accoutrements, reconvened in St. Louis early in 1870, no less than eleven patented models of knapsacks and attendant systems were submitted for consideration. Of these, the board recommended six patterns for further review and testing. Nevertheless, the board qualified its recommendations with a statement that it did not consider any of the knapsacks submitted as a satisfactory solution to the infantry equipment problem.[4]

With well over half a million double-bag knapsacks on hand, the army faced a tough job indeed to justify to Congress the adoption of a new design. But, there were other more subtle, if not more demanding, factors affecting this situation. The army's clothing supply had suffered from the ravages of time and poor storage conditions, and its equipment was hardly better off. In 1870 Quartermaster General Meigs announced that most of the stock of haversacks and knapsacks, both of which were waterproofed with black paint having a linseed-oil base, was ruined. The knapsacks and haversacks had become sticky from age and heat and, in their tightly packed bales, had become stuck to each other.[5]

Meigs promptly announced that nothing could be done to restore the damaged equipment; therefore, it was necessary to procure an entirely new supply immediately. Disregarding the recommendations of the St. Louis Board, Meigs unilaterally placed an emergency order with a San Francisco firm to manufacture a quantity of sealskin knapsacks of a design submitted by Major John C. Tidball, Second U.S. Artillery. An additional two thousand leather and canvas knapsacks of an unidentified pattern were contracted for in Philadelphia. However, these contingency purchases were intended only to mitigate the more serious problem.[6]

This proved to be an opportune time to lay open the entire subject of individual equipment and its adequacy in the light of new U.S. small arms, as well as the equipage trends among European powers. Once again the United States looked to the Old World military establishments for examples. Army observers noted that leading European nations were discarding the traditional shoulder-slung cartridge box and knapsack in favor of integrated load-carrying systems. All of this prompted the organization of a new five-member panel on November 8, 1871, to meet in Washington, D.C., to discuss improvements in infantry equipment.[7]

General Meigs also saw an opportunity in this to divest his department of the responsibility for manufacturing haversacks, knapsacks, canteens, and coat straps by suggesting to the board that these items be produced by the Ordnance Department. Meigs's logic was that most of this work had to be contracted out anyway because his shops were not equipped to manufacture such items. The Ordnance Department, on the other hand, already possessed the necessary facilities, supplies, and human skills required to manufacture all manner of gear. He admitted that this was something he had considered doing back in 1861 but that he had deferred the matter in the face of war. Now the time seemed right to promote the transfer of these responsibilities.[8]

On the facing page:

61. Colonel P. V. Hagner, who graduated from the U.S. Military Academy in 1832. Breveted twice for his service during the Mexican War, Hagner served with the Ordnance Department throughout most of his career. He is credited with a number of accoutrement designs, including the Patterns No. 1 and No. 2 cartridge pouches of 1872 and the swivel used on holsters and bayonet scabbards. (Massachusetts Commandery, Military Order of the Loyal Legion and U.S. Army Military History Institute)

The items sent to the board for evaluation included a full set of British army "brace system" equipments, another set of equipments designed by a British officer, and two sample knapsacks submitted by private inventors. To the board's advantage, a copy of the report of the British army field trials of this equipment accompanied the sample set provided to the American army. However, the board's decision may have been prejudiced from the outset, because Meigs had taken the liberty of showing the various items to General of the Army William T. Sherman before sending them to the board. After examining them briefly, Sherman commented that he favored the British regulation gear. Meeting for all of one day, the board quickly dispensed with all of the samples except the British brace equipment, an outcome that seems more than coincidental.[9]

The brace system was a radical departure from past American infantry equipage. Central to the concept was a pair of leather suspenders attached to the waist belt. Two cartridge boxes, a valise-knapsack, a haversack, and a canteen were all suspended from the brace, the weight being borne by both the torso and the hips. Interestingly, the same principle is used today in U.S. military equipment, as well as that of many other nations. The only significant deviations from the contemporary British pattern were the board recommendations that the brace belts be made of black bridle leather rather than white buff, that the U.S. 1858-pattern canteen be used, and that the British cartridge boxes be modified as necessary to accommodate U.S. ammunition. The board concluded by proposing that five thousand sets be manufactured initially for trial by troops in the field.

On February 14, 1872, the board reconvened to examine the various samples that had been prepared. They approved the sample brace and selected a valise knapsack with a black rubberized flap, though they suggested that the bag itself be made of somewhat heavier linen duck. By the time the first lot of experimental equipments was ready for issue in July, Watervliet Arsenal's commander, Colonel P. V. Hagner (fig. 61), announced that three different kinds of material had been used for the valise flaps—sealskin, vulcanized rubber, and plain linen canvas—to determine which type would be the most suitable.[10] The 1872 equipments introduced the use of new materials, including canvas (linen in 1872, rather than the cotton of later issues), as well as brass for rivets and other hardware throughout. Nearly all of the army's accoutrements before this used copper rivets. The ammunition pouches, variant patterns numbered one and two, were distributed as follows: one thousand sets with Pattern No. 1, two thousand sets with Pattern No. 2, and two thousand sets with one pouch of each type attached.[11] Thus, a set of infantry equipments consisted of a brace yoke, a waist belt, a valise, two cartridge pouches, a steel bayonet scabbard, a pair of coat straps, a canteen, and a haversack (figs. 62 and 63). The officers further recommended that a modified version of the brace be adopted for the cavalry.[12] This special model incorporated a carbine sling as an integral part of the brace suspenders, thus eliminating it as a separate item (fig. 64). The secretary of war quickly approved the board's recommendation that small quantities of each type of equipment be made and issued for trial.

Yet a third board, acting under orders to study horse equipments and to further review the new personal equipments, assembled at Watervliet in April 1872. This time, Hagner himself headed the committee, which included Captain Edwin Vose Sumner (son of the famous dragoon officer) and Captain

Left:

62. Pattern 1872 infantry brace and waist belt.

Right:

63. Rear view of the infantry brace, with the valise knapsack attached to the adjustable suspension rings. The flap of the valise is the type coated with vulcanized rubber.

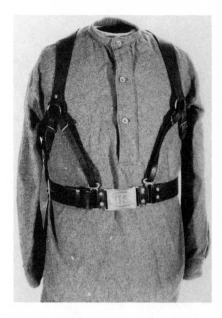

Alfred E. Bates, Second Cavalry. After subjecting the brace system to some practical tests, these officers quickly concluded that it was more a hindrance than an advantage to the mounted man. They particularly condemned the integral carbine sling and advocated retention of the old 1855 cross-belt as being better suited to the cavalry's needs. Even though some of the weight of the carbine rested on the soldier's left shoulder, the socket attached to the quarter-strap ring of the saddle supported most of it. Therefore, they advised against adopting the brace equipment for cavalry because the entire weight of trooper and equipment was actually borne by the horse, not the man. Since the trooper was himself a part of the horse's burden, the perceived weight of his accoutrements was transferred to the animal.[13] Chief of Ordnance Alexander B. Dyer, however, was determined to give the cavalry brace a try, since it already had been approved by the secretary of war. Consequently, the board's recommendations, with the exception of dropping the cavalry brace, were approved by the secretary of war on May 6, 1872.

The experimental cavalry accoutrements consisted of a new saber belt, with provisions to connect the leather suspenders, and the solid-cast rectangular U.S. belt plate. Worn on the belt were a cartridge pouch (several patterns issued for trial), a new flapped holster with swivel attachment, and the old cap pouch, used for holding pistol cartridges. The 1855-pattern carbine sling completed the outfit (fig. 65). Four thousand sets were to be assembled for trial issue among the cavalry regiments. Before long, other company commanders not among the designated trial companies attempted to procure enough new accoutrements to replace all of the Civil War equipment in their units. The chief of ordnance quickly countered this with a circular admonishing: "Requisitions should not be made for any of the horse equipments, cavalry accoutrements, materials, or tools enumerated in G.O. No. 60, June 29, 1872 . . . except to replace stores worn out in service or to supply deficiencies. The order was not intended to direct or authorize a general refitting of companies. Therefore, during the next few years, the accoutrements in the hands of the troops represented a mixture of old regulation and new experimental items, depending on what was requested and what was available at a given time.[14]

INFANTRY ACCOUTREMENTS

Brace Yoke

The foundation of the brace system was the yoke. The soldier wore it suspender-fashion over the shoulders, with all of the other accoutrements attached to it. The yoke was made of black bridle leather in the form of two shoulder straps, each thirty-six inches long. These straps crossed between the man's shoulder blades, where they were joined by one of two methods. In one pattern, apparently the more common one, a brass stud was used. This stud was the type found on the 1855-pattern saber slings and was undoubtedly surplus hardware reused in the experimental equipment. The stud passed through one suspender, the head of the stud being covered by a piece of leather to affix it and to prevent it from chafing the back. The other suspender crossed over and was buttoned on the exposed opposite end of the stud. In the other example, the shoulder straps were connected by leather pieces, seven-eighth inch by twelve inches, sewn and riveted to the undersides of the straps, one overlying the other. This less rigid method permitted the shoulder straps some slippage over each other but restricted them from getting too far out of alignment.

The shoulder straps were 2½ inches wide where they passed over the torso,

Left:

64. Pattern 1872 cavalry brace and saber belt. Note the wider shoulder straps and the attachment of the carbine sling on the right suspender. (J. Edward Green III Collection)

Right:

65. Rear view of cavalry brace, showing special carbine sling, holster, and 1872-pattern Dyer cartridge pouch.

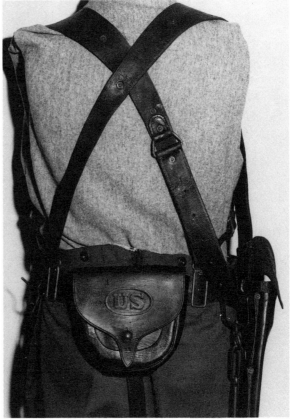

the rear extremity tapering to about 1 inch and buckling to a chape hanging at the side. This chape and the opposite, or front, end of the shoulder strap were stitched to a 1½-inch-diameter brass ring. Each of the rings was backed by a leather pad. Additionally, two narrower stay straps, $^{11}/_{16}$ inch wide with brass wire buckles, were looped through each ring. One of these connected to the respective loop on the waist belt, and the other extended to the rear to steady the valise.

The valise itself hooked to the shoulder straps by means of special movable frame buckles. Each of these two buckles measured 1⅜ inches by 1¾ inches and had a ⅞-inch-diameter brass ring held in a cast eye located along the inner side. These buckles could be adjusted to position the valise comfortably on the wearer's lower back.

On the undersides of each shoulder strap were pieces of leather, shaped like parallelograms, which served as stays for the blanket roll straps. The blanket, folded in a small square, was secured on the shoulders by these straps.

Waist Belt and Plate

An entirely new pattern waist belt was designed as part of the brace system. It was made of black bridle leather, 1⅞ inches wide, with a cast-brass loop stitched and riveted to the left end (fig. 66). To the other side of this loop was riveted a short piece of leather (about 1 inch wide, folded on itself) that embraced a clasp of cast brass for the plate.

The right end of the belt was doubled under and fitted with a brass wire hook mating to a series of punched holes for adjusting the length of the belt. Within this fold was a second brass loop, like that on the opposite end, with an identical leather chape securing the plate to the loop. Each of these fittings had an integral short oval loop at the top, to which the pair of narrow brace straps connected to aid in distributing the weight.

The new belt plate used with the 1872 trial equipment was solid cast brass, rectangular in shape, measuring about 2⅛ inches high by 3¼ inches wide.[15] It was about ⅛ inch thick and slightly curved to conform with the man's body. The right side had a slot for receiving the belt. In relief on the face of the plate were the letters "U.S." encompassed by an oval. The face of the plate also had a raised border. All of these relief portions were polished smooth to highlight them from the recessed area, which was left somewhat rough from the casting. Some examples had stippling applied to the recesses. A ½-inch-wide tongue was cast integrally on the reverse. This plate, even though attractive and easy to maintain, was practically indestructible, an attribute not lost on the military.[16]

Valise-Knapsack

The valise-knapsack was made of linen duck, the main bag measuring 13 inches wide by 12 inches deep, opening at the top (fig. 67). The mouth of the bag was faced with a band of russet leather ¾ inch wide. The bag had a gusset 4 inches wide at the bottom, narrowing to 3 inches at the top. The interior

66. Pattern 1872 infantry waist belt. The brass loops on either side of the plate tended to place the cartridge pouches too far to the rear for the convenience of most soldiers.

67. Valise-knapsack with sealskin flap.
(Arizona Historical Society)

was divided into two compartments by a partition of lightweight linen sewn into the front seam of the gusset. On the front of the bag was a small pocket, 5 inches deep by 6¾ inches, covered by a flap for holding two cartons of reserve ammunition.

According to the instructions issued with the equipment, the valise-knapsack was to be packed with "the softest articles of clothing in the larger sub-division and nearest the body,—then the Trowsers should be folded flat and put in first; then the Shirt also folded; the Boots upright, against the sides, heels outward; then the Blouse, Socks, and Drawers between the Boots. Smaller articles,—Brushes, Comb, Towel, &c.,—should be placed in the smaller subdivision."[17] On the back of the valise were three russet leather straps extending down from the reinforcement around the mouth. Each ended with a standard brass wire buckle, these mating with three matching straps riveted to the underside of the flap.

The mouth and the entire front of the valise were covered by a 14-by-17-inch flap. In its attempts to find the most suitable material for the flap, the Ordnance Department issued the bags with three basic types of flaps: vulcanized rubber, sealskin with the hair on, and plain linen duck.[18] Hagner predicted that the last would prove to be the most practical for field service in North American climates, but the equipment was never adopted officially in any form. The troops apparently liked the rubberized flap, since the question seems to have been settled by the time the 1874 equipments, employing vulcanized covers, were adopted.

Riveted to the upper back of the bag were two sheet-brass hooks for attaching the valise to the movable buckles on the brace yoke. A brass wire buckle was placed at each lower corner, to which the yoke's rear stay straps were fastened. A small iron wire loop attached by a sheet-brass clip between the hooks was probably intended for hanging up the knapsack in barracks.

In the single example of the plain-flap version examined for this study, the flap itself was bound with russet leather, as was the ammunition pocket. Inexplicably, it was made without the buckles at the lower corners for the stay straps and also without the hanger loop.

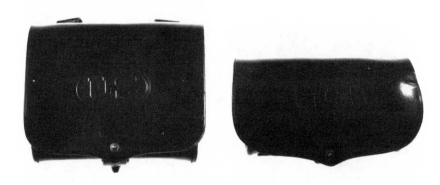

68. Hagner cartridge pouches No. 1
(left) and No. 2 (right).

Cartridge Boxes

No less than forty cartridge boxes and pouches were submitted to the 1870 Ordnance Board for consideration. Only six, however, were selected for final study.[19] Even so, the board members reached a consensus that none of these models were well adapted to the infantry soldier's needs. These devices are presented in appendix I. The board preferred the concept of a rather soft, expandable leather pouch, as opposed to a rigid box. The commanding officer at St. Louis Arsenal, under the direction of the board, made up a shop sample constructed of pliable leather, except for the flap and the front of the pouch. The interior was lined with sheepskin and was made to hold one special carton of twenty-four rounds of .50-caliber ammunition, or the same number if carried loose. The board suggested that up to four of these pouches could be carried in combat, whereas one or two would suffice for garrison duty.[20]

Hagner Pouches

By the time the cavalry board offered its formal recommendations on April 24, 1872, the cartridge pouches of choice were two similar patterns designed by Colonel Hagner himself (fig. 68). Box No. 1 measured about 6 inches wide by 5½ inches deep. It had a full flap cover embossed with the letters "U S" ⅞ inch high within an oval border. A ⅞-inch-wide billet was stitched and riveted to the lower edge of the flap buttoned over a brass stud mounted in the bottom of the box.

The box held twenty-four rounds of .50-caliber ammunition, arranged in three rows of varnished loops. Two of these rows were in one tier in the bottom of the box, with a third row sewn above these on the back panel. The right side of the box had a swelled pocket for holding the rifle screwdriver. A forked leather strap was riveted to the upper corners on the back of the box, the free end buttoning over the same stud used for fastening the flap. A later modification incorporated a narrow horizontal strap riveted to the back of the pouch. The belt yoke could be passed under this strap, effectively shortening the usable portion to accommodate a two-inch waist belt. Conceivably, the belt strap could be unbuttoned, withdrawn from the retainer, and used as a single, wide belt loop. The retainer also may have been intended to allow the soldier to pass the waist belt through the loop below the retainer, thereby positioning the box above his waist rather than below.

Also holding twenty-four cartridges in webbing loops, the Pattern No. 2 box was considerably shorter (3½ inches high) because one row of loops was sewn to the front of the box rather than being on the inside. The other two rows were positioned inside the box proper, as in Pattern No. 1. Thus, all three rows lay in one tier, with the cartridges arranged with the heads up (fig. 69). A strip of heavy leather riveted in the bottom of the pouch had cutouts punched alternately along each edge of its length to raise every other cartridge slightly above those adjacent to it. This made them somewhat easier to grasp with the fingers. In this box, Hagner simply modified the earlier Tileston-pattern box by reducing the number of cartridges from thirty to twenty-four and sewing in the ends to make it rigid.[21] This box also had an implement pocket formed as a swell in the right end panel.

In some of the field reports, the Hagner No. 1 pouch was distinguished as the infantry pattern, and the No. 2 was designated as a cavalry pouch because its shorter height was better suited to mounted service.[22] However, there is no evidence that the Ordnance Department made such a distinction. The pouches were to be issued in pairs, two being worn with the brace for field service. The weight of forty-eight rounds of ammunition counterbalanced the weight of the infantry valise. Since the cavalry did not use the valise, the mounted version of the belt included two sliding brass loops at the back for attaching the yoke suspenders. For garrison duty, one pouch of either type could be worn in back without the brace.

One might assume the pouches were issued in pairs of the same type, and indeed three thousand sets of the initial order for infantry equipments were so arranged. However, an additional two thousand sets were to be set up "with

69. Hagner pouches, open, displaying the two methods for arranging the cartridge loops. Both of these pouches exhibit the modification for .45-caliber ammunition, a change initiated after the adoption of the Model 1873 Springfield rifle and carbine.

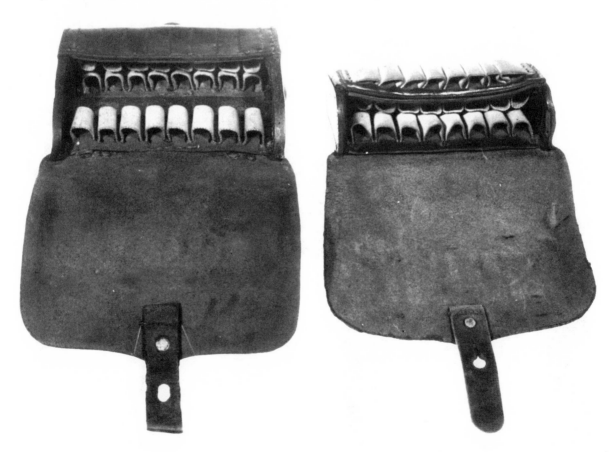

70. Bayonet scabbards: Civil War pattern made entirely of leather (left), steel scabbard with 1870 swivel attachment (center), and steel scabbard with 1872 swivel attachment (right).

pouches both large and small."[23] The Hagner pouches remained in service for at least a decade to come, but with various modifications. These will be discussed in following chapters.

Bayonet Scabbards, Patterns of 1870 and 1872

The bayonet scabbard peculiar to the 1872 equipments resulted from an evolutionary process that began during the Civil War with the Emerson-patent steel scabbard (fig. 70).[24] The 1868 equipment board had previously recommended that the sheet-steel scabbard, 18¼ inches in length, be purchased instead of the old-style leather one, a change that would not be evidenced among the troops for some time afterward because of the enormous number of 1862-pattern scabbards still on hand. Two years later the St. Louis Board advocated the use of a swivel attachment invented by a longtime infantry officer, Brevet Brigadier General William Hoffman, who had only recently retired from the service.

Hoffman's concept for a swivel attachment, patented by him on May 8, 1860, consisted of a frog with a separate belt loop joined to it by a brass stud and washer device.[25] This arrangement allowed the scabbard to pivot through an arc of approximately 120 degrees, rather than hanging at a fixed angle. Thus, the soldier was provided with a scabbard that could be adjusted somewhat to suit his own comfort, especially when the soldier was sitting down.

The actions of these two boards effectively created an entirely new bayonet scabbard. Chief of Ordnance Stephen V. Benet ordered fifty-thousand Emerson steel scabbards, already on hand from the war, to be modified with the Hoffman attachment.[26] The original Emerson frog was cut down, and the belt loop was removed entirely. The remaining stub of leather was cut on a 180-degree curve,

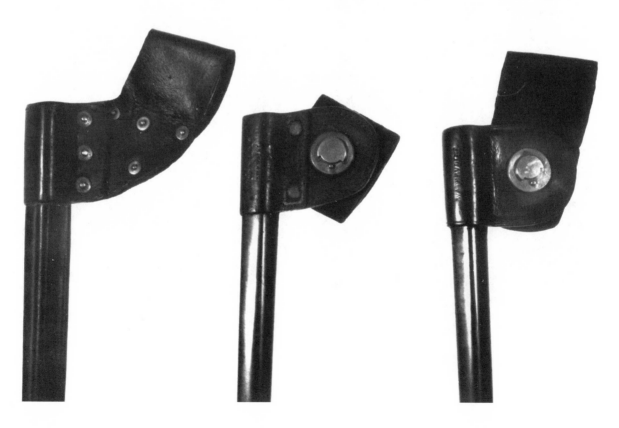

and the severed edges were stitched together. A separate belt loop, wide enough to pass over the standard two-inch waist belt, was affixed by a Hoffman swivel to the reverse of this extension. The 1870 scabbard had two copper rivets fastening the sheath collar to the remaining portion of the belt loop extension, rough side outermost. The original line of stitching across this piece, as well as a portion of the original Emerson markings, usually was evident on the face side. Most, if not all, of these scabbards were stamped "WATERVLIET ARSENAL 1871" on the collar.

A somewhat modified style of scabbard, made especially for the 1872 trial equipments, replaced the patterns of 1862 and 1870. This new scabbard was a direct descendant of the 1870-pattern, utilizing both the steel sheath and the Hoffman swivel attachment. Although similar in appearance to its antecedent, it differed by having a longer belt loop, $4\frac{5}{8}$ inches overall, which dropped the scabbard mouth below the waist belt. This piece had a line of stitching across the midpoint to form the loop proper. This frog was newly made of black bridle leather. Specimens were marked "WATERVLIET ARSENAL," without a date.

Haversack

The equipment board substituted a new linen canvas bag in lieu of the old painted haversack. The trial haversack was issued in two colors, natural and dyed drab. Additionally, as the trials continued, various means of waterproofing were attempted. Some were marked "Waterproof" or "Cowles & Co.'s Patent" inside the flap, reflecting two of these chemical treatments. In construction and size the two styles were identical.

The sack itself measured about $8\frac{1}{2}$ inches wide by 11 inches deep, the back being cut slightly larger, with a $2\frac{1}{2}$-inch-wide gusset (fig. 71). The interior was subdivided by a partition made of lightweight linen, with the rear compartment used to store hard bread and the front one for condiments.

Sewn to the front was an open-topped rectangular pocket, 7 inches wide by $5\frac{1}{2}$ inches deep, for holding the meat can, to be described later. The flap, covering the entire front of the haversack, measured about 13 inches square and had a bound edge of twilled cotton webbing. The same material was used to bind the opening of the bag. The flap was fastened by a $\frac{3}{4}$-inch-wide webbing strap with three brass eyelets. This strap connected to a brass wire buckle, its chape sewn to the gusset.

71. *Pattern 1872 haversack.*

Both styles of the haversack employed a shoulder strap made of 1½-inch-wide cotton webbing. The sling was sewn to the upper rear corners of the bag. The 1872 haversack originally was issued with a one-piece sling that was to be tied either to the brace yoke or to the waist belt, thus disbursing its weight. Without the brace, it could be worn over the shoulder in the usual fashion.

However, it soon became evident that the sling was too short to be worn across the shoulder by most men. By October 1872 the Ordnance Department recognized the deficiency and began making "all haversacks with two-piece straps connected by a buckle to allow for soldiers of different heights."[27] Although the obvious intent was to use some sort of buckle for this purpose, the grim realities of the army budget forced Colonel Hagner to come up with a cheaper solution. As a makeshift answer to the problem, Hagner employed two brass buttonhooks, salvaged from the straps of Civil War double-bag knapsacks. These were poked through one of the straps and mated to corresponding whipped grommets in the other. If a soldier preferred, he could put one hook in each strap to hang the haversack from the brace yoke.

72. Modified canteen stopper attachment adopted in 1872.

Canteen

The 1872 canteen was little changed from its predecessor. With hundreds of thousands of 1858-pattern canteens left over from the war, the army was not particularly interested in proposing anything radically different. Besides, the old one still served the purpose. These surplus canteens continued to be issued in their original form, with only one minor modification.

The pressed-tin canteen body was oblate spheroid in shape, averaging about 7½ to 7¾ inches in diameter. The two halves were soldered together by means of an overlapping joint formed around their edges. A tin flange at the top secured a spout made of either cast pewter or tin about 1 inch long.[28] Three tin sling guides, positioned astraddle the side seam, were located equidistant around the perimeter of the canteen. The shoulder sling was made of a single piece of natural cotton twill, doubled over to a width of ⅞ inch and stitched along each edge.

The 1872 canteen differed from the earlier pattern in only one particular. The iron chain, used previously for connecting the stopper to the body, was replaced by a No. 16 brass jack chain, which was attached to a brass wire loop surrounding the spout (fig. 72). The preformed loop was first passed over the lip of the spout, crimped into an eye, and finally given a quarter twist to tighten it about the neck. The end of the chain was attached to this eye. The reason for using brass rather than iron chain was probably to eliminate the problem of rusting.

One hypothesis for changing the point of attachment is that it reduced the chance that the chain would snag on other equipment, particularly the bayonet, as frequently happened when the chain was fastened to one of the sling guides (fig. 73).[29]

Gun Sling

Since the Springfield rifles Model 1868 and 1870 had shorter barrels than their antecedents, they required only two barrel bands rather than three. The elimination of the middle band lightened the rifle but at the same time necessitated attaching the sling swivel to the new upper band. This two-band arrangement increased by several inches the distance between the guard-bow and upper swivels. Although the Pattern 1850 sling, measuring 46 inches, would suffice for the parade adjustment, it could not be extended. Thus, the 1870-pattern sling was created as an afterthought by combining two of the old musket slings.[30] The hook-portion from one sling was mated with the loop-portion of another, and the cut ends of each were beveled, overlapped, and sewn together.

The 1870-pattern gun sling measured 1¼ inches wide by 63 inches long (fig. 74). One end was folded back on itself to envelop a flat brass hook, for adjustment, extending through a hole in the fold. A standing leather loop was sewn to the opposite end, and two sliding leather keepers were provided to retain the sling on the rifle. The converted slings were distinguished by the splice and its three rows of stitching. Depending on where the cuts were made, some slings retained their original Civil War contract manufacturer's and inspector's markings.

During the 1880s the Ordnance Department manufactured new one-piece Pattern 1870 slings, to augment the supply of converted slings.[31] This sling remained standard until it was replaced by the 1887 pattern, which had a brass double-claw hook.

NCO Sword Frog

In 1868 the old Pattern 1855 sword sling for noncommissioned officers was replaced by a sliding frog worn on the waist belt. The frog was made of a single piece of black leather, folded on itself and stitched down the sides. A horizontal slot in the face allowed the steel or leather scabbard to be passed through; a hole below the slot received the scabbard hook.

CAVALRY ACCOUTREMENTS

Brace Yoke

The cavalry brace yoke was nearly identical to that designed for the infantry. It too was made entirely of black bridle leather with wide shoulder straps tapering to brass rings on the front. From these rings, narrow straps connected to the cast-brass loops positioned on the waist belt to either side of the plate. The wider straps, which led to the rear and which in the dismounted version supported the valise, passed through sliding brass loops on the rear of the belt. Absent were the adjustable buckles with rings for the valise.

The principal distinction was the addition of the short carbine sling, 1½ inches wide. The front end of the sling was attached to a trapezoidal brass wire loop riveted and stitched to the righthand suspender at about the level of the armpit. This end of the sling passed through the loop and was doubled back on itself. On the free end of the sling was a brass hook for length adjustment. The other end of the sling was attached permanently to a similar loop located on the lower rear part of the left suspender, thus suspending the carbine at the right side of the body. The ring on the left side of the carbine was attached to an iron snap swivel, differing from the 1839 pattern only in the width of the yoke, which matched the narrow sling.

73. Iron stopper chain attached to sling guide, as used on Pattern 1858 canteen.

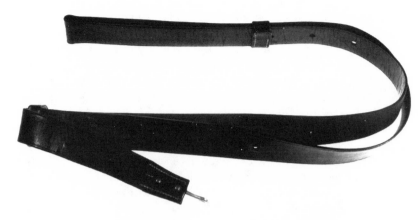

Above:

74. *Pattern 1870 gun sling.*

Below:

75. *Cavalry saber belt, 1872.*

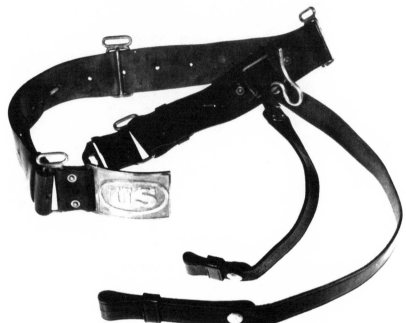

Saber Belt

This belt was constructed of black bridle leather, 1¹¹⁄₁₆ inches wide, in three sections (fig. 75). The plate, averaging 2⅛ inches by 3¼ inches, was made of cast brass with the raised block letters "U.S." on the face, ⅞ inch high. It was joined to a cast-brass loop (intended to take one of the yoke straps) by means of a leather chape fastened with two brass rivets. The belt proper also passed through this loop and was doubled back on itself. A brass adjustment hook and sliding leather keeper were provided at each end of the belt. A brass catch for the plate was affixed to the left end of the belt, in an arrangement similar to that described for the right end.

Two brass wire squares, measuring 1⁷⁄₁₆ inches outside, were located at the left side and the rear of the belt. Each of these was attached to the belt by two leather chapes, placed horizontally and fastened by a single rivet each and by stitching. The hook for attaching the saber in the dismounted position was attached to the front square. On either side of the rear square were two brass sliding loops for attaching the brace yoke. The 1872 saber belt was found in two sizes, numbered either "No. 1" or "No. 2" on the leather chape near the plate.

Saber Slings

The 1872 belt was issued with a pair of black leather saber slings. Each sling had a sheet-metal hook 2¼ inches long on its upper end for attachment either to the squares on the belt or to the saddle rings.

The front sling measured ¹⁵⁄₁₆ inch wide by 15 inches long (excluding the hook), and the rear sling measured 28 inches long. Each sling was provided with a double-head brass stud, ⅝ inch in diameter, for buttoning it to the scabbard rings. The longer sling had two slotted buttonholes for adjusting the length. The doubled lower end of each sling was coupled by a sliding leather loop.

An alternate means of carrying the saber was the Stuart sling (fig. 76). This device was invented and patented in 1859 by First Lieutenant J.E.B. Stuart, later to earn legendary fame as a Confederate cavalry commander. The principal advantage of the Stuart sling was that it connected the saber to the belt at a single point, thus enabling the soldier to quickly transfer the saber from his person to his saddle for fighting dismounted. Not long afterward the War Department, acting on the recommendations of a board, bought the manufacturing rights for the sling. Although only small numbers were issued during the Civil War, Frankford Arsenal produced an order for ten thousand in 1864.[32] The Stuart sling became fairly popular in postwar years, with several hundred being issued annually to the regulars well into the 1870s.

The sling consisted of two bridle-leather straps, each ¹³⁄₁₆ inch wide, riveted to a heavy sheet-brass belt hook 4¼ inches long. The front strap measured 11½ inches long, the rear one 23¼ inches. Like the straps on the 1855-pattern cavalry saber belt, the Stuart sling straps employed ¹¹⁄₁₆-inch-diameter brass studs for attachment to the scabbard rings. Mounted on the plate was a spring bar arranged horizontally beneath the long hook. The purpose of this bar was to facilitate freeing it from the belt and to prevent the sling from twisting.[33] The reverse of the belt hook was marked "U.S." in Old English letters and "FRANKFORD ARSENAL" on the reverse.

Holster

The holster adopted as part of the 1872 accoutrements was designed to fit the single-shot, .50-caliber Model 1871 Remington army pistol (fig. 77). To reduce production costs, the board chose to modify the holster that has been identified as the Pattern 1863, intended for the Remington .44-caliber revolver. This was a black leather holster having a full flap cut either semicircular or somewhat "lobed," with a narrow belt loop riveted and sewn to the reverse. The flap of the 1872 holster, as originally produced, was plain. Those that were not issued until 1875 or later usually were embossed with the letters "U.S." surrounded by a raised oval. The flap was secured by means of a short billet fastening to a brass stud mounted on the holster body. A new and distinguishing feature was the

76. *Stuart saber sling, adopted in 1859 and reissued on a limited basis during the early 1870s.*

Left:

77. *Pattern 1872 revolver holster with cleaning rod. (J. Edward Green III Collection)*

Right:

78. *Obverse of 1872 holster, showing the swivel attachment and the leather tube for the cleaning rod. (J. Edward Green III Collection)*

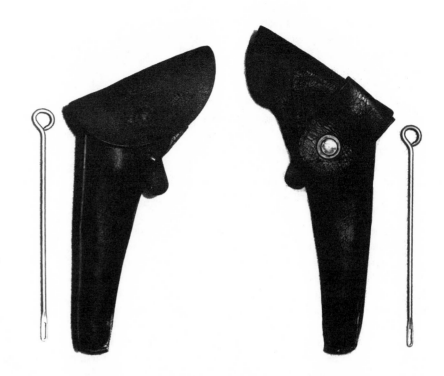

leather tube for holding the cleaning rod. This tube was riveted to the fold of the holster body so that the flap prevented the rod from being lost accidentally.[34]

The Hoffman swivel attachment, already used successfully on the infantry bayonet scabbard, was applied to the trial holster. This was done by cutting off the top edge of the original belt loop and stitching these pieces to the rear of the flap. The swivel, along with a new belt loop, was then mounted to the remnant of the old loop (fig. 78). This version of the swivel, however, had no stop pin. Thus, the holster could revolve a full 360 degrees, an annoying factor that accounted for many lost revolvers.

Pistol Cartridge Pouch

With the advent of metallic cartridges, the board found that the old leather pouch for packets of combustible pistol cartridges could be eliminated. Likewise, percussion caps were no longer needed. However, in deciding what device might best serve to carry the revolver ammunition, the board discovered that the Civil War cap pouch would hold twelve revolver cartridges without any modification being necessary.[35]

Carbine Cartridge Pouch, Pattern 1870

Among the cartridge pouches preferred by the 1870 board was one designed by Brigadier General Alexander B. Dyer, then serving as the chief of ordnance. Dyer's design consisted of a large leather pouch with a single pocket and an expandable gusset for carrying sixty rounds of .50-caliber ammunition (fig. 79). The cartridges were to be removed from their cartons and carried loose in the pouch. In this way, a soldier in the heat of combat had only to reach into the pouch, rather than to extract each cartridge from a drilled wooden block or

79. *Dyer cartridge pouch, 1870, with dual-purpose shoulder and carbine sling.* (Dwight Clark Collection)

loops. The pouch was intended to be slung from a leather shoulder belt that doubled as the carbine sling.

In August 1870 the board authorized a trial sample of one hundred Dyer pouches to be made and issued to cavalry troops on the western frontier. Nearly equal quantities were sent to the arsenals at San Antonio, Fort Leavenworth, Omaha, and Benicia.[36] Depending on the type of arm in the hands of a given unit, the pouch was used to carry ammunition for either the .50/70 Sharps improved carbine or the Spencer carbine.

The pouch was 6¾ inches wide at the mouth by 5¾ inches deep. It had a soft leather gusset 1¾ inches wide when fully expanded. The mouth of the pouch was reinforced by an extra leather strip sewn to the inside, and the interior was fleece lined. The flap, 6½ inches long, had an integral tab that buttoned over a brass stud mounted on the front of the pouch. Leather end pieces were sewn to each side of the flap, covering the mouth of the pouch, to prevent the loss of cartridges.

On the front of the main pouch was an integral pocket, 4⅝ inches deep by 4¾ inches wide, for pistol cartridges. The flap for this pocket measured 4¾ inches wide by 4½ inches long. The flaps of both the main pouch and the pistol cartridge pocket fastened over a common stud.

On the back of the pouch were two belt loops, each 4 inches long, to fit the standard 2-inch belt. Each loop was fastened by a rivet and stitching at each end. In the fold formed at the upper end of each was a brass wire loop to attach the leather shoulder sling. Thus, the pouch could be worn either over the shoulder or on the belt without the sling.

The sling, 1½ inches wide by 82 inches long, was adjusted by a brass hook riveted and sewn to each end. This hook mated with a row of corresponding holes in the belt. A special narrow iron swivel was placed within the folds of the front end of the sling. A cast-brass tongueless buckle could be placed at any point on the sling to retain the doubled sling above the snap swivel. Two sliding leather loops retained the folds just above the pouch.

Carbine Cartridge Pouch, Pattern 1872

Consequent to the field trials, Dyer modified his pouch by reducing the size somewhat. He also dispensed with the sling in accordance with the cavalry equipment board's decision calling for two belt pouches. The 1872 pouch was readily distinguished from the earlier version by its longer, 6½-inch belt loops, which also lacked the brass fixtures for connecting the sling. The outer flap was embossed with "U.S." within an oval border.

Furthermore, the board decided that the standard percussion cap pouch would be used for carrying the cavalryman's pistol ammunition; therefore, the integral pocket on the Dyer pouch would be superfluous. In lieu of this pocket, the 1872 version had a pouch for the combination tool. It was formed by a second layer of leather sewn to the inside of the front panel. The two pieces were left unstitched along their upper edges to form the pocket.

Carbine Sling

The board recommended that the standard Pattern 1855 bridle-leather slings be retained.[37] Although these had been made of black buff leather during the 1850s, and were so described in the 1861 regulations, bridle leather came into general use with the exigencies of war.

The sling measured 2½ inches wide by 56 inches long. At one end was a brass tip secured by four small round-head rivets (fig. 80). This tip was decorative and also served a functional purpose in preventing the wide piece of leather from curling up after being exposed to the weather. At the opposite end of the sling was a large brass buckle with two sheet-brass tongues that mated to corresponding pairs of holes in the belt. The buckle was secured to the belt by turning the end over the center bar of the buckle, rough side out, and fastening it with three rivets and three rows of stitching.

Sliding freely on the sling was an iron swivel made of four parts: the swivel itself (2⅝ inches wide), consisting of a roller and an iron wire eye approximately ¾ inch in diameter; a link 2¼ inches long; and the hook, measuring 4¼ inches long. The overall length was 8½ inches. A variant three-piece swivel, omitting the link, also was produced. This type had an overall length of about 6¾ inches. Since the four-piece swivel was the type described in the 1861 *Ordnance Manual*, it was considered the standard. All of the carbine slings were made under contract by several different suppliers, resulting in variations in the shapes of hooks, the markings on buckles, leather, and swivels, and other minor details.

Even though the board voted against the brace yoke for cavalry service, General Dyer overrode its recommendation before submitting the proceedings to the secretary of war. His objection was based on the fact that the secretary

already had approved the brace system for trials that had not yet occurred and, moreover, the braces were even then being manufactured.[38] So, although the brace yoke sling was tested by troops in the field, the standard carbine sling remained in use by those units that did not have the brace equipments.

Saber Knot

A new and much lighter-weight knot was adopted as part of the experimental equipments. This knot, made of thin black bridle leather, measured ⅝ inch wide by 30 inches long (fig. 81). The specifications called for a braided knot 1½ inches long attached to one end.[39] However, instead of a braided knot, one example had a rectangular tube through which the free end of the strap passed. The surface of the tube was imprinted with crosshatched stippling. The free end of the strap passed through the knuckle bow of the saber, was doubled on itself, and was joined at the knot. One sliding loop was provided to tighten the strap around the trooper's wrist.

Canteen and Haversack

The canteen was the same as for the infantry. Beginning in 1872, the haversack no longer formed a part of the cavalry trooper's outfit but could be issued on special requisition.[40] New linen duck saddlebags, made much larger than the 1859 bags, were intended to hold the soldier's spare clothing and toilet kit (off-side bag), as well as the rations (near-side bag).[41]

Spurs

The only change made in the cast-brass spurs issued under the new regulations was that they were smooth-finished instead of rather rough surfaced, as they came from the mold (fig. 82).[42] The coarse texture of the 1859 spurs made them difficult to keep clean and bright.

Spurs were made in two sizes, No. 1 having a heel depth of 3½ inches and No. 2 measuring 3¼ inches. Relative widths were 3¼ inches and 3 inches.[43] The branches

Left:
80. *Pattern 1855 carbine sling.*

Right:
81. *Saber knot, 1872.*

82. Enlisted cavalrymen's spurs, as issued during and after the Civil War.

of a regulation spur found on the Custer Battlefield tapered in width from about 9/16 inch at the shank to about ⅜ inch at the strap loops. These loops embraced two slots, measuring 3/16 inch wide by 13/16 inch, at the end of each branch. Another specimen recovered from the site of Major Marcus Reno's skirmish line in the valley was nearly identical but was somewhat lighter and had a crude floral design cast into the base of the shank.[44] Shanks for both sizes were 1 inch long, measured to the center of the rowel, or about 13/16 inch overall. Made of blued steel, the rowels measured 13/16 inch and had fourteen stubby points.

The 1859-pattern spurs were issued with a pair of black leather straps ½ inch wide by 19 inches long, creased along both edges. At one end of each strap was a standing loop and an iron wire roller buckle ⅝ inch wide. The straps were modified in 1872 to be ¾ inch wide and employed brass wire buckles.[45]

MISCELLANEOUS

Mess Gear

Before 1872, the army issued no personal mess gear to the rank and file.[46] Cooking in garrison, and frequently in the field, was done by squads or companies, depending on circumstances and the wishes of the company commander. Boiling and baking proved to be the only practical methods for cooking for large numbers of men. Frying meats was discouraged, for both logistical and medical reasons. Therefore, the Quartermaster Department provided only large sheet-iron mess pans and camp kettles, along with cast-iron pots, for cooking purposes.[47]

Although documentation is lacking as to why such essentials were not provided, it may be assumed that the army feared that individual mess utensils would be readily lost or damaged by the soldiers. Someone in the army hierarchy no doubt thought the men would take better care of such things if they were forced to purchase their own utensils. In any event, it was a considerable cost savings to the government.

Each company was permitted to maintain a "company fund," which amounted to petty cash derived from the sale of excess rations. This money was adminis-

83. Meat can adopted in 1872 for use by both infantry and cavalry.

tered by the company officers and used for almost anything that would benefit the men of that unit. In many companies it was common practice to purchase mess gear for issue to the men. In others, the soldiers were left no recourse but to purchase these items from the post sutler, usually at highly inflated prices.

Meat Can

A heavy tin box, termed a "meat can," was adopted as a part of the issue outfit for both infantry and cavalry troops. The concept was to provide a container for the greasy pork ration that soldiers carried into the field. The leaching of grease into everything else in the haversack had been the soldier's bane for years. Some men had put their bacon or salt pork in cotton bags, and others had fabricated ration bags from rubberized poncho material or oil cloth.[48] None of these devices worked very well for any length of time.

The meat can measured 6½ inches long by 1⅜ inches wide by 5³⁄₁₆ inches deep (fig. 83). A large ear-shaped handle was soldered and riveted to one end of the can, the lower end being free so that the can would slip into the specially fitted pocket on the front of either the 1872 haversack or the saddlebags and the handle would pass over the outside of the pocket on the right. The block letters "U.S.," ⅞ inch high and surrounded by an oval border, were pressed into both sides of the can.

The lid, corresponding in size to the top of the can itself and fitted with a collapsible bail handle, had a skirt about 1 inch deep that slipped within the mouth of the can (fig. 84). In theory at least, the can could "also be used if necessary to boil coffee, and the cover for a drinking cup."[49] Desperate indeed was the soldier who resorted to using the rectangular cover as a cup.

Tin Cup

Most soldiers continued to provide themselves with conventional tin cups during the early 1870s. These were more practical and useful than the meat can. The cups available to soldiers on the frontier reflected the basic designs of the contemporary tinner's craft (fig. 85). The pattern most commonly encountered was made of heavy block tin, had straight sides, and measured 4⅛ inches tall by 4¼ inches in diameter across the flat bottom. The upper end of the ear-shaped handle, having rolled wire-reinforced edges, was attached to the cup by the same two heavy-gauge wires, which protruded from the end of the handle. These ends passed through the top edge of the cup beneath the lip and were clinched back over the lip to the outside. The bottom end of the handle was attached by a single rivet and tin burr.

84. Meat can, 1872, with cover removed. Ostensibly, the lid was to be used as a cup.

Examples of this cup, having Civil War provenance, exist in abundance, and several other documented specimens have been recovered at western frontier military sites. This basic style of cup was also illustrated in the mail-order catalogs published by the legendary New York surplus dealer Frances Bannerman. According to Bannerman, these cups had been issued to volunteers during the Spanish-American War. Certainly, this pattern of cup can be considered as the standard that was widely available during the latter half of the century.[50]

Two other typical patterns of tin cups have been recovered from sites all across the West, some of which were not occupied until well after the Civil War. This provenance suggests that both of these types were used by regular army troops. One pattern, considerably shorter than that previously described, typically measured about 2⅞ inches high by 4⅛ inches in diameter, with a slight outward taper from bottom to top. One authority who has studied army cups extensively in the context of the western frontier noted that this short cup has been found at a number of military sites postdating the Civil War. Research suggests that it was indeed used by federal troops, though it was not as common as the larger version.[51]

The third style of tin cup identified was probably of commercial manufacture, since slight variations in size were encountered. Some of these measured 4⅛ inches by 4⅛ inches, whereas other extant specimens with similar characteristics were somewhat taller. This type of cup was distinguished by the handle, which did not have the wrapped wires at the rim. The upper end of the handle was affixed by a bead of solder and usually two rivets, and the lower end was attached by a single rivet. It should be noted that since tin cups were not items of army issue at this time, none were stamped "U.S." on the handle or elsewhere.[52]

Utensils

The styles of knives, forks, and spoons varied more widely than those of cups, owing to the great many styles available on the commercial market. Perhaps the most that can be said is that the knives and forks purchased by soldiers were usually iron with plain, two-piece wooden handles riveted to the shanks with two or three brass pins. Forks were made in both three- and four-tine styles, the former being the more common. Knives averaged 9 inches long, forks about 7 inches long. Spoons were made of either tin or white metal. Again, these were of plain design with spatulate or fiddle-shaped handles. Lengths ranged from 7¼ to 7½ inches.

Other Field Equipage

Poncho and Rubber Blanket   These articles were first issued early in the Civil War. The rubber blanket, authorized in 1861, served as rain gear for dismounted men, who previously had nothing of the kind. For several years before the war, the cavalry had been provided with the talma, a large rubberized raincoat that had full sleeves but no cape. By 1862, cavalrymen were being issued the poncho, which was nothing more than a rubber blanket with a slit for the head so that it could be worn as a cape (fig. 86). Ponchos, probably because they could be made less expensively, soon replaced the talma.[53]

Although ponchos were supposed to be issued to mounted troops and rubber or "gum" blankets to dismounted men, this distinction was seldom made in actual practice. Both ponchos and rubber blankets were used as ground cloths more frequently than for any other purpose. The poncho seems to have been favored by most soldiers. This was simply because it had a slit in the middle so that it could be pulled over the head, whereas the blanket was worn cape fashion around the shoulders and tied with a cord at the neck.

The poncho was made of black rubberized cotton sheeting measuring 45 inches by 72 inches. A slit, 14 inches long, was made laterally across the center and was covered by a flap of the same material. The flap was fastened by a single button, usually of the pressed-tin variety, but one specimen examined had a japanned iron-shank button. Around the perimeter were sixteen ¼-inch-diameter brass grommets by which the soldier could tie the poncho up to trees or brush as a shelter from rain or sun. These grommets, each on a 1¼-inch square reinforcement of the same material, were placed with the centers 1 inch from the edge so as to have six along each side and four on each end. All edges were bound with strips of the same rubber material, ½ inch wide, glued to the face side only.[54]

The rubber blanket was identical to the poncho except that it had no head slit and there were two extra grommets along one side to facilitate tying it around the neck with a cord. One variant examined measured 46 inches by 69½ inches. It had only four grommets along one side and six along the opposite side, with four arranged along each end. This particular specimen had a 12-inch slit (repaired at some later time) in the center, indicating that a soldier had modified it for use as a poncho.

85. Typical mess outfit used by soldiers until the advent of army-issue utensils in 1875.

The principal complaint about the poncho, if not the rubber blanket, was that it simply was too small to adequately protect a man from getting wet. This was especially evident with the cavalry. Captain Theodore J. Wint, Fourth Cavalry, graded the poncho as "worthless to mounted troops" and recommended that it be made seven feet square. A fellow officer lamented the loss of the old talma of antebellum days.[55]

At the end of fiscal year 1870 (ending June 30, 1870), the Quartermaster Department reported it had a total of 363,401 ponchos and 476,106 rubber blankets on hand, plus 6,982 painted blankets. Only 20,289 had been issued during that year and only 27,133 the year previous, when the army had been larger.[56] The Civil War surplus of these items fulfilled the army's needs until 1893.[57]

86. Soldier wearing rubberized poncho, ca. 1866. (Smithsonian Institution)

Shelter Half   The ubiquitous army shelter tent, known to every veteran as a "dog" or "pup" tent, earned its sobriquet during the Civil War. One veteran recalled that it "would only comfortably accommodate a dog, and a small one at that." Trumpeter A. F. Mulford, who served in the Seventh Cavalry during the 1870s, said of the tent's diminutive size: "You enter at one end—that is you crawl in—and you have to stay crawled until you come out. Pup tents are good to keep the sun off but not much protection when it rains."[58] To make matters worse, this first version had no end flaps to keep out the weather.

The 1864-pattern shelter half was made of eight-ounce cotton duck and measured 65 inches wide by 66 inches long (fig. 87). Sewn along the bottom edge were three square reinforcements, also of duck, one at each corner and another in the center. Each of these had two ½-inch-diameter whipped grommets for foot stops made of ¼-inch Manila rope.[59] Two more such reinforcements, each having a pair of grommets, were stitched at the upper corners. Of these, the hole nearest the edge was for attaching the guy rope, and the rear hole for the tenon of the pole.

Along the top, four inches from the edge, was a row of nine pressed-tin buttons, with a corresponding row of buttonholes set ½ inch from the edge. These were used to join the two halves, forming a two-man tent. A similar arrangement of seven paired buttons and holes was placed along both sides, thus permitting additional pieces to be joined for a larger shelter or to be fastened around the ends to keep out wind-driven rain.

Two wooden poles, 46 inches long, supported the shelter tent. Made in two sections for ease in carrying, these poles were made of either pine or poplar, 1 inch in diameter. The upper joint had one end turned down to form a ½-inch tenon that mated with the grommet in the shelter half (fig. 88). The lower end was cut at a sharp bevel corresponding to an identical one on the upper end of the lower joint. Affixed to the lower joint was a tin socket 4 inches long, tacked in place, to hold the two joints together.[60]

Each shelter half was issued with a guy rope 6 feet long made of six-cord Manila, having both ends whipped with stout linen thread to prevent them from fraying. Additionally, four hardwood pins, usually made of oak or hickory, accompanied each shelter half. The peg measured about 9 inches long, the head having the shape of the frustum of a cone, with a neck about ⅝ inch in diameter. The body below the neck gradually swelled to a full diameter of about 1 inch, then tapered to a rounded point.[61]

Above:

87. *Pattern 1864 army shelter tent.*

Below:

88. *Two-piece shelter tent pole and pin.*

In areas where hard or rocky soil prevailed, company commanders often had the blacksmiths make up tent pins of iron. A typical example of this type of pin, found on the site of Custer's camp of June 23, 1876, was made of $\%6$-inch-diameter stock 8½ inches long. A hook for the foot stop was made of the same material and was forge-welded at an oblique angle to the head. The bottom end of the pin was sharpened to a point having four facets. Although these stakes weighed considerably more than the wooden variety, they were practically indestructible.

Blanket   The regulation 1851-pattern blanket, according to specifications, measured 5½ feet wide by 7 feet long and weighed five pounds. Like many of the other contract articles of that time, however, the blankets were subject to variations from the standard. Two extant 1851 blankets in the collections of the Danish Royal Arsenal Museum measured 5 feet 8½ inches by 6 feet 9 inches and 5 feet 8½ inches by 6 feet 3 inches. Their color was brownish-gray, with a black stripe about 3½ inches wide across the width near each end. The ends, unlike blankets made in the twentieth century, were unbound. The letters "U.S.," averaging 4½ inches high, were hand stitched in the center with black yarn.[62] Although these letters often were oriented to read parallel to the width of the blanket, they sometimes ran lengthwise. Apparently, at this early date it was immaterial which way they were arranged.

Although the Woodhull report criticized the wartime army blanket, no immediate action was taken to improve it. Like so many other contract articles, the blankets seldom met the specifications. They often contained shoddy and cotton fiber, were undersized, and were lighter in weight than required. Compounding the situation, the soldier was restricted to the single blanket provided to him at enlistment—and he was not authorized a second one until his third year in service. The woolen blanket was one item a soldier would not be without, either in garrison or in the field. (This was the origin of the soldier slang "Take another blanket," meaning to reenlist.) Despite the regulations, most men managed to obtain several blankets, by purchase either from the Quartermaster Department or from discharged soldiers. An officer wrote from Fort Walla Walla, "Of course no soldier . . . can keep alive in this climate with but two blankets, they all have six or eight, but it seems cruelly unjust to compel soldiers to expend their well earned pay [for] blankets at their own cost . . . or freeze to death."[63]

A special board of officers that was assigned the task of finding a better blanket discovered that the Mission and Pacific Woolen Mills in San Francisco could produce an extremely high quality blanket, better than any available in the East. The specifications for the blanket remained the same, 5½ feet by 7 feet, gray with black end stripes, five pounds in weight. Since blankets always were popular bartering items with soldiers, the letters "U.S.," four inches high, were placed in the center to identify them as government property. Although the specifications were mute as to whether the letters were to be placed parallel with the width or the length of the blanket, one extant specimen has them embroidered in black yarn lengthwise. It is conceivable that some also were made with the "U.S." across the width. Troops on the West Coast were supplied with the "California" blanket immediately, whereas those serving elsewhere were provided with a comparable blanket made under contract in the East.[64]

The Best Small Arms
for the Use of the Army,
1870–1880

THE BREECH-LOADING Springfield rifle models of 1866 and 1868 served the infantry well enough in the years immediately after the Civil War and, perhaps more important, satisfied Congress by their reliance on parts from the available surplus arms. During this same time period, the cavalry utilized the war-tried Spencer and the more recent conversion of the Sharps carbine, modified to use metallic ammunition. Production costs for small arms were thus held to a minimum. These weapons were a stopgap measure, at best, instituted in response to existing economic conditions, rather than an intentional and thoughtful approach to designing an arm suited to the army's needs. Nevertheless, the converted arms served to buy the time necessary to further distance Congress from the war and to allow for more progressive nations to advance their arms developments, by which the United States might benefit.

The Civil War had motivated and provided unparalleled testing grounds for great technological improvements in weapons design. These advancements were not lost on other nations, nations that maintained a keen vigilance over the conduct of the war. During the late 1860s most of the world's great military powers devised ways to convert their old muzzleloaders to breech-loading configurations. By 1871, Austria-Hungary, Germany, Sweden, and England all had adopted new patterns of breech-loading rifles ranging from .41 to .45 caliber. Although all of these were single-shot weapons, they incorporated a variety of revolutionary technological advances, such as Paul Mauser's turn-bolt action. The time had come for the U.S. Army to reexamine its position on small arms in light of these developments.

During the summer of 1869 General William Tecumseh Sherman activated a special board of five officers, headed by Major General John M. Schofield, to review the coordinated system of tactics developed by Lieutenant Colonel Emory Upton. The army had used Upton's tactics for the previous two years. While this board was in session, Sherman, responding to influence exerted on the army by numerous arms inventors, decided to expand its duties by undertaking a study of the small arms and accoutrements that might best suit the service.[1] This extra task was not as unrelated as it might seem initially, since the school of the soldier, fire discipline, and unit tactics were associated directly with the type of weapon with which the troops might be armed. Of continuing concern were the differences between the systems types incorporated in the carbines used by the cavalry and in the rifles used by the infantry. Obviously, the supply of surplus arms was limited, and it was only a matter of time before the Ordnance Department would have to come to grips with the arms issue. Sherman apparently decided, perhaps under the influence of the Ordnance Department, that the time had arrived.

There were no particular limitations placed on the Schofield Board, only that it was to consider all arms submitted to it and to recommend six each of the best rifles, carbines, and pistols for further trial. All arms were to be evaluated for caliber, type of ammunition, simplicity, and parts interchangeability. If the particular arm was a conversion of an existing model, such as the Springfield breechloader, the board was instructed further to consider the existing number and condition of the parent arm.

As the news of the army's quest for improved arms quickly spread, samples began arriving daily at St. Louis Arsenal. By the time of the March 1 deadline, no less than forty-one rifles awaited the board, although only eight carbines and eleven pistols had been submitted. Calibers for all arms ranged from .42 to .50 caliber.

The board's first task was to develop a battery of tests to which all arms would be subjected in an attempt to provide a fair evaluation of their relative merits and deficiencies. The experiments consisted of the following, taken from *Ordnance Memoranda No. 11:*

    I. Simplicity of construction—Each arm to be dismounted, examined, and the number of its pieces to be noted.

    II. Accuracy of fire—Test: fifteen shots to be fired from a fixed rest at a target; distance, 100 yards.

    III. Rapidity of fire—Test: twenty-five shots to be fired from the shoulder; fair aim to be taken at the target; distance, 100 yards.

    IV. Endurance—Test: each gun to be fired at a target 500 times from a fixed rest; distance 100 yards. The arm to be allowed to cool at the end of each 100 rounds, but not to be cleaned during the test. At the end of this test, the arm to be cleaned and examined, to ascertain its condition.

    V. Effects of exposure to the weather and firing—Test: four hundred rounds to be fired without cleaning the arm; one hundred on each alternate day. The arm to be exposed to the effects of the sun and rain (or water artificially applied) during each day of the tests, and the exposure continued for three days thereafter. The arms then to be cleaned and examined.

    VI. Effects of sand and dust on the breech mechanism—Test: eight shots to be fired; then fine dry sand to be sifted over the breech mechanism when closed, and eight shots to be fired; then fine dry sand to be sifted over the same parts when open, and nine shots fired. The sand to be removed in each case by shaking the piece, or using only the hand. The piece then to be examined and cleaned.

    VII. Effects of salt water—Test: the arm to be placed for three hours in brine, covering the breech mechanism and chamber; then to be exposed in the open air until the next day, and fifty shots to be fired.

    VIII. Effects of defective ammunition—Test: the arm to be fired with six cartridges rendered defective in the following manner: 1st, one cut longitudinally from the end of the case to the rim, and placed in the chamber with the cut upwards. 2nd, one cut longitudinally from the end of the case to the rim, and placed in the chamber with the cut downwards. 3d, one to be cut helically from the end of the rim. 4th, one to be cut at the base, so that the firing pin in firing will pierce it.

5th, one to be pierced through the base at four points. 6th, one to be filed through the rim.

IX. Strength of the breech mechanism—Test: the arm to be fired once with a double and once with a triple charge of powder and lead.[2]

By June 10, 1870, the board concluded its deliberations, recommending the following rifles in priority order: .50-caliber Remington; .50-caliber Springfield; .50-caliber Sharps; .42-caliber Morgenstern; .45-caliber Martini-Henry; and .50-caliber Ward-Burton. A carbine version of each of the above was recommended for the cavalry, though the board urged that the Remington action be modified so that the piece could be loaded at the half cock rather than full cock. The following pistols were recommended: .50-caliber Remington, single-shot; .44-caliber Smith & Wesson revolver; .44-caliber Remington revolver No. 2; .44-caliber Remington revolver No. 5; .44-caliber Remington revolver No. 3; and .44-caliber Remington revolver No. 4.

In his review of the board's recommendations for rifles, Chief of Ordnance Alexander B. Dyer was quick to point out that the Remington rolling-block design possessed some faults that had not been readily apparent, or at least reported, in the tests conducted. Because of the Remington's rapid gain in popularity worldwide (the 1867 model having been adopted officially within two years by Sweden, Norway, Denmark, and Spain) the Ordnance Department had initiated limited issues of the rifle in .50/70 caliber before the board's tests. Dyer agreed, however, that the board's top three selections, namely the Remington, the Springfield, and the Sharps, were good weapons. To give these designs practical trials in the field, he recommended that one thousand rifles of each type and three hundred carbines of the respective manufactures be produced and issued in equal numbers to selected companies throughout the army. The experimental arms would be given a one-year comprehensive test, during which company commanders were to report monthly on their experiences with the weapons. Both Sherman and Secretary of War William W. Belknap concurred.[3]

Despite the Schofield Board's recommendations, the National Armory was unshakably wedded to its own design, which the Ordnance Department professionals wanted to keep in production. In his annual report for fiscal year 1870, Dyer subtly suggested that since the armory had nearly completed its current order of fifty thousand Model 1868 rifles, it might just as well bring the reserve stocks up to one hundred thousand, "to meet any emergency" that might arise, especially since more than a year had to elapse before any system could be adopted.[4] With such a large quantity of Springfield breechloaders on hand, Dyer probably calculated that Congress would force the choice on economic grounds, no matter the outcome of the field tests. A sharp-eyed Sherman, however, caught the attempted deception as he reviewed his subordinate's report and overrode the ploy by recommending that further production of the Model 1868 be postponed until the trials were completed (fig. 89). Sherman unabashedly expressed his preference for the Remington, though he betrayed his lack of technical knowledge by suggesting that the Remington system could be applied equally well to rifles, carbines, and pistols, which "would have identically the same caliber and cartridge."[5]

Springfield Armory went to work immediately to manufacture the required quantities of the experimental rifles and carbines. The arms reached the infantry in March 1871, but production problems delayed the carbine issues until that

89. *(Top to bottom) Model 1863 rifled musket, Model 1866 Springfield rifle, Model 1868 Springfield rifle, and Model 1871 Ward-Burton rifle.* (Hayes Otoupalik Collection)

summer. In all, three or four companies in each of sixteen infantry regiments and one or two companies in each of seven cavalry regiments eventually received the new arms.[6]

As something of an afterthought, the Ordnance Department decided to include in the trials a like quantity of the single-shot bolt-action Ward-Burton rifles, also in .50/70 caliber. The Ward-Burton had fallen into last place of those recommended by the Schofield Board, but it finally was included in the trials because of the future possibilities of its turn-bolt action design. The addition of the Ward-Burton provided the army with a good example of four principal breech actions: falling block, upward-swinging block, bolt action, and downward rotating block. As with the other models, one thousand rifles and three hundred of the Ward-Burton carbines were to be manufactured and issued for trial. The Ward-Burtons reached the designated units during the second quarter of calendar year 1872. A survey of the Ordnance Returns indicates that these arms were issued to the same companies selected to receive the other three experimental types.[7]

As the monthly reports accumulated at the Ordnance Office, it became evident that the Model 1870 Springfield was the leading contender (figs. 90 and 91). The chief of ordnance, in eager anticipation that the National Armory's product would be adopted, requested $150,000 to begin manufacturing new rifles and carbines. Congress, however, was not ignorant of the trials then in progress, or of the extensive selection of arms then available worldwide.

Congress, sensitive to the needs of the service as well as the principles of free enterprise, approved the expenditure on June 6, 1872, with the stipulation that none of the funds were to be expended until a second board of officers conducted a further review on the subject. The legislators obviously wanted to make certain that so momentous a decision was based on the soundest data obtainable and that any implication of a bias toward the government's own Springfield design would be dispelled.

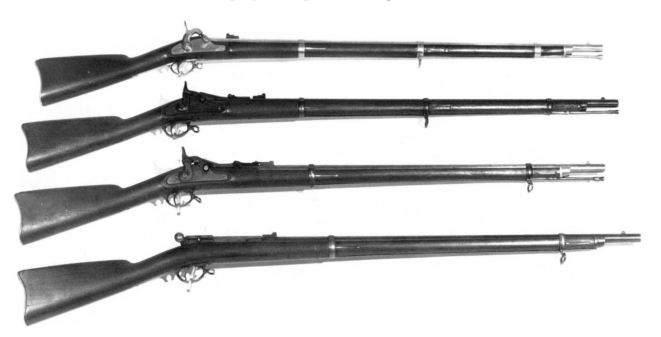

Regardless of the army's general preference for the Springfield, it had been intended only as a temporary measure, the outgrowth of the austere economic environment that existed at the end of the Civil War. The Models 1865 and 1866 were relatively inexpensive conversions, but the subsequent Model 1868 and the most recent example, the Model 1870, incorporated far fewer surplus parts than did the earlier Allin breechloaders. The Model 1870 had, in fact, evolved into nearly a new weapon altogether; the National Armory used many newly made parts, particularly the principal pieces such as the barrel, receiver, breechblock, ramrod, rear sight, and stock.

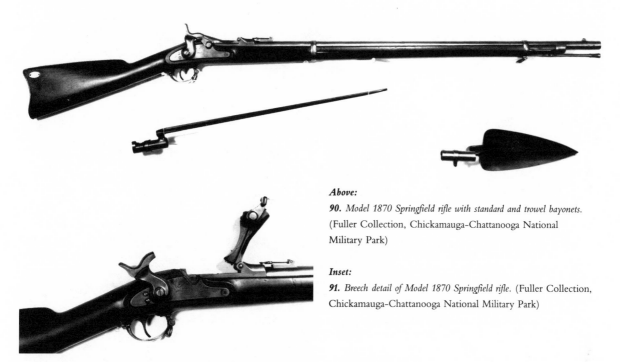

Above:

90. *Model 1870 Springfield rifle with standard and trowel bayonets.* (Fuller Collection, Chickamauga-Chattanooga National Military Park)

Inset:

91. *Breech detail of Model 1870 Springfield rifle.* (Fuller Collection, Chickamauga-Chattanooga National Military Park)

By specifying that "the system, when so adopted shall be the only one to be used by the Ordnance Department in the manufacture of muskets and carbines for the military service," Congress clearly wanted the arms question settled once and for all.[8] There was to be one system, and only one, thus closing the door on any further expenditures for converted and experimental arms.

A second board was directed to undertake a comprehensive approach to selecting an arms system by inviting the broadest possible competition, even from foreign nations. Amid a fanfare of publicity, the officers assembled in New York City on September 3, 1872. The board comprised the following members: Brigadier General Alfred H. Terry, soon to be named commander of the Department of Dakota (fig. 92); Colonel P. V. Hagner of the Ordnance Department; Colonel Henry B. Clitz, Tenth Infantry; Major Marcus A. Reno, Seventh Cavalry; and Captain LaRhett L. Livingston, Third Artillery. Almost immediately, arms began arriving from all of the major domestic arms manufacturers, as well as from several foreign concerns and numerous private inventors. The total eventually reached ninety-nine individual weapons. To establish the highest degree of continuity possible, the Terry Board requested that all arms be

chambered for the .50/70 cartridge, if feasible. Consequently, all but seventeen of the trial samples were of that caliber.

The .50/70 cartridge had been exposed to only moderate testing in its initial development, the object being to adapt surplus weapons to a uniform caliber as determined by the 1866 board of officers, headed by Major General Winfield S. Hancock. Accordingly, the board had requested the chief of ordnance to have Springfield Armory prepare five breechloaders on the Allin system, three of .45 caliber and two of .50 caliber. The former were to have chamber mouths measuring .50, .54, and .58, respectively, and the .50-caliber rifles were to have chambers bored to .54 and .58 diameter. Each chamber size was to have three specially designed test cartridges made for it, containing 60-, 65-, and 70-grain powder charges. The smallest charge was to employ a 450-grain bullet, the larger charges a 480-grain bullet.[9] These experiments resulted in the birth of the .50/70 government cartridge. Notwithstanding the board's recognition of the superior performance of the experimental .45/70 round with a heavy bullet, Ordnance Chief Dyer pronounced it "entirely too long for general service."[10] The difference in range and accuracy, the Ordnance Department concluded, scarcely would be appreciated by the average soldier. Therefore, the board conceded that such a cartridge would not offset the perceived advantage of a shorter round matching the bore caliber of the cavalry weapons then in use, namely the Spencer carbine. But, by 1872 the army was ready to reopen the entire subject of small arms, including consideration of an optimum smaller caliber, since several European powers recently had set the example by adopting smaller bores.

Shortly before the Terry Board met, Special Orders No. 107 established the Small Arms Caliber Board, whose purpose was to test cartridges and barrels of .40, .42, and .45 caliber. These tests, conducted at Springfield Armory, utilized dozens of combinations of caliber, bullet weight, and powder charge, as well as rifling type and rate of twist. In the final analysis the board reported that Barrel No. 16 with Ammunition No. 58 gave the best overall performance, with a mean average deviation of 8.58 inches at a range of 500 yards. This score was attained using a 32½-inch barrel having three wide lands and grooves with a twist of one turn in 22 inches. The best load was of .45 caliber using a round-nosed 405-grain lead-tin alloy bullet with a concave base. The charge was 70 grains of musket powder.[11] The straight-taper copper alloy case contained a cup anvil primer designed by Major S. V. Benet, the commanding officer at Frankford Arsenal. This priming system, adopted by the army in 1868, consisted of a small copper cup seated inside the case head and atop the fulminate compound. Ignition occurred when the firing pin struck the outside of the head and pinched the sensitive compound against the perforated cup anvil. Although the Benet-primed cartridge was virtually waterproof, it could not be reloaded. Thus was born the famous .45/70 cartridge used by U.S. forces through the Philippine Insurrection and by civilian hunters and shooters to the present day.

The ballistics information immediately was passed along to the Terry Board, which quickly requisitioned six sample arms similarly barreled and chambered. Surviving to the final tests were the Ward-Burton (redesigned as a repeating magazine gun), Springfield, Elliot, Remington, Freeman, and Peabody designs. These arms then were subjected to a final battery of tests, including rapidity of fire and use by both experienced soldiers and recruits. The results, combined

On the facing page:
92. Brigadier General Alfred H. Terry. A lawyer before the Civil War, Terry adopted a military career that spanned twenty-seven years. Best remembered for his lackluster leadership of the Dakota Column during the 1876 Sioux Campaign, Terry had headed the arms board three years earlier. (Little Bighorn Battlefield National Monument)

93. *Erskine Allin, master armorer at Springfield Armory, 1850–1875.* (Springfield Armory National Historic Site, National Park Service)

with the previous reports from line units, convinced the board that the Springfield was indeed the best service weapon available at the time.

In view of the incredibly rugged tests imposed on the trial weapons, it was truly remarkable that any of the single-shot arms could pass successfully, much less the repeaters, which by their very nature had more complex mechanisms. That the Springfield emerged almost unchallenged with far fewer broken parts was certainly a tribute to Erskine Allin's simplistic design (fig. 93). Although it could be argued that the function tests were needlessly rigorous, even for military weapons, one must keep in mind several factors influencing the army's attitude at the time. First, it was obvious that the weapon selected would see immediate service on the western frontier, where environmental conditions were extreme and sources of replacement parts remote to nonexistent. It still would be decades before army organization tables would include ordnance units close behind the front lines to provide weapons repair and replacement services for combat troops. Minor repairs, to the extent of replacing broken or worn parts, usually were executed in garrison by an ordnance sergeant. These men were not, however, trained gunsmiths. Replacement of major parts or repairs requiring machine work to restore the arm to service usually meant that the weapon had to be returned to Springfield Armory. Supply lines on the frontier extended hundreds of miles, and a soldier going on patrol, and especially on an extended campaign, had to rely on his rifle or carbine to remain in combat-ready condition for the duration of his field service.

A further consideration was the quality and intelligence of the enlisted soldier himself, for whom most officers did not have a particularly high regard. During the 1870s, nearly one-half of the rank and file was composed of foreign-born men, a number of whom understood little, if any, English.[12] Most recruits, regardless of their origins, came from the lower rungs of the social ladder and had little formal education. To the army's way of thinking, it was only practical to issue small arms requiring a minimum of technical know-how and intellectual sophistication. To what degree this factor influenced the selection of an arm can only be guessed, but it was most certainly a consideration.

As for repeating arms, the service at this time was more interested in the accuracy, power, and reliability of small arms than in the rapidity of fire. There was, in fact, great concern with fire discipline and the conservation of ammunition now that troops were armed with breechloaders. Considering that the average soldier could fire a dozen or more aimed shots per minute with the Springfield and that he carried approximately fifty rounds of ammunition, he conceivably could expend all of his cartridges in a relatively short period of sustained heavy action. Officers feared that their men would fire too rapidly without taking proper aim, thus wasting precious ammunition. That this mode of thinking prevailed during the entire latter half of the nineteenth century is borne out in the reports on the adoption of the .30-caliber Springfield-Krag rifle in early 1892.[13] The Krag, as well as its successor, the famous Model 1903 Springfield, had a magazine cut-off feature reflecting the army's obsession with the concept that even a magazine arm should be used as a single-loader, the magazine being held in reserve to repel a potential rush by the enemy.

The .45 Springfield rifles and carbines were both powerful and accurate (figs. 94 and 95). However, comparisons often are made between the Springfield and the Winchester repeating carbine or rifle, which had magazine capacities of eleven and fifteen cartridges, respectively. The gun most often contrasted with the army's Springfield was the Model 1873 Winchester in caliber .44/40, a popular arm among cowboys, settlers, frontiersmen, and Indians. Despite its greater firepower, it had an inherently weak action, slow reloading time, and an effective range of no more than two hundred yards. Both the 1860 Henry and the Model 1866 Winchester, which were used in significant numbers by warriors in the Custer fight, for instance, were chambered for the even less potent .44 Henry rimfire cartridge.[14] Comparative ballistics are shown below:

	Muzzle Velocity	Muzzle Energy
.45/70 rifle	1,350 ft./sec.	1,525 ft. lbs.
.45/55 carbine	1,150 ft./sec.	930 ft. lbs.
.44/40 Winchester	1,245 ft./sec.	688 ft. lbs.
.44 Henry	1,125 ft./sec.	568 ft. lbs.

Despite the army's experience on the western frontier, the Indian campaigns were viewed as little more than a temporary police action that might be settled at any time. Clearly, the army's focus was on being prepared to fight another large-scale conventional war against a foreign power. Breech-loading small arms were the way of the future and had dictated already revised tactics emphasizing open rather than close-order formations, the utilization of ground cover and rifle pits, and the value of individual marksmanship to break up enemy concentrations at long range. The Springfield breechloader's power, accuracy, and sustained rate of fire made it an effective weapon for such conditions. Of course, this was based on the premise that the troops would be trained as capable combat marksmen. In reality, most soldiers serving in the 1870s were not good marksmen because of the lack of formal training and because of the severe restrictions placed on the amount of ammunition used for target practice. Not until the 1880s would any great advancements be made in the field of army marksmanship.[15]

Above:

94. *Model 1873 .45-caliber Springfield rifle, 1877 stock variation.* (Springfield Armory National Historic Site, National Park Service)

Below:

95. *Model 1873 .45-caliber Springfield carbine, 1877 stock variation.* (Springfield Armory National Historic Site, National Park Service)

A widespread myth attributed to the Springfield carbine is that it suffered from extraction problems to such a degree that it was a factor in Lieutenant Colonel George Custer's defeat at the Battle of the Little Bighorn. Recent archaeological evidence argues against this. Data from the surveys conducted on the battlefield reveal that only 2 percent of the archaeologically recovered .45/55 cases exhibited extraction problems. Combining this figure with all of the other government carbine cases in the Little Bighorn Battlefield collections comes to a total of only 6 percent. The archaeological study concluded that although extraction problems occurred in the fight, this "was not significant to the outcome of the battle."[16] In the interest of evaluating the Springfield's performance in a broader context, one also must look beyond the Little Bighorn to other engagements, such as the Battle of the Rosebud, where at least twenty-five thousand rounds of .45-caliber government ammunition were expended in the period of a few hours. Significantly, no complaints of jamming were lodged against the Springfield after this fight. The 1877 Battle of the Big Hole offers another example, where only one archaeologically recovered .45/70 case bore signs of extraction difficulty.[17]

For the most part, the limited extraction problems encountered must be attributed not to the Springfield's design but rather to the leather cartridge belts that soldiers fabricated for themselves. Uncovered and subjected to the elements, the cartridges soon became grimy and covered with verdigris as a result of the chemical reaction between the copper cases and the tanning compositions contained in the leather. When the gun was fired, the case sometimes stuck fast in the chamber. The only alternative for removing such a case was with either a cleaning rod or a pocketknife, provided the head of the case remained intact. (A jointed cleaning rod for the carbine and a broken shell extractor were provided by 1877.) Soldiers in some units were keenly aware of the problem and were attentive to wiping their ammunition when action seemed imminent. When Indians were reported to be threatening General George Crook's camp near the base of the Big Horn Mountains in August 1876, Sergeant George S. Howard, Second Cavalry, remembered, "The men went to cleaning cartridges and it really looked like a Fight." That both commissioned and noncommissioned officers in the Seventh Cavalry ignored this critical factor is evidenced by their failure to ensure that the cartridges were cleaned and inspected on a regular basis while on campaign.[18] Had such action been taken, the myth of the alleged extractor failure never would have arisen. Such negligence was inexcusable considering that the problem was well-known throughout the army and was, in fact, one of the army's principal arguments against the adoption of a cartridge belt.

The Springfield's power and long range suited it well to most situations of plains warfare, where volumes of fire adequate for handling most situations usually could be produced by company skirmishers. But, there were rare circumstances when the Springfield's single-shot firing capability placed it at a distinct disadvantage. The Battle of the Little Bighorn serves as perhaps the best example of the Springfield's strengths and weaknesses. In those phases of the Custer fight and the Reno-Benteen engagement in which ranges were several hundred yards, Seventh Cavalrymen did relatively well in keeping the warriors at bay.[19] Conversely, when the fighting changed from long to short range in the Custer fight, the warriors were able to bring their shorter-ranged repeaters into play. The greater firepower of the Henry and Winchester Model 1866 rifles at close quarters, when pitted against the slower-firing Springfield, was a decided factor in tipping the scales against the Seventh Cavalry.[20]

The members of the Terry Board were neither so shortsighted nor so parochial that they did not appreciate the advantages of repeating arms, as some of the Springfield's critics have suggested.[21] The board's hesitation to recommend one for official adoption was based on two factors: finding a magazine arm that could handle the .45/70 cartridge; and finding one that was rugged and reliable enough for military service. In its final report the board resolved, "The adoption of magazine-guns for the military service, by all nations, is only a question of time; . . . whenever an arm shall be devised which shall be as effective, as a single breech-loader, as the best of the existing single breech-loading arms, and at the same time shall possess a safe and easily manipulated magazine, every consideration of public policy will require its adoption."[22]

The board was very impressed with the Ward-Burton in its magazine model of .45 caliber. However, the field reports received on the single-shot version indicated that the Ward-Burton was subject to an unacceptable number of broken parts. Therefore, the members were hesitant to recommend it for official adoption but did suggest that a limited number be produced and issued for further trial in the field. The Springfield consequently won out by a narrow margin. The coup de grace for the Ward-Burton was Dyer's disapproval of the board's recommendation. Although he too supported the idea of taking another look at the magazine repeater, he was bound by the congressional restriction that the system adopted would "be the only one used by the Ordnance Department in the manufacture of muskets and carbines for military service."[23]

Acting on the recommendations of the board, Secretary of War Belknap approved the manufacture of the new .45-caliber rifle on May 28, 1873. The Model 1873, one of the finest-quality military weapons of its day, went into production before the end of the year. Although it retained the basic Allin breech-loading system, the new model was noticeably more refined than any of its predecessors. The workmanship throughout was superb. All metal parts were treated with a deep-blue finish, or "browning," a first for a Springfield product. The reduction in caliber from .50 to .45, along with a thinner lock plate and slimmer stock, made the Model 1873 weigh in at nearly three-quarters of a pound less than the Model 1870. It also was fitted with a more sophisticated long-range rear sight. By the end of 1873 nearly 1,942 carbines had come off the assembly line, but only five rifles had been made.[24] This may have been the result of army politics, since the cavalry had been armed with a hodgepodge of different carbines since the end of the Civil War.

With the new weapon standardized at last, nearly all the experimental weapons, except for the Model 1870 Springfields, were called in from the field during 1874. Most of the infantry regiments reverted to using the Model 1868 Springfield, as well as the Model 1870s already on hand, until the .45-caliber rifles were available. By June 30, 1875, all of the foot regiments had received the Model 1873.[25] Manufacture of the carbines in greater numbers, early on, permitted the cavalry regiments to make the transition somewhat faster initially, with the Second and Tenth regiments obtaining the Model 1873 during the first and second quarters of 1874. The remaining units were supplied as quickly as the new arms could be produced and shipped, but with the greater emphasis placed on the production of rifles than carbines in 1874 and 1875, not all of the mounted units were issued new-model arms until mid-1875.[26] It has been suggested that Springfields Model 1868 remained in use as first-class arms until as late as 1880, but ordnance returns fail to reflect this. Although some companies retained a few .50-caliber weapons on their inventories as secondary arms, probably to be issued to hunting parties, the transition to the Model 1873 was virtually complete armywide by the spring of 1876.[27]

The following decade was to see renewed efforts to find a suitable magazine rifle for the army. Yet another board would consider this question in 1878, the only result being the selection of the Winchester-Hotchkiss bolt-action .45/70 repeater, produced jointly by the Winchester Repeating Arms Company and Springfield Armory in 1879. Approximately one thousand Hotchkiss rifles and carbines were sold to the government. Still other repeating arms would be tried without much success during the 1880s. Eventually, the army's quest for a magazine arm merged with a worldwide trend toward smaller calibers using smokeless powder. The result in the U.S. service would be the Model 1892 Springfield-Krag in caliber .30/40, which paved the way for the legendary Model 1903 Springfield.

Out of the plethora of sidearms that flourished during the Civil War, two principal weapons emerged as both mechanically and ballistically superior—the Model 1860 Colt (fig. 96) and the 1858 New Model Remington army revolvers. Even though the Ordnance Department retained reserve quantities of some of the other makes of revolvers, such as the Starr and the Whitney, the army selected the Colt and the Remington as the primary cavalry sidearms after the war because of their proven combat records and the quantities on hand. The Remington, having a solid frame, was preferred somewhat over the less rugged, open-topped Colt. By the middle of 1867, issues of the Remington predominated, though some units retained the Colt or mixtures of both types for several years to come.[28]

Even though these .44-caliber (actual bore diameter was .45 caliber) six-shooters were reliable and powerful, they were slow to load under fire. Both used fixed ammunition, wherein the bullet and powder charge were contained in a chemically treated combustible cartridge. But, the soldier still had to charge each chamber from the front end using the loading lever on the revolver, and each had to be primed with a percussion cap. In most instances, a cavalry action was decided within the time it took for each man to discharge his six rounds in close combat. As noted by Captain William Thompson, Seventh Cavalry, the percussion revolver, once empty, was "of little use to a trooper mounted."[29] Thus, the saber found continued use in hand-to-hand actions.

The army seemed to be in no great hurry to embrace revolvers using metallic cartridges. Technological advances in breech-loading rifles and carbines, notably the Spencer, may have caused ordnance officers to give second thought to the importance of the revolver in future conflicts. The 1868 Ordnance Board reflected this in its recommendations by stating,

> The urgency of the service not demanding the immediate introduction of pistols adapted to the use of metallic primed cartridges, and experiments not having yet determined definitely which of the numerous plans of

96. *Left (top to bottom): Model 1860 Colt .44 revolver; Model 1851 .36 navy revolver; Model 1871 Remington .50 revolver. Right (top to bottom): Model 1873 single-action army .45 revolver; Model 1875 Smith & Wesson .45 revolver. (Hayes Otoupalik Collection)*

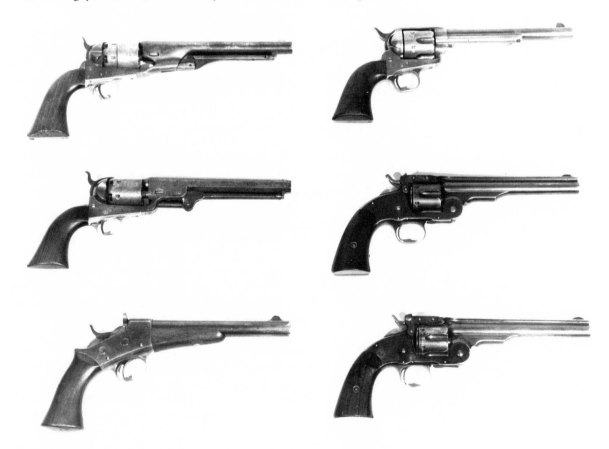

alteration proposed is the best, the Board recommend, that prior to the adoption of any one plan, revolvers altered on the two systems of loading at the front and rear of the cylinder, respectively, be prepared for further trials at Springfield Armory.[30]

However, the troops sent to the frontier were aware of the situation and questioned the army's apparent lack of initiative in providing a more modern pistol. One anonymous officer wrote:

> It is passing strange that while so much is being done in the way of perfecting the rifle and carbine, we hear nothing of an improved Army pistol. There are as many different pocket pistols, revolvers, and repeaters as there are breech-loading rifles, most of them are poor affairs for troops, and Colt's and Remington's Army pistols are still the best we have for the service; but we greatly need a better weapon of this kind. We want a pistol to use the metallic cartridge. . . . Everyone in the Army knows the great inconvenience of loading and capping an army pistol while in motion on horseback, and also the great number of pistol cartridges that are destroyed in the cartridge box, and in loading.[31]

The principal constraint on both the army and the commercial firearms manufacturers was the 1855 Rollin White patent for the bored-through cylinder accepting metallic cartridges. The Smith & Wesson Company had purchased the rights to use this patent before the Civil War, but its production had been limited to small-caliber revolvers that were unsuitable for military purposes. Smith & Wesson would have been delighted to have the army contract outright for a large-caliber revolver, but the service was reluctant to adopt a particular arm without comparative trials. Attempting to salvage something from the dilemma, Smith & Wesson granted limited rights to Remington for that firm to convert some of its New Model army revolvers to adapt them for use with metallic cartridges. This involved making new five-shot cylinders chambered for a .46-caliber rimfire round. Just how many of these may have been produced is uncertain, and most, if not all, were sold on the commercial market. They were identified easily by the altered hammer, an ejector rod added to the right side of the frame, and the cylinder, which was stamped with the Rollin White patent date.

The subject of a new pistol again was considered officially when an ordnance board met in 1870. Of the six weapons recommended by the board, the Remington Arms Company took five places. In first place was its .50-caliber single-shot rolling-block pistol. Surprisingly enough, the board considered this to be an excellent weapon for the mounted service, with the exception that it be modified to load at the half cock, as the board had recommended for the carbine. The board's reasoning, based on its preoccupation with conventional warfare, was revealed in its recommendation that cavalrymen be armed either with the saber and one or two of the single-shot pistols or with the carbine and the revolver. The board considered the revolver to be not only the equivalent of the saber as a close-quarters weapon but also just that, an arm to be used at point-blank range. The board failed to address the question of how well a mounted cavalryman could load a single-shot pistol in the heat of combat. Clearly, the realities of Indian fighting on the plains were not of primary concern to the board.

The rolling-block pistol propelled a .50-caliber bullet at approximately 600-

feet-per-second muzzle velocity, slow by any standards. The heavy ball was a telling man-stopper, unquestionably, but its puny 25-grain powder charge limited the effective range of the pistol to less than 100 yards. No matter how logical the idea may have seemed to the board members, the Remington pistol would have made a highly dubious substitute for the carbine, particularly since it had no provision for a detachable shoulder stock. As with any weapon, it was the soldier's ability to hit his target that became the all-important factor in combat. Troopers armed with only a saber and a single-shot pistol on the Great Plains would have been hopelessly disadvantaged.

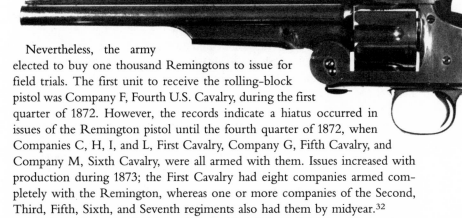

Nevertheless, the army elected to buy one thousand Remingtons to issue for field trials. The first unit to receive the rolling-block pistol was Company F, Fourth U.S. Cavalry, during the first quarter of 1872. However, the records indicate a hiatus occurred in issues of the Remington pistol until the fourth quarter of 1872, when Companies C, H, I, and L, First Cavalry, Company G, Fifth Cavalry, and Company M, Sixth Cavalry, were all armed with them. Issues increased with production during 1873; the First Cavalry had eight companies armed completely with the Remington, whereas one or more companies of the Second, Third, Fifth, Sixth, and Seventh regiments also had them by midyear.[32]

97. Nickel-plated Smith & Wesson .44 revolver issued to Company I, Seventh Cavalry, and used by Second Lieutenant James E. Porter. (Little Bighorn Battlefield National Monument)

The board's second choice was the Smith & Wesson No. 3 revolver, a large six-shooter with a unique hinged frame that, when unlatched, permitted the barrel to tip forward (fig. 97). This exposed the chambers for loading and at the same time actuated a rack-and-pinion extractor milled into the rear of the cylinder, ejecting all six empty cases simultaneously. The board preferred this feature for the mounted service because the revolver was easier to load on horseback. The Smith & Wesson fired a centerfire cartridge, later dubbed the .44 "American," loaded with 25 grains of powder and a 225-grain lead bullet. Frankford Arsenal later produced a slightly more powerful service version of the cartridge employing a 30-grain charge.[33]

Since Smith & Wesson was already manufacturing the No. 3, or First Model American, for the commercial market, it was an easy matter for the company to fill the government's order for the one thousand revolvers required for field trials. The new arms reached the troops in the spring of 1871, the first issues being made to the Second, Third, Fourth, and Fifth cavalry regiments. To determine which finish might be better suited to military demands, two hundred No. 3s were supplied with nickel finish, and the remainder were blued. During the following quarter additional issues of the Smith & Wesson were made to the First and Seventh regiments, the latter receiving twenty nickel-plated and fifty-nine blued revolvers, all of which were assigned to Captain Myles W. Keogh's Company I.[34]

By 1870 the Rollin White patent had expired, and the Colt's Patent Fire Arms Company worked feverishly to catch up with its rival. In January 1871, Colt submitted a prototype of an altered Model 1860 army revolver to the Ordnance Department. This conversion, designed by Colt employee Charles B. Richards, involved machining off the rear end of the cylinder and filling the gap thus created with a recoil plate secured to the frame. This plate contained the firing pin, a hinged loading gate, and a small rear sight mounted on top. The nose of the percussion hammer was faced off flat for use with the frame-mounted pin. No longer needed, the old loading lever assembly was removed and replaced by a spring-loaded ejector in a tubular housing, positioned on the right side of the barrel. The ejector housing was attached by means of an integral pin machined to fit the loading lever aperture in the barrel stud. The revolver was chambered for a newly designed .44 centerfire cartridge having a muzzle velocity of about 650 feet per second. It was loaded with a 225-grain bullet propelled by 30 grains of powder.

Initial shipments of the Colt-Richards revolvers were made early in 1872. A total of 347 conversions were distributed among selected companies of the Second, Third, Fourth, and Sixth regiments by the end of the first quarter of that year. Production apparently fell behind during the second quarter of 1872, for no new issues of the Colt-Richards were made until the fall of that year, when significant numbers of them began to reach the cavalry units in the field.[35]

Military versions of the Colt-Richards were distinguished by the "U.S." property stamp on the left side of the barrel just forward of the cylinder and by the inspector's initials found on various parts. The original serial numbers will be found mixed but are accompanied by an additional set of matching numbers applied at the time the conversion was done.

As the trials continued, Colt introduced yet another revolver for the Ordnance Department's consideration. This example, submitted in November 1872, was an entirely new model incorporating a solid frame and known as the "new model army metallic cartridge revolver," or more popularly as the "single-action army." The first sample Colt sent to the Ordnance Department was chambered for the extremely accurate .44 Russian cartridge, but Major James G. Benton, then commanding Springfield Armory, returned the sample with a request that another be submitted chambered for the .44 American, the same cartridge used in the Smith & Wesson No. 3. Although Colt Company officials tried in vain to convince the army of the inherently superior accuracy of the more recently developed Russian cartridge, Major Benton's position remained unshakable. No doubt his stance was based on a desire to maintain as much uniformity in the tests as possible. Benton got what he wanted in the form of two Colt single-action army revolvers chambered for the American round.[36]

Tests of the new models continued over the next five months, but their direction took a sudden turn when the Small Arms Caliber Board selected .45 to be the standard bore diameter. This decision caused Chief of Ordnance Dyer to request that Colt provide yet another new-model revolver chambered for a .45-caliber cartridge. The company quickly obliged, although Colt employees felt that the .44 caliber was still a better choice. The .44 Russian's long and successful career as a target round was ultimately to prove the company's claim. Having no other options at the moment, however, Colt quickly designed a powerful center-primed cartridge of .45 caliber containing 40 grains of powder (later reduced to 30 grains by the Ordnance Department). The army, convinced of the superiority of the new Colt, dispensed with further testing and adopted it for the cavalry without the benefit of field trials. On June 26, 1873, the Ordnance Department reported that it had been authorized by the secretary of war to purchase eight thousand Colts.[37] The first contract was signed in July, and the government accepted its first shipment of one thousand revolvers in November 1873. By the end of March 1874, eight companies of the previously slighted Tenth Cavalry, along with two companies of the Second, one of the Fourth, and one of the Sixth, were issued the Colt single-action army revolvers.[38]

In May 1873 Smith & Wesson submitted one more eleventh-hour contender for the army's consideration. Major George W. Schofield of the Tenth Cavalry had designed a modification of the No. 3 revolver, incorporating a latch mounted on the frame rather than on the top strap. This provided a much stronger, more reliable means of locking the hinged barrel than on the parent arm. However, Captain John R. Edie, who supervised the revolver tests at Springfield, reported that it reduced the total number of parts in the gun by only one. In his opinion, the basic objection to the Smith & Wesson Model No. 3 still was present in the Schofield modification, that is, it had too many small parts and thus was difficult to disassemble and clean. Edie also thought that the Smith & Wesson suffered from inferior accuracy, was weakened by the hinged barrel, and was subject to jamming due to black-powder fouling.

Although the Smith & Wesson Schofield posed no serious obstacle to the adoption of the Colt, its designer was not yet ready to admit defeat. George Schofield still had a trump card to play. His brother, Major General John M. Schofield, commanded the Division of the Missouri and was a close associate of Commanding General William T. Sherman. Using this influence, Major Schofield was able once again to bring his revolver before an army ordnance board early in 1874. After a careful examination and thoughtful deliberation, the board again rejected the Schofield, citing among other things its awkward grip, the shape of the hammer spur, its weight, and its greater mechanical complexity.

A few months later, still undaunted, Schofield returned with yet another version of his revolver, this pattern based on a modification of the No. 3 Russian model. The most noticeable difference was the shape of the grip, now somewhat larger and lacking the spur along the back strap. The second-finger spur on the underside of the trigger guard was also removed. The cylinder stop was rearranged to make removal of the cylinder easier, and the ejector was simplified to reduce the number of parts. Essential to the pattern was the specially designed latch that prevented the piece from being fired until it was automatically locked by the blow of the hammer. This time the board voted in Schofield's favor, recommending that quantities of the .45 Smith & Wesson Schofield be purchased and distributed to units in the field for trial beside the new Colt.

The army immediately ordered three thousand Schofield revolvers, which began to reach the line units during the spring of 1875. The first companies to receive them were F Company, Ninth Cavalry, stationed at Fort Clark, Texas, and Companies A and G of the Tenth, posted at Fort Concho. By the end of the next quarter the Schofield had been issued to six companies in each of these regiments. During the last quarter the Fourth Cavalry, also stationed in Texas, received enough Schofields to arm six of its companies.[39] This evidence suggests that at least initially all of the available Schofields were routed through San Antonio Arsenal.

A total of 8,005 Schofield Smith & Wessons were purchased during fiscal years 1876 through 1878, but issues were sporadic, depending on the personal preferences of company commanders. From 1876 until 1893, when the .38 Colt double-action army revolver replaced the old .45s, some 5,019 Schofields were issued to the regular army.[40]

The army's lukewarm reception to the Schofield stemmed from both the perceived weakness of the revolver and the discomforting tendency of the gun to become unlatched in the holster. This sometimes happened as the revolver was thrust into the holster. Then, when the revolver was withdrawn, the barrel tipped downward, ejecting all of the cartridges.

The adoption of the Schofield as a secondary sidearm also forced the army to adopt the less-powerful .45 Schofield cartridge. This became necessary because the shorter Smith & Wesson cylinder would not accommodate the longer Colt ammunition. Consequently, Frankford Arsenal was instructed on August 20, 1874, to cease manufacturing the "Colt's revolver cartridges Caliber .45" in favor of a new round intended to be used in both types of weapons.[41] The new cartridge would be designated the "Revolver Ball Cartridge, Caliber .45." The case for this new cartridge was only 1.10 inches long, as opposed to the Colt case, measuring 1.29 inches. Its smaller capacity permitted a charge of 28 grains of powder, and the bullet weighed 230 grains. Like the rifle and carbine cases, the case for the revolver cartridge was made of copper alloy and was Benet cup anvil-primed.

For a brief period, existing stocks of Colt ammunition found their way to troops armed with the Schofield revolver. The longer cartridge simply would not fit in the shorter chamber of the Smith & Wesson. The consternation this created in the field is reflected in Captain Charles King's *Trials of a Staff Officer,* a semifictional account of some of the writer's experiences:

> It so happened that in the summer of 1877 he [Captain Teddy Egan, Second Cavalry] had a mixed armament of Colt's and Smith & Wesson revolvers in his troop. A short time previous X [King] had been ordered to send him five thousand rounds of Colt's revolver ball-cartridges, and did so. One blissful June morning the telegraph operator at the post darted in to X with a dispatch from the chief ordnance officer at Omaha. "Captain Egan reports that the cartridges you sent him will not fit his pistols. What's the matter?" Ten minutes after came another from "Teddy" himself: "Cannot use the cartridges; all too long." . . . X meantime has summoned the ordnance-sergeant, and that veteran glances over the papers and explains the matter in a dozen words. "He's been trying to use Colt's revolver cartridges in his Smith & Wessons, sir," and so it proved. The "revolver ball cartridge" is made to fit both the Colt and the Smith & Wesson, whereas the "Colt's revolver ball cartridge" can be used only in the Colt. This information was telegraphed at once to the captain in the field and the explanation wired to Omaha, but meantime head-quarters had been racked to its foundation at a discovery of so alarming a nature . . . and not with standing our explanation an aid-de-camp was hurried out to investigate; he arrived next day, looked at the two pistols and two styles of cartridges, remarked that it reminded him of the profound philosopher who had two holes cut in his door for his cats, a big hole for the big cat and a little hole for the other, and went back to Omaha.[42]

The Colt single-action army revolver reigned supreme among the troops for the remainder of the century, with the total number purchased by the government reaching 37,060 by 1891.[43] The Schofield Smith & Wessons never were withdrawn from active service during the same period; thus their mere existence in the inventory obligated the army to continue using the underpowered .45 Schofield cartridge.

LONG ARMS

Rifles

Remington Model 1870 Rifle. The Remington rifle was produced at Springfield Armory and issued to selected units for field trial in 1871–74. Chambered for the .50/70 cartridge, this arm also was a single-shot breechloader (fig. 98). However, it differed by having a rolling-block action. It had a 36-inch barrel and an overall length of 51¾ inches, and it weighed 9¾ pounds. The walnut stock was made in two pieces, forearm and buttstock. The barrel was attached to the forestock by two iron barrel bands and with spring retainers.

The adjustable rear sight was graduated to a range of one thousand yards. The receiver was case-hardened, but all other parts were finished bright. Carried in a channel beneath the barrel was an iron cleaning rod having a grooved head with a slot and a single stop shoulder.

On the right side of the frame was an eagle with "U.S. SPRINGFIELD 1870." The tang was marked "Remington's Patent. PAT. May 3d, NOV. 15th, 1864, APRIL 17th, 1868" in two lines. Total production was 1,008.

Remington Model 1871 Rifle (Army). Although this rifle was nearly identical to the 1870 Remington, it was distinguished by the markings "U.S. SPRINGFIELD 1872" on the right side of the frame and "Model 1871" stamped on the left side. Examined by the Terry Board, the 1871 Remington incorporated certain modifications from those presented in the earlier trials, including a double-shoulder ramrod and a larger thumbpiece on the hammer to provide greater leverage in extracting the fired cases. The principal difference was the "locking action," which automatically brought the hammer forward to the safe position when the breech was closed. The finish of the arm was "National Armory bright" throughout, except for the receiver, which was case-hardened.

Most of these rifles were sold to the various states for arming militia units. The Remingtons were not serial numbered. Total production was 10,001.

Sharps 1867 Metallic Cartridge Conversion Rifle. In 1867 the government let a contract with the Sharps Rifle Company to convert several thousand percussion-primed rifles and carbines to chamber the newly developed .50/70 metallic cartridge. The lot included New Models 1859, 1863, and 1865. Some rifles

98. *(Top) Model 1870 Remington rifle; (bottom) Model 1871 Remington army rifle.* (Hayes Otoupalik Collection)

exhibited the respective model designation atop the barrel just forward of the breech, if the date was not polished off during refinishing.

The conversion of the single-shot Sharps included the substitution of a new breechblock, with firing-pin mechanism, and a new hammer. Some of these arms had oversized bores but were within tolerance to engage the .50-caliber bullet. Others, having unacceptably large bores, had to be bored out and relined, in a fashion similar to the Model 1866 Springfield rifles.

In addition, the original legend, "C. SHARPS RIFLE/MANUFG. CO./ HARTFORD, CONN.," appeared on top of the barrel. On the left side of the receiver was "C. SHARPS' PAT./SEPT. 12th 1848." The lock was marked "C. SHARPS PAT./OCT. 5th 1852" and "R. S. LAWRENCE PAT./APRIL 12th 1859." Appearing on the breechblock was "H. CONANT PATENT/ APRIL 1 1856." Lawrence patent markings also were found on the rear sight. Serial numbers were stamped on the upper tang. The prefix letter "C" was used by the Sharps Company to indicate the number 100,000. A distinctive inspector's mark, "DFC" (David F. Clark, government inspector) within a ribbon cartouche, was placed on the left side of the buttstock (center) at the time of conversion. The receivers, butt plates, and barrel bands of the conversions were color case-hardened, but all other metal parts were blued. Total production was 1,086.

Sharps Model 1870 Rifle. Produced at Springfield Armory, this arm was among those issued to selected units for field trial during the years 1871–74. Like the conversions, it also was a single-shot breechloader chambered for the .50/70 cartridge (figs. 99 and 100). The barrel, 32½ inches long, was rifled with three wide grooves and lands. It was fastened to the forearm by two bands and band springs. The two-piece stocks were of American walnut. The rifle was provided with a sliding-leaf rear sight and a single-shoulder ramrod having a grooved and slotted head.

The receiver, lock plate, and lever all were color case-hardened, and all other parts were finished bright. The receiver was marked "C. SHARPS PATENT SEPT 12th 1848" on the right side. Total production was 1,000.

Springfield Model 1866 Rifle (Second Allin Conversion). This rifle was a caliber .50/70, single-shot breechloader. The barrel length was 36½ inches; the overall length of the arm was 55⅞ inches. The rifle weighed 9¾ pounds. It had a full-length stock of American walnut with iron nose cap and butt plate. All Models 1866 were made by converting Model 1864 rifled muskets. This process involved boring out the .58-caliber barrel, then inserting and brazing in place a .50-caliber liner (fig. 101).

The barrel was rifled with three wide lands and grooves and was attached to the stock with three iron barrel bands retained by band springs. The rear sight was of an "L" configuration and was graduated to 700 yards.

All iron parts were finished armory bright, though the breechblock and its hinge piece were blackened by oil quenching. The lock plate had mottled colors, the effect of water quenching. The rifle had a ramrod (cleaning rod) of uniform ¼-inch diameter, without shoulder, carried in a channel beneath the barrel. The rod had a grooved and slotted head ⅞⁄₁₆-inch in diameter at the tulip. The end of the rod was threaded to screw into a plate mounted within the stock to prevent it from slipping from the channel when the piece was fired.

99. *Appendages used with various arms.*
(Left to right) Combination screwdrivers
and mainspring clamps for Model 1866
rifle and Model 1870 rifles and carbines;
Model 1879 and Model 1876 tools for
.45-caliber Springfields.

The lock plate bore an eagle, "U.S. SPRINGFIELD," and either 1863 or 1864 date. On the left-hand flat at the rear of the barrel was a small eagle head. This model was not serial numbered, although rack or unit numbers sometimes were present. The date "1866" appeared over a small eagle head on the top surface of the breechblock. Most Models 1866 bore a cartouche, consisting of the letters "ESA" (Erskine S. Allin), on the left side of the stock opposite the hammer. Most of them also bore the original Civil War–vintage cartouche. Still other examples had only the original marking, without the Allin cartouche. Total production was 52,300.

Springfield Model 1868 Rifle.   A more refined weapon made on the Allin system, this single-shot breechloader was also chambered for the .50/70 cartridge. However, most of its parts were of new manufacture. The overall length of the rifle was 52 inches, with a barrel length of 32½ inches. The weight was 9¼ pounds. It had a full-length stock made of American walnut, having an iron nose cap and butt plate. The barrel was rifled with three wide lands and grooves and was attached to the stock by two split-iron bands. The upper one was provided with a sling swivel, held in place by band springs. The rear sight had an adjustable leaf graduated to 900 yards. All of the iron parts were finished National Armory bright. A cleaning rod was carried beneath the barrel in a groove in the stock. The rod had a grooved and slotted head and a single shoulder to catch the ramrod stop.

On the lock plate appeared an eagle, "U.S. SPRINGFIELD," and dates of either 1863 or 1864. The serial number was stamped on the left side of the barrel, just forward of the receiver. The receiver also bore a matching number, on the left side and forward of the breech. The breechblock was dated either 1869 or 1870, placed above an eagle head and crossed arrows. The master armorer's "ESA" cartouche was placed on the left flat of the stock opposite the hammer. Some specimens exhibited one or more of their original Civil War cartouches as well. Some also had inspectors' initials stamped in small letters below the trigger-guard bow plate. Total production was 52,145.

Springfield Model 1870 Rifle.   This rifle, also a single-shot breechloader of the Allin type, was chambered for the .50/70 cartridge. Its overall length was 51¾ inches. The barrel, rifled with three lands and grooves, measured 32½ inches. The rifle weighed 9¼ pounds. It had a full-length stock of American walnut. Like its predecessor, the Model 1870 had its barrel attached to the stock by two split-iron bands, held in place by band springs. The rear sight had an adjustable leaf graduated to 900 yards. The cleaning rod had a double shoulder, unlike the Model 1868, as well as a slotted and grooved head. The finish of all iron parts was National Armory bright.

On the lock plate were an eagle, "U.S. SPRINGFIELD," and an 1863 or 1864 date. The barrel had no markings, nor was the Model 1870 serial numbered. On the upper flat of the breechblock was the date "1870," beneath which were an eagle head, crossed arrows, and the letters "U.S." Arms produced in 1871 and later had the word "MODEL" placed above the date. On the left side of the stock, opposite the hammer, was an "ESA" cartouche.

The Model 1870 rifle was readily distinguished from the Model 1868 by its shorter receiver nose (like that on the Model 1873), double-shoulder ramrod, and the lack of any serial number. Total production was 11,533.

Springfield Model 1873 Rifle. This rifle also was a single-shot breechloader based on Master Armorer Erskine Allin's system. However, the caliber was reduced to .45/70. It had a barrel length of 32½ inches and an overall length of 51⅞ inches. The length of the barrel was 32½ inches. The rifle weighed 8¼ pounds.

The barrel was fastened to a full-length walnut stock by two barrel bands with retaining springs. The upper band on early-production rifles was of the split type with a sling swivel. Beginning in 1874, a combination sling and stacking swivel was used so that three or more weapons could be securely stacked in the upright position in the field, without fixing bayonets. The rear sight was adjustable, graduated to 400 yards on the base and up to 1,100 yards on the hinged leaf. All metal parts were blued. The cleaning rod, carried beneath the barrel in a channel in the stock, had a grooved and slotted head with double shoulders to lock over a stop. The opposite end had cannelures, to improve the grip, for a distance of three inches from the end.

On the lock plate was an eagle and "U.S. SPRINGFIELD 1873." Those arms manufactured before 1875 bear no proof marks on the breech end of the barrel. However, beginning in the serial range 40,000–60,000, a small "V" (viewed), over a "P" (proofed), over an eagle head was applied to the left side just forward of the receiver to indicate final proof. These markings were somewhat larger on rifles and carbines beginning in the serial range after 60,000.

All Models 1873 were serial numbered atop the rear flat of the receiver. The breechblock was stamped "MODEL 1873," beneath which was an eagle head, over crossed arrows, over the letters "U.S." The stock was proofmarked "P" within a circle on the underside of the wrist, just to the rear of the guard plate. An inspector's cartouche bearing the letters "ESA" (Erskine S. Allin) was stamped on the left side of the wrist. Total production was approximately 50,000.

The Model 1873 rifle and carbine underwent numerous, albeit minor, modifications beginning in 1877 and continuing through 1879. These changes did not greatly influence the external appearance of the arm.

Springfield Officers' Rifle, Model 1875. For several years during the late 1860s and early 1870s it became common practice for officers to order special sporting-type rifles from Springfield Armory. These rifles were based on the standard Model 1868 rifle but usually incorporated half-stocks, special sights, set triggers, and other special features. To lessen the demands on armory workmen, Chief of Ordnance Benet on May 25, 1875, directed the commanding officer at

Springfield to design a standard officers' rifle. Henceforth, it was to be the only sporting-type rifle made by the armory. These were produced from 1875 until 1885, when the model was discontinued. During this period, a total of 477 were made at an initial cost of thirty-six dollars each.

The officers' rifle was chambered in the standard .45/70 caliber only. It was, of course, a single-shot, Allin-type breechloader. It had a barrel length of 26 inches and weighed about 8 pounds. The walnut half-stock had fine checkering on the forearm and wrist, and it had an engraved nose cap of white metal. The butt was thinner than the standard; therefore, the smaller cadet-model butt plate was used. A hickory wiping rod with nickel-plated brass ferrules was carried beneath the barrel. One end of the rod was slotted for a wiping patch; the other was knurled to provide the fingers a better grip for withdrawing it. The rod passes through one thimble mounted on the underside of the barrel and then into a channel in the forearm. A single barrel band holds the barrel to the stock.

The officers' model was provided with a special globe-type front sight, which could be used in either of two positions. The rear sight was the standard leaf-type, graduated as for the issue rifle. There also was a vernier tang peep-sight mounted on the wrist, adjustable to 1,100 yards. The rifle had a hand-fitted set trigger mechanism. The finish basically was like that of the standard rifle, with all principle parts blued except for the breechblock, which was case-hardened, and the white metal nose cap.

All proof and manufacture markings were typical of a standard rifle made in a given year, except that the officers' model was not serial numbered, since it was not intended to be an accountable item. The stocks of rifles made before 1881 bore no inspector's cartouche. The lock plate, hammer, breechblock, tang, top surface of receiver, barrel band, and butt-plate tang were engraved in a rather plain style.

Springfield "Model" 1877 Rifle. Whereas the Model 1877 carbine was recognized officially, a similar designation was not applied to the rifle. However, the modifications pertaining to the carbine were duplicated, for the most part, on the rifle.

Perhaps the most obvious alteration was the extension of the buttstock comb farther forward on the wrist in order to strengthen that weak point. The wrist itself was thickened as well. The bed of the stock, however, remained narrow to fit the first-type receiver.

Whereas the breechblock on rifles of earlier manufacture had a high arch on the underside, the arch was not machined out after mid-1877. This made for a heavier block, though the exact reason for the change has not been determined. The most plausible reason may have been related to the extension of the gas ports along the upper edges of the receiver well, which was implemented at about the same time.[44]

Certain markings on the rifle were changed during 1877, including the omission of the date on the lock plate and a new legend on the breechblock reading "U.S. MODEL 1873." Additionally, the year of inspection was added to the stock cartouche beneath the initials of the master armorer.

The form of the rear sight base was changed by eliminating the four wide, distinct steps for the various ranges. The redesigned base had a curved ramp numbered to 500 yards, and it was marked "R" on the left side to distinguish it from the carbine sight. Total production was 3,943.

During the latter part of 1878 and the early part of 1879 several additional changes were made to the Springfield rifles and carbines. Although the National Armory did not acknowledge an official model change at this time, this variant has sometimes been referred to as the "Model 1879." The principal changes included the following:

1. The "buckhorn" rear sight was modified
2. The receiver was made heavier and wider
3. The barrel bed was deepened and made wider to accept the new receiver
4. The head of the rifle ramrod was countersunk
5. The rifle front sight was changed to a hardened-steel blade cross-pinned to the bayonet stud
6. The stacking swivel was omitted from the carbine band
7. The breechblock hinge pin was made longer

Ward-Burton Model 1871 Rifle. This was yet another of the arms issued to selected units for field trial in 1871–74. The Ward-Burton utilized a bolt action, yet it was a single-shot chambered for the .50/70 cartridge. It had a barrel 32½ inches long and an overall length of 51⅞ inches. The full-length walnut stock was fastened to the barrel by two bands with band springs. All metal parts were finished bright, except for the receiver, which sometimes appeared blackened as a result of the oil-quenching process. The ramrod was the same as the standard Springfield 1868-type, having a single stop-shoulder.

The top of the bolt was stamped "WARD BURTON PATENT DEC. 20, 1859-FEB. 21, 1871." On the left side of the receiver was "U.S. SPRINGFIELD 1871." Total production was 1,011.

Winchester-Hotchkiss Model 1879 Rifle. This was a bolt-action repeater, caliber .45/70. The barrel was 32 inches long, and the overall length of the rifle was 48⅝ inches. The one-piece walnut stock was attached to the barrel by two barrel bands, the upper one having a sling swivel. A five-shot tubular magazine was concealed in the buttstock. The rear sight was of the Model 1877 Springfield leaf-type, graduated to 1,100 yards. The military musket was provided with a steel ramrod carried beneath the barrel. The receiver and butt plate were case-hardened; all other parts were blue-finished.

The receiver was marked "MANUFACTURED BY THE WINCHESTER REPEATING ARMS CO., NEW HAVEN, CONN., U.S.A." and "PAT. OCT. 16, 1860, JUNE 25, 1872, JULY 23, 1878, AND UNDER B. B. HOTCHKISS PATS AUG. 17, 1868, FEB. 15, 1870, NOV. 9, 1875, NOV. 14, 1876, JAN. 23, 1877." The barrel is marked, forward of the receiver, with Springfield Armory's proof, consisting of an eagle head over the letters "VP." On the left side of the stock is the inspector's cartouche "ESA 1878" or "SWP 1879," found on the left side ahead of the wrist. Total production was 513.

Carbines

Remington Model 1870 Carbine. The carbine version was identical in all respects to the rifle except for the shorter 22⅟₁₆-inch barrel and short fore-end. The forestock, which measured 11¾ inches, was of the distinctive Springfield Armory style, rather than the shorter and more angular Remington pattern. It was attached to the barrel by a single band, retained by a spring on the right side. The graduated rear sight was the same as the Model 1870 Springfield pattern. On the left side was a saddle ring bar attached at the front to the frame and to the rear by a plate inletted and screwed to the stock. The receiver was case-hardened and marked with an eagle and "SPRINGFIELD 1870" on the right side. The remainder of the metal parts were finished bright. Total production was 313.

Sharps 1867 Metallic Cartridge Conversion Carbine. Also caliber .50/70, this single-shot, breech-loading carbine was often referred to as the "Sharps Improved." It had a 22-inch barrel, rifled with three grooves. Sharps carbines originally were intended to fire the standard rifle cartridge, which in fact was used by the troops in most instances during the entire period of the Sharps issue.

Above:

100. Model 1879 Winchester-Hotchkiss bolt-action rifle. (Fuller Collection, Chickamauga-Chattanooga National Military Park)

Inset:

101. Breech detail of Model 1879 Winchester-Hotchkiss bolt-action rifle. (Fuller Collection, Chickamauga-Chattanooga National Military Park)

Frankford Arsenal did not begin loading a reduced-charge .50/55 cartridge, especially adapted to carbines, until January 1872.[45]

The carbine had a fixed front sight and an adjustable leaf rear sight, graduated to 800 yards. The buttstock and short forearm were of walnut, with the barrel attached by a single case-hardened band, secured with a band spring on the underside of the forearm. During the conversion process, the old worn stocks on the majority of carbines were replaced. These could be distinguished by the single inspector's cartouche "DFC" (David F. Clark) stamped about midway along the left side of the butt. Original stocks retained the Civil War inspector's cartouche located just above the sling bar, in addition to the Clark marking denoting the conversion. Some of the carbines that retained their original stocks had an iron patchbox with a hinged trap on the right side. Total production was 31,098.

Sharps Model 1870 Carbine. These caliber .50/55 carbines, like the rifles, were assembled at Springfield Armory using only percussion Sharps actions (bearing their original markings) converted to centerfire ammunition. The remainder of the parts were new Springfield manufacture, including a new 22-inch barrel. Two distinguishing features were a Springfield-type butt plate stamped "U.S." and a longer fore-end resembling that of the 1870 Springfield carbine. The rear sight also was of the Model 1870 Springfield type. The receiver and butt plate were color case-hardened, and all other parts were finished bright. Total production was 308.

Spencer Model 1860 Carbine.   One of the most popular arms of the Civil War era, the Spencer carbine was a seven-shot repeater chambered for the 56/56 (caliber .52) rimfire cartridge. It was a rather heavy but compact carbine weighing 9 pounds, 2 ounces, with a barrel 22 inches long, rifled with six grooves. The cartridges were fed from a tubular magazine in the buttstock, accessed by a trap. A finger lever, which formed the trigger guard, was lowered to permit a cartridge to be fed from the magazine to the carrier. Bringing the lever to its closed position chambered the cartridge and locked the breech. The carbine had a large hammer, which had to be cocked manually for each shot, mounted on the right side of the receiver.

The buttstock and forearm were made of walnut, the latter attached to the barrel with one band, retained by a spring on the underside of the forearm. All metal parts were blue-finished, except for the case-hardened receiver. The folding rear sight was adjustable to ranges up to 800 yards.

Marked on the top of the frame was, "SPENCER REPEATING RIFLE CO. BOSTON, MASS PAT'D MARCH 6, 1860." All carbines were serial numbered on the top of the receiver, adjacent to the hammer.

The Burnside Rifle Company also subcontracted to make the Spencer carbine. These arms were identified by the addition of Burnside markings on the receiver. The barrels of the Burnside carbines were rifled with three wide grooves. Total production was 50,000 (approximately).

Spencer Model 1865 Carbine.   The Model 1865 carbine was nearly identical to the older model except that it had a 20-inch barrel and was chambered for the 56/50 (caliber .50) cartridge. It had an overall length of just 37 inches and weighed slightly less: 8 pounds, 5 ounces. The rear sight was an adjustable leaf, graduated to 900 yards.

Approximately two-thirds of those manufactured were provided with the Stabler magazine cut-off, a small turnkey attachment located just forward of the trigger. This device allowed the soldier to block the magazine, holding the seven rounds in reserve, while loading the carbine as a single shot. If more-rapid fire was needed, the cut-off simply could be turned ninety degrees to activate the magazine.

Within a year after the end of the Civil War, Springfield Armory began repairing surplus 1860 model carbines, to bring them up to serviceable condition. Armory personnel soon discovered that the rusted barrels could be drilled out, sleeved with liners, and rebored to .50 caliber. Like the standard Model 1865 carbines, these were rifled with three grooves. Once refurbished, the carbines could fire the newer 56/50 cartridge with far greater accuracy than if they were left in their original .52 caliber. Some twelve thousand Model 1860 carbines were thus modified between the years 1866 and 1874.[46]

The markings on the Model 1865 were identical to those on the 1860 model except that the legend "MODEL 1865" was stamped on the barrel just ahead of the receiver. Total production was 18,959 (purchased by the army).

Springfield Model 1870 Carbine   Although the chamber was the same as the rifle, the carbine was intended to use a less powerful .50/55 cartridge (fig. 102).

(However, it could fire the standard .50/70 just as well.) The carbine was identical to the rifle in all respects except that it had a shorter overall length of only 41⅜ inches. It weighed 7 pounds, 15 ounces. The walnut half-stock measured 29⅞ inches and had a bar and ring attached by the lock screws to the left side. The barrel was 22 inches long, and like that of the rifle, had three wide lands and grooves. The barrel was attached to the stock by a single band with a spring on the right side of the stock.

The sight, like that of the rifle, was the adjustable leaf type, graduated to 700 yards. The finish of the metal parts on carbines sometimes varied. The breechblock was blued; the receiver may have been either blued or left bright. Likewise, the barrel was either bright or blued. The markings were identical to those on the rifle, described above, though the breechblock had the earlier 1870 date without the arrows and eagle head. Total production was 341.

102. Model 1870 Springfield carbine.
(Fuller Collection, Chickamauga-
Chattanooga National Military Park)

Springfield Model 1873 Carbine. The carbine was chambered for the .45/55 cartridge, which utilized the basic .45/70 case, the only difference being the reduced powder charge. The carbine, of course, could fire the more powerful rifle cartridge. Despite the heavier recoil, some cavalry commanders preferred to have rifle ammunition issued to their men.[47]

The carbine was the same as the rifle in all respects except that it had a barrel length of only 22 inches and an overall length of 41¼ inches. It also was lighter in weight, at 7.9 pounds. The half-stock was 29¹³⁄₁₆ inches long and was attached to the barrel by a single barrel band having an open stacking swivel. A bar and ring mounted on the left side by the lock-plate screws served to attach the carbine to the soldier's sling. The butt plate, like that of the rifle, was plain, without a trap. A leaf-type adjustable sight was graduated to 500 yards on the base and up to 1,200 yards on the leaf. All markings were the same as those on the rifle. Total production was 19,938 (approximately, as changes to the Model 1877 were implemented over a period of months).

Springfield Model 1877 Carbine. The carbine incorporated all of the modifications made to the rifle, with one important addition. As a result of the Battle of the Little Bighorn, Springfield Armory was directed to find a way to provide the carbine with a cleaning rod that could also be used to clear a stuck cartridge case from the chamber. Springfield responded by designing a jointed three-piece steel rod that would fit into a receptacle in the butt. This called for a new butt plate as well, having a swivel trap to cover the aperture. It was not necessary to provide this butt plate on the rifle, which already had a one-piece ramrod.

The rear sight also was modified like that of the rifle, except that the base was graduated up to 600 yards. Since the designated ranges corresponded to the 55-grain carbine cartridge, the base was stamped "C" on the left side. Total production was 2,946.

Ward-Burton Model 1871 Carbine.   Like the rifle, the carbine was a single-shot bolt-action, chambered to take either the .50/70 or the .50/55 carbine loading. The barrel, 22 inches long, was rifled with three wide grooves and was attached to the stock by one band with a retaining spring. The overall length of the carbine was 41¼ inches. The stock, made of walnut, was 30 inches long, with a ring bar attached to the left side. The rear sight was the Springfield type, with an adjustable leaf graduated to 700 yards. Most of the parts were finished in National Armory bright except for the receiver, which was blackened by oil quenching. The markings were the same as those on the rifle, described above. Total production was 316.

Pistols and Revolvers

Colt Model 1860 Army Revolver.   One of the principal cavalry revolvers used by federal forces during the Civil War, the Colt Army was a percussion-primed, .44-caliber six-shooter. It had an 8-inch round barrel rifled with six grooves. The front sight consisted of a simple German silver blade; the rear sight was a notch in the hammer lip that was brought into position when the piece was cocked. A hinged loading lever was mounted beneath the barrel.

Most Army Colts were stamped "Address COL. SAML COLT NEW YORK U.S. AMERICA" in a single line atop the barrel. Some early production revolvers were marked "ADDRESS SAML COLT HARTFORD CT." All Models 1860 were stamped "COLTS PATENT" in two lines on the left side of the frame. The trigger-guard strap had ".44 CAL" stamped on the left rear shoulder. The front portion of the cylinder bore a roll-engraved naval engagement scene, and the rear portion was rebated slightly.

The hammer, frame, and loading lever were case-hardened, resulting in mottled colors; the barrel and the cylinder were blued. The back strap and the trigger guard were brass. The Colt was issued with a one-piece walnut grip bearing the inspector's cartouche on the left side. Total production was 200,500 (approximately).

Colt Model 1871 (Richards Conversion).   Modified from the earlier Model 1860, the Richards fired the .44 Colt centerfire cartridge. Like its predecessor, the Model 1871 was a six-shot, single-action revolver, with an 8-inch barrel. It had a one-piece walnut grip and case-hardened frame with a brass trigger guard. All other parts were blue-finished.

The Richards bore the original Colt markings "-ADDRESS COL. SAML COLT NEW-YORK U.S. AMERICA-" in one line on top of the barrel. Stamped on the left side of the trigger guard was ".44 CAL," and on the left side of the frame was "COLTS PATENT." The original roll-stamped naval action scene remained on the cylinder. The left side of barrel was stamped "U.S." and "A" in small letters near the wedge.

This model bore two sets of serial numbers. The original set, on the frame, trigger guard, and back strap, became mixed during the conversion process. A second set, applied at the time of conversion, appeared adjacent to the original numbers. The left grip also bore the original inspector's cartouche. Total converted was 1,200.

Colt Model 1873 Army Revolver.   A six-shot, single-action revolver chambered for the .45 Colt centerfire cartridge, the Model 1873 Army had a 7½-inch-long barrel and a one-piece walnut grip. The frame was case-hardened, but all other parts were blued. It weighed about 2 pounds, 5 ounces.

The barrel was marked "COLT'S PT. F. A. MFG. CO. HARTFORD, CT. U.S.A-" in one line along the top. On the left side of the frame was "PAT. SEPT. 19, 1871" and "PAT. JULY 2, 1872" in two lines. Just to the rear of this stamping were the letters "U.S." Matching serial numbers were placed on the underside of the frame, the trigger guard, and the back strap. The last four digits of the serial number also were stamped on the side of the cylinder parallel with the chambers.

Government inspectors' initials were stamped on the trigger guard below the serial number, on the side of the cylinder, on the underside of the barrel just ahead of the frame, on the back strap just behind the hammer, and for those produced somewhat later, on the frame just above the serial number. The date of acceptance and the subinspector's cartouche were stamped on the left grip. Total purchased was 37,060 (1873–91).

Remington New Model Army Revolver.   First purchased by the government during the Civil War, this six-shot .44-caliber percussion revolver was quite popular among the regulars for several years after the war. It had an 8-inch octagonal barrel with a fixed-post front sight. A rear sighting groove was milled into the top of the frame. The grips were of walnut, made in two pieces; the left one was stamped with the inspector's cartouche.

The barrel was marked, on top, "PATENTED SEPT. 14, 1858/ E. REMINGTON & SONS, ILION, NEW YORK, U.S.A./NEW MODEL." The initials of various inspectors appeared as small letters stamped on various parts of the weapon. One source indicated that the army contracted for approximately 110,000 New Model Remingtons; another gave a figure of 115,563.[48]

Remington Army Model 1871 Pistol.   This unusual pistol was a .50-caliber single-shot with a rolling-block action. Its barrel was 8 inches long, and it had two-piece walnut stocks (grip and fore-end). The receiver and the trigger guard were case-hardened, the breechblock and the hammer were finished bright, and the remainder of the parts were blued.

The markings on the frame were "REMINGTONS ILION, N.Y. U.S.A./ PAT. MAY 3d NOV. 15th, 1864 APRIL 17th, 1866 P s." All Remington pistols were serial numbered. Inspectors' initials were placed on the grip and barrel. An inspector's cartouche was stamped on the left grip. Total production was 5,000 (approximately).

Smith & Wesson Model No. 3.   The Smith & Wesson was a large six-shot, single-action revolver chambered for the .44 centerfire (American) cartridge. Its 8-inch barrel was rifled with five grooves. Government arms were provided in both nickel (two hundred) and blue finishes, with two-piece walnut grips.

Markings along the barrel rib were "SMITH & WESSON SPRINGFIELD, MASS. U.S.A. PAT. JULY 10. 60. JAN. 17. FEB. 17. JULY 11. 65. & AUG. 24.

69." The government property stamp, "U.S.," also is found on top of the rib, forward of the cylinder. On the left grip are the inspector's initials, "OWA." The letter "A" (also for Subinspector O. W. Ainsworth) was stamped on the left side of the frame and the left side of the latch. The letters "A" and "P" appeared on the grip as well. The serial number was applied to the bottom of the back strap. Serial numbers for U.S. cavalry arms range from 125 to 2,199.[49] Total purchased was 1,000.

Smith & Wesson Schofield Model. This large break-top revolver also was a single-action six-shooter, chambered for the .45 Smith & Wesson centerfire cartridge. Its barrel length was 7 inches, and it weighed 2½ pounds. It had two-piece walnut grips and a blued finish.

The left side of the ejector housing was marked "SMITH & WESSON SPRINGFIELD MASS. U.S.A. PAT. JAN. 17TH & 24TH 65, JULY 11TH 65, AUG. 24TH 69, JULY 25TH 73." The company name was stamped on the right side of the ejector housing. The letters "U.S." were stamped on the bottom of the butt. The ordnance subinspector's cartouche and the date were stamped on the left grip. An assistant inspector's cartouche sometimes was placed on the right grip. Total production was 8,969.

EDGED WEAPONS

Bayonets and Entrenching Tools

Model 1855 Bayonet. An angular type bayonet, the Model 1855 had an overall length of 21 inches with a socket 3 inches long, which had a clasp tightened by a screw. The neck between the socket and the blade was 1¼ inches long. The blade, in cross-section, was triangular. The width of the blade was ¾ inch, tapering to a point. The letters "U.S." were stamped on the upper flat near the neck. The finish was bright overall. The Model 1855 bayonet fit the Springfield rifles Models 1866, 1868, and 1870, in addition to other weapons.

The scabbard, made of black bridle leather with a sheet-brass ferrule and tip, had an overall length of about 19½ inches. The belt frog was made of black buff leather doubled on itself, sewn, and riveted with four copper rivets. The frog occasionally was made of bridle leather. The loop was fastened to a leather socket at the top of the scabbard by three rivets. Other scabbards used with this bayonet were the various Hoffman patterns discussed in the previous chapter.

Model 1873 Bayonet. The bayonet for the Model 1873 Springfield rifle was identical to the Model 1855 except that the inside diameter of the socket was only about ¾ inch to fit the smaller .45-caliber barrel. And its finish was blue rather than the traditional armory bright.

The Model 1873 bayonets were newly manufactured until it was discovered that a new cold-press method could be used to compress the socket of the 1855 bayonet. Thereafter, surplus obsolete bayonets simply were shrunk and re-finished. No new bayonets were produced so long as the .45/70 rifle remained in service.[50] This was yet another instance of the army's ingenuity in utilizing surplus stocks of materiel.

The scabbard was a blued sheet-steel tube 18¼ inches long, having a clasp ⅞ inch wide riveted at the top (reverse) with two iron rivets. The clasp held the leather frog in place. A small hole at the tip of the scabbard served as a drain.

The frog was made of two pieces of black bridle leather, one which measured

2⅜ inches wide and which was folded around the tube and stitched. The other piece was 1¾ inches wide, folded on itself and stitched to form a belt loop. This loop was fastened at right angles to the frog by a cast-brass rosette 1¹⁄₁₆ inches in diameter bearing the letters "US" in relief on a stippled background.[51] The rosette permitted the belt loop to swivel a few degrees.

Model 1873 Trowel Bayonet.   Amid the army's general overhaul of equipage arose the issue of an individual entrenching tool for infantrymen. The only previous attempt at providing U.S. soldiers with such an implement had been in the 1840s when the Regiment of Mounted Riflemen was issued large, heavy-bladed knives for this purpose. The concept did not become well rooted, probably because line infantry units still were armed with smoothbore muskets having an effective range of less than one hundred yards. Of necessity, battle lines had to be formed close to each other, and the outcome usually was decided in a relatively short time.

However, the rifled musket changed all of this. The appalling casualties of the Civil War, due largely to the greater range and accuracy of the rifled musket, and to the terribly effective Minnie bullet, underscored the tragically outmoded tactics of the day. By the end of the war, breastworks and trenches were common defenses on the battlefields of Virginia.

The advent of the breech-loading metallic cartridge rifle and its nearly universal adoption by the world's armies caused fundamental changes in infantry tactics. The breechloader outclassed the rifled musket as much as the latter had the smoothbore. The increased effectiveness of breechloaders, in terms of both firepower and long-range accuracy, further rendered close-order battle formations obsolete. The devastation inflicted by the rifled musket during the Civil War sounded a clear signal of what could be expected if massed bodies of troops were to face each other with breechloaders. The breechloader enabled the soldier to fight more effectively as an individual, taking advantage of the protection offered by terrain and hastily dug rifle pits on the battlefield. Modern weapons also gave the soldier the potential to become a deadly marksman and laid the foundation for a formal marksmanship program and a new doctrine of fire discipline.

In July 1872, some two months into its deliberations on small arms, the Terry Board was handed the additional task of evaluating the usefulness of the trowel bayonet. This sparked a heated debate throughout the army about whether or not the bayonet in fact had been made obsolete by the breech-loading rifle. Many officers became convinced that future battles would be fought largely at long range; therefore, troops would have a greater need for an entrenching tool than for the bayonet.

Lieutenant Edmond Rice, a seasoned veteran who had served through the Civil War, rising to the rank of lieutenant colonel of volunteers, learned by experience that shelter on the battlefield was vital to survival. Reasoning that the bayonet probably could not be dispensed with entirely, he pursued the idea of combining the bayonet and the entrenching tool into a single dual-purpose implement. The result was the trowel bayonet, a device with a spadelike blade. It served as a bayonet when fixed to the rifle barrel and as a digging tool when used in the hand. The 1869-pattern trowel later issued for trial incorporated a standard bayonet socket, which doubled as a handle, and a finger ring within the angle of the shank to provide better control when digging. The trowel was

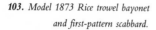

*103. Model 1873 Rice trowel bayonet
and first-pattern scabbard.*

issued with a special leather scabbard with a brass tip and a rigid belt loop much like the regulation 1855 scabbard.

Rice began working on various designs for the trowel bayonet in the mid-1860s. Within five years his concept had attracted enough attention to bring it before the board then meeting at St. Louis. After giving the new implement a preliminary examination, the board felt that the trowel was "a valuable substitute for the common bayonet on account of its great usefulness as an intrenching tool." The board added, "It also appears to be quite a formidable a weapon as the other."[52] The board thereupon recommended that five hundred trowel bayonets be manufactured and issued to companies for field trials.

As it turned out, only Rice's own Fifth Infantry received the new bayonets, the first issues being made during the second quarter of 1871. Nearly the entire regiment continued to use the trowels for the following year, but by the end of 1873 all except two or three companies had exchanged them for triangular bayonets.[53]

Practical tests conclusively proved that the trowel bayonet worked remarkably well for making rifle pits in the field. However, the Terry Board, inheriting the issue late in 1872, felt that the trowel compromised the effectiveness of both the bayonet and the entrenching tool. Two of the members, Colonel P. V. Hagner and Colonel Henry B. Clitz, preferred instead "a light steel intrenching tool with wooden handle."[54] The opinion of the board being divided, Major Stephen V. Benet recommended to the secretary of war that ten thousand of each implement be manufactured at Springfield Armory and issued for trial concurrently.[55]

This resulted in the selection for production of a somewhat modified and more refined trowel bayonet (fig. 103). The principal differences were the socket and the method of locking it to the rifle barrel. The old-style socket and clasp was replaced by a new two-piece device. The entire rear portion of the socket rotated ninety degrees to allow the front sight stud of the rifle to pass through to a mortise in the front section. The rear portion was then turned back to its former position, locking the bayonet on the rifle. However, the troops were given explicit instructions that under no circumstances was the trowel to be used for digging while it was attached to the rifle.[56] The leverage applied would bend the barrel quite easily. Issued with each trowel was a wooden "Chillingworth" plug handle with a pistol-grip extension to improve the grip for digging.

Despite the relatively large number produced, the trowel bayonet was always regarded as an experimental item. The 1874 Infantry Equipment Board reconsidered adopting it but concluded: "Soldiers will be deprived of a very efficient defensive weapon without providing them with an effective intrenching tool. A bayonet has been found to be always more or less necessary, but in our service an intrenching-tool might not be required once in ten years."[57] Although these officers did not attempt to resolve the question, the consensus among them was that the triangular bayonet should be retained and some sort of light shovel be issued when it was necessary to make entrenchments. On April 24, 1874, the Ordnance Department also adopted a leather-covered sheet-metal scabbard for the trowel.[58]

Issues of the Model 1873 trowel bayonet and scabbard began early in 1875. Although the Sixteenth Infantry was the only regiment to be equipped entirely with them, the Fifth, Fourteenth, and Eighteenth were close behind, with eight or nine companies each. By the end of June, the Tenth, Seventeenth, Fourteenth, Eighteenth, Nineteenth, Twentieth, Twenty-third, and Twenty-fifth Regiments were outfitted completely with the new bayonet, and several other units had received partial issues.[59] Eventually, the trowels reached most of the infantry regiments, although a few units never did receive them.

In a surprising move, an army headquarters circular dated September 12, 1876, authorized commanding officers who so desired to turn in their trowels in exchange for standard triangular bayonets. Apparently, the army's high command remained unconvinced of the trowel's effectiveness in its dual roles. Or, it may have been that many field officers simply could not adjust to the rather bizarre appearance of the trowel, preferring instead the less useful triangular bayonet for its visual appeal when fixed during dress parades. Typical of some contemporary opinions of the trowel, one sarcastic wag quipped, "Some genius seeking to transform a soldier into a jack of spades has given him a shovel to wear on the end of his gun."[60] Perhaps the majority of officers considered the entrenching tool of so little utility on the frontier that it simply was not worth burdening the men.[61] In any event, the Twenty-first, Twenty-fourth, and Twenty-fifth applied immediately; other regiments continued to use the trowel bayonet for months and sometimes years.[62] Manufacture of the trowel bayonet ceased by order of the secretary of war on February 25, 1876.[63]

The overall length of the trowel bayonet was 14½ inches. The blade itself (forward of the shank) was 10 inches long by 3½ inches wide. The shape of the blade was that of a spear point, with gracefully tapering sides. The face of the blade was concave, and the reverse was convex with a squared rib running the full length to provide strength. The left edge of the obverse was sharpened for a length of about 4¼ inches to adapt it for scraping and light chopping. The blade was bright-finished.

The socket, curved along the bottom side to fit the hand, was blued and measured 3½ inches in length. Around the socket were six peripheral knurled rings. Forward of the sight mortise was stamped "PAT APR. 16th 72" in very small letters.

The plug handle, made of walnut, measured 5 inches long. The shank measured $^{23}/_{32}$ inch in diameter by 4¾ inches. A ¼-inch-diameter iron stud for locking the trowel in the bayonet's mortise was mounted in the side of the shank about 1½ inches from the handle.

The Pattern 1873 scabbard, made of tin, was 11¼ inches long, its shape conforming to the shape of the trowel's blade. Both front and reverse had a single wide corrugation vertically to provide rigidity. The body was covered with black leather stitched along both outer edges. A brass tip, 1¾ inches long, was attached to the bottom end by a single rivet.

The belt loop, of black collar leather, was formed in two pieces, joined by a Hoffman's swivel. The rosette measured 1¹⁄₁₆ inches and had the letters "U S" cast on the face with stippled background and raised bright rim. The combined unit measured 1⅝ inches wide by 5¾ inches long. It was held to the reverse of the scabbard body by two brass rivets.

Model 1873 Ordnance Entrenching Tool. Although production of the trowel bayonet was approved late in 1873, the design of its competitor, known either as the ordnance or the infantry entrenching tool, was not finalized until the spring of 1874. Two sample tools proposed by Colonel Henry B. Clitz, a Terry Board member, and another submitted by Major James G. Benton, commanding Springfield Armory, were sent to the Ordnance Office for examination. Benet subsequently forwarded these to Springfield, directing Benton to make the selection. On March 7, 1874, the armory commander returned to Benet a smaller version of the tool, presumably a modification of his own design. Benet approved the sample and ordered Springfield to manufacture ten-thousand.[64]

The bright-finished steel blade measured 3½ inches wide by 8 inches long and had a broad rounded point (fig. 104). One edge of the blade was turned at a right angle to make it more rigid for scraping in hard soil. A hardwood handle (ash or oak), 3¾ inches long, was fitted into an iron socket at the butt of the blade. The handle was stamped "U S" near the socket in letters ⁵⁄₁₆ inch high.

The design and manufacture of a suitable scabbard for the entrenching tool, like that for the trowel bayonet, was something of an afterthought. Benet initially had suggested that a ring or some sort of device be attached to the tool itself so that the soldier could sling it to his equipment, but the suggestion was not adopted. It was not until March 4, 1875, that a final design for the scabbard was approved.[65] This scabbard, made of corrugated tin and covered with russet leather, had an iron staple riveted to its brass throat. The staple held a split-iron ring by which the scabbard could be "fastened to any part of the equipment at pleasure . . . [and] covered with leather as a protection to the clothing from rust."[66] The scabbard measured 4 inches wide by 8¼ inches long. The letters "U.S." were stamped in the upper left corner of the scabbard face.

Soldiers commonly modified the scabbard by removing the ring and substituting in its place a more practical leather belt loop.[67] One example of a modified scabbard had a leather belt loop ¾ inch wide by 4⅜ inches long, fabricated from an overcoat strap. The ends simply were overlapped

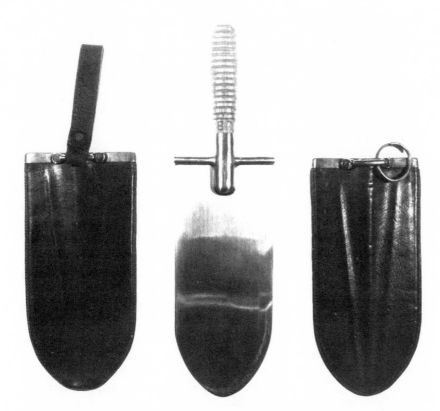

104. *Hagner entrenching tool, 1873, flanked by field-modified scabbard with belt loop (left) and standard scabbard (right).*

on the rear side and fastened with a single brass rivet passing through all three layers.

Swords and Sabers

Noncommissioned Officers' Sword, Model 1840. Company sergeants of infantry continued to carry the Model 1840 sword, even if only for dress parades, until the promulgation of General Orders No. 77, dated August 6, 1875. This order, the result of a recommendation by the 1874 Infantry Equipment Board, discontinued the NCO sword as a part of the equipment for company-grade sergeants.[68]

The noncommissioned officers' sword had an overall length of 37½ inches (fig. 105). The blade, finished bright, measured ⅞ inch wide at the hilt by 31¾ inches long. A fuller ran from the ricasso to within 1½ inches of the point. The obverse of the ricasso was stamped with the letters "U.S.," the inspector's initials, and the date of manufacture in three lines. The reverse usually bore the name of the maker.

The hilt was formed of cast brass with a grip of false wire wrapping. A flattened knuckle-bow crossed the blade and curved to the rounded pommel. The bow usually bore inspector's initials stamped on the obverse at about the midpoint. A double-kidney-shaped counterguard was cast integrally with the knuckle-bow.

The scabbard was made of either black bridle leather or black japanned sheet steel. Both types had a brass throat and tip with drag. A cast-brass hook on the obverse, pointing downward, supported the scabbard in the sling or frog. As has been mentioned elsewhere, the 1868 Ordnance Board recommended that the manufacture of leather scabbards be discontinued in favor of steel scabbards. At the same time, a sliding leather frog replaced the old cross-sling.

Musician's Sword, Model 1840   The sword issued to trumpeters and bandsmen of infantry was essentially the same as the NCO sword except that the blade was 4 inches shorter and the double-kidney counterguard was omitted. The shorter length of this sword was attributed to the fact that most army musicians in the mid-nineteenth century were boys, some as young as twelve years old. Their generally shorter stature dictated a shorter sword.[69]

The blade measured 28 inches long by ¾ inch wide at the hilt; the overall length of the sword was 34½ inches. The scabbard also was like that of the NCO sword, except shorter in length.

Foot Officers' Sword, Model 1850.   Infantry officers used the Model 1850 sword from its adoption until 1872, when it was replaced by the Model 1860 staff and field officers' sword.[70]

The more useful foot officers' sword measured 37 inches overall (fig. 106). The slightly curved blade measured 32 inches long by 1⅛ inches wide at the hilt. It had a false upper edge extending back about 8 inches from the point.

It was distinguished by its etched blade, consisting of floral designs, an American eagle, military trophies, and a scroll bearing the motto "E PLU-RIBUS UNUM." The reverse side was etched similarly, except that the letters "U.S." were substituted for the motto. The manufacturer's name appeared on the ricasso.

The wooden grip was covered with fish skin (gray in color) wrapped with brass wire. The brass guard had a single knuckle-bow that flared toward the blade to form an oval counterguard. The knuckle-bow was engraved with scrolls and branches. The pommel was decorated with oak leaves.

105. (Top to bottom) Model 1858 light cavalry saber; Model 1840 light artillery saber; Model 1840 noncommissioned officers' sword; and Model 1840 musicians' sword, with their respective scabbards. (Hayes Otoupalik Collection)

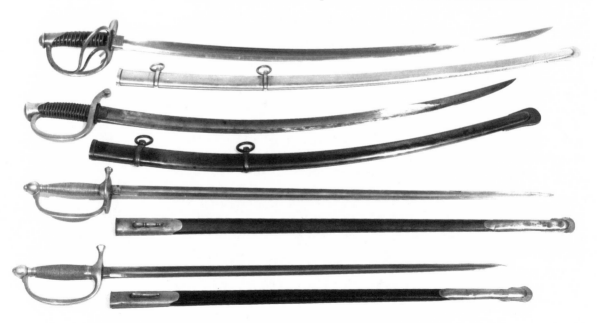

The scabbard for the Model 1850 sword was made of black bridle leather with throat, middle band, and drag all of brass. Suspension rings were attached to the throat piece and the middle band. Some of these swords were issued with blued or blackened steel scabbards with brass mountings.

Light Cavalry Saber, Model 1858.   The introduction of the light cavalry saber saw the similar, but heavier, Model 1840 phased out, although both types were used extensively throughout the Civil War. Long termed the "Model 1860" among scholars and collectors alike, the light cavalry saber was conceived in 1857, when the Ames Company was requested to design a new saber for cavalry use. A prototype was provided, and on its approval, Ames was awarded a contract for eight hundred of the new sabers on April 9, 1858.[71]

The Model 1858 is readily distinguished from the older saber by its lighter blade, having a rounded back. The earlier model had a thicker, square-backed blade. The regular army was issued the light cavalry saber exclusively during the Indian campaigns.

Throughout the postwar era, a debate raged over the future usefulness of the saber. The question never was settled, and cavalrymen continued to carry the saber well into the next century. Experienced cavalry commanders, however, usually ordered their men to omit the saber from their field gear on active frontier service. Its weight on the already overburdened mounts failed to be offset by the almost nonexistent potential that it might be used in combat.

The saber had a curved blade 34⅝ inches long by 1 inch wide at the hilt. The overall length was 30¾ inches. The blade had fullers on both sides, extending nearly its entire length. A brass guard consisted of a knuckle-bow and double

106. (Top to bottom) Two Model 1850 foot officers' swords; Model 1872 cavalry officers' saber; Model 1860 staff and field officers' sword. (Hayes Otoupalik Collection)

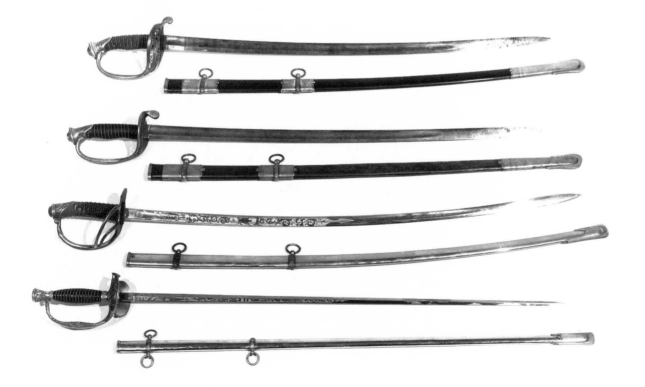

branches. The grip was made of wood covered with leather, over which was a wrap of doubled and twisted brass wire. The obverse ricasso was stamped "U.S.," with inspector's initials and date of manufacture; the reverse usually bore the maker's name.

The scabbard was made of sheet steel with mouthpiece, two rings, and a drag, which usually bore inspector's initials. The scabbards were finished bright.

Officers' Light Cavalry Saber, Model 1860. Many officers purchased this utilitarian saber for field use. It was quite similar in appearance to the enlisted man's light cavalry saber.

The single-edged, curved blade duplicated that of the enlisted version. It was 1 inch wide at the hilt by 35 inches long. (A foreign example made by E. Horsier had a blade measuring 1⅛ inches by 34 inches.) The only difference was that both sides of the officers' saber were etched with military and floral designs. On the right was an eagle with the national motto, "E Pluribus Unum." On the reverse were the letters "U.S."

The wooden grip was covered with fish skin and had a wrapping of doubled gilt-wire wrapping. The pommel was decorated with a pattern of leaves along the edge where it joined the grip.

The hilt was gilded brass throughout. The guard consisted of two branches, like those on the enlisted saber, except that each bore floral stampings, inside and outside, at the ends nearest the counterguard. A similar floral design appeared on the knuckle-bow where it joined the pommel. The inside of the counterguard bore an engraved eagle and floral design.

The iron scabbard was blued with two brass bands with brass rings. Both were cast with floral designs. The tip also was of brass.

Staff and Field Officers' Sword, Model 1860. The 1872 uniform regulations prescribed this light dress sword for all officers of the army except light artillery, cavalry, paymasters, and the medical department.

The straight blade, diamond-shaped in cross-section, had straight-tapering edges from the hilt to near the point. It measured 31 inches in length by ⅝ inch wide at the hilt. Both sides of the blade were etched for about half its length, a light gold wash covering the etched portions. The obverse bore the letters "US" (upside down), along with military equipage consisting of a Union shield, flags, and bugles intermixed with floral designs. The reverse had similar floral etchings and trophies, including flags, drums, and cannon. Additionally, there was an arms of the United States, a spread eagle with ribbon. Etched just above the ricasso was the maker's name, "U.S. Armory Springfield, Mass." Inspector's initials appeared on the ricasso.

The hilt was made of gilded brass. The knuckle-bow had flattened sides decorated with scroll. It was pierced near the pommel with a slot for the sword knot. The pommel itself was an inverted, truncated cone decorated with shield and eagle. The pommel cap was covered with leaf and berry designs.

At the point where the knuckle-bow turned up, there was a single branch on the obverse. This branch joined a kidney-shaped counterguard decorated with flags and an eagle. The guard on the reverse was hinged to fold down, making it more comfortable to the wearer. An iron push-button catch released this portion of the counterguard or locked it in either position. The grip was covered with black fish skin and wrapped with gilded wire.

The scabbard was made of nickel-plated steel. It had two gilded-brass bands with two rings on the upper and one on the lower. It had a brass tip and drag.

Cavalry Officers' Saber, Model 1872.   This very lightweight saber replaced the more utilitarian Model 1860 light cavalry officers' saber authorized previously. No doubt many of the latter continued in use throughout the Indian campaigns among those officers who preferred to carry the saber in the field.

The saber had an overall length of 38 inches, with a blade measuring 32¼ inches by ¾ inch at the hilt. The blade was slightly curved with a single blunt edge. A false edge extended back from the point approximately 6½ inches. Each side had a single broad fuller. The obverse was etched with military trophies, floral designs, and a spread eagle. The reverse had similar decorations but, rather than the eagle, bore the letters "U.S." in Old English script. The manufacturer's name was etched on the blade.

The guard was made of brass and was of the half-basket pattern with two branches between the hilt and the knuckle-bow. These branches were engraved with leaf patterns, as was the pommel. The latter also bore a shield. The counterguard was decorated with an eagle clutching a palm branch, with arrows above the grip and a circle of thirteen stars below the grip. The grip was covered with fish skin and wrapped with gilded wire.

The scabbard was nickel-plated steel with gilded-brass throat, rings, and drag.

UNTIL THOSE NOW ON HAND
ARE EXHAUSTED

CLOTHING, 1874–1877

THE YEAR 1874 SAW the army's transition to new clothing well under way, but several problems arose to impede the changeover. As well intentioned as the combined efforts of the 1872 Uniform Board and the Quartermaster Department may have been, the workings of bureaucracy soon presented several obstacles to the program. Moreover, some of the new uniform items simply did not live up to the soldier's needs and expectations. It was in this era that the American soldier and his frontier experience exerted great influence on military authorities to change the clothing to better adapt it for service in the West.

In his annual report for 1873 the quartermaster general announced that surplus stocks of old clothing were being sold off at auction as rapidly as possible, both at the depots and at posts around the country. Alerted to these sales, someone in Congress investigated and discovered that huge inventories of "old-pattern" clothing remained on hand in army storehouses. However, the alarmist failed to recognize that most of this surplus was unfit for issue and had been for some time, being either of substandard quality or of sizes too small or too large for most of the men in the army. Apparently ignorant of General Meigs's previous reports, Congress nevertheless took decisive action to halt what it perceived, incorrectly, as being a flagrant abuse of public funds.

On June 16, 1874, Congress, in passing legislation for the army's annual budget, stipulated that "none of the money appropriated should be used in the purchase of hats, uniform caps, forage caps, uniform coats, uniform jackets, flannel sack coats, and unlined coats, but that these articles should be issued from the supply on hand known as the old pattern; and that none of the articles enumerated should be purchased until those on hand were exhausted." No sooner had this order been issued than the quartermaster at Jeffersonville Depot (Indiana), where the bulk of the remaining surplus lay, reminded higher authorities of the size shortages and the unusable condition of the bulk of the clothing. The headgear, particularly forage caps, cap covers, and 1858-pattern hats, had suffered the ravages of moths and poor warehousing. This damaged stock was peremptorily condemned before anyone could again change their minds. Contracts for new-pattern replacement items were issued immediately. Although Meigs acknowledged the size deficiency in many articles of the old-pattern clothing, he ordered the available stocks to be issued nevertheless. A full range of sizes was on hand only in cavalry and light artillery uniform jackets, unlined sack coats, and ordnance uniform coats. Infantry dress coats could be provided only in sizes 1 and 2, and lined sack coats were available only in the medium sizes.[1]

In an effort to make the situation somewhat more palatable, Military Store-keeper John F. Rodgers suggested that a portion of the new blouses, trousers, and overcoats be sent out to the posts unmade. Rodgers recognized that many men took enough pride in their military appearance to pay the company tailors to alter their uniforms for a better fit. His new idea was to issue all of the pieces for a particular garment precut and bundled with appropriate trimming materials, buttons, and thread. This would allow the soldier to indulge himself in a custom-fitted uniform more easily and at less cost than having to remake finished goods. Despite the obvious merits of the suggestion, the army was not yet ready to adopt so radical a concept simply to benefit the enlisted soldier. According to the military authorities, this would present a temptation to the men to take too many individual liberties in having their uniforms made, which could affect the basic concept of uniformity itself.[2]

In the wake of the reversal for issuing the new uniform, the army assumed a decidedly motley appearance (fig. 107). This, of course, contradicted the purpose of adopting the new clothing in the first place. Meigs had proudly announced in his annual report of 1873 that nearly all the troops had received the new 1872 uniform, but photographic evidence suggests that many men still wore components of the old uniform, especially for fatigue and field duty. The new restrictions only compounded the supply problem in 1874. One exasperated Tenth Infantry officer protested that his men at Fort Stockton, Texas, were in such dire need of clothing that "it was sometimes necessary to excuse men from parade for want of decent covering, and the Troops presented in many instances a ragged appearance which could not be avoided."[3] The yoke placed on the army by the 1874 act would plague the troops for several more years as the military attempted to rid itself of the Civil War surplus clothing once and for all.

Despite these complications, distribution of the new uniform progressed. But, as the fanfare and back-patting in Meigs's office subsided, results from the acid test of soldier opinion began to come in from the field. Even though Captain Rodgers had predicted that the 1872 uniform would prove to be infinitely better than the old one, the troops gave it a typically mixed review. Reactions, herein synopsized from field reports, ranged from tacit acceptance to no less than vehement disgust.

The dress headgear items for both mounted and dismounted troops were generally accepted by the rank and file, though the cavalry helmet was less well liked than the infantry's shako. No strong opinions were lodged against the latter, except that some foot soldiers felt slighted by not receiving a helmet. However, the cavalry dress helmet was criticized for its excessive weight and long, sharply angled visors, which forced the soldier to either push the helmet back on his head or tilt his head back in order to see. These problems would be overcome eventually when the helmet pattern was revised in 1881 and issued, with distinctive branch trimmings, to both mounted and dismounted troops.

Soldiers soon discovered that for all of the splendor, there were times when the helmet cords were a nuisance. The cords had a practical purpose in that they were intended to link the helmet to the soldier so that the helmet would not be dropped accidentally while the soldier was mounted. There were occasions, however, when troopers needed to rid themselves of the helmet, such as at

formal social events. For a solution to the problem they had only to look to the officers' helmets, which had cords detachable by means of a small snap hook just below the tassel. It did not take the ingenious enlisted men long to improvise a similar connection by cutting the cords, sewing the ends together, and adding a hook and eye under the tassel. Other men severed the cords above the tassel, then sewed the ends together again with the cord looped through the scroll and ring.[4]

"The forage cap," according to one officer, "is in every respect a great and marked improvement over the old and miserable cap heretofore issued, the new one has all the requisites of a good cap, the material . . . is good, the top does not touch the hair."[5] This popular piece of headgear was the one most commonly seen around the posts, not only because the men liked it but also because an 1873 order forbade them to wear the campaign hat except when they were doing physical labor.[6] Because of its general acceptance throughout the service, the basic style of the 1872-pattern cap remained the army standard for another twenty-three years.

Confusion had reigned over how to properly wear the cap insignia since the promulgation of the 1872 uniform regulations. The ambiguous language of the regulations suggested that either the branch insignia or the company letter was to be worn on the front of the cap. This, it would appear, left the matter in the hands of post or company commanders for the first few months after adoption of the new uniform. The oversight was soon discovered, however, and a new general order was issued on June 25, 1873, stating that both the letter and the branch insignia were to be displayed on the front of the cap. Still, this order failed to specify how they were to be placed relative to each other. Colonel George L. Andrews, commanding the Twenty-fifth Infantry, wrote from his headquarters at Fort Davis, Texas, "I notice a great difference in the views of company commanders regarding the insignia to be placed within the bugle, some require the letter of the company to be worn, others the number of the regiment, while others omit both."[7]

At the same time, numerous complaints were leveled at the quality of the insignia, which one officer rated as "the most flimsy articles possible, the metal thin as paper and the soldering of the loops and eyes too weak for use."[8] Soldiers quickly improvised various ways of contending with the frail insignia. Some men drilled small holes through the pieces so that they could be sewn directly to the cap. A more popular method was to fill the backs of the branch insignia with molten lead, which, when set, greatly reinforced the pieces. More creative types soldered the numbers and letters directly to the branch device and frequently added a wire pin on the reverse so that the unit could be removed easily for cleaning. The Quartermaster Department eventually took notice of the many complaints and began stamping the insignia from heavier (No. 20) sheet brass in 1877.[9] However, the practice of using a lead fill had by that time become so popular that it continued among the troops for as long as such devices were issued.

In 1875, army headquarters decided the infantry's bugle insignia was outmoded; instead the insignia should reflect the principal weapon of the infantry, as did the insignias for cavalry and artillery. Orders were issued on November 19 establishing crossed rifles as the official cap insignia for infantry, a symbol that has continued in use to the present day.[10] Exempt from the order were the field and band musicians, who retained the bugle, with the regimental number in the center and the company letter above.[11]

On the facing page:

107. Officers and civilians of Lieutenant Colonel George A. Custer's Black Hills Expedition, August 1874. Custer (lying on the ground, center) appears in his typical buckskins. The other officers exhibit a variety of clothing, including homemade blue woolen shirts with white or yellow edging. Many wear the 1872 folding campaign hat, others have on the forage cap, and yet others wear civilian hats. Note the men (left of the photo) who wear fabricated leggings. (Little Bighorn Battlefield National Monument)

Yet, this decision was not applauded universally. The army was filled with officers and soldiers who had served under the bugle ornament for many years and were loath to give it up. One old soldier, signing himself only as "Infantry," commented in the *Army and Navy Journal*: "The time honored bugle is to be done away with. Now we are to have 'crossed rifles without bayonets.' 'Yes, but that is so much more appropriate for the infantry.' That's so, and by the same token let's give the engineers crossed quills, nibs upward, or if they prefer it, a pick and a spade. For what do they have to do with castles unless they are in the air?"[12]

If nothing else, the change to new insignia served to focus official attention on the arrangement of the numbers and letters. The new crossed rifles were to have the company letter in the upper angle and the regimental number below.[13] At last, the directions were clear-cut, for the infantry at least. Meanwhile, the cavalry still operated under the ambiguities of the 1873 order calling for branch device and letter only. Just as the doughboys began to sport their new insignia, letters uppermost, army headquarters had another change of mind. Unable to leave well enough alone, the staff issued yet another directive in March 1876, specifying that henceforth the number would be placed in the upper angle of the rifles and the company letter in the lower angle.[14] Nearly a year later, the army command noticed the continued inconsistency in the way the different branches displayed their cap insignia. The problem was resolved by the promulgation of a final order on the subject. Thereafter, all line personnel wore the number in the upper angle of the branch device and the letter in the lower. Noncommissioned officers of the regimental staff wore only the number.[15]

The folding campaign hat, which was supposed to be so practical, provoked intense, widespread criticism. In a memorable exchange, Captain Oddment Butler, commanding a company of the Fifth Infantry at Fort Dodge, Kansas, in 1874, complained that the 1872 hats became unserviceable within a matter of weeks after his men drew them. Butler's letter eventually wound its way through channels and into the hands of the imperious military storekeeper, John F. Rodgers, at the Philadelphia Depot. Rodgers, true to form, immediately responded that he had received no other complaints and that the hats worn by the Fifth Infantry were just like those issued to everyone else. Attempting to mollify the outraged captain, Rodgers nevertheless suggested that Butler send in some of the supposedly faulty hats for his examination. Captain Butler was only too happy to accommodate, and he included written testimony by eight of his men, who stated that their hats had begun falling apart after one week of wear. Rodgers immediately rejected this evidence, suggesting that Butler's men had hoodwinked the captain into a "hasty and unjust condemnation of a good article." He further contended that no one could have worn out a hat as quickly as these men claimed. Captain Butler, now thoroughly aroused, picked up the gauntlet thrown down by the quartermaster and counterattacked with a sheaf of statements by no less than forty-four soldiers, plus several officers, denouncing the hat in no uncertain terms.[16]

If Butler's complaint was the first Rodgers had heard, he certainly did not have long to wait for others to arrive. Typical of these was First Lieutenant William H. H. Crowell's observation that the campaign hat was "of such poor quality, that the broad brim when not hooked up—particularly in bad weather—breaks and falls down over the eyes making it necessary either to narrow the brim, or wear it always hooked up." Furious about the hat, Captain Loyd

Wheaton denounced it as "a failure in every respect. Unserviceable, hot, un-comfortable, hideous in appearance, and of worthless material." Surgeon William H. Forwood, writing from Fort Richardson, Texas, chimed in by stating that in his opinion the hat had "not even the redeeming quality of durability or usefulness to offset its horrid ugliness."[17] Reports from all over the West proved that the campaign hat would not last more than six to eight weeks in the field. If the assessments of scores of officers were not enough, Inspector-General Edmund Schriver gave the hat its death blow when he called it "ridiculous in design . . . faulty in manufacture . . . better suited to a wet nurse than a soldier in the ranks."[18] Other reports from the field stated that most men, if forced to draw folding hats, threw them away at the first opportunity.

Although some soldiers attempted to make use of the folding hat by cutting down its brim, many soldiers, perhaps the majority, resorted to buying their own hats from the post traders (fig. 108).[19] Even though the Quartermaster Department finally admitted that the 1872-pattern hat was a failure, it was slow to act on finding a replacement, since some forty-one thousand of the wretched things remained on hand. For the next few years soldiers wore an indescribable variety of hats, ranging in color from black, gray, and drab to off-white.[20]

Meantime, the Clothing Branch went back to the designer of the original sample hat, Warnock & Co. of New York, and attempted to find out if subsequent contractors had strayed from the specification materials. The Warnock hatters determined that the composition of the felt corresponded with their formula but that they had made an error in the formula in the first place. Although they offered to provide a better-quality felt, there simply was too much evidence against the hat to continue its production. Even if the material had been improved, the design still was unacceptable to the troops. In view of the stigma attached to the hat, the men would likely never have been convinced that it was a good one. Recognizing this, the secretary of war in 1875 directed that samples of new hats be obtained and forwarded to Washington. One of these, made by P. Hurst & Co. of Philadelphia, impressed both General Meigs and the secretary of war. Belknap subsequently ordered one hundred of these hats be made up and sent to troops in Arizona for trial.[21] This new hat, described more fully later in this chapter, would be adopted the next year.

The dress coat, favored for its jaunty style and looser fit, drew two main criticisms. Most men found that it was too short in the waist. When the waist belt was worn at its proper level, that is, through the loops sewn into the waist seam, the lower ribs were painfully compressed. When the soldier drew a size that fit properly in the waist, the coat was usually too large for his neck. Consequently, most of the men had to pay the company tailors to alter the coats by moving the belt loops, lowering the waist, or changing the neck size. Likewise, it was nearly impossible for small men in the infantry to use the belt loops when both cartridge boxes were worn because the boxes conflicted with the belt loops. However, another officer observed, "When the soldier is equipped as he generally is for garrison purposes, minus the shoulder braces and one cartridge box, the waist seam strap can be used as intended."[22] Fault also was found with the facings, particularly those on the infantry coats. "The material . . . is worthless," an Eleventh Infantry officer wrote from Fort Richardson, Texas, "as it fades to a dirty blue (in this climate) in less than three months."[23] Both of these shortcomings would be corrected, but not for years to come.

At the bottom of the opinion scale, alongside the folding campaign hat, was the pleated blouse that Surgeon Woodhull had lauded so highly. What was logical in theory proved to be a dismal failure. The men bitterly complained that the pleats billowed in the wind and collected so much dust that the men could keep them looking clean for only a short time. As a work and campaign garment, which it was supposed to be, the blouse proved impractical because the pleats snagged on almost everything. To improve the utility of the blouse, many men resorted to having the company tailors stitch down all of the pleats, thereby negating their purported advantages. When asked whether the allowance of blouses was adequate, one officer responded sarcastically that it "was more than sufficient in quantity—one blouse of such a pattern in a lifetime is more than sufficient." Veteran Colonel Frank Wheaton summed up general opinion of the pleated blouse by contemptuously branding it "an absurd garment." Photographic and documentary evidence indicates that pleated blouses commonly were relegated to campaign use as late as 1876–77 (fig. 109).[24]

Compounding the lack of uniformity in the ranks was the discovery of perfectly good 1857 dress uniform coats stored at various depots. Since these fell under the congressional order to be issued, the men had little choice but to draw them. Some were altered for dress purposes, and others were converted for use as fatigue garments (fig. 110). Sixth Infantryman Wilmot P. Sanford, serving at Fort Buford, Dakota Territory, bought three of the old coats and immediately remade one of them into a blouse.[25] Converting these coats presented a challenge to the company tailors; nevertheless, they managed to alter the coats into suitable work garments. The standing collar was removed and replaced by a short, rollover style. The long skirt was shortened to hip length, usually with the front corners rounded like a sack coat. The cuffs sometimes were altered by removing the overlay of cloth with the decorative braid, leaving them plain.

As a result of the congressional mandate, men in the same unit wore four-button sack coats, pleated blouses, and the modified 1857 coats (fig. 111). General orders issued as late as 1877 reminded the army that these items were to be charged at the rates established in 1871 and that contracts for duplicate items of the new pattern were not to be let until the surplus was consumed.[26] For a time this mélange of blouses in the ranks exasperated company commanders and contributed to a most un-uniform army.

Some soldiers serving in the Southwest were decidedly more un-uniform than others. They discarded the woolen uniform altogether, preferring instead to wear their stable clothing or commercial hunters' outfits. "Dust, soot, rain, and grime," wrote Captain John G. Bourke, describing his Third Cavalry comrades, "had made their impress upon the canvas suits which each had donned, and with their hair uncut for months and beards growing with straggling growth all over the face, there was not one of the party who would venture to pose as an Adonis."[27]

If the rank-and-file soldier of the mid-1870s presented a motley appearance in the field, his officers frequently bore an equally distant and practical departure from the uniform regulations (fig. 112). Captain Charles King, serving as adjutant of Colonel Wesley Merritt's Fifth Cavalry in 1876, contrasted the appearance of the officers of General Alfred H. Terry's Dakota Column with that of General George Crook's command.

On the facing page:
108. *Cavalrymen at Fort Grant, Arizona, ca. 1876. The dress of these men reflects the hodgepodge of clothing worn in the mid-1870s. Seen here is a variety of headgear, including civilian hats and a forage cap; the soldier at the left wears the regulation 1872 campaign hat. Others in the group may have on folding hats that have had the brims cut down to various widths. Note the concurrent use of the 1858-pattern sack coat, the pleated blouse, and the 1874 blouse.* (Arizona Historical Society)

On the following page:
109. *First Cavalrymen in the field during the Nez Percé Campaign, July 1877. Although several of the men wear 1874-pattern blouses, the old folding campaign hat is still very much in evidence. Some of the soldiers in the background appear to have the 1875 dark-blue flannel shirts. Others wear white shirts of either flannel or cotton.* (Douglas D. Scott Collection)

Facing the following page:
110. *Twentieth U.S. Infantrymen drilling as crew members for a one-inch Gatling gun at Fort McKean, Dakota Territory, on the eve of the 1876 Sioux Campaign. First Sergeant Hugh Hynds, (left) wears a four-button sack coat with outside breast pocket. He appears to have the old Civil War–style bugle on his cap, with the regimental number within the loop. The sergeant behind him wears a Civil War frock, converted for use as a blouse. The three privates wear the 1874-pattern fatigue blouse, with the cuff and collar braid removed. The man standing at the wheel has added two buttons to the regulation one on his cuffs. Two of the men have thimble belts with wide canvas loops; the belt worn by the private in the right foreground has narrow leather loops.* (Little Bighorn Battlefield National Monument)

General Terry, as became a brigadier, was attired in the handsome uniform of his rank; his staff and his line officers . . . were all in neat regimentals, so that shoulder straps were to be seen in every direction. General Crook, as became an old campaigner and frontiersman, was in a rough hunting rig, and in all his staff and line there was not a complete suit of uniform. Left to our fancy in the matter, we had fallen back upon our comfortable old Arizona scouting-suits, and were attired in deerskin, buckskin, flannels, and corduroy; but in the Fifth Cavalry you could not have told officer from private. It may have been suitable as regarded Indian campaigning, but was undeniably slouchy and border-ruffianish.[28]

King described himself as clothed in "an old shooting coat, an indescribable pair of trousers [described elsewhere as 'buckskin trousers fringed and beaded, but much the worse for wear'], and a straw hat minus ribbon or binding, a brim ragged as the edge of a saw and a crown without a thatch."[29]

Officers' hats, more often made of felt than of straw because of the greater durability of felt, ran the gamut of styles and colors. Although some officers preferred the regulation 1872 folding campaign hat, others opted for conventional-style black hats obtained on the civilian market. Photographs indicate that these hats frequently had rather narrow brims and high crowns. Other officers chose to wear light-colored felt hats of the "slouch" or "sombrero" styles with broad brims and low crowns. Most officers wore no insignia on their

On the facing page:

111. Camp of Eighth U.S. Infantry in the desert near Fort McDowell, Arizona Territory, ca. 1875. The enlisted men standing in the background wear a mixture of sack coats, 1872 pleated blouses, and 1874 blouses. The man standing at the right, with his hand on a chair, wears a thimble belt fabricated from a cavalry carbine sling. The stacked rifles are Model 1868 Springfields, without slings. (B. William Henry Collection)

Below:

112. Fifth U.S. Cavalry officers in the Black Hills, 1876, far from the parade ground, and resembling border ruffians. Officers and soldiers alike dispensed with formality and wore practical garb in the field. (Paul L. Hedren, National Archives)

hats, though a rare individual would sew on the regulation dark-blue oval patch bearing the branch device.

Officers wore blouses into the field, though these represented a variety of styles. Period photographs suggest that some officers wore the regulation 1872 blouse but that many preferred to buy enlisted-pattern blouses for campaign use rather than sacrifice their more expensive jackets (fig. 113). Some of the older officers, who had been in the service before the new regulations were issued, elected to wear their obsolete four-button sack coats. Perhaps the majority, depending on the particular commanding officer, wore no shoulder straps on their blouses. The insignia were expensive to purchase, and there was always the chance that Indian sharpshooters might single out anyone with distinguishing features.

Since officers did not have a regulation shirt, they wore shirts either made by wives or company tailors or purchased on the civilian market. Many officers of the Seventh Cavalry, for instance, wore dark-blue shirts with wide collars having the regimental number handworked on the points. Others opted for the double-breasted shield front, or miner's, shirt of dark blue, gray, or perhaps red (fig. 114). Still others wore common pullover shirts buttoning halfway down the front, not much different from those of the enlisted men except that they often had one or two breast pockets. Some "swells" in the officer corps had the edges of either the shield or the placket bound in white or branch-colored twill.[30]

Officers also wore a variety of styles of trousers. John Ryan, who served with the Seventh Cavalry in 1876, recalled that most of the officers wore only the regulation sky-blue kersey, but others, including Lieutenant Colonel George A. Custer and his brother Captain Thomas W. Custer, had the plainsman's fringed buckskin trousers, as described by Captain King. Whereas some officers, like enlisted men, lined the seat and legs of their woolen pants with canvas to prolong the life of the pants in the field, others simply purchased the corduroy or canvas pants used by miners, cowboys, and other western outdoorsmen.

Officers' footgear also varied from one individual to the next. The majority of officers appear to have preferred high-topped cavalry boots of one style or another, some boots as high as, or higher than, the knee. However, many officers, particularly infantry officers who marched with their men, wore the brogan or the short Wellington boot. With these, the officers often chose to wear commercially made canvas leggings, which were lighter and cooler than boots (fig. 115).

Captain Rodgers, chagrined by the army's rejection of the vaunted pleated blouse, immediately set his patternmakers to work on a new style. The secretary of war approved this pattern on February 27, 1874, as a substitute for the 1872 blouse.[31] The basic style of the new blouse, with only minor modifications through the years, would serve the army until after the turn of the century.

A survey of field reports on the new clothing indicates that the pattern 1874 fatigue blouse went into production immediately (fig. 116). The troops received initial supplies of them as early as March 1875.[32] However, to save face and avoid a confrontation with Congress, the quartermaster general directed that the new blouse was to be issued "as fast as the existing stock of the old pattern [1872]" was exhausted.[33]

The trousers proposed by the 1872 regulations were to be "sky blue mixture, pattern now worn, waistband three and a half inches wide, to button with two buttons in front; pockets in front, opening at top." The stripes for noncommis-

On the facing page:

113. *Officers of the Second U.S. Cavalry posed in the Black Hills as members of General George Crook's column in 1876. The garb worn by these officers reflects typical field attire of the mid-1870s. Represented are a sack coat, a double-breasted Civil War–vintage blouse, the 1872 regulation blouse, a canvas coat, and a miner's shirt. The man at the far right wears canvas-lined trousers. (Paul L. Hedren, National Archives)*

Below:

114. *Corporal Daniel Ryan, Company C, Seventh U.S. Cavalry, sports a double-breasted miner's shirt, a civilian hat, and a leather prairie belt. Although the Model 1873 Springfield carbine was regulation issue, the 1858 Remington percussion revolver may have been a personal weapon or a photographer's prop. (Little Bighorn Battlefield National Monument)*

sioned officers were to be made of facing cloth, rather than worsted lace, because it was more durable and cost less.[34] Initially, a very limited quantity of the new-pattern trousers was made and issued to units for trial at various eastern posts.[35] These experimental trousers had barely reached the troops when instructions were issued to Schuylkill Arsenal at Philadelphia to manufacture 15,600 pair of mounted trousers and 8,000 pair of foot trousers.[36] However, the 1872-pattern trousers, with their wide waistband and curved frog-mouth pockets, cost more to produce, at a time when the appropriation already was insufficient to meet the dictates of the revised uniform regulations. The higher-priced trousers attracted the attention of the secretary of war, who quickly amended the orders and directed that the 1861-pattern with side-seam pockets be continued.[37] The trousers were made from surplus kersey, on hand from the Civil War. With the exception of the inspector markings and dates, these trousers were indistinguishable from those made during the war. Thus, the "new" trousers were simply newly manufactured copies of the old style. However, they were made in five sizes, as called for in the 1872 regulations. This, at least, eased the problem of size shortages.

The troops were not so easily fooled. One suspicious officer wrote that the material was "the same as that issued before '73 when the new uniform was prepared though they cost the soldier $2.03 more per pair."[38] Had anyone given Military Storekeeper Rodgers's annual report for 1873 a close reading, it would have confirmed their suspicions. Rodgers determined that as of June 30, 1873, there was still enough old kersey on hand "to make all the trousers and capes for overcoats . . . required during the present year."[39]

Discrepancies also were reported from other sources. At Fort Randall, Dakota Territory, an officer from the Inspector General's Office noted, "The new Trousers received from Schuylkill Arsenal are not made according to regulations in regard to pockets and waistbands."[40] Not only the troops but also the army staff had been deceived.

Before long, many of the same complaints heard in previous years arose once again. The weight of the kersey used for trousers was reportedly "a source of much discomfort and resultingly many loud complaints during the hot months."[41] There were also objections about the un-uniform color, since it was common to see several different shades of sky blue in any company formation. The soldiers' greatest dissatisfaction with the pants, however, was their fit. A Twenty-first Infantry officer wrote: "The Trowsers are a source of annoyance, by being out of all proportion as regards length and circumference, being invariably too large around the waist and without any shape that would fit any ordinary man. The men always have to expend from $2. to $ 3. per pair, to have them 'Altered,' which is to make them entirely over again."[42]

Captain Edward G. Bush, Tenth Infantry, complained that the trousers were "too baggy in the seat"; he suggested that the cuffs be lined with canvas, "to give them shape."[43] The disproportionate sizing forced many soldiers to wear makeshift belts to support their pants, a "slovenly and injurious" practice that prompted at least one medical officer to suggest that the army begin issuing suspenders as part of the clothing allowance (fig. 117). Several more years passed before the army became that magnanimous.[44]

Above:

115. Buckskin leggings typical of those worn by some army officers for field service. (Hayes Otoupalik Collection)

On the facing page:

116. Private John B. McGuire, Jr., Company C, Seventh U.S. Cavalry, in regulation garrison uniform and under arms, ca. 1876. At the Battle of the Little Bighorn, McGuire was fortunate to be assigned to the packtrain guard. Most of the men of his company were killed with Custer. (Little Bighorn Battlefield National Monument)

117. Privates George Walker (left) and Timothy Donnelly (right), Seventh U.S. Cavalry, ca. 1875. Whereas Walker appears to wear a civilian shirt, Donnelly wears the 1874-pattern gray flannel shirt. Following a fairly common practice among enlisted men, Donnelly uses a homemade belt for his trousers. Note that neither man has cap insignia. Both men were killed in action at the Battle of the Little Bighorn. (Glen Swanson Collection)

Faced with such widespread discontent in the ranks, the Quartermaster Department adopted new standards for kersey on November 12, 1874. The new fabric was used in the manufacture of trousers beginning in 1875, but considering the slow turnover rate, it was some time before these new trousers reached the troops serving on the frontier.[45]

The gray flannel shirt, which the Quartermaster Department had conveniently overlooked two years before, became the focus of criticism about this same time. A Fourteenth Infantry officer described them as "a very poor article." He explained: "The texture is coarse, the seams so narrow that the shirt soon comes to pieces in washing, and they shrink badly. A large proportion of the enlisted men do not wear them at all, preferring to buy cassimere shirts for winter, and percale shirts for summer.[46]"

The most annoying of the problems with the gray shirt was its tendency to shrink drastically after a few washings. To economize, the wartime contractors did not preshrink the fabric, preferring instead to make the troops suffer the loss in yardage on their backs. As a result, the shirts became so small that a man's normal movements in them broke the seams and elbows. Likewise, the tails became so short that the men could barely tuck them inside trousers. Even the Woodhull report of 1868 had pointed up the tendency of the gray shirt to shrink to a length slightly below the navel, whereas it should have reached to the thighs. Faced with these shoddy gray pullovers, many soldiers opted to draw the old prewar white flannel shirts whenever possible.[47]

Reacting to the volley of complaints leveled at the regulation shirt, the Clothing Branch moved quickly to draw up specifications for a new shirt, which was adopted on August 5, 1874. The new shirt was made of a better-quality "Army standard gray shirting flannel," which, presumably, was preshrunk (fig. 118).[48]

Some line officers had suggested that shirts for enlisted men be made of "heavy dark-blue material, shrunk before making. Troops in hot climates [could] then march in their shirt sleeves and still be uniform in appearance."[49] Although the Quartermaster Department did not seriously consider these suggestions initially, circumstances in 1875 unexpectedly resulted in the production of such a shirt. In the wake of the problems caused by the war-surplus cloth, the Clothing Branch was casting an increasingly critical eye at the quality of materials used in making the new uniform items. On one occasion, when a large quantity of dark-blue blouse flannel was found unsuitable for its intended purpose, someone (likely the ever-efficient Captain Rodgers) decreed that it would be used, instead, for making shirts. No surviving example of this shirt is known, but Rodgers, in all likelihood, used the existing pattern for the 1874 gray shirt. By the summer of 1875, some ten thousand of these blue shirts had been produced and issued to the troops, who regarded them as "comfortable and convenient" for field service.[50] Unwittingly, the Clothing Branch had given the soldier something he liked a great deal and would demand more of in the future. Coincidentally, that decision had a far-reaching effect. It not only heralded a new look for the army, with the blue flannel shirt being adopted as regulation in 1881, but also served as the genesis for the world's popular image of the blue-shirted frontier soldier.[51]

Encouraged by the Quartermaster Department's responsiveness to their needs, the troops exercised their newfound influence on some of the less-obvious clothing items. Drawers, for instance, had been a long-standing source of irritation, literally. Troops in hot climates complained that the drawers were too heavy; those on the northern plains countered that the drawers were not

118. Pattern 1874 gray flannel shirt manufactured at Jeffersonville Depot during fiscal year 1875–76. (Smithsonian Institution)

heavy enough. Typical of the objections were those of Captain Augustus W. Corliss, Eighth Infantry, an old soldier and former enlisted man himself, who recommended, "Cotton cloth (*not cotton flannel*) drawers and shirts, for summer wear . . . would tend to remedy the evils of 'Eczema' (prickly heat) now a source of considerable annoyance."[52]

On the opposite end of the scale were the troops serving at Fort Totten, Dakota Territory. One officer there complained that January temperatures for 1875 averaged nineteen degrees below zero. Consequently, his men had to wear two shirts and two pair of drawers, in addition to their outer garments.[53]

The other major complaint about the drawers was their sizing. As one veteran officer of the Twentieth Infantry caustically observed: "The cut of the drawers is such that they can be worn with comfort only to the smallest user, they are too small in the seat. The contractors evidently working up to their general rule [of] the greatest number of the article from the least quantity of material."[54] The poor sizing and bad construction caused the drawers, like the shirts, to rip out long before they were worn out. Drawers also were part of the stock remaining from the Civil War; therefore, soldiers still were feeling the effects of the contractor deficiencies a decade later. An improved pattern was adopted on April 24, 1875 (fig. 119).[55]

"The stockings," recorded the Fort Craig surgeon, "are certainly the most inferior article of clothing issued to the soldier."[56] Reports from the field claimed they would last only about a month in garrison and not more than ten days on campaign. Few details are known except that they were, "woolen . . . generally miserable in texture."[57] Judged by the official Quartermaster Department photograph, they appear to have been dark in color and probably were the brown socks for which specifications finally were prepared in 1876. Just why these shoddy stockings were not improved during the general overhaul of clothing in 1872 is unknown, but by 1875 the protests were so numerous that Meigs was moved to take action. By this time, most soldiers were purchasing their own socks from the post traders rather than tolerate the issue ones. Meigs soon authorized the purchase of twenty-five thousand pairs of worsted stockings on the commercial market during fiscal year 1876.[58]

As for the overcoat, perhaps the main criticism was the variety of patterns that had resulted from the niggardly congressional appropriation for clothing. An officer writing from Fort Richardson, Texas, lamented: "The present issue is of different patterns, poor material, varying in color, and altogether fails to answer the purpose designed. The color of the coats, as presented by a Company, doing frontier duty, ranges from sky blue (a new coat) to a nondescript greenish yellow."[59] The problems with the different hues and quality of the old war-contract kersey thus continued to plague the army.

Troops on the northern plains complained that the blanket-lined overcoats introduced in 1871 still were not heavy enough to keep a man warm in sub-zero weather. At about the same time, the Quartermaster Department discovered that the supply of inferior blankets used to line these coats was almost exhausted. Faced with this new predicament, the Clothing Branch decided to substitute either dark-blue woolen cloth or sky-blue kersey, as available.[60] These circumstances soon led to yet another revision of the enlisted overcoat.

The troops also demanded warmer gloves or mittens. Numerous complaints were lodged against the woolen mittens, one officer going so far as to say, "If warmth is the object, the mittens now provided are a failure, they keep

119. *Responding to widespread complaints, the Quartermaster Department issued a new gray flannel shirt in 1874 and new-pattern drawers in 1875, both pictured here.* (U.S. Army Quartermaster Museum, courtesy Smithsonian Institution)

the hands of the men clean but serve no other purpose that I have discovered."[61]

Captain John G. Bourke, a member of General George Crook's staff, provided a detailed description of the winter clothing used by the command in the early phases of the 1876 Sioux War:

> For underwear, individual preferences were consulted, the general idea being to have at least two kinds of material used, principally merino and perforated buckskin; over these was placed a heavy blue flannel shirt, made double-breasted, and then a blouse, made also double-breasted, of Mission or Minnesota blanket, with large buttons, or a coat of Norway kid lined with heavy flannel. When the blizzards blew nothing in the world would keep out the cold but an overcoat of buffalo or bearskin or beaver, although for many the overcoats made in St. Paul of canvas, lined with the heaviest blanket, and strapped and belted tight about the waist, were pronounced sufficient. The head was protected by a cap of cloth, with fur border to pull down over the ears; a fur collar enclosed the neck and screened the mouth and nose from the keen blasts; and the hands were covered by woollen gloves and over-gauntlets of beaver or musk-rat fur.[62]

In the fall of 1876, Colonel Nelson A. Miles established a cantonment, later christened Fort Keogh, on the Yellowstone at the mouth of Tongue River. Miles announced his intention to prosecute an unrelenting campaign against the Sioux and Northern Cheyennes during the coming winter in an effort to break the power of the Indians. However, the troops needed clothing better adapted to field service on the northern plains in order to pursue the Indians into their winter haunts (fig. 120). Miles appealed to Meigs to supply the Fifth Infantry with buffalo overcoats. Although Meigs was willing to comply with Miles's request, he found that the Quartermaster Department had only three coats remaining from a small supply purchased in 1868–69.[63] There was little he could do until the Clothing Branch was able to procure a supply of robes and have them made up into coats. Allowing no delays in his plans, the aggressive Miles arranged to have the garrison at Fort Buford manufacture enough buffalo overcoats to outfit his command (fig. 121). These coats were to be "large sizes, long, coming below the knees, double breasted, and high rolling collar, such as can be turned up about the ears."[64]

Miles's Fifth Infantrymen further adapted themselves to winter campaigning in Montana by building on their experiences of two years earlier in the Texas Panhandle region. Both officers and soldiers fashioned extra-heavy under-

120. Colonel Nelson A. Miles and officers of the Fifth U.S. Infantry near the cantonment on Tongue River, Montana, January 1877. Miles's relentless campaign against the Sioux and Northern Cheyennes through the winter of 1876–77 led to the official adoption of specialized winter clothing. Second Lieutenant James W. Pope, third from the left, wears an enlisted man's pleated blouse. (National Archives)

121. Guard mount at Fort Keogh, Montana. The heavy buffalo coats proved to be more practical for garrison purposes than for field service. (Little Bighorn Battlefield National Monument)

clothing from army blankets. They also procured warm "buffalo moccasins," combining them with wrappings of burlap as a frost barrier.[65] Miles's surgeon, Dr. Henry R. Tilton, described the clothing he wore as protection against temperatures of forty degrees below zero:

> I wore two pair of woolen socks, buffalo mocasins and leggins [*sic*], and buffalo overshoes; 2 pr drawers, one of them buckskin; 2 pr pants, one made out of blanket; 5 shirts, one of them buckskin and one made out of blanket; a coat and buffalo overcoat; blanket cap, which would cover the face when necessary; a comforter; [and] buck-skin gloves inside of blanket lined buckskin mittens—and yet, on two days when marching in the face of a snow and wind storm, I felt as if there were no blood in my body.[66]

No doubt, Tilton's outfit was typical of those worn throughout the command. These harsh experiences and the makeshift garments devised by the troops influenced the Quartermaster Department to further develop specialized clothing to meet the needs of troops stationed on the western frontier (fig. 122).

In 1876–77 the Quartermaster Department attempted to respond to requests from troops in the field by procuring a small number of Canadian-made felt boots. These were issued experimentally to units serving at high altitudes on the northern plains. But, they failed to meet the needs of frontier troops, likely because they were suited to use in dry snow only. During a thaw they would become saturated with moisture.[67]

Many soldiers, like Seventh Infantryman Eugene Geant, a member of Colonel John Gibbon's 1876 expedition into the Yellowstone country, resorted to the time-honored practice of greasing their shoes. "The worst is," Geant observed, "the snow will penetrate through the leather of the shoes, and the shoes are too

low, allowing the snow to get in at the top. A pair of leggins [*sic*] 'come in handy just now.'"[68]

The 1872-pattern shoes and boots contributed to the soldier's misery in another way. Doctor Tilton recorded: "The cable screwed shoes would have a deposit of frost around each piece of metal, on the inside of the sole, every cold morning. Many of the boots and shoes would be coated with a cake of ice inside when they were not dried out in the night."[69]

For a proper evaluation of the clothing authorized under the 1872 regulations, General Orders No. 6 of 1875 requested that all commanding officers submit reports on the suitability of clothing under actual use. After these reports were compiled, army headquarters promulgated Special Orders No. 264, dated December 27, 1875, which directed a board of officers to meet at Philadelphia to make further recommendations in the clothing. Through the field reports, the officers and enlisted personnel of the army once again directly influenced additions and refinements to uniforms and other clothing. Over the next two years many of their suggestions were manifested in the new or improved articles described below.

POST-1872 ALTERATIONS AND ADDITIONS TO THE AUTHORIZED UNIFORM

Campaign Hat, Pattern 1876

Specifications for a new hat to replace the hated folding campaign hat were adopted on June 14, 1876. The new hat was made of black "XXX" wool with a crown 6 inches high in the center and 5½ inches deep front and rear (for size 7⅛, other sizes varying 1/16 inch per size). In each side of the crown was a brass "Bracher's Pattern Ventilator." These vents measured approximately ½-inch in diameter, and each had a small revolving fan mounted on an axis (fig. 123). The

122. *These soldiers of the Fifth U.S. Infantry, on an ice-cutting detail at Fort Keogh, Montana Territory, display a variety of winter fatigue clothing. Several of the men wear their blouses tucked into their trousers for extra warmth. Most of them wear regulation muskrat caps, although some appear to wear knit or canvas civilian caps. Virtually all of these soldiers wear the arctic overshoes.* (Little Bighorn Battlefield National Monument)

idea was to permit an air flow through the vent, thus preventing heat buildup in the crown while keeping out rain.[70]

The brim measured 2½ inches front and rear and 2⅝ inches on the sides. The edges were turned ⅜ inch on the upper side and stitched down with two rows of black stitching, which usually faded to an olive or drab shade.

The base of the crown was trimmed with eight-ligne black hatter's ribbon, machine-stitched in place, with a bow on the left side. The sweat was made of brown japanned leather, turned along the top edge, 1¾ inches wide. The specimens examined revealed the maker's name imprinted in silver in the top of the crown.

The Quartermaster Department contracted with John T. Waring & Co. to produce the initial supply of fifteen thousand of these hats. However, Meigs postponed their issue until April 1877 in order to use up some of the remaining stock of the folding campaign hat. Burdened with a large stock of the 1872 hats that few soldiers could be induced to draw, Meigs eventually found a way to salvage part of the investment. He negotiated a contract to have the brims cut down and the crowns reblocked to simulate the 1876 campaign hat. This cosmetic surgery was accomplished at a cost of fifteen cents per hat. The soldiers who drew these hats quickly discovered the ruse because the material was, of course, of the same poor quality that had led to the quick demise of the folding hat in the first place. In a final, desperate act to rid the army of the folding hats, Meigs generously offered to sell these counterfeits to the officers at the current price of a regulation model. Finding few officers so gullible, he capitulated and ordered the remaining hats, both altered and unaltered, to be issued to the inmates at Fort Leavenworth Military Prison.[71]

The 1876 hat corrected most of the faults found with the folding hat. Just why the army stuck with the black color, however, remains a mystery. Wide-ranging opinion from the field clearly favored a lighter color that would better reflect solar heat. Nevertheless, the idea would not materialize until the adoption of a regulation drab-colored campaign hat in 1884.[72]

The branch-colored worsted cords, originally intended for use with the 1858 hat, remained an item of the clothing allowance throughout the 1870s (fig. 124). The extent of their use, however, is reflected in the annual statement of articles issued for the year ending June 30, 1877. Deputy Quartermaster General J. D. Bingham reported that the army had no less than 444,000 cords on hand at the first of the fiscal year but that only 20 were issued during the following twelve months.[73]

Above:

123. Campaign hat, 1876. Reflective of civilian hats of the period, this hat had a narrow brim with a stitched edge to add a degree of stiffness. Bracher's-patent ventilators released heat from the crown while keeping out rain. (Smithsonian Institution)

On the facing page:

124. Sergeant Charles N. Loynes, Seventh U.S. Infantry, bedecked his 1876 campaign hat with full insignia and hat cord, a rare occurrence. Loynes was a veteran of the Battle of the Big Hole, August 9, 1877. (Historical Photograph Collections, Washington State University Libraries)

Officers' Fatigue Blouse, Pattern 1875

Continuing a trend toward more practical uniforms, the officer corps adopted a simpler-style blouse, similar in outward appearance to that of the enlisted men. The new blouse omitted the mohair braid on the front and the cuffs, since it tended to snag on brush in the field, as well as the slashes at the sides.[74] These blouses generally were made of finer woolen broadcloth or serge than the flannel used for enlisted men's blouses. The sateen or silk serge linings ranged in color from dark green to black, and occasionally even burgundy. Likewise, most of these tailor-made blouses exhibited double rows of stitching around the outer edges of the collar, along the edges of the front opening, and at the wrists.

Fatigue Blouse, Pattern 1874

The 1874 fatigue blouse was not too different in outward appearance from the old 1858 sack coat. The principal exceptions were that it had five brass eagle buttons (Pattern 1855) closing the front, rather than four, and the blouse was more closely fitted to the body (fig. 125). The flannel used for its construction initially was, in fact, leftover Civil War blouse material.[75]

The improved design consisted of a four-piece body, two of which were in the back rather than the one-piece back used for most of the sack coats. The sleeves were one piece, the seam running along the back of the arm, but were cut somewhat smaller in circumference than those of the sack coat. Whereas the sack coat had very pronounced rounded corners at the bottom of the front opening, the 1874 blouse had rounded corners of a distinctively smaller radius.

The 1874 blouse was produced in both lined and unlined versions. The specifications for lining called for "gray twilled mixed flannel" for the body and unbleached muslin for the sleeves.[76] The actual color of this material was a rather light greenish-gray hue. Inside the breast were two slash pockets without facings, let into the lining, one on either side. Branch-colored worsted cord trim, approximately ⅛-inch in diameter, was sewn along the outer edge of the collar (fig. 126). The cuffs had an inverted "V" of the same cord, with one vest-size eagle button located at the juncture of the trim and the sleeve seam.

125. *Pattern 1874 fatigue blouse.* (Smithsonian Institution)

Trousers, Pattern 1876

The basic deficiencies of the 1861-pattern trousers and persistent complaints about them, despite the higher-quality kersey, prompted the Clothing Branch to make another attempt to improve the fit and quality of trousers. On November 30, 1874, Captain Rodgers at Philadelphia Depot submitted two samples that incorporated some of the features originally in the stillborn 1872 trousers. Rodgers's model trousers had the front top-opening pockets as earlier envisioned. To offset the cost of the better pockets, and to make the trousers fit more comfortably, Rodgers recommended that they be made without a waistband. His superior, Colonel L. C. Easton, endorsed the new pattern and forwarded the samples to the quartermaster general's office for approval. Early in the next year, Meigs authorized the manufacture and issue of five hundred pairs for trial.[77]

The 1876 Uniform Board considered the comments received from the field and urged that the new trousers, with a few refinements, be adopted. In addition to the frog-mouth pockets and no waistband, the trousers were to have an

126. *Sergeant Benjamin C. Criswell, who served in B Company, Seventh U.S. Cavalry, from 1870 to 1878. In this view, probably taken about 1875– 76, Criswell wears a tailor-made version of the 1874 blouse. It is distinguished by a short, squared collar and double-row stitching along the front opening. Note that he has added officers' buttons, a not-uncommon practice among NCOs. The chevrons appear to be the pre-1872 style.* (Little Bighorn Battlefield National Monument)

adjustment strap and buckle on the back, a slight spring, or flare, at the cuffs, and a watch pocket. Revised specifications incorporating these changes were adopted on March 25, 1876.[78]

Pattern 1876 trousers were made of the improved sky-blue kersey adopted two years earlier. It was of medium shade and had a distinctive twill weave. Trousers for mounted men had an additional oval-shaped layer of kersey, termed a "saddle piece," which covered the seat area and extended down the insides of the legs.

The new trousers, as suggested by Rodgers, had no waistband and there was a pronounced rise at the rear to fit the small of the back (fig. 127). Around the waist were six tin four-hole buttons, $^{11}/_{16}$-inch in diameter, for suspenders, two pairs of buttons at each side and one pair at the rear. A single button of the same type fastened the waist. The fly had five smaller tin buttons, $^{17}/_{32}$-inch in diame-

Left:
127. Pattern 1876 trousers, front.

Right:
*128. Rear view of 1876 trousers showing
high waist and belted back.*

On the facing page:
*129. Company of the Fifth U.S. Infan-
try in camp in Montana, 1878. Photograph by Stanley J. Morrow. (Montana
Historical Society)*

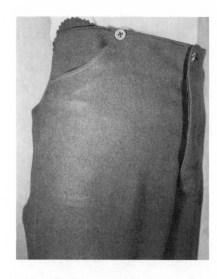
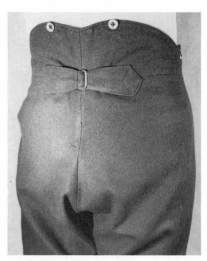

ter. Two pairs of small tinned buttons were sewn inside the cuff openings, a pair astraddle each seam, for attaching the cloth instep straps. The straps were intended to prevent the trousers legs from riding out of the boots, but it is doubtful that many cavalry soldiers used them. Although the straps were mentioned in the specifications, no dimensions were given.

The trousers had two curved, open-top pockets on the front, but there were no rear pockets. A watch pocket was let into the top edge of the waist above the right front pocket. It had a backing of kersey extending from slightly above the rear edge of the opening into the pocket to facilitate insertion of the watch. On the rear of the pants, below the edge of the waist, was a cloth belt and double-pronged brass buckle for adjusting the fit (fig. 128). The trousers were made in five sizes, with the waists ranging from thirty-two to forty-two.[79]

In recommending the cuffs have a "spring," the board acknowledged a fashion trend in civilian garments of the period. The slightly flared bottoms allowed for a less full cut in the leg, yet the trousers leg would fall smoothly over the shoe (fig. 129). Although the functional purpose was the same as the split-cuff formerly used, the spring-bottom was neater in appearance.

The waist was lined with 8-ounce natural cotton duck to provide a degree of stiffness or body to the pants. The pockets were made of like material. A circular inspection stamp, bearing the name of the depot and the fiscal year, was inked on the waist lining at the rear.

Shirt, Pattern 1874

This pullover shirt, adopted on August 5, 1874, was made entirely of gray flannel with a two-piece body.[80] A plait, 2 inches by 11 inches, covered the breast placket. The shirt front closed with three $^{17}/_{32}$-inch-diameter tinned-iron buttons, two on the plait and one at the neck, with a second one spaced horizontally on the neck band for adjustment. The shirt also had a short rollover collar and separately applied sleeve cuffs, each having a single button. The tail was made considerably longer than that of the Civil War shirt, extending nearly to midthigh, but the drop-shoulder cut was retained. As a concession to the troops stationed in hot climates, the army adopted a thinner shirting flannel in 1876 and thereafter made shirts in two weights.[81]

130. *First sergeant's overcoat chevron, 1876. Dark-blue chevrons were worn by infantry noncommissioned officers to contrast with the sky-blue kersey of the coats. The chain stitching, as well as the diamond for a first sergeant, was white.*

Overcoat, Pattern 1876

Military Storekeeper John F. Rodgers submitted a pattern for a new coat meeting the 1872 regulations. Its external appearance was quite similar to the 1861 mounted greatcoat except that it was made of 1874-specification sky-blue kersey. The body was made double-breasted, with five large regulation eagle buttons, so that it could be buttoned from either side. It had a wide falling collar 5 inches deep. The single unlined cape, buttoning with eight to ten vest-size eagle buttons (depending on size), reached to the ends of the sleeves. An improvement was the larger circumference of the sleeves, making it easier to put the coat on over other garments. Like the cuffs of the 1861 overcoat, those for the 1876 coat were made of a double thickness of material about 5 inches deep and were intended to be worn turned up, unless needed to keep the hands warm. The overcoat also had a belt on the back, fastening with two large eagle buttons. The body was lined with dark-blue twilled flannel extending down to the top of the slit in the skirt. There were two inside breast pockets opening horizontally.[82]

Since the army followed its usual practice of using up existing stocks of old-pattern goods first, the 1876 overcoat actually was not produced until the fiscal year beginning July 1, 1878. Even then, the 1861-pattern coats and the variations thereof continued to be forced on the troops, regardless of their objections. During the first year of manufacture, only larger sizes of the new coats were made to replace depleted supplies.[83]

Chevrons

The 1872 uniform regulations called for the chevrons of noncommissioned officers to be worn on the dress coat and the overcoat, but the soldier's most common garment, the blouse, apparently was overlooked. Nevertheless, the noncoms insisted on wearing their chevrons on their blouses, regardless of the regulations. Noting this universal practice, the army acquiesced by issuing General Orders No. 21 on March 20, 1876, which officially authorized chevrons to be worn on blouses.

The same order acknowledged that the infantry's sky-blue chevrons were hardly distinguishable when worn on the kersey overcoat, an obvious oversight by the 1872 Uniform Board. Thus, a new chevron of contrasting dark-blue cloth with stripes delineated by white chain-stitching was mandated for use specifically on the overcoat. The diamond on the chevron for first sergeants was fashioned of white facing cloth (fig. 130). These chevrons were worn above the elbow on both sleeves. The fact that the overcoat cape covered the chevrons was an oversight not rectified until 1883.[84]

Forage Cap Covers, Pattern 1872

Cap covers proved to be a needless item, probably because the forage cap itself offered such poor protection from rain. When men had to be out in a downpour, they universally wore the campaign hat to shed water away from their necks. Since there were few requisitions for cap covers, the quartermaster general dropped them from the supply table in 1877.[85]

Shoes and Boots, Pattern 1876

Both shoes and boots continued to be made with double brass-screwed soles (fig. 131). Some of the complaints from the field centered on the screws, which occasionally worked their way through the insole. On investigation, the Quartermaster Department discovered that the operators of the screw-making machines sometimes ran them too fast, resulting in screws that were cut off improperly. Once this was corrected, most of the complaints subsided. Soldiers also criticized the screws because they conducted heat and cold directly to the wearer's foot. Eventually, the army abandoned the concept of screwed soles and returned to hand-sewn ones.[86]

The only improvement made in the 1876-pattern shoe was a longer tongue, a feature requested by the troops to better prevent sand from entering the shoe. Thus, the tongue was lengthened to extend about one-half inch above the top of the shoe.

The term *bootee,* heretofore applied to infantry shoes, had led to much confusion and numerous errors in filling requisitions. To correct the situation, the army officially changed the nomenclature early in 1875.[87] Thereafter, infantrymen were issued shoes, rather than bootees.

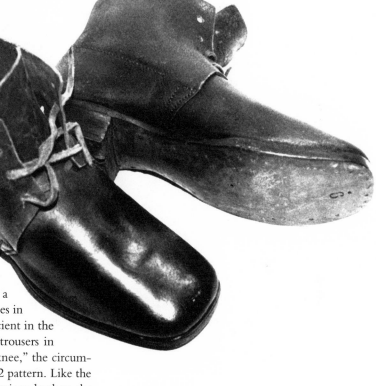

131. Pattern 1876 shoes. These had brass-screwed soles and slightly longer tongues than preceding styles.

During 1873 it came to the attention of army headquarters, probably via the eagle-eyed Meigs, that infantrymen frequently drew or purchased boots rather than shoes. Some soldiers obtained issue boots to wear as more suitable footwear for mud and snow; others simply preferred them to shoes for general wear. However, an order promulgated that year flatly prohibited foot troops from receiving issue boots, which were to be reserved for the cavalry.[88] As a result, many soldiers of both branches bought commercially made boots, "to gratify their personal pride in having a more comely boot or shoe."[89]

The subject of cavalry boots was addressed separately by the 1876 Uniform Board. The troops requested and received a taller boot, having a leg 15½ inches high in front and 14 inches in back. Since there were complaints that the boots were "deficient in the size of the legs, too narrow to permit the retention of the trousers in them and so short as to permit the rain to soak in from the knee," the circumference of the leg was made somewhat larger than in the 1872 pattern. Like the earlier boots, the new ones were made of black South American leather; the dressed side of the leather, which was frequently too stiff to conform well to the foot, was turned outermost.[90]

Stockings, Pattern 1876

Adopted on May 31, 1876, these socks were made of brown woolen yarn with fashioned toes and heels. They were produced on a commercial knitting machine and were furnished in three sizes: 10, 10½, and 11. The leg for all three sizes measured 14 inches long.[91]

Stockings, Pattern 1877

These all-wool stockings, adopted on June 4, 1877, in lieu of the worsted stockings, were medium gray in color with white toes. The weave of the heels

ran parallel with that of the leg and at nearly right angles to that of the foot (fig. 132). The legs were 14 inches tall, and the feet were to be made in sizes 9½, 10½, and 11½. The size was stamped in ink on the toe of each sock.[92]

Arctic Overshoes, Pattern 1876

The buffalo "snow excluders" were effective in cold climates and dry snow when used with several pairs of socks and a layer of burlap as a frost guard. However, they were all but worthless in wet snow, slush, and mud. Once they became wet, the moccasins were difficult to dry and in that condition posed a serious hazard to the men's feet. As a result, the army adopted a new overshoe on May 5, 1876.

The arctic overshoe was made with a vulcanized rubber sole, with a foxing of the same material about 1 inch deep around the sides (fig. 133). On the toe was a scalloped piece about 2 inches long at the center. The upper was made of "black tweed waterproof" material lined with gray felt. The average height of the boot was about 7½ inches from the heel to the top. The front was joined to the quarter on each side by a gore of the same material, thus forming a waterproof expansion joint that made the boot easier to slip on. A twilled cloth strap and a black japanned buckle were used to fasten the front over the foot.[93]

Blanket, Pattern 1873

The specifications for blankets adopted on August 15, 1873, have not been located. It is presumed these described the "California" blanket adopted by the army the previous year (fig. 134).

Blanket, Pattern 1876

This gray woolen blanket was the same as the pattern of 1873 except that the end stripes and the "U.S." were applied in indigo blue rather than black. The letters were either stamped on or woven into the blanket, at the preference of the manufacturer. The specifications called for the blanket to measure 66 inches by 84 inches and to weigh five pounds.[94]

One example of this blanket measured 63½ inches by 79½ inches, probably having shrunk somewhat through washing. The letters "U.S.," 3⅝ inches high, were rather crudely stenciled in the center, parallel with the ends. The stripes, one across each end, measured 2⅜ inches wide and were spaced 5 inches from the ends.

The color of another specimen was faded to a butternut hue. The 2¾-inch-wide end stripes had assumed a shade close to royal blue. The badly faded letters, 3½ inches high, were stenciled on one side only, parallel with the width. This blanket measured 68½ inches by 78½ inches.

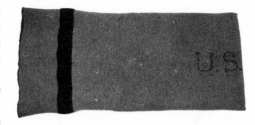

Above:
134. Gray woolen army blanket, 1873.

Below:
135. Army muskrat fur cap.

Winter Clothing

Sealskin Cap and Gloves, Pattern 1876.   These items were recommended by the 1876 Uniform Board, and specifications were adopted on May 23, 1876. However, no surviving examples are known, so only the barest description offered in the quartermaster general's report remains: "Caps: To be of the 'wool seal' skin, with ear-flaps, cape, and visor, according to pattern. Lining of Turkey-red chintz, padded with cotton wadding. Gloves: To be made of the 'wool seal' skin, according to pattern. Gauntlets to be at least five inches deep and of sufficient fullness to admit cuff of dress coat or blouse."[95]

It is presumed that the external appearance of these caps did not differ greatly from that of the muskrat variety described below. The clothing bureau contracted with Edmund R. Lyon of Philadelphia on June 22, 1876, to produce 2,000 such caps. The bureau also contracted for a similar quantity of sealskin gloves. During fiscal year 1877 the army bought an additional 6,158 caps and 5,437 pairs of gloves. But, field experience with these new items soon proved that sealskin was not strong enough for military purposes. Moreover, it became brittle after being wet and then dried.[96]

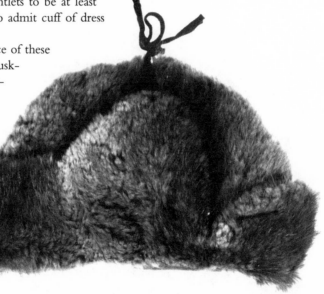

Muskrat Caps, Pattern 1878.   Muskrat was selected as a superior skin for making winter caps and gloves and was used exclusively in their manufacture beginning in 1878.[97]

The cap was made with the fur side outermost and had an inside depth of about 6 inches (fig. 135). It was lined with brown cotton chintz or silesia, with cotton wadding for insulation layered between the lining and the outer skin. This was machine-stitched with two widely spaced concentric lines. On the front was a visor, measuring about 2¼ inches deep, that folded up against the body of the cap.

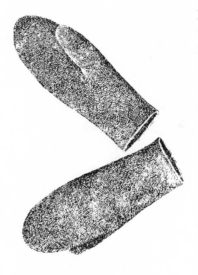

The cap was provided with folding ear flaps about 4½ inches deep, joined by a neck cape 2 inches deep. A tie string made of black twill tape, approximately ½ inch by 16 inches, was sewn into the end of each flap. The ear flaps could be worn up, with the strings tied over the head, or down and tied under the chin.[98]

Muskrat Gauntlet Gloves, Pattern 1878.   The muskrat gauntlets had separated fingers and a thumb, the palms being lined with grayish sheepskin (fig. 136). The specifications of March 12, 1879, called for each glove to have a gauntlet at least 5 inches deep and wide enough to admit the coat sleeve. However, a regulation specimen examined had gauntlets only about 4 inches deep. Whereas the cuffs were lined with either red or dark-blue flannel, the hands had lining of closely cropped natural lamb's fleece.[99]

Woolen Mittens, Pattern 1873.   Circular No. 8, 1875, noted that these mittens were originally accepted as standard effective July 3, 1873. Because no specimen was available for examination, the specifications adopted on May 31, 1876, provide the only description: "To be made of pure gray woolen yarn, doubled and twisted; thumb and forefinger formed. To be of three sizes, viz: 10, 11, and 12 inches in length." The specification drawing shows them to be a simple mitten with a straight, rather than a gathered, wrist (fig. 137).[100]

Buffalo Overcoat.   Although no specifications for this coat have been found, it may be tentatively designated as the pattern of 1877, that being the first year buffalo coats were purchased by the Quartermaster Department.[101]

The outer shell of this coat was made from a winter hide, hair side outermost, and extended to the wearer's calves (fig. 138). Although the pattern of the coat did not differ greatly from civilian styles of the period, it did have some diagnostic features.

The double-breasted front closed with five black hard-rubber buttons measuring 1¾₆ inches in diameter. These buttons had a plain concave face with four holes and were marked on the reverse "Goodyear I. R. [India Rubber] Co. Pat. 1851." They fastened to loops made either of cable-twist cotton cord or of black mohair braid about 2 inches long.

The collar measured fully 8 inches deep at the center. Below it and on either side of the front opening were lapels measuring about 6 inches wide at their points. At the front opening, on the underside of the collar, were two additional buttons, ⅞ inch in diameter, to be used for fastening the turned-up collar by means of a 3½-inch loop attached to the left side.

The rear of the skirt was slit up the midline for a distance of 24 inches. It could be fastened shut, for dismounted activities such as guard duty, with two ⅞-inch buttons spaced 4 inches and 11 inches, respectively, from the bottom. Or it could be opened for ease of marching or riding.

The types of body linings varied, for no discernible reason. Whereas commercially made coats usually were lined with black or dark-green cotton sateen, often quilted, army coats were lined in either dark-blue twilled flannel or drab-colored cotton drill. Those with drill probably date from the 1880s, since they frequently bear stenciled unit markings on the linings. The sleeves were lined either with corset jeans, a natural-colored cotton material with a soft, smooth finish, or with drab cotton drill.

The coat had two slash pockets located at the waist. The mouths of the pockets were placed at an angle and measured about 7 inches wide. The pockets themselves were made of dark-blue flannel.

Buffalo coats were company property and were not issued to the men as part of their clothing allowance. They were sent only to northern posts, where they were kept boxed in company store-rooms during warm seasons, and were issued to the men only in winter.

138. *Buffalo overcoat provided to soldiers serving on the northern plains.* (John A. Doerner Collection)

New Schemes for Inflicting Something Wonderful on the Soldier

Equipment, 1874

THE 1872 EQUIPMENTS were in the hands of the troops hardly long enough to give them a fair trial when reports from the field clearly indicated that they were not meeting the army's expectations. The Ordnance Department still failed to recognize that even though the theory of weight distribution was sound enough, conditions on the western frontier were not comparable to those in Europe, or in the eastern United States for that matter. Frontier regulars, of necessity, did most of their campaigning across vast expanses of rugged terrain, where they seldom enjoyed the luxury of anything that might be termed a road. Practicality and sheer survival dictated that soldiers carry only the bare essentials if they were to remain an effective fighting force against the highly mobile Indians of the trans-Mississippi West. Officially, the U.S. Army seemed bent on forcing the soldier to carry a load of field equipment that was both unnecessary and unwanted by the soldier.

The brace-yoke concept proved to be an utter failure, for both cavalry and infantry troops. Cavalrymen lodged bitter complaints that the yoke constricted the clothing on hot days and that the motion of the horse caused the yokes to chafe the shoulders "to such an extent, in many instances, that they cannot be worn at all."[1] Echoing the opinions of many other cavalry officers, Captain Moses Harris, First Cavalry, pointed out that the yoke "only constricts a man's movements and does not support the weight of the equipments." Other officers pointed out that the weight of the carbine on the integral sling produced a most uncomfortable traction to the left shoulder and caused the waist belt to pull up unless it was cinched tightly. Tightening the belt around the abdomen, of course, nullified the basic purpose of the shoulder braces. Clearly, most cavalrymen wanted to return to the old-style separate sling. A Fourth Cavalry officer simply dismissed the brace as "a useless expense to the government" and strongly recommended that it be abolished, for mounted troops anyway.[2]

Although a few infantry officers endorsed the brace system, probably because their men had not used it in the field for any length of time if at all, most disliked it. Just the appearance of a soldier in the yoke system, according to one Twelfth Infantry captain, made him "look like a well-packed mule"; the captain added that his men never wore the equipments except when ordered to do so. Another officer claimed his men were "rendered completely helpless" in the outfit. When Company I, Seventeenth Infantry, embarked on the Black Hills Expedition in the summer of 1874, the men wore "this simple but evil contrivance," as the post surgeon described it. Within the first eight miles of the march, he reported, nearly the entire company was incapacitated. The other infantry company on the expedition, outfitted in the usual "light marching order," had only three men fall out in the same distance.[3]

The 1872 infantry equipments were an arguable improvement over the poorly designed 1859 double-bag knapsack, but the brace did have the advantage of not constricting circulation into the arms. Additionally, unlike a regular knapsack, it placed the weight of the valise near a man's center of gravity, rather than high on his back. However, when both the overcoat and the blanket were packed in the prescribed fashion, their weight tended to have the same effect. Significantly, the concept failed to consider that the weight and encumbrance of the equipments themselves, without their contents, posed a handicap to the doughboy. A Twentieth Infantry officer reported from Fort Totten, Dakota Territory: "The Brace Yoke Style of Knapsack meets with no favour. The men find it too complicated—too many straps and buckles—it cannot be made to rest high up on the shoulders."[4]

Conversely, the blanket roll, preferred by most foot troops during and after the war, was made up of the essential items themselves, with no additional weight imposed by any sort of knapsack or harness. The roll was relatively comfortable to carry on long marches, was easy to throw off at rest halts, and was quickly made up without the complex folding of the blanket and placement of the other items in the precise order to fit in or fasten on the devices designed by the Ordnance Department.

Troops in the field gave the new 1872 cotton-duck equipments a mixed review. Most infantrymen found the valise-knapsack too heavy and cumbersome. Moreover, it rode too low on the back, causing the weight to pull uncomfortably on the shoulders. The haversack, on the other hand, was generally liked by doughboys who had used it in the field for periods of up to several months. Their only recommendations were that it be provided with an improved sling adjustment and a better means for waterproofing the flap.

The men also rejected both patterns of the Hagner cartridge pouch for anything other than parade-ground use. The principal disadvantage was the difficulty the soldiers had in extracting the ammunition. Since the pouches were located on the front of the body, they were almost impossible to access when the soldier took either the kneeling or the prone position, the two positions encouraged by the breechloader and Emory Upton's new tactics. The No. 2 pouch, though somewhat smaller than the No. 1, made it especially difficult to withdraw the cartridges because the three rows of loops were so close together. One company commander reported that his men, when anticipating action, avoided the problem by transferring their cartridges from the pouches to their pants pockets.[5]

The Dyer pouch, shaped much like a pocket, enjoyed rather widespread popularity for field use among cavalrymen. Cartridges were carried loose in the pouch, rather than being held in loops, thus permitting the breechloader to be fired fairly rapidly. One soldier went so far as to state: "For continuous rapid firing . . . there is nothing surpassing the pouch. . . . [A]ny soldier who has been in action once with a pouch, will not be without it if he can buy, borrow, or steal it."[6] In fact, of thirty-nine cavalry company officers surveyed, twenty-six favored the Dyer pouch for field service, compared with nine voting for the thimble belt.[7] Just why the Dyer pouch would not have served the infantry's needs as well is not apparent, nor was it ever officially suggested. Nevertheless, an examination of the 1875 field reports shows that on the whole, troops serving on the frontier still overwhelmingly preferred the "field" or "prairie" cartridge belt for active campaigning. Several extant examples of these belts are described at the end of this chapter.

Another component of the cavalry outfit that failed the field tests was the holster. "The swivel frog pistol holster," complained one Fourth Cavalry officer, "is unsafe travelling faster than the ordinary gait the holster revolves, becomes unbuttoned and the pistol lost. Four pistols have been lost [in his company] since the issue of this holster."[8] This is only one example of many such objections made about the new Hoffman attachment.

An item common to both the cavalry and the infantry was the 1872 meat can, and neither horse nor foot soldiers had anything positive to say about it. Typical of the comments are those of Captain William McC. Netterville: "The Meat Can I consider worthless for the reason that unless a man has time to cut all the meat off the bone that would be issued and carefully pack it in the can he could not carry meat enough to last him a day. They are of no use to boil coffee nor to use as a drinking cup and besides they are continually in the way, interfering with the free use of the left hand and arm."[9] For obvious reasons, most men much preferred the regular quart-size drinking cup to the long, narrow lid of the meat can. The army's universal dissatisfaction with the meat can caused the Ordnance Department to reconsider the question of a ration container, with the intent of designing something better.

By the fall of 1873 Chief of Ordnance A. B. Dyer, already receiving some feedback on the trial equipments, concluded that the time was right to formally evaluate those for cavalry. He therefore recommended to the secretary of war that another board, comprising both cavalry and ordnance officers, be convened for that purpose at some point west of the Mississippi. That Dyer made a point of stipulating the meeting be held at a western location was significant. His insistence on this point signaled that troops stationed on the frontier were now influencing army equipment development, in addition to clothing design, to a much greater degree than before. Since, in fact, all of the cavalry was then posted in the trans-Mississippi, we see for the first time a turning of the army's attention away from the European scene. The groundwork was being laid for the future design of military equipage for decades to come, design based on the American frontier experience.

The board, ordered to meet early in January 1874, was first slated to assemble at Fort Riley, Kansas. But, the location was changed to Fort Leavenworth, probably because of the production facilities and expertise offered at Leavenworth Arsenal. Once there, the board approached its task by examining examples of the various items and sharing opinions offered in communications sent from the field. This preliminary survey afforded the members the opportunity to become more familiar with the technical aspects of the equipment and to evaluate it firsthand, based on the experience of other officers.

Field reports concerning the brace yoke were nearly all negative. Soldiers and officers alike saw no need for a cavalryman to wear the suspenders, since the perceived weight of his accoutrements was borne by the horse, not the man. Therefore, the brace was disposed of quickly by a unanimous vote against its adoption and a subsequent recommendation to retain the old 1855-pattern carbine sling, which nearly everyone had continued to use anyway.

The board recommended a somewhat modified saber belt. With the deletion of the brace, the brass loops on either side of the plate could be omitted, as well as the sliding loops on the rear of the belt. The 1872 belt plate and the saber slings were retained in their original form, but the method of attaching the slings was changed. Although a clear majority of the surveyed officers favored the Stuart sling, the board compromised by recommending a belt with two sliding brass loops and separate slings. This permitted the soldier to detach the saber easily and, if desired, hang it by the slings from the rings on the saddle. Additionally, the slides allowed the trooper to adjust the position of the separate slings on his belt, thereby having the advantages of both the 1872 belt and the Stuart sling.

The adoption of the Model 1873 Colt single-action army revolver led the board to endorse a modified holster, which omitted the full flap and substituted a wide strap to secure the pistol. The new revolver, using metallic ammunition, obviated the need for a flap, the purpose of which was to protect a percussion weapon from rain. The 1874-pattern holster also lacked the pipe for holding the pistol-cleaning rod, and the Hoffman swivel attachment was modified to restrict movement of the holster to an arc of forty-five degrees.

As has been stated, the Hagner pouches found few advocates in the mounted service, whereas both the Dyer pouch and the thimble belt had strong support for field use. Again, the board came up with a compromise, recognizing the advantages of both the pouch and the cartridge belt. The popular Dyer-pattern pouch was redesigned to be slightly smaller but retained the same basic shape as the 1872 version. The lower ends of the belt loops were shortened to just clear the two-inch belt and were riveted to the back of the pouch rather than to the gusset.

To supplement the forty rounds of carbine ammunition, the board recommended the issue of carbine cartridge "loops" designed by Colonel William B. Hazen, Sixth Infantry. Each set consisted of a double row of leather loops, twenty in all, sewn to a central strip of leather. Two sets of loops were to be issued to each man for campaign service, the loops sliding onto the saber belt to convert it to an ersatz cartridge belt. These units, along with the Dyer pouch, provided each trooper the capability of carrying eighty rounds of carbine ammunition. As appealing as this may have seemed in theory, most troopers, being small or at least slim men, did not have waists large enough to permit all of these items (along with the holster and the pistol cartridge pouch) to be worn at the same time. Thus, the physical characteristics of the men largely negated any potential advantages.

The board urged adoption of a smaller version of the Dyer pouch for carrying the revolver ammunition. This pouch lacked the screwdriver compartment on the front but was otherwise nearly identical in construction to its larger brother.

The board decided that the smooth-finished brass spurs and the wider straps adopted in 1872 needed no further improvements. Likewise, the members found the saber knot functional enough, but they suggested an additional sliding loop, presumably so that one loop could be snugged up to the saber guard and the other used to tighten the strap against the trooper's wrist.

The cavalry board completed its work early in May 1874. All of the findings were summarized in a list of detailed resolutions that were subsequently forwarded to army headquarters for approval. Neither Dyer nor General of the Army Sherman had any reluctance in ratifying the final recommendations, but the two men agreed that none of the new equipment should be issued until like articles of the old patterns were exhausted. The secretary of war, concurring in this restriction, approved the new-pattern accoutrements on May 20, 1874.[10] Ironically, the aging Dyer died on the same day.

The restrictions on the issue of the 1874 equipments, consequently, gave little urgency to their manufacture. And, diminished military appropriations, an effect of the financial panic of 1873, further delayed fabrication of the new equipment. Data concerning the production of the 1874 cavalry accoutrements are sketchy at best. That a few of the items were produced immediately is suggested by the newly appointed Chief of Ordnance S. V. Benet's June 17, 1874, order directing Watervliet Arsenal to make "2,000 wool lined carbine cartridge pouches 'to conform strictly to the recommendations of the Board on Cavalry Outfit and drawings herewith sent'" (fig. 139). Captain Clifton Comly, commanding San Antonio Arsenal, had specifically requested these pouches for issue to the Fourth and Tenth cavalry regiments then stationed in Texas.[11]

There were, of course, thousands of Pattern 1863 holsters in storage, in addition to the 1872 holsters still on hand at arsenals and in the hands of troops. Nevertheless, some 1874 holsters were made, as indicated by official correspondence and extant examples, but their numbers were limited.[12] Another equally important factor effecting the short life of the 1874-pattern holster was the adoption of the Smith & Wesson Schofield revolver the following year. The larger frame of the Schofield would not fit in the new holster; consequently, the pattern had to be widened in the upper portion, a change executed in August 1875.[13] All other features of the 1875-pattern holster remained the same.

In a further effort to comply with the new regulations, Watervliet Arsenal developed a method late in 1875 for altering the percussion cap pouch to serve for carrying the pistol cartridges. This alternative was both logical and economically sound, since some thirty-five thousand of these pouches were available and could be altered less expensively than new pouches could be made. This large stock lasted the army until the advent of the .38-caliber Model 1892 Colt revolver. Therefore, the regulation 1874 pistol cartridge pouch was never produced.[14]

As noted earlier, the cap pouch had been adopted for carrying pistol cartridges in 1872 simply as a temporary measure. In actual use, it was found that the double flaps were unnecessary for protecting metallic ammunition and they interfered with extracting the cartridges. The alteration consisted of removing the sheepskin strip, cutting away the central portion of the inner flap, and stitching down the remaining leather "ears" on each side to cover the openings on both sides of the mouth. This prevented the cartridges from slipping out from beneath the flap. The letters "U.S.," centered within an oval, were imprinted on the face of the flap, per the 1874 specifications.[15]

The record for the saber belt is even more vague. Certainly, some four thousand Pattern 1872 belts and plates were either available or already in the hands of the troops. This left the majority of the cavalry in the mid-1870s still using the old Civil War–vintage belt with the eagle plate. Contemporary photographic evidence, limited as it is, indicates that some troopers continued to use the 1855 belt, without the support strap and its attachment loop, for several years after the adoption of the 1874 equipment. Moreover, the 1851 eagle belt plate was commonly used with the 1874 saber belt, either by choice or by coincidence, a practice that continued well into the 1880s.[16] Conversion to the 1874-pattern belt and plate, as a unit, obviously was a long and fitful process.

139. *Brigadier General Stephen V. Benet. Beginning his military career on the eve of the Mexican War, Benet later served as the chief of ordnance, from 1874 until his retirement early in 1891.* (National Archives)

The ink was hardly dry on the cavalry board's papers when later that same month the Ordnance Department prevailed on Secretary of War Belknap to authorize a similar assemblage of infantry officers to review the foot soldier's kit and recommend improvements. This board consisted of Lieutenant Colonel William R. Shafter, Twenty-fourth Infantry, Lieutenant Colonel Alexander McD. McCook, Tenth Infantry, Lieutenant Colonel Thomas C. English, Second Infantry, Major Alexander Chambers, Fourth Infantry, and Captain M. H. Stacey, Twelfth Infantry. Like their cavalry counterparts, the members of the infantry board initially elected to meet at Fort Leavenworth and began their deliberations by reviewing reports that had been submitted from line units during the previous year. They also had on hand, for comparison, examples of all the previous infantry accoutrements dating back to 1861. Within two weeks, it became apparent to the board that Fort Leavenworth lacked the facilities necessary to construct or remodel equipments for consideration. To accomplish its task, the board requested that the meetings be moved to Watervliet Arsenal in New York, where complete shops and skilled workmen were available. The secretary of war approved, and the board reconvened at Watervliet on August 19, 1874.[17]

Deliberating through the summer and into the fall, the board spent nearly five months evaluating literally scores of items, ranging from accoutrements dating back as far as 1850 to new varieties of knapsacks, belts, and cartridge-carrying devices submitted by inventors. Inventors sent, or personally demonstrated, everything from eating utensils to a knapsack that could be transformed into both a poncho and a shelter tent.

In contrast to its cavalry counterpart, the infantry board accepted the brace-yoke concept. Despite a majority of field reports to the contrary, these officers felt that the theory was sound, the principal drawback of the 1872 system being its weight and the unwieldy valise knapsack. An alternative contrivance was submitted by Lieutenant George H. Palmer, a veteran of the Civil War who had later served with the Twenty-seventh Infantry on the Bozeman Trail. Palmer's brace was made of lighter-weight leather and had better adjustment features than the earlier version (fig. 140). The bulky valise gave way to a "clothing bag" made of duck material with a rubberized cover, the waterproofing method that had found favor among the troops. This bag was suspended at the left hip from straps attached to the brace. On the opposite side was a haversack, modified from the 1872 pattern. This bag was of similar size but was made of stouter cotton duck with a rubberized flap like that of the clothing bag. It was also provided with both a shoulder sling and buckles for attaching it to the brace yoke.

The belt and plate were also new, but their ancestry in the experimental pattern was unmistakable. The cast-brass plate was identical to the 1872 plate except that both the plate and the catch had small, oval-shaped loops atop their upper edges for the brace suspenders. This belt, suggested by Colonel Hagner, thus omitted the separated loops and leather spacers of the previous infantry belt. The repositioning of the brace loops allowed the cartridge boxes to be worn directly in front of the body rather than to the sides; thus the boxes would not interfere with arm movements. This simplified arrangement was also cheaper and easier to manufacture.

Of the many ammunition-carrying devices tried, the looped cartridge belt remained the average soldier's preference. But, it seemed that the army, in its determination to resist the belt, would go to almost any length to find an alternative. The most eccentric of these alternatives was a cartridge-block device submitted to the board by Lieutenant Henry Metcalfe of the Ordnance Department. Actually, Metcalfe had presented his invention to the Terry Board several months earlier, but that board had politely declined it. Undaunted, he appeared personally before the equipment board to make a second pitch.

In simple terms, Metcalfe had designed a rectangular wooden block, bored along its upper edge for eight rifle cartridges, that could be attached to the side of the Springfield rifle just ahead of the lock (fig. 141). This cartridge block was affixed to the weapon by means of a special lock mechanism inletted into the stock. Several of these blocks, filled with cartridges, were to be carried on a special waist belt using a clip carrier made of spring steel with a leather fastening strap for each block. The blocks were to be made and loaded with cartridges at

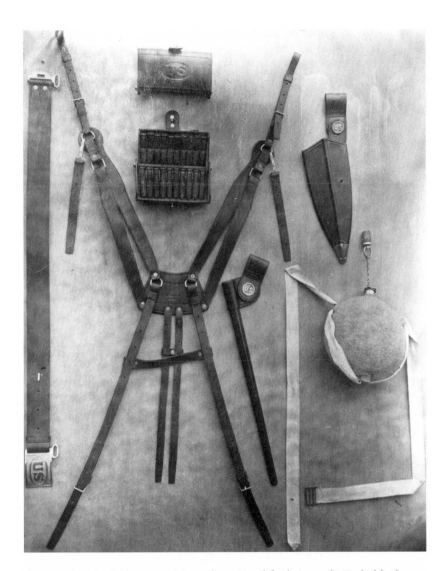

the army's principal ammunition plant, Frankford Arsenal. Each block was wrapped in a waterproofed-paper label describing the contents. In theory, the soldier would draw ready-made blocks of ammunition, place them in the belt clips, and then either use them directly from the belt or move blocks to the rifle as needed. Metcalfe made numerous claims for his system, the principal one being that it increased the rapidity of fire. But, even though having eight cartridges at hand on the rifle may have saved a bit of time and motion, the system as a whole did not offer any significant advantage over the cartridge belt. The Terry Board arrived at this very conclusion, but the equipment board was intrigued enough to recommend that a quantity of blocks, accoutrements, and altered rifles be produced for trial. Springfield Armory records indicate that one thousand rifles were adapted for the Metcalfe device. Six thousand carriers and thirty-one thousand blocks filled with cartridges also were made. To date, no records have been found to indicate that the Metcalfe rifles and blocks were actually issued for trial.[18] In all probability most of the rifles were later dismantled and restocked.

141. Model 1873 Springfield rifle with Metcalfe cartridge block attached (top) and Model 1875 officer's rifle (bottom). (Hayes Otoupalik Collection)

Among the many cartridge boxes submitted to the board was one designed by First Lieutenant Samuel McKeever, Second Infantry. This box was destined to become the last and best-known leather cartridge box for rifle ammunition used by the U.S. Army. It was made in two sections, rectangular in shape and hinged together, with belt loops on the rear. When the soldier folded the front of the box forward and down, opening it like a book, two rows of ten webbing cartridge loops were exposed. Leather bellows sewn to the upper edges of each row of loops allowed the heads to angle outward, making them easier to grasp. The board liked the advantages presented by the McKeever box, since it combined the neatness and military appearance of a leather box with the facility of the cartridge belt. It also protected the cartridges from the elements and from accidental loss. It was intended that the boxes be issued in pairs, under normal circumstances, giving a soldier a total of forty rounds of ammunition. However, the board also acknowledged that one box would suffice for garrison duty and suggested that four might be carried under some circumstances.[19]

Troops in the Southwest sometimes lamented that the canteen was not large enough for desert conditions, but a great many more throughout the West reported that its sling was too narrow, causing it to cut into the shoulder. Also, its length could not be adjusted for men of different heights. Experimenting with buckle and eyelet arrangements during the board's deliberations, Major Chambers struck on a simple tongueless buckle with three slots that would allow the strap to be threaded in such a way as to lock on itself. A wider version of this buckle was also adopted for use on the haversack. Although the cavalry board had decided the canteen should have double covers, a suggestion voiced by both foot and horse soldiers on the frontier, the board made no mention of the sling. This was probably because the mounted soldier usually had the canteen attached to his saddle; therefore, the sling was of no particular consequence to him. Whereas Sherman saw no need for a canteen with two covers, the new sling passed his review. The result was a canteen with its original woolen cover, a brass chain connecting the cork to the spout, and a webbing sling with the Chambers buckle. The sling was threaded through the three tin guides or loops on the canteen. This type of canteen was then issued to both infantry and cavalry beginning in 1875 as older patterns were turned in, marking the second modification of the Pattern 1858 canteen.[20]

In addition to the canteen, the individual mess gear proposed by the 1874

board was used universally among the army's various branches. Voicing a widespread pet peeve in the army, one officer urged, "Knives, forks, spoons, tin plates, and cups should be gratuitously issued to the soldiers, heretofore . . . these desirable articles have been bought from the Company fund."[21] In response to this universal plea, the army began issuing utensils and a tin cup to each soldier in 1875 (fig. 142). However, General Sherman, concerned about what he obviously considered an extravagance, quickly stipulated that if any of the items from the mess kit were lost or broken, the cost would be deducted from the man's pay. Both the knife and the fork, submitted by Lamson, Goodenew & Company, were made of steel with nearly indestructible cast-iron handles. Both were provided with sheaths made of scrap leather to prevent the sharp points from damaging the haversack. The large, sturdy spoon was made of tin-plated iron. All three utensils were stamped either "U.S." or "U.S.A." to identify them as government property.

Since reports from the field left no doubt in anyone's mind that the 1872 meat can was a failure, the infantry board adopted a new design that was destined to establish the basic style for all American "mess kits" up to the present day. It consisted of two oval halves, or dishes, that fit together to form a container, supposedly grease-tight, for storing the meat ration on the march (fig. 143). The deeper dish was fitted with an iron handle, hinged to one end, which could be folded over the unit to lock the two together or could be extended as a handle to make a frying pan. The more shallow, upper pan was to be used as a plate, although most soldiers simply used the frying pan for both purposes.[22] Needless to say, no one mourned the quick passing of the 1872 meat can.

Further illustrating the army's enlightened attitude toward mess gear, the

Left:

142. Pattern 1874 haversack (left) and clothing bag (right) with new meat can, cup, and utensils as adopted in 1874. (West Point Museum Collections)

Right:

143. Haversack and clothing bag, open, showing the two pans that formed the meat can. (West Point Museum Collections)

 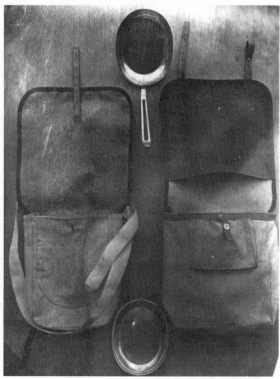

infantry board made a long-overdue recommendation that a standard tin cup be issued to the rank and file for field duty. The responsibility for providing the cups fell to the Ordnance Department, since it had the shop facilities for manufacturing them. This cup, described in greater detail at the end of this chapter, was made of heavy block tin and measured approximately four inches high by four inches in diameter, a size used widely among the troops during and after the Civil War. It had a distinctive ear-shaped handle, which was affixed to the side and was smaller than those on earlier cups. The handle was stamped with the letters "U.S." on the upper face.[23]

144. *Pattern 1874 McKeever cartridge boxes. The upper box is the first style. The lower one exhibits the swelled end to hold the rifle screwdriver, as modified in 1876.*

When the infantry equipment board concluded its meetings on November 24, 1874, the members were satisfied that they had done the job to the best of their abilities and were confident that "the principles involved in the equipment" were correct. The board noted, "Practical trials in actual field service [will] demonstrate what further improvements can be made."[24] With Secretary Belknap's approval of the recommendations, manufacture of the new infantry equipments was ordered to begin on July 1, 1875. Watervliet Arsenal, directed to manufacture two thousand sets of equipments, took the lead in perfecting the final designs, probably because the board had conducted most of its meetings there. Watervliet then sent a sample set to Rock Island Arsenal as the pattern for its first order of three thousand sets.[25]

Even though General Sherman did not stipulate the restrictions he had placed on the distribution of the new cavalry equipment, Chief of ordnance Benet certainly interpreted them to apply universally. Congressional appropriations still were quite limited; therefore, the 1874-pattern equipment was to be issued initially only "to replace similar articles of other patterns" that had become "unserviceable."[26] Nevertheless, among infantry troops on the frontier, the changeover to the 1874 equipments seems to have progressed rather rapidly during the first several months of 1876.

One of the first items to go into production was the McKeever cartridge box. Benet placed an initial order for four hundred with Watervliet Arsenal on January 15, 1875, less than two weeks after the infantry board's recommendations were approved.[27] Other orders for both McKeever boxes and Dyer pouches followed in rapid succession at both Watervliet and Rock Island arsenals.[28]

In approving the McKeever box, the board had noted its lack of any provision for carrying the screwdriver but had quickly dismissed this oversight by advising that the tool could be inserted into one of the loops. And, there were always clothing pockets for such things. However, by late in the first year of production, the Ordnance Department began looking for a way to stow the tool inside the cartridge box to ensure that the soldier had it when he needed it. One of Colonel Hagner's workmen came up with an idea for making a "swell" on one end of the box into which a shortened screwdriver could be placed (fig. 144). It was held in place by a short leather bar across the inside of the pocket. Benet approved this design for an order of five thousand boxes on February 18, 1876, and shortly thereafter Rock Island was provided with a sample box as a pattern. A like number of the modified screwdrivers were ordered to be made at Springfield Armory at about the same time. From then on, all McKeever boxes were made with the swelled end, though for a while both types were issued concurrently in order to utilize the earlier ones with flat ends.[29]

The demand for the 1874 equipments was heavy, and the chief of ordnance was soon forced to concede that funds were insufficient to supply the army's needs. Benet soon found an expedient that would ease the financial strain and, at the same time, provide the necessary equipment to the troops. Major D. W. Flagler, commanding Rock Island Arsenal, devised a way to alter the 1872 cartridge pouches to accommodate .45-caliber ammunition. He proposed attaching new, longer billet straps to accommodate the longer cartridges. But Lieutenant Colonel Julian McAllister at Benicia Arsenal suggested instead that by simply repunching the stud hole to lengthen it, the army would accomplish the same purpose without additional cost.[30] Some pouches, therefore, have elongated holes in the billets.

The No. 2 pouch, having a row of loops on the front, posed a different problem, since the .45-caliber cartridge was over a quarter of an inch longer than the .50/70. Smaller in diameter, the .45 slipped through the loop up to its rim. Flagler suggested that a narrow strip of heavy leather be stitched above the outer row of loops to increase the tension on the cartridges and to catch the rims at a higher point, thus preventing them from dropping down. He further recommended that the billet strap be fastened to the bottom of the box, rather than the flap, to prevent it from being unbuttoned by the downward pressure of the longer cartridges (fig. 145). Some No. 2 pouches were altered in this manner, but others were modified on a plan advanced by Benet himself. This was done by cutting strips of thin leather to form rows of tapered "fingers," which were then inserted into the cartridge loops of both No. 1 and No. 2 pouches. A few stitches along the upper edges secured the strips in place. This simple method of shimming the loops made up the difference in size between the .45- and .50-caliber cartridges.[31]

145. Hagner No. 2 pouches. The upper pouch is the standard pattern. The lower example reflects the alternate method of fastening the flap.

Rock Island Arsenal began altering Hagner pouches in November 1875 when an initial quantity of 1,239 were modified. Within the next few months Watervliet, Benicia, and San Antonio arsenals were directed to follow suit by modifying all of the Hagner boxes currently on hand and all that were turned in at those points. These modified pouches were then issued either singly or as components of some of the 1874-pattern infantry equipment sets in lieu of the McKeever boxes.[32] Hagner pouches No. 1 and No. 2, thus modified, composed about 15 to 20 percent of the total issues through 1879, after which year their numbers were almost negligible. Because the useful life of a cartridge box was several years under normal circumstances, the Hagners were seen on army parade grounds well into the 1880s.[33]

During the Sioux Campaign of 1876, the army had an unparalleled opportunity to field-test the new cavalry and infantry equipment (fig. 146). On the eve of the campaign, Captain Otho E. Michaelis, chief ordnance officer at Fort Abraham Lincoln, Dakota Territory, labored intensively to supply the outbound troops with everything they would need in the coming weeks. In the process of issuing ammunition, new saddle girths, canteens, and a multitude of other equipage required by General Terry's men, he discovered no less than fifty sets of brand-new infantry equipments. What better opportunity, he thought, than

to issue them to the doughboys departing to fight the Sioux. Offering them to the officers of the Montana-bound companies, Michaelis discovered, to his astonishment, that he "could not induce the Infantry Officers to give them a trial during the campaign; the mere sight of a man 'in harness,' as they referred to it, was sufficient to condemn the system for field service."[34]

Crook's infantry battalion was commanded by none other than Lieutenant Colonel Alexander Chambers, former member of the infantry board and inventor of the buckle used on the canteen and haversack straps. When Terry's and Crook's columns joined forces on Rosebud Creek in August, Captain Michaelis was surprised to find that the Fourth and Ninth infantrymen under Chambers's command were "in light marching order, and never under any circumstances use[d] the carrying brace." He added, "I saw two companies of the 14th Infantry, [commanded by Chambers] . . . which had been supplied with the new model, under circumstances which required them to make forced marches, and yet not a single soldier wore the brace."[35] When Michaelis questioned Chambers as to why his men had left their braces in the wagons, the latter responded that in his view the system had been designed as a substitute for the knapsack. Pondering this, Michaelis concluded that the whole concept of the brace was flawed because either the men were "in light marching order, carrying their few necessities in blankets or pieces of shelter tents slung across the shoulder or their impedimenta [were] transported in pack or wagon trains."[36] Private Richard Flynn, marching with Crook's column, recorded that he and his comrades of the Fourth Infantry started the campaign "with 150 rounds of ammunition per Man, one blanket, one Over Coat, and no change of under clothing."[37] Witnessing this firsthand and having the opportunity to speak with seasoned campaigners in the field, Michaelis arrived at a startling revelation that had entirely escaped the equipment board. Troops engaged in Indian campaigning on the plains simply did not need a knapsack—therefore, they did not need the Palmer brace (fig. 147). The army, in its fixation with conventional warfare in eastern environments, had once again ignored the realities of its current mission on the frontier and, in so doing, had underestimated the American soldier's propensity for using only that which was practical. Michaelis got to the heart of the issue when he observed, "The New Model equipments as an entirety do not meet the want of Indian Campaigning." This should have been clearly evident to the board, had the members of the board only seen the field reports on the 1872 brace, reports that came in some months after they adjourned. The obvious conclusion is that the Palmer brace was adopted both prematurely and unnecessarily; the decision was based on a faulty premise and lacked timely feedback about the field soldier's dislike of the trial brace.[38]

Equally unnecessary in the doughboy's kit was the bayonet. Michaelis reported, "Not a single triangular bayonet was carried by the infantry in General Terry's and Crook's columns, and it is hardly conceivable that circumstances should ever demand its use in Indian warfare."[39] Regardless, Michaelis did not overlook the potential value of the trowel bayonet as an entrenching tool in siege situations like that experienced by the combined battalions of Major Marcus A. Reno and Captain Frederick W. Benteen at the Little Bighorn. The trowel, he thought, might be useful to cavalry units as well as infantry. To conserve weight, he proposed that it could double as a picket pin. Reno, who had occupied a seat on the board that had recommended the trowel three years earlier, might have contemplated that himself as he and his men attempted to

On the facing page:
146. Infantry soldier, ca. 1875, equipped with the Palmer brace yoke, belt, and Hagner No. 2 pouches. (U.S. Army Military History Institute)

147. Obviously posed for photographer Stanley J. Morrow, these members of General George Crook's command nevertheless represent an authentic view of soldiers at the end of a hard campaign. (Stanley J. Morrow Collection, W. H. Over Museum)

scratch out rifle pits with knives and tin cups during that memorable night of June 25. Despite these circumstances, no action was taken on Michaelis's suggestion.

The cavalry saber, like the bayonet, was a useless weapon in Indian warfare. Michaelis noted sabers were entirely absent from the Second, Third, Fifth, and Seventh cavalry companies that participated in the 1876 campaign. However, he added that given the nature of the fighting at the Little Bighorn and at the Battle of the Rosebud a week earlier, cavalry officers might want to reconsider carrying them. He recommended that in the future, the saber should be attached to the saddle, not the belt. Although the saber would not be abandoned until the passing of the horse cavalry itself, Michaelis's prediction that it would be carried exclusively on the saddle was to prove true.

Arsenal orders for components of the new gear, beyond those for "sets of equipments," infer that at least some items of the 1874 equipment found their way to line units of both infantry and cavalry before the beginning of the Sioux War. Despite widely held opinion that the 1859 haversack was still being issued to troops in the spring of 1876, the author has found no evidence supporting this contention.[40] On the contrary, it must be remembered that the primary impe-

tus for a new haversack was Meigs's 1870 report stating that most of the old painted ones left from the war were no longer fit for issue. At least 20,500 haversacks of the 1872 pattern were manufactured and presumably distributed during the years 1872–76, in compliance with Sherman's orders to issue obsolete patterns first. Accelerating the integration of new articles was a directive to issue 1874-pattern haversacks to recruits of all branches en route to their permanent assignments.[41] Therefore, both the 1872 and the 1874 patterns would have been represented among the infantry and some of the cavalry outfits in the field that summer.

By the summer of 1876 some cavalrymen still carried haversacks, but by no means were they all equipped with haversacks. Ordnance returns indicate that some of the companies had received the 1872 or the 1874 saddlebags and that others had not, which was entirely consistent with the army practice of issuing new items only when the old ones became unserviceable. General Orders No. 60 of 1872 made no provision for troopers to be issued haversacks, since the larger saddlebags were intended to serve that purpose. This policy was modified by *Ordnance Memoranda No. 18*, which authorized the issue of haversacks to cavalrymen while on dismounted duty. But, if a trooper had the misfortune to draw a pair of the tiny 1859 saddlebags, he had no choice but to use a haversack for his rations. Apparently a question arose as to whether this was to be a special type of haversack, but Dyer clarified the point by stating that haversacks "in all respects like the one now issued to Infantry" would be issued to cavalry on requisition. It is known that some companies still used the 1859 saddlebags as late as the Sioux War, and they probably carried haversacks of the newer patterns.[42]

Michaelis revealed that some cavalrymen, equipped with the new, larger saddlebags, no longer carried haversacks on the 1876 campaign. He wrote:

> The new saddlebags [Pattern 1874] are entirely too heavy. It is a grave question whether it would not be better to abolish them entirely. The temptation to carry useless articles is too great. The brush and comb are invariably packed in the nosebag, and a few days' rations can, if necessary, be carried in the haversack attached to the saddle, or in the forage sack described below. . . . The infantry haversack with short leather sling should be issued to the Cavalry for use when required.[43]

The new canteen, like the haversack, suffered from a sling that was still too narrow. Michaelis observed that the webbing slings on both tended to "string with use" after they became wet and twisted.[44] The intended advantage of the wider sling was thus negated, and the weight of the canteen and haversack was painfully accentuated on the wearer's shoulder. Michaelis also noted that the sling was useless to the cavalry, since the men always tied the canteen to one of the saddle rings. He suggested that arsenals provide a short leather strap and snap hook instead, a fabrication he probably saw in use during the campaign. This field fabrication, adopted by the Ordnance Department in the early 1880s, allowed the canteen to be easily attached to one of the saddle rings.[45]

Extensive and hard field use of the 1874 canteen proved that the traditional woolen cover alone would not stand up under such conditions. By the spring of 1877 the Ordnance Department was issuing canteens with an outer cover of drab-colored cotton duck drawn over the original woolen cover. Besides being more durable, the double cover (when wet) helped to keep the water cool by evaporation. It is believed this alteration of the canteen was effected in April or

On the facing page:
148. Some of General Crook's dough-boys, wearing preferred cartridge belts, butcher a mule on the "Starvation March," September 1876. (Stanley J. Morrow Collection, W. H. Over Museum)

May 1877, based on an inquiry by Major D. W. Flagler to the chief of ordnance on March 30 asking how he should go about filling requests for canteen covers. Flagler advised that the arsenal supply "petersham covers only," a recommendation that Benet approved. This suggests that the subject of double covers had been broached but that no official decision had been rendered. Accordingly, canteens were still being shipped from the arsenals with only the single cover at that time. But, just two months later, First Lieutenant William B. Weir, an ordnance officer stationed at Watervliet who had recently inspected the used equipment turned in from the Department of Dakota, described "the canteen as at present made [with] two covers."[46]

The new mess gear seems to have been issued almost universally by the spring of 1876, and for once, the troops had no complaints. The men were happy to have their common tin cup back again, and almost everyone thought the oval meat can was a wonderful improvement over the square one. The only exception was Lieutenant Weir, who had to deal with the pile of filthy, grease-soaked haversacks turned in after the Sioux War. Weir pointed to the meat can as the culprit. Since a soldier usually did not have the means, or the inclination, to clean the cooking-fire soot from the bottom of the pan, this grime rubbed off in the haversack's fitted pocket. On the march the sun heated the can containing the meat ration, causing the grease to run out of the overlapping joint between the two halves. Since the pocket was permanently sewn to the front panel of the haversack, there was no way to keep it clean, other than to wash the whole bag. As for the mess utensils, Michaelis added the suggestion, evidently based on some incident of the campaign, that the pointed mess knife be rounded on the end to preclude its being used as a dirk.[47] His recommendation was not adopted by the army, but similar commercially made table knives had rounded ends.

Throughout his service with the expedition, Michaelis was deeply impressed by the all-but-universal preference the soldiers had for cartridge belts rather than the regulation cartridge boxes or pouches (fig. 148). "In the very companies of the 14th Infantry, furnished with the new waist belt and boxes," he wrote, "I saw men with prairie belts. Some had slung the regulation belt over the shoulder, and wore the loop belt about the waist, others wore both belts and others again evidently for want of material, had converted the regulation into a quasi loop belt by cutting slots in couples around it."[48] Michaelis's statement suggests that the two companies of Chambers's own regiment were ordered to wear the regulation belts and boxes, since there was an ever-watchful ordnance officer present in the command. Complying with the letter of their instructions, the soldiers did wear the required gear but made a nonverbal statement by also wearing their homemade prairie belts. Michaelis simply could not believe that the efforts of the equipment board had been for naught. Determined to vindicate the Ordnance Department, he scoured the camps of the Bighorn and Yellowstone Expedition to find just one soldier who preferred to use the cartridge box. His search was eventually rewarded when he encountered an old Irish sergeant who still had his leather box. But, when the captain asked what he carried in it, the weathered sergeant exposed the contents and calmly replied, "Lunch, sur."[49]

Soldiers who took the field in the 1870s still bemoaned the fact that they had no proper leggings (fig. 149). Said Colonel Frank Wheaton: "No regiment of our Infantry army can leave its Barracks tomorrow and accomplish a successful 30-days march, unless every soldier and Company Officer makes a decided

change in his uniform, this he will do by wrapping his trowsers around his ankle, pulling his stockings over the pantaloons and tying them in place. He actually cannot march in wet grass or on a muddy road unless he does resort to some such device."[50]

149. Private William Earl Smith, Fourth U.S. Cavalry, as he appeared at the conclusion of Colonel Ranald S. Mackenzie's expedition against the Cheyennes in the fall of 1876. Note the full-length leggings Smith wears. (Charles Watts Collection, Courtesy Sherry L. Smith)

This simple but archaic method was a poor substitute for leggings. Although it kept the pants cuffs from flapping about and snagging on brush or caking with mud, the soldiers' stockings wore out all the faster. And, gravel, seeds, and burrs funneled down the uncovered shoe tops to quickly incapacitate even the hardiest doughboy. Although most European nations had remedied the problem by issuing canvas gaiters or short marching boots, the American infantry was destined to tie up its socks for another decade.

In the aftermath of the Little Bighorn disaster, reinforcements were concentrated in southeastern Montana. One of these units was Colonel Nelson A. Miles's Fifth Infantry, then stationed at Fort Leavenworth, Kansas. Most of the Fifth's companies sped northward by train to the operations zone. On reaching Fort Abraham Lincoln, Miles's vanguard disembarked to be inspected "to see that all the paraphernalia and equipments that were supposed to be demanded for such a campaign as was before it, had been supplied. The command was found in perfect condition, having all the equipments required by the regulations." After inspection, the troops boarded river steamers to continue the journey to Montana via the Missouri and Yellowstone rivers. They had no sooner gotten under way when orders were given to pack up "all the paraphernalia" that they had found in their "experience with the southern Indians to be not absolutely essential. . . . In place of cartridge boxes, [the soldiers] gladly buckled about their waists the more useful equipments of cartridge belts."[51]

Among the rank and file of the Fifth Infantry were many men who were veterans of the 1874 Red River War. The recruits, as in any war, looked to these more experienced men for advice about what they considered necessary equipment for active field service. So great was the veterans' advocacy of the cartridge belt that the new men fabricated prairie belts aboard the steamer by using their suspenders to make loops for their waist belts.[52]

Cavalrymen likewise preferred the prairie belt, despite the surveys taken by the 1874 Cavalry Equipment Board. Although some men wore the Dyer pouch on the leather saber belt, most chose the cartridge belt (fig. 150). These field belts took a variety of forms, actual examples of which are described in the following section. A feature that apparently was unique to the belts of the Seventh Cavalry was a "pendant looped arc on the left side for pistol cartridges."[53] There is no known surviving example of a field belt of this type, but presumably the arc had loops for about twelve cartridges. Troopers who chose not to avail themselves of this invention probably carried their revolver cartridges in their trouser pockets. Some may have constructed their prairie belts with a space or other provision to accommodate the converted cap pouch.

150. *First Sergeant John Comfort,*
Fourth U.S. Cavalry, in campaign
clothing, including cartridge belt
ca. 1876. (National Archives)

The Sioux War clearly influenced Chief of Ordnance Benet and other high-ranking figures. As we have seen, the Ordnance Department had steadfastly refused to adopt a regulation cartridge belt, even though the troops themselves had been making and using them almost since the advent of breech-loading arms. By the mid-1870s their use was so widespread as to make any other method of carrying ammunition in the field the exception. Michaelis went so far as to say, "The prairie or loop belt is universally demanded, and is always worn by both Infantry and Cavalry." Unwilling to be censured for not providing "the boys in blue" with everything they needed to whip the Sioux, Benet approved the manufacture of a standard cartridge belt on December 14, 1876, and authorized Watervliet Arsenal to make two thousand of them immediately.[54] There was very little high-level review and quibbling over this belt, nor was there any thought of test models and field trials.

The regulation 1876-pattern cartridge belt was a direct descendant of the thimble belts that soldiers had been making for themselves. Yet, there were

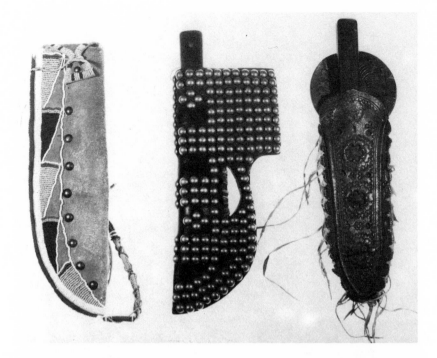

151. Typical knife sheaths procured by soldiers for field use. The commercially made example at the right was used by First Sergeant Joseph W. Hunting, Fifth U.S. Infantry, during the Red River War of 1874.

some important improvements. The problem with leather belts and verdigris had been noted early on and had weighed heavily against adoption of the belt. Verdigris was a greenish substance that resulted from the chemical reaction between tannic acids, used in producing leather, and the copper in the cartridge cases. When a cartridge coated with verdigris was fired, the heat welded the case to the chamber of the weapon, thus preventing, or greatly inhibiting, its extraction. In the field, soldiers had to either wipe their cartridges frequently or risk having jammed weapons in combat.

To eliminate this problem, the army designed the regulation cartridge belt as a leather belt completely encased in brown-dyed canvas. The leather belts were obtained at no cost by salvaging the shoulder slings from Model 1855 cartridge boxes left over from the war.[55] To this belt were sewn fifty-four loops made of varnished cotton webbing. This virtually eliminated the verdigris problem. At the right end of the belt was a leather billet that mated with a brass open-frame buckle on the other end. The belt was simple and it worked. The army's acceptance of the cartridge belt stands as a monument to the common soldier's persistence in using only the tools that best suited his trade. Never again would the American army wear the cartridge box for anything other than dress parades, and even there its days were numbered.

Thus, the Sioux War saw the frontier regulars equipped with a variety of gear representing a mixture of parts and pieces of the 1860, 1872, and 1874 patterns. Significantly, there was little attempt to use the equipment in the integrated systems for which it was originally intended. With but few exceptions, virtually all of the men were wearing prairie belts of some type. The cavalryman's antiquated carbine sling, like the doughboy's blanket roll, had survived all of the reforms simply because the Ordnance Department had been unable to design anything better so far as the soldier was concerned. Most units had abandoned the saber and the bayonet in favor of the more useful sheath knife, worn on the

152. Pattern 1874 cavalry saber belt. The saber slings have the nonregulation snap hooks popular with many soldiers.

belt (fig. 151). Each infantryman carried a haversack of either the 1872 or the 1874 pattern, the common tin cup dangling from the flap billet. Cavalrymen usually fastened their cups to the saddlebag flap. Both branches still carried the basic 1858 canteen, but by this time many of the canteens seen in the hands of the troopers had been modified according to either the 1872 or the 1874 specifications.

CAVALRY EQUIPMENT

Saber Belt, Pattern 1874

The saber belt was made of black bridle leather in two lengths, 38 inches and 42 inches by 1¹³⁄₁₆ inches wide (fig. 152). On the right end was a brass wire hook used for adjusting the length of the belt. The right end of the belt folded back on itself, and the two thicknesses were held together by a sliding leather loop. On the left end, held in a fold of leather fastened by two brass rivets and three lines of stitching, was a cast-brass catch that coupled to the plate. The plate used was the standard 1872-pattern rectangular brass plate bearing the letters "U.S." within an oval border, described earlier in this volume.

On the belt were two sliding brass loops for the saber slings. The forward loop had a sheet-brass hook. On dismounting, the trooper fastened the saber to this hook, guard to the rear. The slings, only slightly modified from the Pattern 1872, had sheet-brass hooks, 2½ inches long, at the upper ends. The slings measured 1 inch wide by 16¼ inches and 29¼ inches long. The longer strap connected to the rear-most brass loop, thus allowing the saber to hang at the proper angle when the trooper was mounted. Each strap was provided with a brass stud and a sliding leather loop to button the doubled ends to the rings of the scabbard. Some soldiers purchased polished-brass snap hooks and attached these to the lower ends to dress up the belt and to simplify attaching the saber.

Holster, Pattern 1874

Constructed of black bridle leather, the holster was 11 inches long, measured from the mouth, with a 1-inch-diameter leather plug in the muzzle end

Left:
153. Pattern 1874 holster.
(Michael A. Ward Collection)

Center:
*154. Reverse of 1874-pattern holster
showing the Hoffman swivel.*
(Michael A. Ward Collection)

Right:
*155. Pattern 1875 holster. This differed
from the 1874 holster only in its slightly
wider mouth and the addition of "U.S."
embossed on the body.*
(Dwight Clark Collection)

(fig. 153). The flap was cut on a curve, 3¼ inches at its widest point by 7¼ inches long, the free end tapering to a width of 1 inch. It had a single hole to secure the flap over the finial.

The belt loop, about 2½ inches wide, had the brass Hoffman swivel with stop pin to restrict its movement to an arc of 45 degrees (fig. 154). The swivel was mounted to the holster body by means of a piece of leather, 2¼ inches by 4⅜ inches, stitched and riveted with three brass rivets, which also secured the upper end of the flap. This model was made specifically to fit the Colt single-action army revolver and was produced in very limited quantities.

Holster, Pattern 1875

This pattern was nearly identical to the 1874 holster except that the upper portion of the holster was made slightly larger, the mouth being about ½ inch wider, to accommodate the Smith & Wesson Schofield revolver (fig. 155). The brass finial closing the flap was placed nearer the seam to give the strap a higher angle to fit the Schofield's larger grip. All other features, including the narrow belt loop and Hoffman swivel attachment, were the same.

This holster was readily distinguished from the Pattern 1874 by the letters "U.S." embossed on the body. The letters were ⅞ inch high and were surrounded by an oval border.

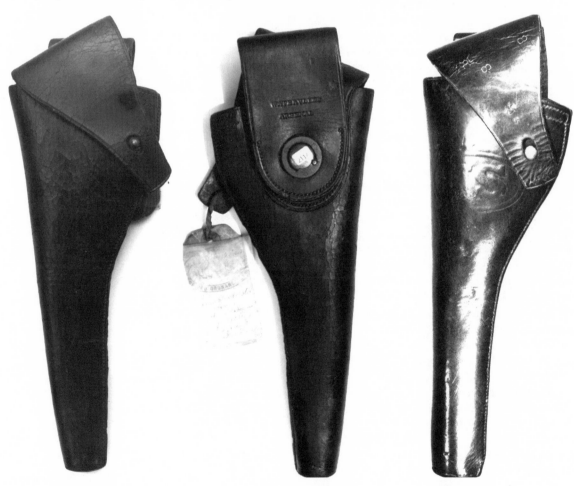

Hazen Cartridge Loops

These cartridge holders consisted of twenty leather loops arranged in two rows and stitched to a central piece of leather rectangular in shape (fig. 156). There were twelve loops on the outer row and eight on the inside row, along with three belt loops. The loops of specimens examined varied from 1¾ to 2 inches in depth. The unit measured approximately 7¾ inches long and was dyed black.

Carbine Cartridge Pouch, Pattern 1874

This pouch measured 4¼ inches deep by 6 inches wide at the mouth with a gusset about 1⅜ inches wide (fig. 157). The bottom and sides of the pouch were cut on a continuous curve, forming an arc. The gusset and extension tabs on the upper corners of the front overlap were riveted together to prevent the cartridges from bouncing out of the pouch. The interior of the main pocket was lined with sheepskin.

On the front of the pouch was a screwdriver pocket, measuring 4¼ inches wide at the top and 3⅜ inches deep, which was formed by a separate piece of leather sewn to the inside of the front piece. The mouth of this pocket fastened with a small brass button. At the bottom center of the front was a larger finial for fastening the flap.

The flap measured 6¾ inches wide, the back of the pouch being a continuation of the same piece of leather. The bottom edge of the flap was cut with a short extension forming a closure tab. On this tab was a brass escutcheon with a keyhole used to reinforce the leather so that the hole would not become enlarged. Pouches made at Watervliet and Benicia arsenals usually exhibited an elliptical escutcheon on a horizontal axis measuring ¹⁵⁄₁₆ inch by 1½ inches. This type was fastened with two brass pins. The Rock Island product invariably had a vertically oriented escutcheon. Also elliptical in shape, it was oriented on a vertical axis and was much more rounded than the football-shaped style used on the other pouches. The exterior surface of the flap was embossed with the letters "U S," ¹³⁄₁₆ inch high, surrounded by an oval border. Riveted and stitched on the back were two loops just large enough to pass over the saber belt. The pouch was intended to hold forty rounds of .45-caliber carbine ammunition.

Pistol Cartridge Pouch, Pattern 1874

The pouch for revolver cartridges, recommended by the 1874 Cavalry Equipment Board, never saw production beyond a few arsenal samples.[56] As designed, it was to be made of black leather and lined with sheepskin. A simple flap with an integral tab buttoned to a small brass stud on the front. On the back were two belt loops.

The pocket measured about 3⅜ inches wide, with an equal depth. The front and back panels were to be made of somewhat heavier leather than the gusset to provide a degree of stiffness so that the flap could be buttoned down easily.

The gusset on the completed pouch was about ¾ inch wide, the ends of which extended beyond the front and back panels to prevent the cartridges from jolting out from beneath the flap.[57]

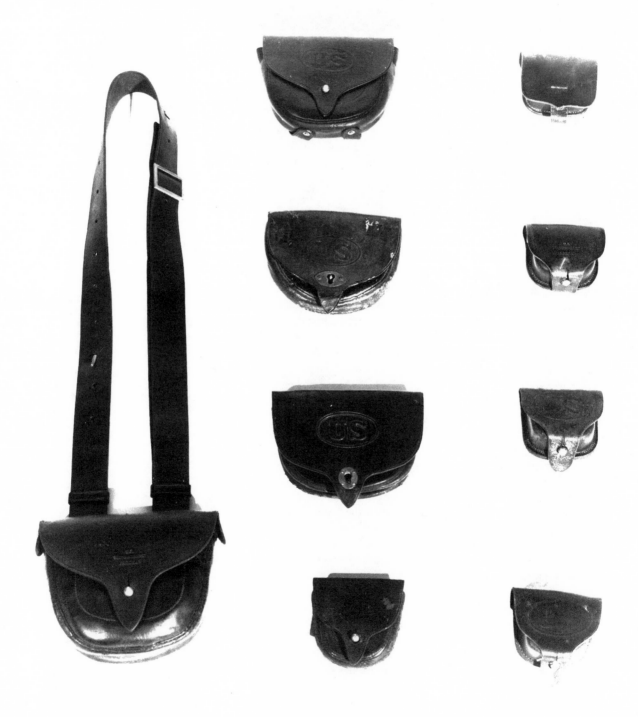

Pistol Cartridge Pouch, 1874 Conversion

This was the standard black leather percussion cap pouch, modified by cutting out a 1½-inch portion from the inner flap. The rear edge of the flap was left in place inside the back of the pouch. The small angular pieces of the flap remaining at each side were shortened, folded over the sides of the pouch, and stitched down to prevent the cartridges from jolting out. The flap was embossed with the block letters "U S" surrounded by an oval border, 1⅝ inches by 2⅝ inches. (Many unaltered cap pouches continued to be used for carrying revolver ammunition throughout the period.)

Saber Knot, Pattern 1874

The new-model saber knot was identical to that prescribed in 1872 except that it was to have two sliding loops rather than one. The strap measured ⅝ inch wide by 30 inches long and had a braided knot, without tassel, 1½ inches long on one end. The saber knot, like the Dyer-pattern pistol cartridge pouch, probably was not produced in quantity, since many thousands of the old style lay in storage.[58] A survey of period photographs indicates that few cavalrymen on the frontier actually used the saber knot; the majority of those who did had the Civil War type.

INFANTRY EQUIPMENT

Palmer Brace

This device, made entirely of black bridle leather, consisted of a rather complex arrangement of suspenderlike straps extending from a pad situated high on the soldier's back between the shoulder blades. The back pad, measuring about 4 inches wide across the top, 6½ inches across the bottom, and 3¾ inches high, was intended to centralize the load at a man's strongest point. From here the weight was further distributed by the leather suspenders. To the pad were riveted four straps, one at each corner, about 1 inch in width, two straps for each shoulder. The outside strap was about 12 inches long, the inner one about 15 inches. The longer strap was tapered to pass through a brass ring and then was doubled back, terminating in a tongueless buckle. The outer strap passed through this square and was riveted to the outside of the inside shoulder strap about 3 inches above the ring. Two waist-belt straps, ⅝ inch wide by 20 inches long, were secured to the brass rings and attached to the loops on each side of the belt plate.

The haversack and the clothing bag were attached at their rear corners by two straps, ⅝ inch by 14 inches, riveted to the lower edge of the back pad, 1 inch apart. The front corners of each bag were connected by straps ¹¹⁄₁₆ inch by 11½ inches, which were attached by brass wire hooks to the front rings of the brace. The haversack was provided with a special strap, riveted to the bottom of the gusset, that buckled to the clothing bag. This arrangement prevented the two from working forward while the soldier was marching, especially at double time.

On the upper corners of the back pad were two brass D-rings, held by the same rivets that fastened the upper shoulder straps, through which the blanket straps were passed. These blanket straps measured ¹¹⁄₁₆ inch by 42 inches. A connector strap, 8 inches long and formed with a loop at each end, was placed on the blanket straps, passing underneath the bag support straps, to hold the blanket firmly in place when marching at double time.

On the facing page:
157. (Left) Dyer 1870 cartridge pouch and sling; (center, top to bottom) 1872 Dyer pouch, two variations of the 1874 Dyer pouch, and board-sample 1874 pistol cartridge pouch; (right) standard and modified cap pouches used for carrying pistol cartridges. (Hayes Otoupalik Collection)

Waist Belt, Pattern 1874

The waist belt was made of black bridle leather 1¹³⁄₁₆ inches wide by either 38 or 40 inches long, depending on the size (fig. 158). A brass wire adjustment hook was fastened with two rivets to the right end, which was doubled on itself. This hook mated with a series of adjustment holes punched in the belt. A sliding loop secured the fold thus formed. On the left end was a cast-brass catch with an integral ¹³⁄₁₆-inch loop on its upper edge. This catch was fastened with two brass rivets and three lines of hand stitching.

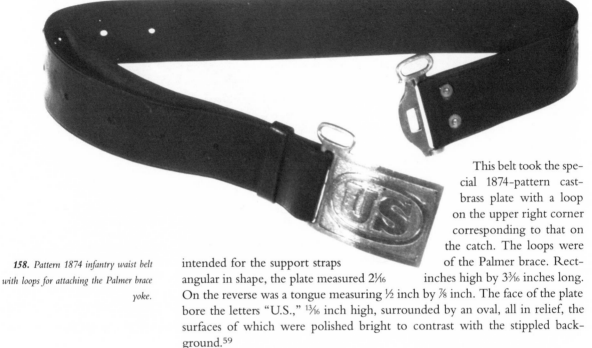

This belt took the special 1874-pattern cast-brass plate with a loop on the upper right corner corresponding to that on the catch. The loops were of the Palmer brace. Rect-

158. Pattern 1874 infantry waist belt with loops for attaching the Palmer brace yoke.

intended for the support straps angular in shape, the plate measured 2¹⁄₁₆ inches high by 3³⁄₁₆ inches long. On the reverse was a tongue measuring ½ inch by ⅞ inch. The face of the plate bore the letters "U.S.," ¹³⁄₁₆ inch high, surrounded by an oval, all in relief, the surfaces of which were polished bright to contrast with the stippled background.[59]

McKeever Cartridge Box, Pattern 1874 (Type 1)

Made of black bridle leather, the box contained twenty rounds of .45-caliber government ammunition (fig. 159). The box measured approximately 3³⁄₁₆ inches by 6½ inches long. On the reverse were two loops, 3⅛ inches long, for the waist belt. The front and rear sections of the box were hinged at the bottom on a brass rod so that the box opened by lowering the front half. At the top, on the front section, was a brass stud that mated with a leather tab, 3 inches long, sewn to the rear half. The hole in this tab was reinforced with an elliptical brass escutcheon attached by three pins. The upper corners of the box were reinforced with brass straps ³⁄₁₆ inch wide. When the box was open, the cartridges were exposed in two rows of varnished webbing loops 1¼ inches wide. These were sewn to russet leather bellows. The front of the box was embossed with "U S" in letters ⅞ inch high within an oval border.

McKeever Cartridge Box, Pattern 1874 (Type 2)

This box, introduced early in 1876, was merely a modification of the one described above, differing only in the screwdriver pocket formed in the left

159. Pattern 1874 McKeever cartridge box in the open position.

end. The pocket was nothing more than a swell approximately ¼ inch deep, with a small piece of leather sewn across the inside to hold the Springfield screwdriver.

Haversack, Pattern 1874 (Type 1)

This haversack was characterized by its black rubberized flap measuring 13½ inches wide by 13¼ inches long (fig. 160). It was bound with black leather ⅜ inch wide. The flap was secured by means of a russet leather billet, sewn and riveted to the flap, which mated to a brass wire buckle held by a leather chape on the bottom of the gusset. The bag, constructed of natural cotton duck, was divided into two pockets, front and rear. It measured approximately 8½ inches wide by 11 inches deep with a gusset 2½ inches wide at the bottom. Sewn to the inside of the gusset were two fitted pockets, one on the right side for the spoon and fork and another on the left for the mess knife. The fork and knife were provided with split-leather sheaths to prevent the points from cutting the material.

On the front of the bag, covered by the flap, was a separately applied pocket with a rounded bottom corresponding to the meat can. The pocket was closed by a large-size regulation eagle button. Oddly enough, the button could not be fastened with the can in the pocket.

On the upper rear corners of the haversack were russet leather buckle chapes,

Left:

160. Pattern 1874 Haversack

Right:

161. Reverse of a Pattern 1874 haversack showing the brace yoke buckles and strap. This example is shown with one of the replacement slings used primarily for clothing bags.

4 inches long, for attaching it to the brace. There also was a permanently attached webbing sling, 1½ inches wide, made in two pieces connected by a brass Chambers buckle. Riveted to the gusset, along its right side, was a russet leather strap, ¾ inch by 11½ inches, for buckling the haversack to the clothing bag when the two were used with the brace (fig. 161). When not in use, this strap was passed through a small leather retaining loop affixed to the gusset. Although all 1874-pattern haversacks were made originally with these brace attachments, few survived with them intact. Since they were useless to the soldier and tended to snag on other gear, most soldiers removed them. But, the rivet holes and stitching lines remain, indicating where the brace straps once were attached.

Most 1874 haversacks had "U.S." stenciled in white letters, 1½ inches high, on the front of the flap, but some were made without markings. Unit markings, when used, usually were applied to the outside of the flap. However, an example exists with unit markings stenciled on the meat-can pocket.

Some 1874 haversacks had flaps bound with ¾-inch drab webbing. This variation was a result of their being reconditioned at Watervliet Arsenal.[60]

Haversack, Pattern 1874 (Type 2)

By the fall of 1877 it had become apparent to Colonel Hagner that the leather parts on haversacks and clothing bags could be replaced with cotton webbing at a considerable cost savings. This also would allow them to be washed by the soldiers or laundresses. Acting on this idea, the chief of ordnance authorized the arsenals to thereafter make both articles with webbing flap binding and straps in place of leather (figs. 162 and 163).[61] This type also differed in having a flap made of two thicknesses of drab duck and a meat-can pocket of the same dimensions as the front panel instead of the short, rounded version.

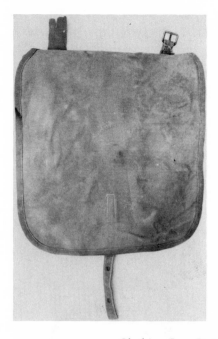 

Left:
162. *Pattern 1874 haversack, Type 2.*
(Tom Wilder Collection)

Right:
163. *Pattern 1874 haversack, Type 2,*
reverse, showing the webbing chapes and
straps. (Tom Wilder Collection)

Clothing Bag, Pattern 1874 (Type 1)

This bag had a leather-bound, black rubberized flap like that of the haversack except that it measured 13 inches by 15 inches (fig. 164). On the inside was a flat pocket, 11½ inches deep, for holding socks or other minor articles. Two leather straps near the lower corners of the flap mated with brass wire buckles on the gusset. Like the haversack, the clothing bag displayed the letters "U.S." stenciled in white block letters 1½ inches high on the outside.

The main pocket measured about 9½ inches wide by 12 inches deep. A pocket, 6¾ inches wide by 5¼ inches deep by 1½ inches, was sewn to the front. This pocket held one carton of spare rifle ammunition or miscellaneous small articles of the soldier's kit. The contents were secured by a leather tab passing over the top of the pocket and fastening to a large regulation eagle button on the front of the pocket.

There were two leather chapes and brass wire buckles at the upper rear corners for attaching the clothing bag to the Palmer brace. Another buckle chape was sewn to the bottom of the gusset to take the connector strap of the haversack.

Clothing Bag, Pattern 1874 (Type 2)

This bag was the same as the standard described above except that it was made of "lead colored" duck and did not have the black rubberized flap. Apparently this style was made for a brief time in 1876–77.[62] Although production of the clothing bag began in 1875, the chief of ordnance directed Watervliet Arsenal to begin the use of lead-colored duck for infantry equipments early in 1876. Just why this was done has not been determined; possibly, soiling was not as noticeable on this color. However, the arsenals continued to use the natural-colored material whenever the dyed duck was in short supply.[63]

Left:

164. *Pattern 1874 clothing bag.*

Right:

165. *All-canvas clothing bag, bearing the
"RECRUIT" identification ordered in
1876.*

Clothing Bag, Pattern 1874 (Type 3)

This variant bag utilized webbing throughout in place of leather for the various chapes, straps, and the binding around the flap. (Refer to the description above for the Type 2 haversack.) It also omitted the layer of rubber in the flap because it was found that a double thickness of duck served the purpose just as well. Examples will be seen that obviously have been modified from the Type 1 by being dyed and having all of the leather parts replaced, leaving old stitching lines and rivet holes visible. The eagle button was sometimes left intact as well.

A further modification of this type, introduced in 1878, had a ⅝-inch-diameter "patent button" of tinned iron to fasten the outer pocket. This shank button cost only $.35 per gross, as opposed to $1.35 for the army eagle buttons used previously.[64] The new button also saved a considerable amount of labor, since the eagle buttons were attached by means of a short piece of rawhide lace being passed through the loop and whipstitched in place to anchor the button.

As early as 1875, clothing bags and haversacks, particularly the former, were issued to recruits for holding their meager belongings when they left the depots to join their assigned units. On arrival at their stations, the new men were to turn in all of these articles, which were deemed "unnecessary, unsuitable, or unserviceable." These were then packed and shipped back to Watervliet Arsenal to be cleaned, reconditioned, and reissued at the recruiting depots. Apparently, many company commanders elected to keep the bags, or at least failed to return them. Therefore, the articles were stenciled on the flap with the word "RECRUIT" in a split oval border (fig. 165). This presumably

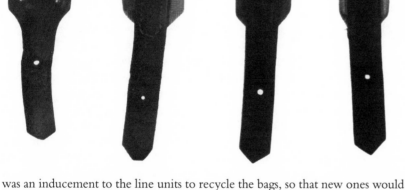

166. *Four varieties of clothing bag slings.*

was an inducement to the line units to recycle the bags, so that new ones would not have to be manufactured.[65]

Shoulder Strap, Clothing Bag

As an afterthought, the army issued separate shoulder slings for the clothing bag so that it could be used without the Palmer brace. In the absence of a knapsack, recruits had to have something in which to carry their kit for the few months they would spend at one of the depots in the East or Midwest. During this period, infantry recruits had no need for a full set of brace equipments, and cavalry recruits would not be mounted (and thus not have access to saddlebags) until being assigned to a line unit. The clothing bag therefore became the only available option. So that the bags could be used without the brace, Chief of Ordnance Benet authorized separate detachable slings to be made for the clothing bag so that bags could be used without the brace (fig. 166). The pattern for this sling was designed at Watervliet Arsenal and submitted for approval late in 1875.[66]

In fiscal year 1877, clothing bags and slings totaling 4,181 in number appear on the statements of materials issued to the army, reflecting the department's decision to issue a sling with each bag so that it could be used either with or independent of the brace.[67] It is also conceivable that the extra sling could be used as a replacement for a worn-out sling on the haversack, provided the brace buckles were intact.

There were several variations of this sling. The most common style was constructed of drab webbing, 1½ inches wide, in two pieces. On each end was a 4-inch-long leather billet with a single hole for attachment to the buckles. The pieces were joined and made adjustable by a Chambers buckle. This same style also appeared in a narrower, 1¼-inch width in both drab and natural colors. Another and scarcer variation was made of a single piece of 1½-inch-wide drab webbing with a leather billet riveted directly to the Chambers buckle.

MISCELLANEOUS

Canteen, Pattern 1874 (Type 1)

The initial version was the standard 1858 canteen, complete with its two-piece woolen cover (fig. 167). The covers usually had a brownish-gray hue, though some were sky blue. The sling was made of 1³⁄₁₆-inch-wide brown cotton webbing, in two sections, and was fitted with a distinctive variation of the Chambers buckle made of light sheet brass. The buckle had three slots and measured 1⁷⁄₁₆ inches wide by 1¼ inches. The outer edges of the top and bottom bars were convex, and the sling was sewn to the second bar rather than to one of the end bars, as in later examples of the 1874 canteen.

Because this version simply represented a further modification of the Pattern 1858 canteen, the stopper was usually found attached according to the 1872 configuration, that is, with a 4½-inch length of brass jack chain hooked to a neck ring of brass wire. The loop for attaching the chain was formed by a twist of the wire, which also tightened the ring about the neck of the canteen. The last link in the other end of the chain was hooked around the finger ring of the stopper. Some canteens remained unaltered, with the original iron chain attached to one of the upper sling guides, per the 1858 design. Interestingly, the type-specimen photographed at the conclusion of the board's deliberations shows a neck ring with pinched loop and brass safety chain. Although Type 1 canteens are rarely if ever encountered with these features, the photograph suggests it was the board's intent to use this method for attaching the cork. One hypothesis for this contradiction is that older versions already in use were provided with the new sling early on, without bothering to change the cork attachments. Later on, 1858-pattern canteens drawn from stock for conversion received all of the prescribed alterations outlined below for the Type 3 canteen, including the pinched neck ring.

Canteen, Pattern 1874 (Type 2)

This variant of the 1874 canteen was distinguished by its outer cover of brown duck (fig. 168). Also unique to this type was the leather welt sewn into the cover's seam, probably for added strength if the canvas shrank (fig. 169). This modification is an enigma so far as the historical record is concerned, but the rather crude manner in which the cover was put on suggests that it may have

167. The first style of the 1874-pattern canteen.

Left:

168. Example of canvas-covered 1874 canteen, which may represent a department depot or field-level modification.

Right:

169. Side view of the canteen in figure 168, showing the leather welt in the seam.

been an early method of double covering the canteen.[68] A key point was the bottom sling guide, which remained intact under the cover, with the strap passing through it. The upper sling guides likewise lay beneath the cover. The cover simply may have been pulled over the Type 1 canteen, then closed by hand stitching from the upper guides to the base of the neck.

Although this style of canteen was less common than either the Type 1 or the Type 3, several examples were encountered. All of those examined were nearly identical in construction, suggesting that this rather crude conversion may have been done at one of the western depots rather than at either the arsenal or the unit level. All three styles of cork attachments were seen on this type: iron jack chain, brass jack chain with twisted neck loop, and brass safety chain with neck loop.

Invariably, the covers were ill fitting, but the unique method of hand stitching was consistent from one specimen to another. The only documentary evidence discovered thus far that may relate to this canteen was a requisition submitted by Captain O. E. Michaelis in December 1877 for "1600 canteen covers, straps, and corks."[69] These may or may not have been the leather welt covers. In any event, the telegram indicated that the Fort Abraham Lincoln Depot was reconditioning the canteens turned in from the Sioux and Nez Percé campaigns.

Canteen, Pattern 1874 (Type 3)

The specifications for the 1874 canteen provided with double covers were eventually standardized, probably during the summer or fall of 1877. This final version was distinguished by the presence of only the upper two sling guides, and the leather welt was omitted from the duck cover (fig. 170). The bottom guide was removed as unnecessary because the duck cover alone was sufficient

Above:

170. Later version of the 1874 canteen, as finally standardized. The "U.S." marking, however, is not common.

Below:

171. Detail of the neck ring and chain stopper attachment used on late-manufacture 1874 canteens.

to hold the sling in place. The cover also fit more evenly and tightly without it. The duck itself was usually of a lighter-shade drab, as compared with the brown dye used on earlier patterns.

The Chambers buckle employed on this version was made of much heavier brass (about 1/16 inch thick) and measured 1¼ inches by 1⅝ inches. The sides were straight, rather than being curved as on the earlier types, and the sling was invariably sewn to one of the outer bars of the buckle. Lieutenant John Pitman's photographs of the 1874 board samples reveal the same Chambers buckle and method of attachment. However, no example of a Type 1 canteen with this arrangement has yet been encountered. All of the examined canteens display the lightweight buckle attached as described earlier.

The arsenals used brass safety chain exclusively for attaching the stopper (fig. 171). The neck ring, rather than being a twist of wire, was made of heavier brass wire, pinched at one point to form a loop for the chain and at the same time to tighten the ring about the spout. This last type of neck ring, with safety chain, may be found on any of the earlier canteens, since it would have been applied to canteens turned in for reconditioning with missing or broken chains.

One subtype of this canteen has been encountered and may bridge the Type 2 and Type 3 modifications. It had the later version of the Chambers buckle, as well as the stopper chain and ring. However, the bottom sling guide still was present under the cover. The cover, stenciled with "U.S." in block letters ½ inch high, and the sling were dyed brown. It should be noted that this particular variation was the only Pattern 1874 canteen encountered having arsenal-applied U.S. property markings.

Meat Can, Pattern 1874 (Type 1)

Oval in shape and made of stamped-block tin, the meat can comprised two halves, or pans, that fit together (fig. 172). The bottom pan, measuring 6⅝ inches wide by 8¼ inches long by ¾ inch deep, was provided with a folding iron handle hinged at one end of the pan. The handle was stamped "U S" (3/16 inch high) near its outer end. The cast-iron hinge was attached to the pan by three roundheaded rivets. The handle on the Type 1 can had a slot, ¼ inch by 5¼ inches, down the middle to diffuse heat.

The upper pan, intended to be used as a plate, measured slightly smaller so that it would fit within the overlapping lip of the fry pan. The depth was the same as that of the bottom half. At the outer end was a ¾-inch oval ring attached by a fold of tin riveted to the side. The ring served both as a pull for separating the two pans and as a lock for the handle. Both pans were distinguished from later versions by having somewhat smaller bottoms due to the longer, straight-beveled sides.

Meat Can, Pattern 1874 (Type 2)

Similar in overall appearance to the Type 1 meat can, this variation incorporated several minor improvements. The most obvious change was the elimination of the slotted handle, probably because it bent too easily. The improved solid handle, also stamped "U.S.," measured ⅞ inch wide and was made of lighter-weight iron. A longitudinal rib formed down the center added rigidity. The cast hinge was replaced by one formed of heavy stamped iron. One specimen, bearing a larger ¼-inch "U.S." marking and "WATERVLIET" in small letters, was recovered from the Seventh Cavalry's retreat route in the Little Bighorn Valley, suggesting that the solid-handle can was being issued as early as 1876.

The sides of the pans were formed convex, rather than having flat chamfers. This made the bottoms of the pans approximately ¼ inch larger than on the Type 1 meat can and better adapted the pans for holding soups and other liquids.

The fry pan was not so elongated in shape as earlier, measuring 6½ inches by 8 inches. The upper pan was made shallower, having a depth of only ⅝ inch. The exact date of the introduction of this meat can remains uncertain; however, a Watervliet Arsenal drawing dated May 1880 illustrates the Type 2 meat can as the one being produced at that time.

172. Variations of the 1874-pattern meat can.

173. Pre-1874 tin cup (left) and regulation 1874-pattern cup (right).

Meat Can, Pattern 1874 (Type 3)

This, the most common and the last version of the 1874 meat can, was identical to the Type 2 except that the pull-ring was mounted on the plate in an offset position to the right of center. The reason for this change has not been determined.

Ordnance Memoranda No. 29 of 1885, a summary of the horse equipments and cavalry accoutrements in use at that time, stated that the upper and lower pans of the meat can were to be ¾ inch and 1 inch deep, respectively, but actual specimens uniformly measure ⅝ inch and ¾ inch, respectively.[70]

Tin Cup, Pattern 1874

The cup as finally standardized by the 1874 board measured, on average, 4 inches in diameter by 4⅛ inches high (fig. 173). It was made of "XXXX" block tin with a rolled lip and flat-crimped bottom affixed by a wiped solder joint. A folded and soldered seam extended up the side under the handle. The small ear-shaped handle measured 1⅛ inches wide at the top and ⅝ inch wide at the bottom. It was fastened to the side of the cup by two roundheaded iron rivets at the top and one at the lower end. Stamped in the handle were the letters "U.S" ⅜ inch high.

Utensils, Pattern 1874

The 1874 knife had a steel spearpoint blade 5¼ inches long with an integral cast-iron handle (fig. 174). The blade was stamped on the left side "U.S." or "U.S.A." in block letters measuring either ⅛ inch or ³⁄₁₆ inch high. On those examined, the "U.S.A." marking was invariably in the larger-size letters and probably was the earlier form of marking utensils. A knife bearing this style of marking was found on the Little Bighorn Battlefield. Overall length of the knife varied from 9 inches to 9⅛ inches. Some examined specimens had handles with straight, tapered sides narrowing toward the blade, whereas others had curved edges making a handle ¹³⁄₁₆ inch wide in the middle.

Also made of steel, the fork had three tines and a cast-iron handle. Overall length was 7½ inches. The same type of "U.S." or "U.S.A." markings as on the knife appeared on the reverse of the shank of the fork, between the handle and the tines.[71] Contradicting the theory that all army utensils of the period are so marked is a Pattern 1874 fork found in the Reno-Benteen rifle pits on the Little

174. *Mess utensils adopted in 1874.
Leather scabbards were provided for the
knife and fork.*

Bighorn Battlefield. This particular specimen is in relatively good condition and
bears no markings whatsoever.[72]

Constructed of heavy tinned iron, the spoon measured 7⅜ to 7½ inches in
length. The bowl was 1⅝ inches wide by about 2¾ inches long. A pressed rib
extended longitudinally from the bowl for nearly three-quarters the length of
the handle. The handle was stamped "U.S.A." (lengthwise), in letters ³⁄₁₆ inch
high, on the flat near the upper end.[73]

Utensil Scabbards

To prevent damage to the haversack pockets, the army provided scabbards made
of scrap leather, simply folded and sewn along two sides, for both the knife and
the fork. The dressed side was turned outermost so that the smooth side would
be inside and would not snag the sharp utensil points. The sheath for the fork
measured 1¾ inches wide by 6¼ inches long. The knife scabbard was about 1½
inches wide by 8¼ inches long.

Hagner Pouches, Pattern 1872, Modified

Both the No. 1 and the No. 2 pouches were modified to accept .45-caliber rifle
and carbine ammunition. Only one method of alteration for the No. 1 pouch
and two variations for the No. 2 have been observed. The principal modification employed for both types was the addition of strips of thin leather shims
hand stitched above each row of cartridge loops. These extended into the loops
to reduce the size sufficiently to grip the smaller-caliber cartridges. Some shims
had the dressed side of the leather exposed, whereas others had the smooth side,
dyed black, outermost.

The alternate method, observed only on the No. 2 pouch, was the addition of a strip of bridle leather stitched in place just above the row of loops on the front of the pouch. This provided sufficient friction to prevent the cartridges from slipping all the way down to their rims. In some instances, the leather fingers were omitted from the loops on the inside of a No. 2 pattern pouch simply because the cartridges were supported by the bottom of the box itself.

Some No. 2 pouches also were altered by the removal of the tab from the flap. The finial was moved to the flap, and the tab was attached to the bottom of the pouch, where the stud formerly was located, with two brass rivets. This modification, devised by Major D. W. Flagler at Rock Island Arsenal, prevented the longer .45-caliber cartridges from slipping down and unbuttoning the billet strap.

Thimble or Prairie Cartridge Belts

Field-fabricated cartridge belts took a variety of forms and were used by both soldiers and civilians on the frontier. Certain common features have been noted among examples with known or probable military provenance. The use of a cast-off army belt plate, either the 1851 eagle plate or the 1839-pattern U.S. oval, was a distinctive feature of belts of military origin, although period photographs show many civilians wearing them as well. Because of their ready availability, military harness buckles and other hardware were incorporated into the belt. Thimble belts often were made of black leather, since the soldier had access to regulation belts and other military leather. In most instances, when a regulation waist belt was used as the foundation for the cartridge belt, the style was unmistakable. The descriptions below represent several belts in various public and private collections that are characteristic of soldier-made cartridge belts of the 1870s.

Thimble Belt No. 1.　This specimen was constructed using a regulation Pattern 1851 NCO buff-leather waist belt, complete with its eagle plate (fig. 175). It had thirty-seven loops of black bridle leather for .45-caliber cartridges. On the left side was a space 2¾ inches wide, probably intended for a knife scabbard. Size adjustment was made by the addition of a russet leather strap, 1¼ inches wide, hand stitched to the inner right side of the belt. This strap had a series of holes to accept the original belt hook.

Thimble Belt No. 2.　Made of black bridle leather, this belt measured 1½ inches wide by 34½ inches long. The end of the belt, part of which was missing, formed the billet. This mated to a common black japanned roller buckle. The

176. *Prairie belt, made from two infantry waist belts. This well-made belt may have been one of the samples submitted by Colonel W. B. Hazen to the 1874 Infantry Equipment Board.*

buckle chape enclosed a ¾-inch-wide standing loop, which served as a keeper for the free end of the billet. The belt had forty-three black leather .45-caliber loops.

Thimble Belt No. 3.   This unusual belt was fabricated by using two Civil War infantry waist belts, one of which was its original full length with the oval Pattern 1856 plate on the right end (fig. 176). Forty .50-caliber loops were hand stitched to this belt. A second belt, with its original standing loop intact, was slipped under the outer belt, the loop connecting the two. The end near the plate was fastened to the outer belt by the stitching for the first cartridge loop on that end. The two belts were stitched together at the midpoint to prevent the outer belt from sagging under the weight of the ammunition. Both belts were creased along their outer edges.

Judged by its unused condition and its unique construction, this belt may be one of the two submitted to the 1874 Infantry Equipment Board by Colonel W. B. Hazen. Such belts are listed on the inventory presented in *Ordnance Memoranda No. 19.*[74]

Thimble Belt No. 4.   This black leather belt measured 1⅞ inches wide by 40¾ inches long, with a 1-inch black japanned-iron roller buckle on the left end (fig. 177). The buckle was attached to the belt by a chape 1 inch wide by 2⅞ inches long with a standing loop. On the right end of the belt was a billet, 1 inch by 8½ inches, with four adjustment holes. The belt was partially covered by a canvas sleeve 28½ inches long.

The .45-caliber loops were made of a single piece of natural cotton duck folded to three thicknesses and hand stitched through the belt and its cover. The belt had a capacity of forty-four rounds.

Thimble Belt No. 5.   The belt itself was constructed of a piece of No. 12 drab duck folded to six thicknesses 3 inches wide (fig. 178). The .45-caliber loops, 2¼ inches wide, were similarly made of three folds of duck, thus forming forty-one loops along the length of the belt. At the left side was a space, 1⅜ inches wide, stitched along the bottom. This tiny pocket, formed by the flat loop, would have been a convenient place to store the Springfield carbine screwdriver or the shell extractor.

The thirteenth loop from the right end of the belt was made of leather and shows evidence of once having been the anchor point for a holster strap extending toward the buckle. The billet, sewn to the left end, measured 1³⁄₁₆ inches wide by 11⅜ inches long.

Thimble Belt No. 6.   This was a black bridle-leather belt 1½ inches wide by 33¼ inches long. A billet, 1 inch wide by 8½ inches long, was riveted to the right end of the belt; on the other end was a chape with a standing loop and iron horseshoe buckle. Forty .45-caliber loops, also made of black leather, measured 1⅛ inches wide.

Thimble Belt No. 7.   A regulation Pattern 1874 waist belt incorporating an 1851 eagle belt plate was used as the foundation for this rather crudely made cartridge belt. It had forty-five loops of black leather for holding .45-caliber ammunition. There was no provision for adjustment, other than the original holes in the belt. Thus, the hook is forced into one of the loops from the back side.

Thimble Belt No. 8.   This belt was made of black, lightweight leather of the type normally associated with officers' belts. Both edges of the belt and the loops were creased with double lines. At each end of the belt was a group of four loops separated from the rest by a space. On the right side of the belt, this space measured 5 inches and probably accommodated the holster. The space on the

177. (Top to bottom): All-leather .50-caliber thimble belt; canvas-covered belt, .45-caliber; removable canvas cartridge loops; 1874-pattern saber belt; two sets of Hazen cartridge loops and an experimental cartridge wristlet to speed the loading of the single-shot Springfield.
(Hayes Otoupalik Collection)

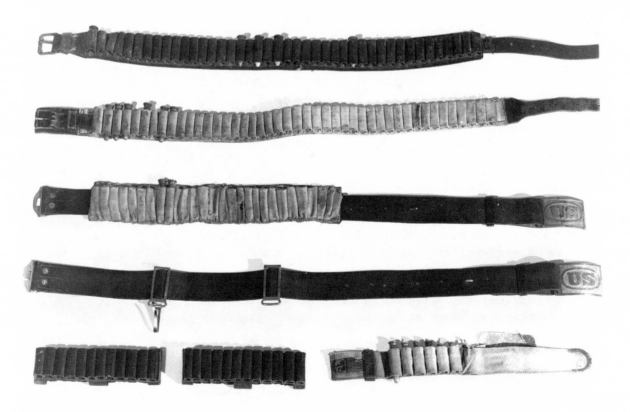

left side measured 2½ inches and may have been used for the pistol cartridge pouch. The leather loops, hand stitched with either linen or cotton thread, were 1⅜ inches wide and held .50-caliber ammunition. The standard hook arrangement on the doubled right end of the belt was used for adjustment. A sliding loop, ⁷⁄₁₆ inch wide, held a one-piece cast-brass officer-type eagle plate. This mated with a standard brass catch attached to the left end of the belt by three rows of stitching.

Thimble Belt No. 9. Also based on a Civil War–period officers' field belt, complete with its brass wire adjustment buckle, this belt had twenty-nine .50-caliber loops. The loops also were of black leather. It used an 1851-pattern eagle plate with a three-piece German silver wreath, affixed to the belt by two copper rivets.

Cartridge Belt, Pattern 1876 (Type 1)

This regulation item was a leather belt with a 2-inch-wide drab-colored canvas covering hemmed along the bottom edge (fig. 179). Sewn to the belt were fifty-four cotton webbing loops 1¾ inches wide (according to specifications) for .45-caliber ammunition. However, on the belts examined, the loops actually measured somewhat less, averaging nearer 1⅝ inches. Belts were made in two lengths, 38 inches and 44 inches, as measured from the buckle bar to the end of the billet. The leather belt protruded from the end of the canvas covering to form a billet measuring 1⅝ inches wide by 12½ inches long. The billet was backed with a layer of thin leather, smooth side outermost and stitched around

Above:

178. (Top to bottom): Removable canvas cartridge loops made for use on the waist or saber belt; leather thimble belt; thimble belt fabricated entirely of canvas, except for the chape and billet. (Ralph Heinz Collection)

Below:

179. Pattern 1876 cartridge belts (top to bottom): standard Type 1; standard Type 3; Type 3 belt, shortened, with strap added for bayonet or knife; Type 2 belt made for .50-caliber ammunition.

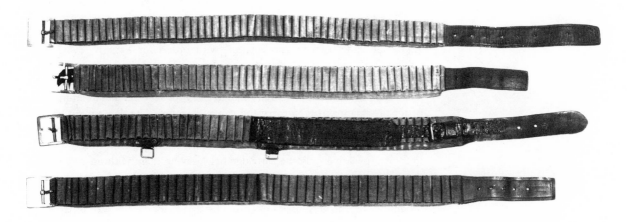

180. Detail showing difference in width between the Type 1 and Type 3 belts.

the edges. The belt was coupled by a brass frame buckle measuring 2⅛ inches wide by 2⁵⁄₁₆ inches high. Five thousand of these belts were manufactured early in 1877.[75]

Cartridge Belt, Pattern 1876 (Type 2)

A variant of the basic belt described above, this version had varnished-webbing loops measuring 2 inches wide (or slightly less) sewn to a canvas belt 2¼ inches wide. This change was made when Watervliet Arsenal was unable to procure enough of the narrower webbing to fill its orders.[76] Since this belt used the wider webbing, the width of the covering had to be increased by ¼ inch. All other features were the same as described for the first type.

On February 13, 1878, Captain O. E. Michaelis, still commanding the ordnance depot at Fort Abraham Lincoln, requested Watervliet Arsenal to manufacture three hundred belts in .50 caliber.[77] These likely were intended for issue to the various Indian auxiliaries, guides, and civilian teamsters who invariably accompanied the army into the field. When those individuals did not have their own weapons, ordnance officers often provided them with "second-class" arms, such as Model 1867 Sharps improved carbines or various models of .50-caliber Springfield rifles. All of the examined .50-caliber belts correspond to the Type 2 dimensions. Although an example of this belt in .45 caliber has yet to surface, ordnance records indicate that such belts were produced.

Cartridge Belt, Pattern 1876 (Type 3)

Authorized by the chief of ordnance on November 30, 1877, this version of the 1876 belt differed from its predecessor in that the width of the belt was increased to 2½ inches.[78] By making the skirt of the canvas covering wider, the cartridges could be inserted all the way to the rims, yet the wider skirt would protect the uniform from being smudged by the lead bullet (fig. 180). Watervliet produced 12,500 of these belts in combination with orders for Pattern 1874 infantry equipments.[79]

In its haste to adopt a cartridge belt, the Ordnance Department failed to make any provision for the cavalryman to carry the revolver and its ammunition or for the infantryman to carry the trowel bayonet. The department absurdly assumed that the soldier would wear both the leather waist belt and the cartridge belt. On taking the field, however, most soldiers simply sacrificed the waist belt in favor of wearing only the cartridge belt, leaving them with no way to carry the other equipment. It was not long before soldiers developed some expedients to alleviate this problem. As a result, these belts will be found with various field modifications. Infantry-used belts often have a separate leather strap attached to the inside of the belt on the left. This strap, often fabricated from a piece of 1872 brace leather, usually has punched into its free end a hole that fastens over the buckle tongue. The bayonet or entrenching tool scabbard was slipped onto this strap and was thus suspended below the cartridge belt.

Cavalry belts were distinguished by the addition of a leather billet over the outside of the cartridge loops on the right side. The free end of the strap either was fastened with a small harness buckle at the junction of the loops and billet or was simply laid over the billet and fastened to the belt buckle. In this way, the holster with its 2-inch-wide belt loop could be slipped over the attachment and, for that matter, so could the pistol cartridge pouch.

TO THE GREAT RELIEF AND SATISFACTION OF THE ARMY

EQUIPMENT AND CLOTHING, 1878–1880

ACTIVE CAMPAIGNING ON the northern plains during the years 1876 to 1878 pointed up several lingering deficiencies in army equipage. These extended military operations, involving great marching distances, extremes of weather, and numerous engagements, were a proving ground of incomparable value for the new clothing and equipments. Yet, in spite of all of the effort and testing devoted to improvements in equipage, certain problems had not yet been resolved. Captain J. W. Reilly, chief ordnance officer for the Division of the Missouri, observed:

> The equipment adopted by the Infantry Board of 1874 is too complicated and cumbersome for field service, however neat and well adapted it may be for garrison duty. I think it will be accepted as truth that the equipment best adapted to our service is that which the men themselves spontaneously adopt after the experience of several campaigns; and such experienced soldiers will not cumber themselves with the regulation equipment, but limit their burden to a cartridge belt, canteen, haversack for rations and the blanket roll. The "carrying braces," the essential feature of the equipments of '74, were all discarded by the men in the recent Sioux and Nez Perce campaigns. Although "regulation," the troops in the Department of Dakota are no longer required or permitted to wear them. It is a useless expense to furnish them for garrison duty. We should take what the soldiers themselves find convenient and necessary and make them uniform and neat for garrison duty. The adoption of the cartridge belt seems to be universally spontaneous. This seems a conclusive argument against the "pouch." I think the Cavalry accoutrement and equipment the best any troops ever had, and with some slight exceptions as to material and manufacture of smaller parts, eminently satisfactory.[1]

Not all were against the brace system, however. A soldier signing himself as "Vindex" retorted, "Troops in other Departments have worn these equipments on other campaigns than that against the Sioux and Nez Perces, and with most satisfactory results, the infantry soldiers being able to lend a helping hand to their comrades in the cavalry, with the little conveniences for cooking which they carried by means of the brace system."[2]

The search for optimum designs for the soldier's individual equipment continued to perplex the army, fueling further debate. The most annoying problem still was how best to carry the infantryman's field kit. All of the inventions tried up to that time had been flawed in one respect or another. The 1872 brace system, for instance, was designed so that the weight of the cartridge boxes on the belt would serve to counterbalance that of the valise suspended on the man's lower back. Theoretically sound, the yoke failed because it seriously constricted both breathing and circulation, as had the breast straps of the old double-bag knapsack of the Civil War. Palmer's system, also using a yoke from which the clothing bag and haversack were suspended, interfered with the soldier's balance and movements.

Central to reform was the army's realization that soldiers simply would not "carry anything more" than they were "compelled to."[3] The troops resorted almost universally to the blanket roll. As one officer put it, "[This is] not so much because it is the best way of carrying the kit as because all other devices thus far adopted or tried have been comparatively so much inferior."[4] Appealing for the army to simply adopt what the soldiers preferred to use, a correspondent writing under the name "Just One More" editorialized in the *Army and Navy Journal* that infantrymen should carry only "the rifle, the bayonet . . . the haversack with food supply, and the ammunition." He added: "The knapsack containing clothes the soldier can get along without, seems to him an additional burden that it is better to lose than to waste his strength carrying. If it is considered necessary that the troops carry tents and clothing, a few needful articles may be rolled up in their shelter tents, instead of using the knapsacks or canvas bags. The haversack and canteen answer the purpose for which they are designed very well."[5]

Even Generals William Sherman and Philip Sheridan were strongly influenced by the army's service on the plains. Both expressed their preference for a commonsense light marching order for infantry by advocating the adoption of the blanket roll, the "hunting pouch" or cartridge belt, the entrenching knife, and the best rifle available. They likewise broke with tradition by recommending that the cavalry abandon not only the saber but the whole idea of fighting from horseback in favor of simply being equipped and trained as mounted infantry.[6]

Addressing the secretary of war in the spring of 1878, Chief of Ordnance Benet conceded: "The equipments as now made are very expensive. If the recent field experience in the Departments of the Platte, Dakota, and Columbia will result in simplifying them and reducing their cost, it is a matter well worth consideration."[7] A short time later, Secretary of War George Washington McCrary directed the army to assemble another board of officers, the seventh board within a decade, to consider "the whole subject of intrenching knives, intrenching bayonets, trowel bayonets, and intrenching tools for Army use, and also the equipment of troops generally."[8]

In mounting this new effort, the army compiled a representative team of distinguished and field-experienced infantry, cavalry, and artillery officers to grapple with all the issues at hand. Chairing the board was no less a figure than Colonel Nelson A. Miles, whose Fifth Infantry had been singularly successful against the Sioux and Cheyennes in the closing episodes of the Great Sioux War. Equally notable was the Fourth Cavalry's Colonel Ranald S. Mackenzie, who had been instrumental in subjugating the Kiowas and Comanches in Texas. Lieutenant Colonel Henry A. Morrow, who first experienced military life as a volunteer private during the Mexican War and eventually rose to general officer rank by the end of the Civil War, brought an additional perspective. In the postwar era he had served as second in command of the Thirty-sixth and later

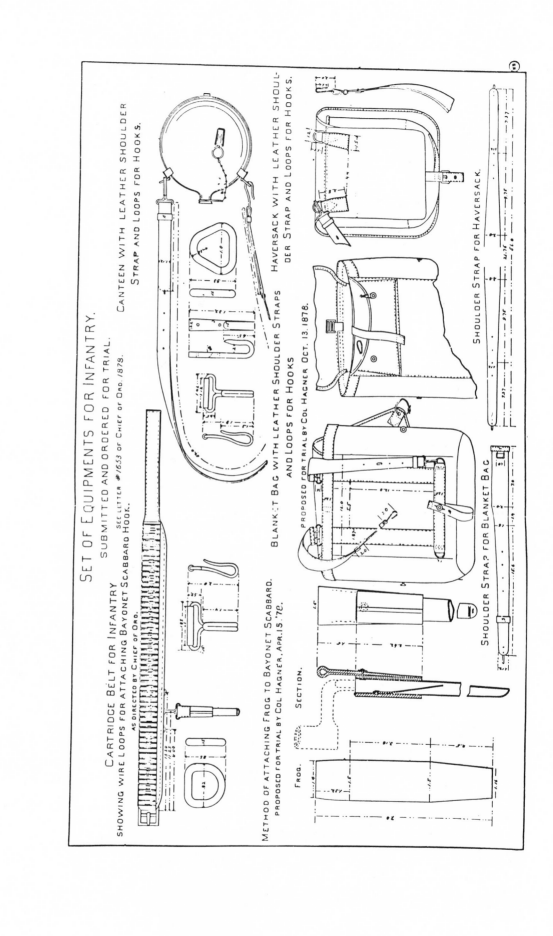

SET OF EQUIPMENTS FOR INFANTRY.

CARTRIDGE BELT FOR INFANTRY.
SUBMITTED AND ORDERED FOR TRIAL.
SEE LETTER #1653 OF CHIEF OF ORD. 1878.
SHOWING WIRE LOOPS FOR ATTACHING BAYONET SCABBARD HOOK.
AS DIRECTED BY CHIEF OF ORD.

CANTEEN WITH LEATHER SHOULDER
STRAP AND LOOPS FOR HOOKS.

HAVERSACK WITH LEATHER SHOUL-
DER STRAP AND LOOPS FOR HOOKS.

SHOULDER STRAP FOR HAVERSACK.

METHOD OF ATTACHING FROG TO BAYONET SCABBARD.
PROPOSED FOR TRIAL BY COL HAGNER, APR. 15 .'78.

SECTION.

FROG.

BLANKET BAG WITH LEATHER SHOULDER STRAPS
AND LOOPS FOR HOOKS
PROPOSED FOR TRIAL BY COL HAGNER OCT. 13. 1878.

SHOULDER STRAP FOR BLANKET BAG.

the Thirteenth infantry regiments. Major George B. Sanford had followed the fortunes of the First Cavalry since joining the regiment at the outbreak of the Civil War. His frontier experience included campaigns against the Apaches in Arizona, the Modocs in the Northwest, and the Nez Percé in Idaho. Also a Civil War veteran officer, Captain Daniel Webster Benham had marched with the regular army's Eighteenth and Thirty-sixth infantry regiments before transferring to the Seventh Infantry in 1869. He too had served against the Sioux and the Nez Percés. Breveted twice during the war, the board's recorder, Captain Joseph P. Sanger, had served with the First Artillery since 1861. In 1881 he and Lieutenant Colonel Emory Upton would make a global tour of other armies.

Responding to the field reports submitted by Captain Michaelis in 1876, the resourceful and aggressive Colonel Hagner put his people at Watervliet to work designing improvements in the various pieces of equipage months before the board was called to order (fig. 181).[9] It was obvious that the Palmer brace concept had failed, but Hagner noted that some of the individual components had met with some success during the campaigns of 1876–77. The haversack, for instance, was generally acceptable in size and shape. Its webbing sling posed the main problem because it twisted and rolled up after being used for a short time. Soldiers with field experience advocated a leather sling. Additionally, Hagner saw several other ways to improve the haversack. The first of these was to construct it, like the canteen cover, of drab duck so that it would not show soiling as readily as the natural color. He also found that a cost savings could be realized by substituting a flap made of a double thickness of duck in place of the vulcanized rubber material. The double flap was just as resistant to rain, and it did not absorb heat and flake off as did the rubber flap. A correction was also made in the undersized meat-can pocket of the original 1874 pattern. The remodeled haversack included a considerably larger pocket, like that of the Type 2 Pattern 1874, which was of the same dimensions as the front section of the bag. Rather than having form-fitted utensil pockets, Hagner's new pattern incorporated square-cut pockets of width equal to that of the gusset so that they could simply be sewn into the front and back seams, thus saving a construction step. Further economy was effected by abandoning the eagle button and its costly method of attachment in favor of the patented shank button. Drab webbing was substituted for all of the leather parts, including the flap binding and buckle chape, and of course, the brace attachments were done away with altogether. All in all, the final product hardly resembled the 1874 haversack except in overall size and shape.

With the widespread complaints about the webbing canteen sling, Hagner devised a method for attaching a 1-inch-wide russet leather sling to the canteen body (fig. 182). This was accomplished by first removing the bottom sling guide from the original 1858-pattern body, if it had in fact survived the previous modification. Then, as with the last version of the 1874 canteen, the body was given the double cover of petersham cloth and drab duck. Hagner added a triangular iron wire loop, fastened by a light iron strap, to each of the upper sling guides (fig. 183). Brass hooks on each end of the adjustable leather sling were used to attach the canteen.

Hagner designed a replacement for the clothing bag in the form of a larger drab duck knapsack designed to be worn on the back in conventional fashion. This "blanket bag," as he called it, was made commodious enough to carry the folded blanket, an extra pair of shoes, underclothing, and toilet items. The

On the facing page:
*181. Watervliet Arsenal drawings of
Pattern 1878 equipments.* (William E.
Meuse Collection)

Left:

182. Pattern 1878 canteen and leather sling.

Right:

183. Side view of 1878 canteen, showing modification for sling attachment.

On the facing page:
184. Watervliet Arsenal drawing of sample Pattern 1876 cartridge belt modified for carrying the bayonet scabbard.
(William E. Meuse Collection)

shelter half and poncho could be rolled and strapped to the top of the pack. A large flap covered the main pocket and the front of the bag, and detachable leather slings were fitted to the back.

The 1876-pattern cartridge belt had been an instant success with the troops and by 1878 was an established article of equipment. Still, it had its shortcomings. The arsenal version lacked any means by which the doughboy could carry his trowel bayonet, entrenching tool, or standard bayonet. Since the entrenching tool could be of no use unless the soldier carried it into the field, Hagner added three brass rings along the bottom left edge of the belt to accommodate it. He also recommended modifying the standard triangular and trowel bayonet scabbards by substituting a brass wire hook in place of the leather belt loops (fig. 184). Using these hooks, the soldier could easily attach the bayonet to the cartridge belt; the spacing of the three rings permitted adjustment for different waist sizes so that the bayonet would ride comfortably on the left hip.[10]

This belt has been misidentified as being a modification performed at the Fort Abraham Lincoln Ordnance Depot.[11] The error arises from misinterpretation of a statement contained in Captain Stanhope E. Blunt's 1882 annual report of operations, wherein he stated: "The woven belt (Mills) is now in the hands of about one-half the troops in the department. All these belts have, before issue,

PLAN FOR ATTACHING THE FROG TO THE TROWEL-BAYONET SCABBARD
AND FOR ATTACHING THIS SCABBARD TO THE CARTRIDGE-BELT.

PROPOSED BY COL. P. V. HAGNER.

FIG. A.

THIS BELT ANSWERS ALSO FOR THE
ORDINARY BAYONET SCABBARD ALTERED
BY TURNING IT IN THE FROG AS IN FIG. A.

been altered by the addition of rings for the bayonet scabbard." Blunt made it unmistakably clear that he was speaking of modifications to the Mills woven cartridge belt, not the Pattern 1876 belt. Therefore, a so-called prairie belt with brass rings most certainly was not the Fort Lincoln modification. Rather, it was the most common variety of the 1876 cartridge belt.[12]

Like those before it, the Miles Board invited samples of equipage inventions by anyone who wanted to submit them. This time an inordinate number came from within the army itself, perhaps reflecting current interest in the subject and concern that the troops be provided with equipment that worked in frontier conditions.

Of the several patterns of infantry equipments delivered to the board, one in particular made a favorable impression on the officers. This was a light steel yoke, covered in leather, worn across the body in blanket roll fashion, to which a modified clothing bag was attached. This bag, designed by Colonel Hagner, held the blanket, spare underclothing, and incidentals. The overcoat and shelter half were rolled and strapped atop the bag. The principle, apparently, was that this spring yoke would not compress the lungs or blood vessels.

The board was also intrigued by an equipment system submitted by James Sherlock, who had laid the same design before the 1874 Infantry Equipment Board. Sherlock's invention relied on a brace and a knapsack, the latter being fitted with special pockets for two square canteens. It also included two small haversacks, one hanging on either side of the body, and a waist belt. But, after the recent campaigns and the great outcry against the Palmer system, the army remained skeptical of any design based on a brace. The proceedings of the Miles Board suggest that one hundred sets of the Sherlock equipments were issued for trial, but further information as to whether or not this was carried out has not been located.

The board, in an apparent contradiction, expressed great confidence in the concept of the steel yoke yet recommended that only one hundred sets be manufactured at Watervliet Arsenal for field trials. On the other hand, they concurred with the manufacture of one thousand sets of the Pattern 1878 blanket bag equipments, the system designed by Colonel Hagner and his people at Watervliet Arsenal. The Ordnance Department had already started production of these equipments early in May 1878, and Hagner had reported these ready for issue near the end of August, but action was delayed because of the army's impending review of equipments.[13] However, the equipments were distributed to the troops immediately after the board concluded its business. It would appear that none of the other trial equipments proved as successful as the Pattern 1878 blanket bag equipments, which emerged as the officially adopted pattern.[14] In all fairness, however, it must be taken into consideration that ten times as many of these were issued as either of the other two, if indeed the steel yoke and the Sherlock equipments ever were released. This factor alone may have greatly biased rank-and-file opinion in favor of the Ordnance Department's preferred design. The Pattern 1878 blanket bag equipments were produced in large numbers over the following twenty years, remaining the standard field equipment for infantry until after the turn of the century (figs. 185 and 186). Nevertheless, the time-honored blanket roll simply would not go away and continued to enjoy wide popularity through the 1890s.[15]

Although the Pattern 1876 cartridge belt, as modified by Hagner, remained as the regulation belt for a time, its days were clearly numbered. The Miles Board

185. *Soldier modeling Pattern 1878 blanket bag.* (National Archives)

186. *Side view of equipment. Note the Type 2 1874 haversack and 1874 canteen, as standardized.* (National Archives)

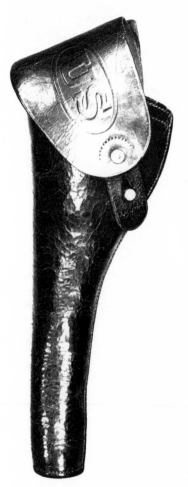

187. Pattern 1879 holster.
(Dwight Clark Collection)

greatly favored a belt designed by First Sergeant J. F. Unger but at the same time recommended the Mills method for weaving cartridge belts of cotton webbing with integral loops. After some experimentation, it was found that the double-wide Unger belt could not be made on the machinery designed by Mills. In the end, no Unger belts were produced by the Ordnance Department. General Sherman, on being advised of the situation, ordered that single-webbing belts with a capacity of fifty rounds of .45-caliber ammunition be adopted. If more ammunition was needed, two belts could be laced together by means of four grommets placed in the ends of the belt and worn as a bandolier. It would be another two years, however, before the Ordnance Department negotiated contracts with Major Mills to supply the army with his belts.[16] The various types of the Pattern 1876 belt were used by both cavalry and infantry well into the 1880s before the Mills belt eventually replaced it.

For the most part, the cavalry had few complaints about the 1874 accoutrements. Exceptions, however, were the 1874- and 1875-pattern holsters. These were deficient in two aspects: the unreliability of the Hoffman swivel attachment and the size of the button hole in the flap. As discussed previously, the swivel attachment frequently broke loose from the holster, allowing the revolver to fall to the ground. Numerous revolvers were reported lost in this manner. The hard field service of the Sioux Campaign also pointed up the fact that the buttonhole was too large to fit snugly over the stud. After moderate use, the hole became elongated and the flap could not be fastened.

Hagner, having become aware of these problems, began work to remedy them in 1877. His answer for the elongated hole was to cut off and round the lower end of the flap. To this shortened flap he added a short, narrow strap with the buttonhole, similar to that found on the old Civil War holsters (fig. 187). The Hoffman swivel was abandoned in favor of a regular belt loop made of leather. This modified holster was approved for manufacture on February 4, 1879.[17] The Miles Board saw no reason to change the design and merely recommended that the 1879-pattern holster be retained in service.

Like their infantry brethren, cavalrymen insisted on using the cartridge belt for field service. Despite the overwhelming popularity of the belt, the board remained dogged in its conviction that a cartridge belt would not present a proper soldierly appearance, considered so necessary in garrison. Since the majority of the troops did not favor the Dyer pouch for active campaigning, the board recommended that its manufacture be discontinued and that the McKeever box be issued in lieu of it for garrison duty. That the McKeever was difficult to use while mounted was unimportant because its use was relegated to the parade ground and guard duty, most of which was performed dismounted anyway. By adopting the McKeever box for the mounted service, the army achieved a further measure of uniformity and economy. Now all branches were to be issued the same style of cartridge box.

The board recommended several changes in the army's clothing, but few of these passed Sherman's critical review. For instance, the board advised that the troops of all line branches be issued a dress helmet, similar to that of the cavalry, to the exclusion of the French cap. It also recognized the need for a special white duck summer uniform and cork helmet, which would give both officers and men some relief from the insufferably hot woolen uniforms. The Quartermaster Department had experimented with cork helmets as early as 1875 when 100 British helmets were purchased and sent to troops serving in Arizona. This innovation was slow in gaining the acceptance of high-ranking officers, and it was not until three years later that an additional 350 helmets were procured for issue to troops in Texas and at the artillery school at Fort Monroe, Virginia.[18] This second issue was just in time to attract the attention of the Miles Board.

Miles and his fellow officers, no doubt cognizant of the British army's use of cotton duck for making uniforms that were well adapted to desert climates, strongly recommended similar clothing for troops stationed in the American Southwest. "It is also within the knowledge of the Board," they stated, "that when allowed by those in command[,] officers are generally glad to wear white duck or linen coats and pants in summer, and that in warm climates, when campaigning[,] Cavalry soldiers wear their overalls and stable frocks whenever permitted."[19] The board recommended that these uniforms have removable buttons for easier washing and be trimmed in white braid for officers, with noncoms having white braid chevrons.

Additionally, the board moved to change the branch color of the infantry back to white, as it had been before 1851, due to the fugitive nature of the sky-blue dye used for uniform facings. The intense sunlight in the West quickly faded the trimmings to a light bluish-green hue that spoiled the appearance of the uniform. For officers, the board advocated the abolition of the shoulder strap and its replacement by collar insignia. Also, the board sought to replace the buttons and gold lace cuff trim on the officers' dress coat with Russian knots or, as an alternative, to make the coats plain, without any decoration.

For many years the bane of the infantryman had been the dust that permeated his pants and stockings, irritating the skin, and the brush that tore at the cuffs of his trousers. In rainy seasons the misery was compounded with wet, muddy cuffs and socks. The board officially acknowledged these problems by reporting: "The universal custom on marches of tying the pantaloons at the bottom and pulling the socks over them to save the feet and ankles from dust, which chafes them, and to prevent the pantaloons from flapping about the legs when saturated with mud, has . . . suggested leggings as a necessary part of the uniform of foot-soldiers for field service."[20]

The crusty Sherman, however, was not inclined to concur with what in his opinion were frivolities, and he struck down all these suggestions with the single exception that officers' cuff lace could be omitted, simply because the change would cost nothing. He thought the present dress cap for foot troops was "good enough," even if the men found that it was difficult to balance on their heads and that it rode heavily on their brows. Loath to contradict a tradition of nearly thirty years, Sherman also rejected the idea of changing the branch colors. They were by this time familiar to everyone, and he saw no good reason to switch.

Sherman did consider the summer uniforms and leggings to be reasonable enough indulgences, so long as the troops procured them at their own expense. He also left it up to the whim of the individual post commanders as to whether or not summer uniforms were to be sanctioned. This decision struck deeply at the individual soldier's comfort and provoked widespread reaction from both officers and the rank and file. One soldier, signing himself as "100 deg. in the shade," retorted:

With all due respect for the General's opinion, that summer uniform is sadly needed in the Army, and to the certain knowledge of the writer has been earnestly wished for by rank and file for many a year back, and ought to be adopted in General Orders from the War Department, and fixed so that it would not be left to the caprice, whim, or will of any commanding officer during the months of June, July, August, and September. The present uniform during the summer months is simply killing. Let us have the "summer uniform," please, and furnished by the Government to the men—not out of their own pockets—and that both officers and men be allowed to wear it at all times, both on duty and off, including officer of the day, dress parades, and inspections.[21]

Another officer went so far as to compare Sherman's conservative stance to that of "a grandmother dictating to a young society lady how to dress."[22] The objections piled up until finally, by sheer weight of numbers, the Quartermaster Department was compelled to disregard Sherman's veto. A sample summer helmet, based on the British pattern issued for trial two years earlier, was submitted to the secretary of war, who approved the specifications on May 5, 1880 (fig. 188). The first contract for the manufacture of the helmet was let that summer with the famed Horstmann Brothers & Company of Philadelphia.[23]

One of the things Sherman did approve, surprisingly enough, was the lining of the soldiers' overcoat capes with branch-color flannel corresponding to the uniform facings. The exception to this rule was the infantry, who were assigned dark-blue flannel to complement the distinctive overcoat chevrons. Actually, Sherman and Meigs had decided two years earlier to allow this change whenever the supply of overcoats dwindled to the point that additional manufactures were needed. The board recognized that soldiers throughout the army had been doing this for some time, at their own expense, because the lining added some warmth to the coats. Perhaps more important to the men, the lined capes contributed an element of flare to the outfit.[24]

Sherman also agreed that a blanket-lined canvas overcoat would be as warm as the buffalo coat yet lighter in weight. Troops engaged in active campaigning

188. The summer helmet recommended by the Miles Board and issued beginning in 1880. This helmet proved more popular in garrison than in the field. (Hayes Otoupalik Collection)

during the winter complained that besides being too heavy, the buffalo coats were too long for marching in snow.[25] A number of these "Miles overcoats," as they were known, were manufactured and issued to troops experimentally. These coats were made of a kersey-lined blue canvas outer shell, with an attached hood. However, for reasons that remain unclear, the enlisted men did not favor the canvas coats and refused to draw them. The remainder of the stock eventually was sent to posts in the Department of Dakota for gratuitous issue, as were the buffalo overcoats. Nevertheless, the decline of the buffalo herds made it obvious to the Quartermaster Department that a substitute would have to be found for the hide coats. In 1883 a refined version of the Miles overcoat, made of brown canvas, was adopted and continued in use until World War I.[26]

In 1877 ten thousand modified shirts were issued for trial, and as a result, a final version of the gray flannel shirt was designed and adopted on January 16, 1878.[27] In the fall of that year Deputy Quartermaster General James D. Bingham reported: "The troops have been in the habit of cutting off the collars of their shirts. Inquiry having shown that this habit was general, shirts are now made without collars."[28] This change resulted in a collar much like that found on civilian dress shirts of the period and made for a more comfortable fit beneath the blouse collar (fig. 189). Since soldiers normally were not permitted to appear outdoors in shirtsleeves, except while on fatigue or in the field, the old collar had little purpose. On campaign, a neckerchief had proven to be better protection against sunburn.

The blue flannel shirt had come about as a fluke yet had proven so popular with soldiers that the field reports on the subject were forwarded to the Miles Board for its consideration. The overwhelming evidence in favor of a blue shirt swayed the board to recommend it for adoption as standard issue. Even the conservative Sherman gave a nod to this revolutionary change, one that was to have a far-reaching effect on the army. A series of delays, however, prevented its official production and issue until early in 1881.[29]

The board supported the two grades of gray shirting flannel adopted early in 1876 and went a step further by gaining approval for stockings of a lighter weight for warm climates. These turned out to be made entirely of cotton and in three different colors, brown mixed, gray mixed, and white unbleached, something entirely new in army thinking. (The service has stuck to the ever-popular olive drab for most of the past century, even though enlisted personnel have not worn anything but boots for the past fifty years.) Although the stockings were not good marching socks, they were more comfortable for garrison wear. The board's proposal to also make drawers in two weights met, inexplicably, with Sherman's opposition.

189. *Collarless gray flannel shirt adopted in 1878.* (Smithsonian Institution)

The effect the Miles Board had on equipage was to consolidate and refine all the previous efforts made during the decade of the 1870s (fig. 190). Its recommendations recapitulated certain changes that had come about in the interim following the other boards, and it gained approval for many of its own initiatives. And, the board officially argued for further reforms in the army's matériel. Even though some of these measures were not immediately approved, the Miles Board nevertheless profoundly influenced the army's equipage and related philosophy on several key issues throughout the remainder of the nineteenth century.

The breech-loading rifle and the army's frontier service had prompted serious debate as to whether or not the bayonet and the saber were viable weapons for modern warfare. The Miles Board advocated the retention of the traditional bayonet for close-in fighting in woods and trenches and at night. And, there was always the possibility of having to quell civil disturbances, in which the bayonet might well have effective psychological if not practical value. Prophetically, during the decades since the Miles Board, the army has encountered these very conditions in numerous instances the world over, thus prolonging the life of the bayonet to the present day. As for the saber, the board was less decisive, but it is clear it envisioned the day when weapons development would negate any advantages still held by that near-sacred symbol of the horse soldier. Evading the issue for the moment, the board took the position that the question would "find its solution at the hands of those . . . required to use them." The board added, "While believing that the saber is practically useless in Indian campaigns . . . it should be continued in the service, at least so long as the cavalry regard it as a necessary part of their equipments."[30] Although the saber never again would play an important role as a combat weapon, its demise would not come until 1934, just nine years before the end of the horse-mounted cavalry itself.[31]

Coupled with the bayonet and saber issue was that of providing the individual soldier with a suitable entrenching tool. Evolving conventional tactics, prompted by the worldwide adoption of long-range breechloaders and by the army's frontier experiences—such as those of the Reno-Benteen battalions at the Little Bighorn, Colonel John Gibbon's regiment at the Battle of the Big Hole, and Miles's own command at Bear Paw Mountain—argued persuasively for the value of individual entrenching tools. The board proposed that each soldier be provided with an entrenching tool, which he could use individually to conceal himself from enemy fire. This concept, manifested in a long line of compact entrenching tools, has guided U.S. Army doctrine ever since.

The ingenuity of Major Anson Mills influenced military equipments both here and abroad far beyond what even that visionary officer himself could have foreseen. Over the years he had persisted undaunted in his efforts to gain military acceptance of his cartridge belt. His methods and machinery for weaving heavy cotton webbing into various forms of accoutrements eventually revolutionized the industry. His original cartridge belt concept was so successful that within ten years of its adoption by the U.S. Army it was used to the exclusion of any other type. The woven belt was also embraced by Great Britain, and before long Mills broadened the concept to include the manufacture of a variety of equipment belts, braces, and even revolver holsters. Eventually, his equipments would be used by nations the world over. The basic Mills-inspired pocket cartridge belt, for instance, remained as standard issue in the U.S. services well into the 1950s.[32]

On the facing page:

190. Infantry detachment in Yellowstone National Park, ca. 1878. These soldiers present a more uniform appearance than did soldiers of just two years before. Nearly all wear the 1876 campaign hat, the 1874 blouse, and the regulation cartridge belt. (Historic Photograph Collection, Yellowstone National Park)

Blanket Bag, Pattern 1878

The blanket bag was a large knapsack made of drab duck with removable leather shoulder slings. The main pocket measured 12¾ inches wide by 15½ inches deep and was bound around the outside of the mouth with 1½-inch-wide webbing. Sewn inside the mouth of the bag, one each front and rear, were pieces of 1-inch-wide webbing, averaging 8 to 10 inches long, that could be used to tie the bag closed. The gusset, 5 inches wide, was reinforced on each side with an additional layer of material sewn to the inside to help retain the shape of the knapsack. Sewn to the front of the body near the mouth was a pocket with a flap measuring 5 inches deep by 1¾ inches wide (fig. 191). The flap had two leather string loops, which fastened to buttons riveted to the pocket. A flap measuring 15 inches square and stenciled in black with the letters "U.S.," 1⅜ inches high, covered the main pocket and front of the knapsack (fig. 192).[33] The flap was made of two layers of duck bound around the edge with drab-colored webbing. The flap was secured on each side by leather loops that were sewn to webbing chapes under the lower corners of the flap and that attached to pressed-tin buttons on the gusset.

All buttons were of the pressed-tin variety with a concave face measuring ¹¹⁄₁₆ inch in diameter. Examples of early manufacture exhibited a plain-faced style, whereas later issues employed tinned-iron buttons with stippled rims, as adopted in 1885.[34] Both types had a single hole and were attached by means of a single tubular rivet.

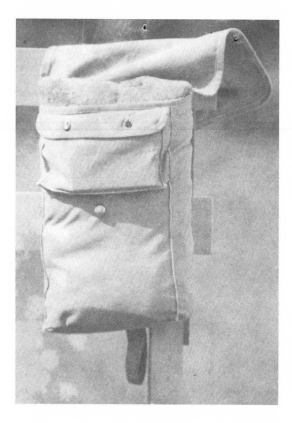

The adjustable shoulder slings, 24 inches long, were made of russet leather measuring 1¹⁵⁄₁₆ inches wide at their upper ends, tapering to 1⅛ inches. A square brass loop was fitted at the top of each sling to hold straps, ⁹⁄₁₆ inch by 65 inches, for securing the rolled shelter tent. At the lower end of each sling was a doubled brass wire hook, which connected to a brass D-ring at the corresponding bottom corners of the bag.

A webbing strap measuring 1 inch by 7 inches, for attaching the tin cup, was sewn into the center of the bottom seam of the bag. The free end of this strap was fastened by a tin button.

Canteen, Pattern 1878

This was the standard 1858-pattern oblate spheroid canteen body, modified by the removal of the bottom sling guide and the addition of triangular iron wire loops to the upper guides. These loops were secured by strips of light iron, ⁵⁄₁₆ inch wide, which were wrapped around the guides and soldered in place.

The body of the canteen was covered with a layer of petersham cloth for insulation, plus an outer cover of drab duck. The hem of this cover was turned inside up to the sling guide openings. The hems of the two halves were machine sewn from the guides to the neck, with the two joined on the canteen by overhand stitches. The "U.S." marking was applied in the same peculiar block lettering style as used on the blanket bag, described above.

The shoulder sling was made of black collar-leather 1 inch by 56 inches. The sling was made adjustable by means of a brass wire hook at each end fastened by two small brass pins. The ends of the sling were doubled back through leather slides, and the hooks mated to any of the five holes provided on each end of the sling. The sling also was provided with two 2-inch-long brass wire hooks with rollers, one at each end, which fastened to the triangular loops of the canteen.

The stopper was attached to the neck in the usual manner with a brass safety chain and a pinched ring encircling the neck.

Haversack, Transitional 1874–78

Although not an officially recognized pattern, this haversack represented the further evolution of the 1874 haversack discussed in a previous chapter. It is included here because the example encountered during the course of this study exhibited marked features from both the 1874 and the 1878 patterns.

The entire haversack was constructed of drab duck. The flap, uncoated and made of two layers of material, measured 12¾ inches wide by 13¾ inches long. It was bound with drab cotton webbing, yet it was sewn to the body in the manner unique to the Pattern 1874.

The haversack used brass D-rings for the sling, a webbing fastening strap on the flap, and an internal divider sewn into the back seam, all of which were incorporated in the 1878 pattern. Likewise, the meat-can pocket covered the front panel of the bag. However, the ancestry of this haversack was clearly evident in the fitted mess utensil pockets sewn inside the gusset, as well as the eagle button used to close the meat-can pocket.

Haversack, Pattern 1878

Constructed entirely of drab duck and webbing, this haversack served the army through the Spanish-American War and the Philippine Insurrection. It had a flap measuring approximately 12 inches by 14 inches, though dimensions varied

Left:
193. *Pattern 1878 haversack.*

Right:
194. *Reverse of 1878 haversack,
showing method of attaching the leather
shoulder sling.*

somewhat on those examined (fig. 193). The edges of the flap were bound with drab webbing 1 inch wide. Examples had both styles of "U.S." markings on the flap, as discussed above for the blanket bag. A strap ¾ inch by 8 inches, sewn to the underside of the flap, connected to a brass frame buckle on the bottom of the gusset. Examples of early Watervliet Arsenal manufacture often bore the date of manufacture below the arsenal marking.

The body, measuring approximately 8½ inches by 11 inches, was constructed with an inside pocket sewn into the back seam and a meat-can pocket sewn to the front. The meat-can pocket was closed at its upper end with an ¹¹⁄₁₆-inch-diameter tinned button. (Examples dating from the late 1880s and 1890s had stippled buttons.) Inside the gusset, on each side of the main pocket, were 9-inch-deep rectangular pockets for holding the mess utensils.

The black collar-leather sling was 2 inches wide in the middle, tapering to 1⅛ inches at the ends. Both ends had a series of adjustment holes to accept the brass hooks riveted to either end. The sling attached to the haversack with two brass wire roller hooks (though the rollers were omitted at some later date) in the folds of the tapered ends of the sling. These connected with two brass D-rings held by webbing chapes to the upper rear corners of the bag (fig. 194).

Cartridge Belt, Pattern 1876 (Type 4)

Like those before it, this variant of the 1876 belt utilized a leather belt with a 2-inch-wide covering of drab duck with fifty-four loops for .45-caliber ammunition. The loops, measuring 2 inches deep, were made of drab webbing. On the left end was the standard open-frame brass buckle with single tongue measuring 2⅛ inches by 2¼ inches. Extending from the right end of the belt was a black leather billet of varying lengths.

The 1876 belt was authorized to be made in two lengths, 38 and 44 inches overall. However, the billets of unaltered belts examined ranged from 7 inches to 13 inches in length. In some instances, uncommonly small men modified their belts by cutting off a few loops from the right end of the belt and reattaching the billet to get a proper fit.

The Type 4 belt had three brass ½-inch-diameter D-rings mounted along the bottom edge of the left side beneath the fifteenth, nineteenth, and twenty-second loops (fig. 195). These were affixed by means of a piece of leather fitted inside each ring, the units then being inserted into the seam and secured with small roundheaded brass rivets passing through the leather inserts. The seam on either side of each ring was restitched, by hand. Approximately one-third of the lower portion of each ring was left exposed to accept the bayonet scabbard hook.

Although this variation of the 1876-pattern belt was intended to be a part of the Pattern 1878 blanket bag equipments, the Ordnance Department made no special counterpart belt for the cavalry. Records of manufacture suggest that no particular effort was made to produce belts in numbers corresponding to those of other component parts of the infantry equipments. In fact, many Type 3 belts already on hand may have been converted by the addition of the rings. It may be assumed that the Type 4 belts, along with the earlier versions of the 1876 belt, found their way into mounted units because there was nothing to prohibit their use by cavalry.

Above:

195. *(Top) Pattern 1876 cartridge belt, Type 4 with three brass D-rings attached to the lower edge for the bayonet scabbard; (bottom) reverse of Type 4 1876 cartridge belt.*

Below:

196 *(Top) Rock Island Arsenal experimental 1876 cartridge belt, modified to attach the bayonet scabbard or entrenching tool; (bottom) reverse of R.I.A. experimental belt.*

Cartridge Belt, Pattern 1876, Rock Island Arsenal Experimental

One example of the Ordnance Department's official efforts to improve the 1876 belt for carrying the triangular and trowel bayonets was initiated by Captain Jesse Alvin Penn Hampson, stationed at San Antonio Arsenal. In October 1878 Hampson submitted a design to the chief of ordnance, who in turn thought it merited production in limited quantities for trial issue.[35] Rock Island Arsenal was directed to make one hundred of these belts, which differed from the standard by measuring only 2¼ inches wide and having fifty unvarnished loops (fig. 196). A black leather strap, 1¾ inches wide by 12 inches long, was hand stitched to the inside of the belt on the left side between the eighteenth and

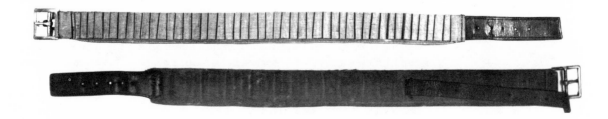

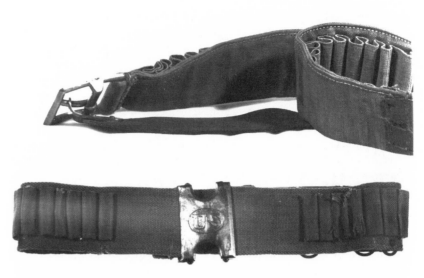

Above:

197. Detail of Rock Island Arsenal experimental belt, showing the bayonet strap with its brass tip attached to the buckle.

Below:

198. Pattern 1880 Mills woven cartridge belt.

nineteenth loops. Riveted to the free end of the strap was a curved brass tip having a ¼-inch-diameter hole to fit over the buckle tongue (fig. 197). The belt was stenciled on the inside "R. I. A. EXPERIMENTAL" in black letters ½ inch high. Hampson's belt, obviously, was nothing more than a professionally executed version of what the soldiers themselves had been fabricating in the field.

The following month Hampson requisitioned one thousand of the brass tips for use in converting the cartridge belts on hand in the infantry companies in the Department of Texas. General Benet approved the request and ordered Rock Island Arsenal to provide them. Presumably, Hampson used these to modify belts of the earlier styles.[36]

Cartridge Belt, Pattern 1880

The first contract for this belt, recommended by the Miles Board, was let to Anson Mills on November 17, 1880, with production beginning early the next year. The belt, 3 inches wide, was woven of drab-colored cotton and had either forty-five or fifty loops for .45-caliber ammunition (fig. 198). On each end of the belt, spaced ½ inch on centers from the edge, were four brass eyelets for the purpose of lacing two belts together to form a bandolier, if circumstances dictated.[37] The ends were left raw-edged, though they had two lines of stitching to prevent them from fraying.

The plate was made of stamped sheet brass 3⅛ inches high by 2¼ inches wide. Around the edge was a raised border ¼ inch wide, top and bottom, and ³⁄₁₆ inch wide on the right side. The left side of the plate was plain, the border being formed by the left edge of the matching catch. A tongue ¾ inch wide was brazed on the reverse. On the reverse of both plate and catch were double bars through which the belt was threaded and locked. The inner bars of each piece were scalloped with points; these caught the fold of the belt to prevent it from slipping once the end was passed back through the outer bar. The catch measured 1 inch wide with a D-shaped hole, ⁷⁄₁₆ inch by ¹³⁄₁₆ inch, within a stamped recess in the center to accept the buckle tongue.

(Although the Mills belt was included in this section for convenience, the reader should note that it was issued to cavalry as well as infantry.)

Bayonet Scabbard, Pattern 1878

This scabbard employed the standard triangular blued-steel sheath 18⅛ inches long but was distinguished by a two-piece black collar-leather frog and brass hook (fig. 199). Whereas the Pattern 1873 scabbard had been made with the flat side of the sheath next to the wearer's body, the flat side was turned opposite on the 1878 scabbard. This in turn rotated the bayonet socket so that it stood away from the body rather than being held tightly against the cartridges in the belt. The frog was secured with a single brass rivet just beneath the mouth of the scabbard.

The socket, through which the sheath passes, measured 1½ inches wide at the top by 2⅜ inches long. This socket was stitched to a loop approximately 3¾ inches long, the fold of which held a brass wire hook 1½ inches long with roller. The purpose of the hook was to facilitate attachment to the Pattern 1876, Type 4, cartridge belt. Production of this scabbard began in the fiscal year 1880 (1879–80) with an initial issue of 1,208.[38]

Trowel Bayonet Scabbard, Pattern 1878

This was the same as the standard Pattern 1873 leather-covered tin sheath with brass tip, having an overall length of 11¼ inches. Beginning in 1878, a short leather chape 1⅜ inches wide was substituted for the original leather belt loop. In the fold of this loop was a brass wire roller hook like that used on the triangular bayonet scabbard. The chape was fastened to the scabbard with two brass rivets, using the two original holes in the sheath.

199. (Top to bottom): A Model 1873 triangular bayonet; a Pattern 1878 scabbard with brass hook for attaching to the cartridge belt; a trowel bayonet; a Pattern 1878 trowel scabbard with attachment hook.

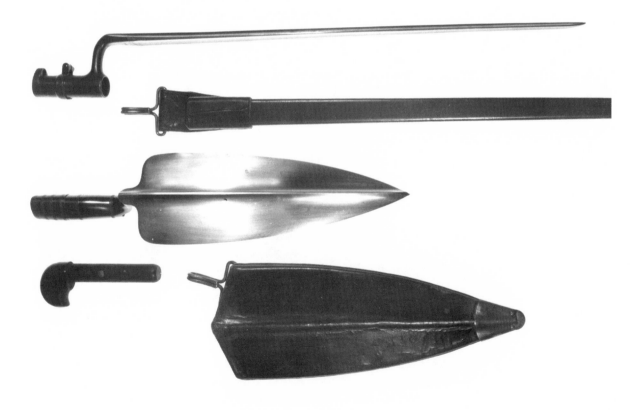

Bayonet Scabbard, Unknown Date

This scabbard incorporated a standard triangular steel sheath and Hoffman frog. It differed from the 1873 pattern, however, in that the leather belt loop was considerably longer, measuring 5¼ inches. The loop itself was 3½ inches deep, which was large enough to pass over all of the Pattern 1876 belts, loaded with cartridges. But, the loop will not admit a Mills belt. One authority contends that this scabbard was designed for use with the interior scabbard strap of the Rock Island Arsenal experimental belt described above.[39] Indeed, the long frog lowers the scabbard mouth far enough below the belt to allow the bayonet to be handled without difficulty. Contradicting this is Captain Jesse A. P. Hampson's statement in which he claimed his belt modification would permit "carrying the bayonet with the frogs now on hand in Infantry companies in this Department."[40] This compelling evidence suggests that his only motivation was to adapt the cartridge belt to accommodate the 1873-pattern scabbard, which it does. Indeed, the long-loop scabbard may have been developed in response to the interior bayonet strap. Or, it may have been intended to be worn over the belt or worn either way, at the pleasure of the soldier.

CAVALRY EQUIPMENT

Holster, Pattern 1879

Distinguished by its narrow flap and vertically embossed "U S" with oval border, the 1879 holster was otherwise identical to the Pattern 1875. It had the somewhat wider body to accommodate either the Colt or the Smith & Wesson Schofield revolver. Overall length was slightly more than 11 inches, the muzzle end being plugged with a leather washer having a drain hole in the center.

A billet strap, 1 inch by 2¾ inches, was stitched and riveted to the end of the flap. This fastened to a brass finial positioned on the front of the holster near the side seam, about 2¼ inches below the mouth. The flap itself measured approximately 3¼ inches wide in the center. A loop, 3¾ inches long for the standard saber belt, was riveted and sewn to the reverse of the holster.

Spurs, Mills Pattern

Although recommended by the Miles Board and officially adopted in 1879, these spurs were not produced until 1881 (fig. 200). At that time one thousand pairs were manufactured at Rock Island Arsenal. This quantity was divided evenly between two variations of the spur, designated "Model A" and "Model B." The principal difference between the two lay in the manner of attaching the leather straps. Model A employed a rather wide strap, 2 inches over the instep by nearly 11 inches long, riveted to the body of the spur. Model B used the more traditional method of threading a narrower strap through two parallel slots at each end of the yoke. Both styles had a small brass center-bar buckle for attachment.

Each spur consisted of a No. 16 sheet-brass yoke formed to fit the heel of the boot. Model A measured approximately 2⅛ inches at the heel, and Model B measured somewhat less than 2 inches. A brass rowel plate with a 1-inch-diameter steel rowel was riveted to the heel of the yoke.[41]

200. *Mills-patent spur.*

CLOTHING

Summer Helmet, Pattern 1880

Specifications for this helmet were adopted on May 5, 1880.[42] The body was composed of cork covered on the outside with a layer of white cotton drill, and on the inside of the dome with a finer-quality slate-colored drill." The helmet had broad rounded visors, the front one measuring 2 inches deep and the rear 2⅜ inches. The edge of the visor was bound all around with white cotton twill.

The outer covering was made of four pieces with top-stitched seams. The visor was lined with emerald-green merino, a light woolen cloth. The depth of the dome was about 6 inches. Around the base of the dome was a band of white drill 1¹¹⁄₁₆ inch wide; the seam at the rear was covered by a loop of like material. Atop the dome was a tin ventilator covered with drill and having three ports, each approximately ⁵⁄₁₆ inch wide along its lower edge. The ventilator was provided with a brass stud, which screwed into a threaded tube supported by a brass fixture in the top of the helmet.

The leather sweat, 1⅜ inches wide, was separated from the shell by a series of ten cork spacers arranged around the interior. A two-piece chin strap of white enameled leather with a brass slide was attached at both sides of the helmet by two brass hooks mounted under the sweatband.

The specifications for the officers' version of the summer helmet were not approved until the following year. It differed only slightly from the enlisted version, mainly in the finer-cloth covering, brass side buttons, leather-backed

*201. Pattern 1879 stable frock worn
by cavalry soldiers while performing
stable duty.*

chin chain, and optional brass spike with oak-leaf base. The shape was somewhat more squat, and the visors were broader and flatter.

Shirt, Pattern 1878

Abandoning the time-honored practice of using the one-piece body with drop shoulders, this shirt incorporated three-piece construction with a yoke across the shoulders. It was made of army-standard gray shirting flannel in two weights, 5 ounces and 6 ounces per linear yard. The yoke was lined with the same material. This improved pattern did away with the archaic drop shoulder by introducing somewhat narrower sleeves let into the body. Like the 1874-pattern shirt, it had a plait, 2 inches by 12 inches, with one four-hole tinned-iron button (⁹⁄₁₆ inch in diameter) at the neck, with an additional two buttons spaced equidistant on the plait. The plait, rather than being squared as it was on the Pattern 1874 shirt, terminated in an angular point.

The shirt was collarless, having only a band, because of widespread dissatisfaction with the collar's bulkiness when worn under the blouse or dress coat. The long tail was cut nearly square at the corners. Specifications were adopted on January 16, 1878.[43]

Stable Frock

This new frock is something of an enigma, since no references have been found for a change in pattern from the garment worn during the Civil War. The 1875 Quartermaster Department photographs leave no doubt that the old pattern survived the general uniform change of 1872. Although the Miles Board focused considerable attention on the subject of white duck summer clothing, it

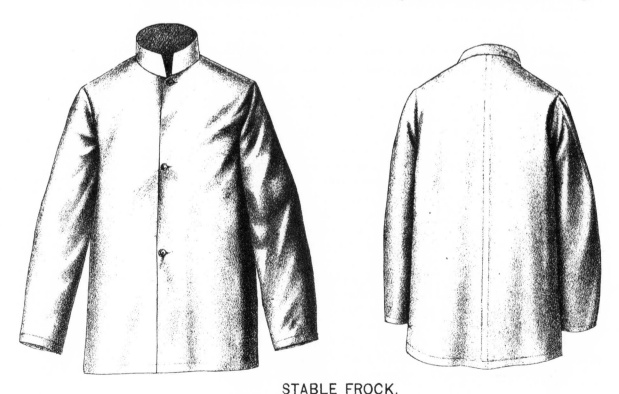

STABLE FROCK.

made no mention of the stable frock other than to recommend its abolishment after the issue of the recommended (but not adopted) white clothing. Whatever the reason, the army adopted new standards for the stable frock on March 12, 1879.[44]

The modified frock was made of white duck weighing about 8 ounces to the yard. It had a standing collar about 2 to 2½ inches high, depending on the size, to prevent dust, horsehair, and hay from entering the shirt opening at the neck. The body was unlined, but the hems were felled to form finished edges (fig. 201). The front was closed with three four-hole tinned-iron buttons having stippled faces (¹¹⁄₁₆ inch in diameter) and spaced equidistant from neck to waist.

Stockings, Cotton

These were issued in three colors: gray mixed, brown mixed, and white (unbleached). They were made with fashioned toes and heels, the heels to be extra thick. The ribbed tops were woven integrally with the leg, about 4½ inches deep, with a welt around the upper edges. The colored stockings were made somewhat heavier than the white ones, probably because the latter were intended to be worn for light or off-duty wear. All were made in five half-sizes ranging from 9½ to 11½. The first specifications for these stockings were adopted on October 17, 1879.[45]

Great Coat, Canvas Lined

An example of this coat was not located; therefore, the only available description is in the brief specifications published by the Quartermaster Department:

Pattern: To be according to pattern, with two (2) outside pockets and a waist belt, and to be of two (2) sizes corresponding to the Regulation great coats of sizes 3 and 4.

Materials—The outside to be of cotton duck weighing nine and one-half (9½) ounces to the square yard, dyed blue to the shade of standard sample. The inside or lining to be of Army standard twenty-two (22) ounce 6/4 sky-blue kersey. The cords and tassels to be of blue worsted according to pattern—one for the neck to be sixty (60) inches long, and two (2) for the hood to be each forty-two inches long; the latter to be fastened at the outer edge of neck and drawn at the center of the hood or cape. Seven (7) rubber buttons on front and two (2) on belt, as on sample. Adopted August 18, 1880.[46]

EPILOGUE

To many in the army, William Tecumseh Sherman represented an obstacle to the modernization of the service. There can be no doubt that he left his mark on the army, and in many ways he helped to strengthen it. But, in his approach to new equipage, Sherman was conservative at best. In the months and years following the Miles Board, a ground-swell effort to override Sherman's decisions gained momentum, eventually forcing many of the changes suggested by that visionary group. Within two years after the board adjourned, all foot troops had the black felt dress helmets Sherman had denied them, although the new model had distinctively shorter visors than the pattern adopted by the cavalry and light artillery in 1872. Such helmets were standard at dress formations throughout the army until the design of an entirely new uniform after 1902.

The Quartermaster Department itself finally faced the reality that the sky-blue facings on infantry dress coats simply would not withstand exposure to the sun, and in 1884 it changed them to white.[1] Except for the retention of the traditional "army blue" uniform, the army had radically altered its appearance between the years 1870 and 1880. No longer did its clothing and equipments simply mirror those of the great armies of the Old World, as they largely had through the 1860s. In spite of the army's continued tendency to emulate those nations, the western experience had proven to be a key factor influencing the evolution of the army's matériel. The trend, firmly established by 1880, was toward a more practical field outfit, with the exception that dress uniforms would reflect strong European influence for the remainder of the nineteenth century.

The decade of the 1870s was marked by a more professional approach to designing and manufacturing matériel for the army. By the end of the 1870s the army had established a foundation of documented specifications for its numerous items of clothing and, to a lesser degree, individual equipments. The Ordnance Department still relied primarily on the traditional system of "approved samples," carefully prepared standard models that were then duplicated by the arsenals. In any event, the industrial revolution brought about technological advancements and manufacturing methods that resulted in constant improvements in military equipage. In his annual report for 1879, Quartermaster General Meigs announced:

> The department endeavors constantly to improve the quality and the
> pattern of the clothing and equipage provided for the Army. It is believed

that it is kept fully up to the advanced condition of modern manufacture, and it is procured under the system of fully advertised contracts, at the lowest prices, and of excellent quality . . . [and] that the improvement in the quality of clothing of the Army has been carried almost too far.[2]

Meigs explained that the troops had come to expect such high standards that they now complained at the slightest deficiencies, details that would have gone unnoticed a few years earlier. In fact, it was this very persistence on the part of the American soldier that caused the army to consider many items that it might not have otherwise issued. Whereas soldiers in other armies had little freedom or power to influence such matters, the democratic principles of the American system created an atmosphere in which even the lowliest private could voice his opinion.

The no-nonsense regulars of the postwar era were quick to demand the clothing and equipment that they found to be best for getting the job done. When the army would not or could not provide for their needs, they invariably found alternative ways to obtain the items. By so doing, they often established, at the field level, designs that eventually were implemented officially. The Pattern 1876 cartridge belt is a salient example.

The decade witnessed the demise of the old Civil War uniform, which was neither liked by the army nor well adapted to the army's needs in the West. The stockpile of surplus clothing, considered an asset immediately after the war, came to be an albatross for the Quartermaster Department. Even though the army attempted to rid itself of the old clothing, Congress adamantly insisted that the clothes be force-fed to the troops, one way or another. Happily, and no doubt with a great sigh of relief, General Meigs reported in 1880:

> All of the larger sizes had been consumed, so that from what remained on hand it was not possible to fill requisitions for any body of troops. Moreover, it had deteriorated by effect of time and ravages of moths, and on the 19th December last, the War Department determined to condemn the whole of it . . . which has been done, to the great relief and satisfaction of the Army. Only what is known as the new pattern clothing is now issued to troops.[3]

While the Clothing Branch groped for a solution to the surplus problem, it also made many concessions to the soldier's comfort. This marked the beginning of a reformation that developed rapidly in the years to follow. The adoption of light and heavy weights of shirts and stockings heralded the coming of entire uniforms suited to seasonal and climatic changes. In the Apache campaigns in New Mexico and Arizona, soldiers commonly wore their white canvas stable clothing in order to withstand the extreme desert heat. This practice, along with the official sanction of white linen or cotton trousers as recommended by the Miles Board, led eventually to the adoption of white duck uniform blouses and trousers in 1888 to complement the cork helmets. By the time of the Spanish-American War, troops were provided drab-colored duck field uniforms for tropical climates. In future decades, the army expanded its catalog of climatically adapted clothing as the nation's involvement in international events spread around the globe.

Conditions in the West also motivated the army to adopt specialized winter clothing. The Quartermaster Department, reluctantly following the example of soldiers on the frontier, eventually conceded that plains winters demanded clothing adapted to the prevailing weather. No longer able to ignore the situation, the miserly General Meigs finally was induced to issue fur caps and gloves, as well as coats made of buffalo hide and, later, lined canvas.

Soldiers expressed a clear preference for the blue flannel overshirt. But, this probably had more to do with the weight and texture of the material, and the fact that it could be worn in lieu of the blouse, than it did with color. The "gray shirting flannel" used for the Patterns 1874 and 1878 shirts was extremely coarse and heavy. The blue flannel, conversely, was somewhat softer and lighter and was more comfortable to wear. In 1883 the army adopted a dark-blue wool pullover shirt with two breast pockets and a half-button front. The basic design of this shirt was to serve the army until well into the 1920s, long after army blue had given way to olive drab.

Likewise, the campaign hat clearly was a product unique to the army's western experience. Soldiers in those regions, far more than their eastern counterparts, were outdoorsmen of necessity. The scorching summer sun, punctuated by fierce thunderstorms, was common to almost all frontier stations. Field service could be especially grueling, and the broad-brimmed hat, better than anything else, was useful in deflecting both sun and rain. A drab-colored campaign hat, the color of choice worn by many officers and soldiers serving in the West, was at last sanctioned officially in 1883. This hat remained little changed until the classic "doughboy" hat with the Montana peak was adopted in 1912. The basic design of this hat remained unchanged until early in World War II. To this day, NCO drill instructors wear a descendant version of the frontier army's campaign hat.

The canvas leggings so strongly urged by the Miles Board eventually were produced and issued to the infantry in 1888, despite General Sherman's original objections. In any kind of field service in the West, soldiers encountered brush, dust, sand, and mud, all of which worked into the shoes, stockings, and pant legs and caused extreme discomfort, if not outright disability. As late as 1884, soldiers in Texas, desperate for relief, used gunny sacks "tied closely around the leg from the knee down over the shoe, making a heavy and clumsy legging."[4] The regulation brown canvas legging, when it finally made its debut, proved so popular that its issue was extended to the cavalry in 1894 to replace the heavy, hot, and expensive leather boots.[5] The laced legging remained a trademark of the American soldier until the latter part of World War II.

Of the plethora of clothing and equipment items to appear during this era, perhaps the most uniquely American was the looped cartridge belt. Its precise origin remains unknown, but there is little doubt that it was the invention of frontiersmen who devised belts to carry metallic cartridges in a convenient, accessible manner. Soldiers quickly imitated the civilians by fabricating their own belts. After several years, the army finally succumbed and issued arsenal-made belts. Looped cartridge belts of the Mills type remained standard issue until after the turn of the century, when the clip-charged Model 1903 Springfield rifle led to the production of pocket cartridge belts. Such belts, in slightly varying forms, were used by the U.S. Army for another sixty years, until they eventually were replaced by a load-carrying system not unlike the 1872-pattern infantry equipments.

The decade of the 1870s truly was an era of experimentation and evolution. As this study has shown, the developments of that period resulted in changes that led to greater standardization of equipage during the remainder of the century. Although the army continued to refine the soldier's outfit, there were relatively few entirely new items introduced. Nearly everything adopted in the decade after 1880 was rooted in the reforms of the seventies. The soldier who emerged from this long process—wearing his drab campaign hat, the simple five-button blouse or the blue shirt, and a bristling cartridge belt while clutching a .45 Springfield—was distinctively American, a product of frontier service. His appearance influenced the U.S. Army well past the threshold of the twentieth century. Indeed, one has only to survey the works of premier artists Frederic Remington and Charles Schreyvogel, or the movies of the immortal John Ford, to witness the powerful effect on the characterization of the U.S. soldier of that era.

SAMPLE CARTRIDGE BOXES OF THE ST. LOUIS BOARD, 1870

A PHOTOGRAPHIC ESSAY

DENNIS L. GAHAGEN

In the following essay, Dennis L. Gahagen, a longtime collector and student of American military accoutrements, presents the cartridge boxes and other devices from the 1870 St. Louis Board. Gahagen's contribution is the result of years of effort on his part to locate the extant specimens of these extremely rare, mostly one-of-a-kind pieces. This photographic exhibit represents a unique assemblage of the board samples and graphically illustrates the otherwise sterile published proceedings.

General Orders No. 60 dated August 6, 1869, created a board of officers to examine, among other things, infantry accoutrements. After much serious work the board completed its task of evaluating the cartridge boxes and pouches submitted. The following are listed according to the board's order of merit:

1. Lieutenant J. G. Butler's pouch (figs. 202 and 203)
2. Lieutenant J. G. Butler's box
3. General A. B. Dyer's pouch
4. Lieutenant C. L. Best's box (figs. 204 and 205)
5. Major S. Crispin's box
6. Lieutenant Colonel B. S. Roberts's box (figs. 206 and 207)
7. Board pouch (fig. 208) (the board submitted its own sample in the form of a pouch that would hold twenty-four cartridges)

The chief of ordnance later ordered the following boxes and vest manufactured:

1. Captain W. Clifford's vest, as modified (figs. 209, 210, 211, and 212)
2. Colonel P. V. Hagner's box (right and left) (figs. 213, 214, 215, and 216)
3. E. Tileston's pattern box (figs. 217, 218, and 219), as modified, three different types[1]

Each box or pouch was marked "U.S. Watervliet Arsenal" in three lines. Each was also stamped with a large letter to avoid influence in evaluating the boxes in cases where the originator might otherwise be known. Some boxes and pouches were also marked with the same size letter in green paint, usually on the rough side of the leather. All boxes and pouches were intended to hold .50/70 caliber ammunition and to be carried on a waist belt of some type.

The following is a list of cartridge boxes made at Wavervliet Arsenal, New

York, in compliance with instructions, dated August 19 and 24, 1870, from the chief of ordnance.[2]

RECOMMENDED BY THE ST. LOUIS BOARD	NUMBER MADE	LETTER CODE
Lieutenant C. L. Best's box	100	A
Lieutenant Colonel B. S. Roberts's box	100	B
Lieutenant J. G. Butler's pouch	100	C
with buckle		
with button	100	C
Major S. Crispin's box	100	D
General A. B. Dyer's pouch	100	E
Lieutenant J. G. Butler's pouch (figs. 220 and 221)		
with tin cartridge holder (fig. 222)	100	F
with curved wood holder (fig. 223)	100	F
Pouch proposed by the board	100	L

The following additional equipments were made in compliance with subsequent orders from the chief of ordnance:

RECOMMENDED BY THE ST. LOUIS BOARD	NUMBER MADE	LETTER CODE
Captain Clifford's vest, as modified at Watervliet Arsenal (right and left)	50 pairs	H
Tileston pattern, as modified at Watervliet Arsenal, with leather loops	50	K
Colonel P. V. Hagner's box (right and left)	50 pairs	M
Tileston pattern, lined with waxed ticking loops of waxed webbing	50	N
Tileston pattern, lined with varnished ticking loops of varnished webbing	50	P

The remaining two boxes were not located for examination or photographing: the "E" pouch (General Dyer) and the "D" box (Major Crispin). The "E" pouch, or Dyer pouch, would probably be the second-style Dyer pouch, with the large belt loops that fit over the 1872 cavalry yoke-system belt. The outer flap should have a three-quarter-inch or one-inch "E" stamped on the outer flap and "U.S./Watervliet/Arsenal." There may also be a green "E" stenciled on the underside of the flap. The "D" box by Major Crispin would probably have had a three-quarter-inch or one-inch "D" stamped on the flap along with "U.S./Watervliet/Arsenal." There may have been a green "D" stenciled on the underside of the flap.

On the facing page:

Above, left:
202. Butler pouch with buckle (closed)

Below, left:
203. Butler pouch with buckle (open)

Above, right:
204. Best box (closed)

Below, left:
205. Best box (open)

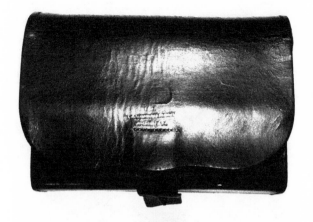

Above left:

206. *Robert's box with button fastener*

Below left:

207. *Robert's box (open)*

Above right:

208. *Ordnance Board pouch*

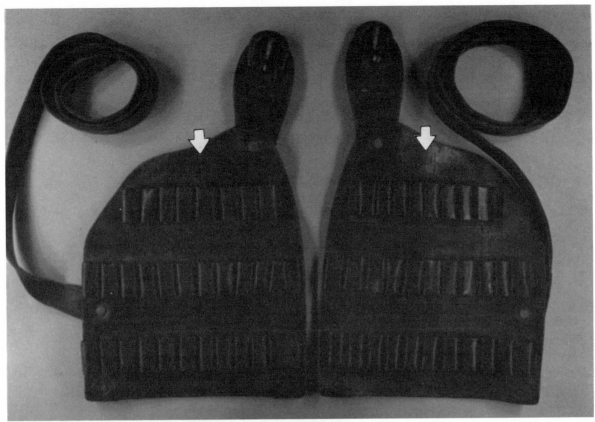

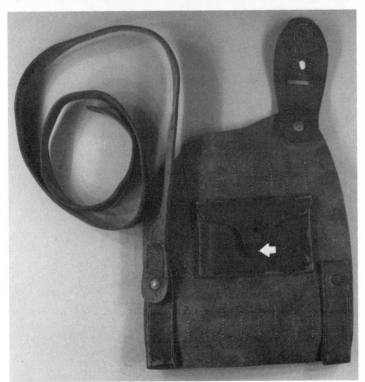

Above:

209. *Clifford vest, leather (front view)*

Left:

210. *Clifford vest, leather (reverse view)*

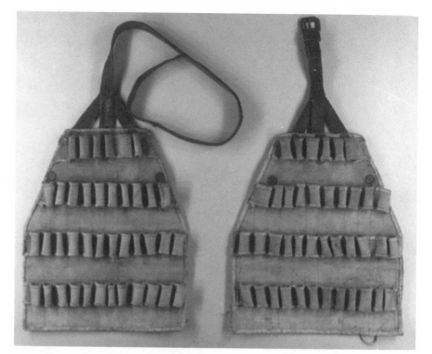

Above:

211. *Clifford vest, canvas (front view)*

Below:

212. *Clifford vest, canvas (reverse view)*

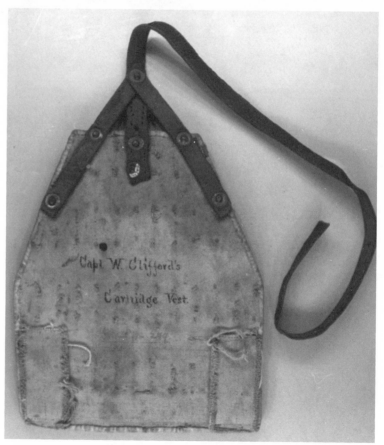

Below left:
213. *Hagner box*

Above left:
214. *Hagner box (open)*

Above right:
215. *Hagner box (reverse view)*

Below right:
216. *Hagner box (close view)*

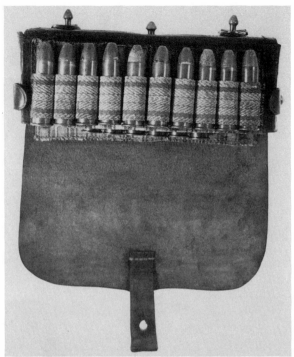

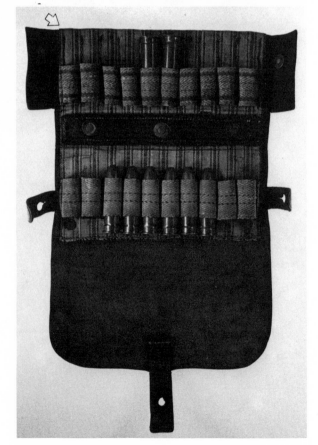

Above left:
217. Tileston pouch

Above right:
218. Tileston pouch, flap open

Right:
219. Tileston pouch, completely open

Above:
220. *Butler pouch (top view)*

Below:
221. *Butler pouch with tin cartridge holder*

Above:
222. Butler pouch (front view)

Below:
*223. Butler pouch with wood cartridge
holder (open)*

DIRECTIONS

FOR

FITTING INFANTRY EQUIPMENTS,

U. S. ARMY.

WATERVLIET ARSENAL,

West Troy, N. Y.

SPRINGFIELD, MASS.:
PRINTED AT NATIONAL ARMORY.
1872.

INFANTRY EQUIPMENTS.

The Equipments consist of—

1 *Waist Belt.*
1 *Bayonet Scabbard, steel, with swivel frog.*
2 *Cartridge Boxes, to hold each* 24 *Metallic Cartridges, carried in loops, (of two patterns for trial.)*
1 *Valise to hold Clothing, with pouch under flap to receive two packages extra cartridges* (40).
1 *Brace Yoke.*
2 *Coat Straps.*

While the object is to provide means of carrying a good supply of ammunition and all the necessary articles a soldier is likely to require during a campaign, it is not intended that the whole equipment should be always worn, or that all the requisite articles should of necessity be in the Valise; on the contrary, it is proposed to carry only one Cartridge Box on ordinary occasions, in peace, and to place in the Valise merely such articles as may be wanted at the time. The object is, in fact, to leave the soldier as unencumbered as possible, except when there is a necessity for weighting him.

The length of the Brace Straps will be found to suit tall and middle-sized men, but for small men it may be necessary to shorten them. This should be done after trial of a few days, so that the best length for comfortable wear can be determined. Sometimes it may improve the fit of the shoulder straps to shape the inner edge on top of the shoulder a little, as the inner edge may press too much. This slight cutting (if allowed) should be done under the supervision of an officer, and then only after some days' wear of the equipment, as the strap may accommodate itself to the shape without cutting. Fresh holes may also be necessary in some of the straps. During drills, or on garrison duty, when the Valise is not carried, it is proposed that only one Cartridge Box holding 24 rounds be carried. This is sufficiently supported by the Waist Belt and may be placed either in front or behind. See Fig. 1.

Fig.1.   Fig.2.

If 48 rounds are required, two boxes may be carried, and should be worn in front. As this weight is too great to be supported by the Waist Belt alone, the Brace Yoke should be put on. See Figs. 2 and 3.

It will be seen that the longest of the two straps attached to each of the Brace Rings in front, is the strap reaching to bottom of Valise. These can be unbuckled from the Ring as well as from the Valise; habitually they should be left attached to the Valise, as they are only needed when it is worn.

If it is desired to carry the great coat, without the Valise, it can now be put on and also the Blanket if wanted. The coat straps would be passed through the loops on the cross straps behind, from below upwards, and the coat or blanket, or both, secured by them. The blanket and coat are best carried when folded about 10 in. high and 15 or 16 in. wide; if the cartridge pouches are full this load rides very steadily. See Fig. 4.

Fig. 3.   Fig. 4.

Figs. 5, 6 and 7 show the Valise and how it is attached and worn. Particular care should be taken, at first, about this. The Valise should be packed neatly,—the softest articles of clothing in the larger subdivision and nearest the body,—then the Trowsers should be folded flat and put in first; then the Shirt also folded; the Boots upright, against the sides, heels outwards; then the Blouse, Socks and Drawers between the Boots. Smaller articles,—Brushes, Comb, Towel, &c.,— should be placed in the smaller subdivision.

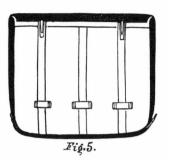

Fig. 5.

After the Valise is packed and the Buckles with Rings moved to the most suitable holes on the Brace Straps, and the strap ends of the Braces fastened to their buckles, the Valise-hooks are passed into the Rings and the straps from the bottom of the Valise to the front Brace Rings. The proper adjustment of length of these straps, as well as the proper distance between the rings, is important to the comfortable wearing of the Valise; and each man should try two or three holes until he finds the one most comfortable. The Equipment when once adjusted and straps connected can be put on like a coat (see Fig. 6) and secured to the Waist Belt. The Valise should be worn just high enough to allow the wearer to sit without interference. The side strap should not be too tight under the arm; a comrade should alter this until it is easy, and in like manner the strap to the bottom should be tried at different lengths until the proper support is found to be given to the Valise.

By taking a little trouble at first, a man will find exactly how tight the straps should be and where the Valise rests most easily.

When the Haversack is worn, it can be attached to the Brace Belt either at the Rings, or behind, according as experience may prove best, taking care to bring the weight upon the shoulder without pressure upon the chest. See Fig. 8.

The Haversack body is

Fig. 6.

made to form two sacks, in the larger of which the bread is carried and in the other the sugar, coffee, etc., etc., in separate small bags.   Under

Fig. 7.   Fig. 8.

the flap is a pocket for the meat can, which will contain four days' rations of pork or of condensed meat. This can may be also used if necessary to boil coffee, and the cover for a drinking cup. See Fig. 9.

Fig. 9.   CANTEEN
Fig. 10.

Fig. 11.

A Canteen of Tin, covered with woolen cloth is also issued and will be worn attached to the Braces, or over the shoulder, as may be preferred. See Fig. 10.

On the march, the soldier may unclasp the Waist Belt Plate at times, and thus give himself temporary relief without detriment to the stability of the load. See Fig. 11.

Three kinds of materials for Valise flaps are proposed for trial, viz.:—Seal Skin, Vulcanized Rubber Cloth and heavy Linen Canvas —the body of the Valise being of Canvas in all patterns. The Canvas flap being lighter, more durable, and less objectionable on account of warmth in the sun, will be, it is thought, preferable for use to either of the others in our climate; especially as the Poncho recommended for issue to the soldier will, when worn, sufficiently protect the whole equipment from rain.

Respectfully submitted,

P. V. HAGNER,

Col. of Ordnance.

Watervliet Arsenal, July 12, 1872.

Commanding Officers of Companies using these Infantry Equipments are requested to make Monthly Reports, as to their merits, direct to the Chief of Ordnance.

Approved.

By Order,

S. V. BENÉT,

Maj. of Ordnance.

Ordnance Office, July 15, 1872.

Instructions for Assembling and Wearing the Infantry Equipments, Blanket Bag Pattern

Captain A. L. Varney, Ordnance Department

[Within a short time after their adoption in 1879, the blanket bag equipments saw wide distribution among infantry and artillery units. To secure some uniformity in the items carried and the way in which they were packed in the blanket bag, the Ordnance Department issued the following instructions. They were prepared by Captain Alomon Libby Varney, a Civil War infantry veteran from Maine, who spent the remainder of his long military career as a professional ordnance officer. The document was first published in the report of the chief of ordnance contained in the *Annual Report of the Secretary of War*, 1882.]

The Blanket Bag now supplied by the Ordnance Department is a substitute for the Clothing Bag of the pattern of 1874 (described in Ordnance Memorandum No. 19), and is designed to be worn without the "Carrying Brace."

Two "Blanket-bag Straps" are supplied in lieu of the brace system, each 23 inches long, 2 inches wide at one end, and 1⅛ inches wide at the other. On the wide end is sewed a standing leather loop, open, on the undressed side of the strap, and having a small brass-wire loop, to receive the coat strap, on the blackened side, attached by a chape sewed and riveted under the leather loop.

A double brass-wire hook is attached to the small end of the strap, which is passed through its eye (the back of the hook toward the undressed side) and secured by another hook riveted on and passing through holes punched in the strap to regulate the length. A sliding loop slipped over the fold in the strap keeps the double-wire hook in place. The straps are attached to the bag by means of two rectangular brass-wire loops at the top. To attach the strap, remove the double-wire hook and the sliding leather loop; pass the strap through the rectangular brass loop at the top of the bag from the back of the bag toward the side of the flap, holding the blackened side of the strap toward the bag and observing that the straps are "rights" and "lefts." The straight edges of the straps should be toward the middle of the bag. Next, pass the small end of the strap through the standing leather loop at the wide end and draw the noose thus formed up close to the rectangular wire loop on the bag. The small brass loop on the strap should be drawn through the brass loop on the bag so as to remain on the outside. Next put on the sliding leather loop and then the double-wire hook.

Source: Transcribed from *Annual Report of the Chief of Ordnance to the Secretary of War, 1882,* appendix 24, pp. 285–86.

Adjust the strap to the desired length by means of the hook at the end and pass the sliding loop over the fold in the strap.

To attach the Coat Strap, slip the sliding loop down to the buckle and pass the billet end through the small brass loop on the blanket-bag strap, holding the blackened side of the coat strap toward the bag; pull the strap through to within one foot of the buckle; pass the billet through the sliding leather loop and push the latter down close to the brass loop through which the strap passes. The coat strap should be inserted in same direction with regard to the bag as the blanket-bag straps—that is, so that when the strap hangs double over the flap of the bag the buckle end will be outside.

To sling the bag, first hook the left-hand strap to the D-ring on the lower left-hand corner of the bag, pass the left arm through this strap, grasp the end of the other strap with the right hand, swing the bag over the shoulders carrying the right-hand strap over the head; bring this strap down over the right shoulder and hook it into the D-ring at the lower right-hand corner of the bag. The webbing loop with button and buttonhole at the bottom of the blanket bag is designed to carry the tin cup.

When the bag is filled, the flap is fastened down by passing the leather loops at the corners over the buttons on the gussets.

A haversack strap is also made of leather and supplied with double-wire hooks at each end like those on the blanket-bag straps. These hooks are inserted into the buckles at the top of the haversack. No change has been made in the haversack except to enlarge the pocket for the meat-ration can. It can be used with either the carrying brace or the haversack strap now provided.

A leather strap similar to the haversack strap (only narrower) is now provided for the canteen. Iron-wire loops are attached to the sides of the canteen to receive the double-wire hooks on the strap.

NOTES

FOREWORD

1. One of these articles was subsequently published as a separate monograph, James S. Hutchins's *Boots & Saddles at the Little Big Horn: Weapons, Dress, Equipment, Horses, and Flags of General Custer's Seventh U.S. Cavalry in 1876* (Fort Collins, Colo.: The Old Army Press, 1976).

2. See Sidney B. Brinckerhoff, *Military Headgear in the Southwest, 1846–1890* (Tucson: Arizona Pioneers Historical Society Museum Monograph No. 1, n.d.), and the same author's other two works, *Metal Uniform Insignia of the U.S. Army in the Southwest, 1846–1902* (Tucson: Arizona Pioneer Historical Society Museum Monograph No. 3, 1965), and *Boots and Shoes of the Frontier Soldier* (Tucson: Arizona Historical Society Museum Monograph No. 7, 1976).

3. Chappell's two publications from the Arizona Historical Society in Tucson were released as Museum Monographs No. 4 and 5, published in 1966 and 1972 respectively. The author's *Summer Helmets of the U.S. Army, 1875–1910* was published in Cheyenne by the Wyoming State Archives and Historical Department in 1967.

4. *They Continually Wear the Blue* was written by John P. Langellier for Barnes-McGee Press of San Francisco in 1976. The headgear studies are Edgar M. Howell and Donald E. Kloster, *United States Army Headgear to 1854*, Vol. 1 (Washington, D.C.: Smithsonian Institution Press, 1969), and Edgar M. Howell, *United States Army Headgear, 1855–1902*, Vol. 2 (Washington, D.C.: Smithsonian Institution, 1975). William K. Emerson's *Chevrons: Illustrated History and Catalog of U.S. Army Insignia* was published in 1983.

5. Another useful reprint is *U.S. Army Uniforms and Equipments, 1889* (Lincoln: University of Nebraska Press, 1986).

6. Frederick P. Todd, *American Military Equipage, 1851–1872* was published in three volumes by the Company of Military Historians between 1974 and 1978.

7. Randy Steffen, *The Horse Soldier, 1776–1943*, 4 vols. (Norman: University of Oklahoma Press, 1978).

INTRODUCTION

1. Colonel Philip Regis De Trobriand to Adjutant General, USA, March 15, 1875, Papers Relating to the Army Equipment Board 1878–1879, File 7721 AG0 1878, Letters Received by the Office of the Adjutant General (Main Series) 1871–1880, Records of the Adjutant General's Office, Record Group (RG) 94, National Archives (NA), Washington, D.C., Microcopy 666, Role 436 (hereinafter cited as Army Equipment Board, 1878).

2. Robert M. Utley, *The Contribution of the Frontier to the American Military Tradition*, Harmon Memorial Lectures in Military History, no. 19, (Colorado Springs: U.S. Air Force Academy, 1977), p. 6.

CHAPTER 1

1. An anecdote illustrating this point is found in Cordy and Yeh, "Thread Colour Change in United States Civil War Uniforms," p. 95. The authors relate the fraud exposed when the blouses of troops returning to Washington, D.C., after less than four months' service, were faded badly, as compared with others within the same unit. It was found that logwood dye, costing much less than the required indigo, had been used by the contractor.

2. *Army and Navy Journal,* October 19, 1872, p. 154 (hereinafter cited as *ANJ*).

3. Chappell, *The Search for the Well-Dressed Soldier,* p. 2.

4. Woodhull, *Medical Report,* p. 25.

5. *Revised United States Army Regulations,* pp. 169–171.

6. *ANJ,* September 28, 1872.

7. Woodhull, *Medical Report,* p. 4.

8. McConnell, *Five Years a Cavalryman,* p. 104; Rickey, *Forty Miles,* pp. 94.

9. *Revised United States Army Regulations,* p. 463.

10. Ibid., p. 10.

11. Todd, *American Military Equipage,* pp. 106–8.

12. McConnell, *Five Years a Cavalryman,* p. 230.

13. Captain Jeremiah Schindel, Co. H, Fifth U.S. Infantry to the Adjutant General, Headquarters of the Army, March 7, 1872, Letters Received, Records of the Adjutant General's Office, RG 94, NA.

14. Regulations prescribed that all soldiers wear both number and letter above the branch device, yet official army photographs taken in 1866 contradict this. The infantry model is posed with regimental number within the bend of the bugle. Although this was possible with single digits, the horn's loop was not large enough to admit two figures for the higher-numbered regiments. *Revised United States Army Regulations,* p. 467; *Uniform Regulations for the Army, 1861,* p. 26.

15. Chappell, *Well-Dressed Soldier,* p. 2.

16. Woodhull, *Medical Report,* p. 5.

17. *ANJ,* August 31, 1872, p. 42.

18. Circular No. 2, Department of the Platte, December 20, 1869, Circulars and Orders, Fort Fetterman, Wyoming Territory Records, Wyoming State Museum and Archives.

19. The French term *kepi* is a misnomer frequently applied to this cap. The forage cap had a tall, floppy crown unlike the low, stiff crown of the true kepi. Moreover, the term *kepi* was never used officially by the American army in reference to any regulation headgear during the nineteenth century.

20. Woodhull, *Medical Report,* p. 5.

21. For example, on June 30, 1867, there were 917,272 lined and 744,613 unlined sack coats on hand at the various depots. Two years later the respective figures were 590,759 and 482,988, indicating that the troops were drawing large numbers of the lined blouses. *Annual Report of the Quartermaster General to the Secretary of War for the Year 1867,* pp. 538–39 (these reports are hereinafter cited as *QMG, Sec. of War,* with year). See also *QMG, Sec. of War,* 1869, p. 337.

22. Woodhull, *Medical Report,* p. 11.

23. Todd, *American Military Equipage,* pp. 57–58.

24. *Revised United States Army Regulations,* p. 481.

25. Todd, *American Military Equipage,* p. 53.

26. Adjutant General's Office, *General Orders No. 108,* December 16, 1861 (hereinafter cited as A.G.O., *G.O.,* with specific order numbers).

27. One problem reported with this reinforcement was its raw edges, which rapidly frayed out, leaving a fringe of threads around the perimeter. Woodhull, *Medical Report,* p. 18.

28. Ostrander, *An Army Boy of the Sixties,* p. 154.

29. White flannel shirts became regulation in 1852 and remained an item of limited

issue until the mid-1870s. The gray flannel shirt apparently was adopted in 1862. Todd, *American Military Equipage,* p. 67; Kloster, "Uniforms of the Army," p. 6.

30. Woodhull, *Medical Report,* p. 15.

31. Ibid.; *QMG, Sec. of War,* 1867, pp. 538–39, and 1869, p. 335.

32. Kloster, "Uniforms of the Army" p. 9.

33. Woodhull, *Medical Report,* p. 13.

34. Ibid., p. 19.

35. Ibid.

36. Brinckerhoff, *Boots and Shoes,* p. 3.

37. Rickey, *Forty Miles,* p. 124.

38. Captain J. S. Poland, Sixth Infantry, Military Station, Standing Rock, D.T., to Adjutant General, U.S.A., March 15, 1875, and Lieutenant Colonel L. C. Hunt, Twentieth Infantry, Fort Totten, D.T., to Adjutant General, U.S.A., March 10, 1875, both in Army Equipment Board, 1878.

39. Hill and Innis "The Fort Buford Diary," p. 28.

40. Woodhull, *Medical Report,* p. 23.

41. *Revised United States Army Regulations,* p. 524. This provision was contained in the additions of 1863, probably as the result of two years of war. Another consideration behind this change may have been that the dark coats of officers would distinguish them immediately in a battle formation, such as that at Fredericksburg in December 1862.

42. Kloster, "Uniforms of the Army," p. 14.

43. Surgeon Edward P. Vollum to Post Adjutant, Camp Douglas, Utah, March 17, 1875, Army Equipment Board, 1878.

44. Rickey, *Forty Miles,* p. 123.

45. Typical of the complaints were those lodged by officers at Lower Brule Agency, D.T., Fort Rice, D.T., Cheyenne Depot, Wyo. Terr., and Fort Cameron, Utah, all in Army Equipment Board, 1878.

46. Woodhull, *Medical Report,* p. 22.

47. Circular No. 20, December 18, 1874, Orders and Circulars, Fort Laramie, Wyoming Territory, Records of U.S. Army Continental Commands, RG 393, NA.

48. Ibid., p. 6.

49. Woodhull, *Medical Report,* p. 24.

50. Giese, *My Life with the Army,* p. 18. Farmer described typical infantry dress during the Seventh Infantry's march to Utah, during the so-called Mormon War, as "uniform trousers and white flannel shirts, blouses with light felt hats, purchased from the Company Fund."

51. The 1862-pattern scabbard was distinguished by the lack of stitching on the frog, except at the mouth of the sheath. Rather, it was fastened to the scabbard by a row of three copper rivets; four more rivets were used to form the belt loop. The rivets simplified manufacture and were more durable. Reilly, *Socket Bayonets,* pp. 158–59.

52. *Proceedings of the Ordnance Board,* p. 25.

53. Phillips, "Emerson Steel Bayonet Scabbard," pp. 97–98.

54. A survey of ordnance returns revealed that although most regiments used the slings to some extent throughout the postwar era, their popularity varied, even from one company to the next within the same regiment. For instance, in 1867 only the companies of the Eighteenth Infantry used them without exception. Their issue was sporadic to nonexistent in most units during the same reporting period. During 1870, in the Seventh Infantry and the Tenth Infantry, only one company from each used slings. Conversely, in the Eighth Infantry, only one company did not have slings. Other infantries, like the Thirteenth, Fifteenth, Eighteenth, and Twenty-fifth, used them universally, whereas not one was reported in the Twenty-first Regiment. Statements for Quarters Ending June 30, 1867, and December 31, 1870, *Summary Statements of Quarterly Returns of Ordnance and Ordnance Stores on Hand in Regular and Volunteer Army Organizations—Infantry and Miscellaneous Organizations, 1864–1876,* Records of the Office of the Chief of Ordnance, RG 156, NA (hereinafter cited as *Ordnance Returns*).

55. Ordnance returns for the last quarter of 1870 list the following patterns of cartridge boxes: Hagner's, Benton's, Butler's, Burton's, Crispin's, Hoffman's, Howlett's, McGinness's, and Wall's. The number of trial cartridge boxes was always small and fluctuated somewhat with the passage of time. Not all infantry regiments were issued experimental boxes. Of those that were—principally, the Third, Fourth, Fifth, Seventh, Ninth, Tenth, Eleventh, Thirteenth, and Twenty-fourth regiments—only one or two companies were partially equipped. Statements, Quarter Ending December 31, 1870, *Ordnance Returns.*

56. *Proceedings of the Ordnance Board,* p. 25.

57. Ibid., p. 27.

58. In this period, the returns for only two quarters have survived. However, both reports reflect similar statistics on the NCO sword sling. Although a few were reported in nearly every regiment, usually only in certain companies, their numbers were comparatively small. Exceptions to this were the Eighth and Eighteenth regiments, which used the slings universally. Statements, Quarters Ending June 30, 1867, and December 31, 1870, *Ordnance Returns.*

59. *Ordnance Manual for the Use of the Officers of the United States Army,* pp. 229.

60. Todd, *American Military Equipage,* pp. 194, 199. Several examples of the special brass slides have been recovered at Fort Davis, Texas (1867–91), and Little Bighorn Battlefield (1876).

61. Frasca and Hill, *The .45–70 Springfield,* p. 290; Waite and Ernst, *Trapdoor Springfield,* pp. 6–7.

62. The Twelfth Infantry, stationed in the District of Columbia, was the only regiment to be armed entirely with the Model 1865 Allin breechloader. Company A, Eighteenth Infantry (Fort Casper, Wyoming Territory) was issued fourteen 1865 models, and two companies of the Twenty-first, posted in Virginia, were partially armed with them. Statements, Quarter Ending June 30, 1867, *Ordnance Returns.*

63. Frasca and Hill, *.45–70 Springfield,* p. 295.

64. Ibid.

65. Butler, *United States Firearms,* pp. 152–53; Garavaglia and Worman, *Firearms of the American West,* p. 21.

66. *Ordnance Returns.*

67. Company I, Twenty-seventh Infantry, stationed at Fort Reno, Wyoming Territory, had the Model 1866. Records indicate that an additional 115 Allin conversions were in the hands of detachments, perhaps recruits en route to join the regiment. Statements, Quarter Ending June 30, 1867, *Ordnance Returns.* Former Private Samuel S. Gibson recalled that seven hundred Model 1866 Springfields arrived at Fort Phil Kearny on Gilmore and Porter's bull train in June 1867. Hebard and Brininstool, *The Bozeman Trail,* pp. 41, 43. General Order No. 20, referenced in that post's returns for the same month, supports this. Post Return, Fort Phil Kearny, June 1867, Records of U.S. Army Continental Commands, RG 393, NA, microfilm copy in Wyoming Room, Fulmer Library, Sheridan, Wyoming. For accounts of the fights in which the Allin rifle played prominent roles, see Hebard and Brininstool, *The Bozeman Trail,* and Keenan, *The Wagon Box Fight.*

68. Statements, Quarter Ending June 30, 1867, *Ordnance Returns.*

69. Statements, Quarters Ending September 30, 1870, December 31, 1870, and March 31, 1871, *Ordnance Returns.*

70. Ibid.

71. *Annual Report of the Chief of Ordnance to the Secretary of War for the Year 1869,* p. 442 (these reports are hereinafter cited as *Chief of Ordnance, Sec. of War,* with year).

72. Butler, *United States Firearms,* pp. 152–53.

73. Upton, *A New System of Infantry Tactics,* pp. iii–iv, 97–124.

74. *Ordnance Memoranda No. 19,* p. 38.

75. Ibid.; See also *Proceedings of the Ordnance Board,* p. 26.

76. *Ordnance Returns.*

77. Ibid.

78. Todd, *American Military Equipage,* p. 188.

79. The inventor of the famous woven cartridge belt, Anson Mills, employed the cartridge belt concept when, serving as a captain in the Eighteenth Infantry, he provided his men with leather thimble belts. This probably occurred while Mills was stationed at Fort Bridger, Wyoming Territory. Mills, *My Story,* p. 310. Colonel John E. Smith, Twenty-seventh Infantry, allowed seventy-five of his men at Fort Phil Kearny to use thimble belts of a pattern designed by Lieutenant Thomas Connolly. The men were "unanimous in their expression in favor of the Belt with loops," Smith reported. Monthly Report on Breech-Loading Arms, June-December 1867, for Cos. A, B, C, F, and K, Twenty-seventh Infantry, Hagen Collection, Wyoming Room, Sheridan Public Library, Sheridan, Wyoming.

80. Hutchins, *Boots and Saddles at the Little Big Horn,* p. 49.

81. A pattern date of 1853 for the double-bag knapsack is applied by Katcher, *U.S. Infantry Equipments,* p. 20. However, no source is provided for this information.

82. Captain Loyd Wheaton, Twentieth Infantry, Fort Pembina, D.T., to Adjutant General, U.S.A., March 10, 1875, Army Equipment Board, 1878. This is just one example of many such testimonials found in this group of records.

83. Sylvia and O'Donnell, *Civil War Canteens,* p. 72. For further details, see also Phillips and Carter, "Canteens," p. 67.

84. *Revised United States Army Regulations,* p. 23.

85. *QMG, Sec. of War,* 1869, pp. 219–21, and 1870, p. 250.

86. Ibid., 1871, p. 125.

87. Ibid., 1870, p. 148.

88. Ibid., 1867, pp. 538–39, and 1869, p. 337.

89. Ibid., 1870, p. 148.

90. Ibid.

91. Woodhull, *Medical Report,* p. 26.

CHAPTER 2

1. Woodhull, *Medical Report.*

2. *QMG, Sec. of War,* 1870, p. 149.

3. A.G.O., *Special Orders No. 260,* July 3, 1871.

4. A.G.O., *G.O. 76,* July 27, 1872; Jacobsen, *Uniform of the Army, 1872.*

5. *QMG, Sec. of War,* 1873, p. 120.

6. Ibid., 1873, p. 142. Meigs's statement appears to be inconsistent with the fact that Civil War contract fabric was used until 1877 for blouses and drawers, and nearly that long for trousers. Since no entirely new overcoats were produced, only the dress coats might have been made of new material. However, numerous examples of 1872-pattern coats produced in the mid-1870s appeared to be made of the same cloth used for 1858 uniform coats. Ibid., 1878, p. 193.

7. Ibid., 1873, pp. 120–21.

8. Ibid., 1873, p. 152.

9. Ibid., pp. 120–21.

10. A.G.O., *G.O. 81,* August 25, 1877.

11. Further elaboration on the origins of the 1872 dress helmet may be found in Howell, *United States Army Headgear,* pp. 41–42, and in Chappell, *Brass Spikes,* pp. 1–9. Chappell attributes the origin of the helmet style, used by several nations, to the Germans, who had been using such headgear since the 1840s. However, Colonel Henry J. Hunt's comments, written in 1875 and presented in Howell, suggest that the U.S. helmet was directly influenced by a pattern used in the British service in the early 1870s.

12. Howell, *United States Army Headgear,* p. 42.

13. Ibid., pp. 42–43.

14. Although the Bracher Patent vent was supposed to be standard, a Bent & Bush specimen exhibited a small pressed-brass ventilator with three vertical bars and four slots.

15. Howell and Kloster, *United States Army Headgear,* p. 54.

16. One example of the enlisted hat was labeled "P. Herst Manufacturer," without date, but it presumably was from one of the two contracts let to that firm late in 1872. This example adheres quite closely to the Smithsonian specimens cited in Howell, except that it has three vent holes, one-eighth inch in diameter, punched in an equilateral triangle arrangement in each side of the crown. Despite the hat's apparently unused condition, it must be assumed that the vents were made either as a field alteration or as an experimental issue.

17. Jacobsen, *Uniform of the Army, 1872,* p. 10.

18. Two surviving examples of the 1872-pattern coat worn by Lieutenant Colonel George A. Custer depart from the regulations by cuff braid one-half inch wide and of a type identical to that used for 1884-pattern enlisted dress chevrons. The double stripes on cuffs were eliminated after January 1, 1880. A.G.O., *G.O. 76,* July 23, 1879, p. 42.

19. Jacobsen, *Uniform of the Army, 1872,* p. 17.

20. *ANJ,* August 17, 1872, p. 10.

21. Jacobsen, *Uniform of the Army, 1872,* p. 8.

22. The best photographs of officers in the field during the 1870s were those taken by Stanley J. Morrow, as published in Hedren's *With Crook in the Black Hills,* pp. 25, 51–63.

23. These small tongueless buckles are exactly like those used on the 1858 forage cap and probably were, in fact, surplus left from the manufacture of the earlier headgear.

24. Each of these rosettes had a brass-wire loop that passed through the plume base, connecting it to the helmet body. On a helmet worn by Sergeant William C. Williams, Seventh Cavalry, these ornaments, as well as the eagle plate, were keyed in place by rectangular pieces of very thin leather measuring approximately three-fourths inch by two inches. These appeared to be original to the specimen.

25. Howell, *United States Army Headgear,* p. 44.

26. Initially, the regulations did not specify a uniform manner for wearing the cords. Some men wore the tassels suspended from a button on the chest, in the manner of the 1864-pattern artillery cap; others looped them to the left epaulet button. A.G.O., *G.O. 67,* June 25, 1873, prescribed the latter method.

27. The specimen pictured in Howell, *United States Army Headgear,* p. 38, clearly has an unbound visor, whereas the visor on a J. H. Wilson contract example was bound in thin leather.

28. This marking was found in most of the headgear of the period, particularly in those items manufactured after 1878, including dress caps, forage caps, and campaign hats. *QMG, Sec. of War,* 1878, p. 243. The late nineteenth century saw a great proliferation of military goods for state, local, and veterans' organizations. Some of these were made according to federal specifications, but others departed to a greater or lesser degree from the standards of the Quartermaster Department. Only those specimens bearing Quartermaster Department and/or federal contract markings can be relied on as regular army issue.

29. The table of clothing allowances permitted a soldier to draw one cap annually during each year of his enlistment. Howell, *United States Army Headgear,* p. 48.

30. The regulation 1872 cap, compared with commercial versions made in the 1880s and 1890s, had a distinctive crown that was noticeably higher than its counterparts. There was a trend toward lower crowns on officers' and other commercially made caps during the following decade, but this was not reflected in the regulation enlisted caps. For a brief discussion of this, see Howell, *United States Army Headgear,* p. 48.

31. Howell, *United States Army Headgear,* p. 54. One officer commented that the hat's brim was "too large for a man on horseback, as the least wind [kept] it flapping in his face." First Lieutenant Henry Sweeney, Fourth Cavalry, to Post Adjutant, Fort Richardson, Texas, February 16, 1875, Army Equipment Board, 1878.

32. Howell, *United States Army Headgear,* p. 53.

33. Jacobsen, *Uniform of the Army, 1872,* p. 9.

34. Steffen, in *Horse Soldier* 2:135, illustrated the cavalry insignia worn with only the letter in the lower angle. However, this arrangement was not suggested by the regula-

tions, nor has any evidence been found to indicate that the insignia was actually used this way.

35. *QMG, Sec. of War,* 1874, p. 122.

36. Howell, *United States Army Headgear,* p. 52.

37. Woodhull, *Medical Report,* pp. 10–11.

38. The slashes on the coat worn by Sergeant William Williams, Seventh Cavalry, measure 7½ inches deep.

39. Woodhull, *Medical Report,* p. 13; Entry 2176, September 10, 1872, Register of Letters Received, Office of Clothing and Equipage 1870–1872, Records of the Office of the Quartermaster General, RG 92, NA, (hereinafter cited as Reg. of Letters Rec'd, Clothing Branch, 1870–1872).

40. Woodhull, *Medical Report.*

41. General Meigs originally alerted Schuylkill Arsenal to manufacture 15,600 pair of mounted and 8,000 pair of dismounted trousers. Entry June 25, 1872, Reg. of Letters Rec'd, Clothing Branch, 1870–1872. Records indicate that only five pair of each type and size, mounted and dismounted, were made for trial. The mounted trousers were sent to light batteries at Fort Hamilton and Fort McHenry, and the dismounted ones were to be sent to posts near Philadelphia. Entry 2182, Act. QMG James D. Bingham to Colonel Langdon C. Easton, January 3, 1874, Box 78, Letters Received, Philadelphia Depot, Records of the Office of the Quartermaster General, RG 92, NA.

42. General Edward S. Godfrey, "Godfrey Describes Mounts, Uniforms, and Equipment," in Graham, *The Custer Myth,* p. 346.

43. A.G.O., *Circular No. 9,* October 12, 1883. There is some evidence, such as the illustrations contained in Jacobsen, *Uniform of the Army, 1882,* to suggest that musicians informally adopted double stripes before the official order. Further reference may be found in Hardorff, *The Custer Battle Casualties,* p. 112, wherein Lieutenant Charles De Rudio recalled identifying, by the trouser stripes, one badly mutilated body as that of a trumpeter.

44. Nine of these buttons were recovered from the Custer Battlefield, plus two from the Reno-Benteen defensive position. See Scott, Fox, Connor, and Harmon, *Archeological Perspectives,* p. 198.

45. Although trumpeters are sometimes portrayed with a bugle insignia on one or both arms, this device was not authorized by the U.S. Army until after the beginning of the twentieth century. Emerson, *Chevrons,* p. 147.

46. Ibid., pp. 254–60.

47. Cavalry regiments were not authorized principal musicians; therefore, the chevron for this grade was made only for infantry and artillery regiments. Ibid., p. 90; Heitman, *Historical Register,* table, "Organization of the Army under the Acts of June 16 and 23, 1874, March 2 and 3, 1875, and June 26, 1876," pp. 612–13.

48. Kautz, *Customs of Service,* pp. 77–78.

49. A.G.O., *G.O. 107,* December 14, 1872.

50. Before 1869, enlistments had been for three years. However, an act of Congress in 1866 extended cavalry terms to five years, whereas those for infantry remained at three. Then the act of March 3, 1869, mandated five-year enlistments for all branches. Ganoe, *The History of the United States Army,* pp. 306, 307, 325.

51. A.G.O., *G.O. 92,* September 15, 1873.

52. Woodhull, *Medical Report,* p. 15. The 1872 uniform regulations indicated that consideration was given to issuing a lighter-weight shirt after the old ones had been consumed. Jacobsen, *Uniform of the Army, 1872,* p. 20.

53. Kloster, "Uniforms of the Army," pp. 6, 8.

54. Lieutenant Colonel George A. Woodward, Fourteenth Infantry, to Adjutant General, U.S.A., March 30, 1875, Army Equipment Board, 1878.

55. Hutchins, *Boots and Saddles,* pp. 5, 13–14.

56. *Revised United States Army Regulations,* p. 464. The wording, "shall be buttoned or hooked at the collar," may account at least in part for the frequency with which we see

soldiers photographed with only the top button of the blouse fastened. The letter of the regulations was met, but greater comfort was achieved by leaving the rest of the buttons undone.

57. Woodhull, *Medical Report*, p. 19; Kloster, "Uniforms of the Army," p. 6.

58. First Lieutenant John M. Ross to Post Adjutant, Ft. Walla Walla, Washington Terr., February 23, 1875, and First Lieutenant Charles H. Greene, Seventeenth Infantry to A.G., U.S.A., March 17, 1875, both in Army Equipment Board, 1878.

59. Woodhull, *Medical Report*, p. 20.

60. *QMG, Sec. of War*, 1873, p. 179.

61. Ibid., 1878, p. 267. It was only in 1876 that the army began publishing detailed specifications. Before this time, samples were either made up or procured on the commercial market, provided with an official wax seal, and delivered to the contractors to use as models. Therefore, many of the articles for which specifications were published in the late 1870s, regardless of the stated date of adoption, had been in use for some years.

62. Woodward to A.G., U.S.A., March 30, 1875, Army Equipment Board, 1878.

63. In 1868 Surgeon Woodhull recommended issuing the mounted coat to all soldiers. He also recommended the heavier lining. Woodhull, *Medical Report*, p. 21. Army regulations specified a stiff, standing collar, as on the dismounted coat. Only with the promulgation of new regulations in 1861 was the mounted overcoat modified to have the falling collar. *Regulations of the Army of the United States, 1857*, p. 450, and *Regulations for the Uniform, 1861*, par. 121. The collar on one specimen measured 5 inches deep at the rear and 4⅝ inches at the front corners.

64. Ryan, *Ten Years with General Custer*, p. 47.

65. Specimen bears an original tag from Jeffersonville Depot inscribed "Great Coat Mtd.—Blanket Lined—O[ld] P[attern]."

66. Meigs to Bingham, February 23, 1872, Reg. of Letters Rec'd, Clothing Branch, 1870–1872.

67. Billings, *Report on the Hygiene*, p. lii.

68. *QMG, Sec. of War*, 1873, pp. 151–52.

69. A.G.O., *G. O. 67*, June 25, 1873.

70. *QMG, Sec. of War*, 1873, p. 153.

71. Ashburn, *History of the Medical Department*, p. 114.

72. Circular No. 20, December 18, 1874, Orders and Circulars, Fort Laramie, Wyoming Territory, Records of U.S. Army Continental Commands 1821–1921, RG 393, NA.

73. Billings, *Report on the Hygiene*, referring to A.G.O., *G. O. 9*, February 3, 1871, p. liii.

74. Captain John H. Patterson Twentieth Infantry to A.G., U.S.A., March 20, 1875, Army Equipment Board, 1878.

75. General Montgomery C. Meigs to A.G., U.S.A., August 6, 1872, Correspondence Relating to Changes in the Uniform of the Army, File 3028 AGO, Letters Received by the Adjutant General's Office (Main Series), Records of the Adjutant General's Office, RG 94, NA.

76. The specifications for white gloves, adopted on May 31, 1876, note the measurement of the elastic strip as ¼ inch by 1 inch; however, those on an original pair measure 1½ inches long. They meet the specifications in all other respects.

77. The Equipment Board of 1878–79 (Miles Board) stated in its report, "When campaigning, Cavalry soldiers wear their overalls and stable frocks whenever permitted." A.G.O., *G. O. 76*, July 23, 1879.

78. Bourke, *On the Border with Crook*, p. 211.

79. *QMG, Sec. of War*, 1871, p. 126. Judging by the number of iron heel plates found at various western sites, their use appears to have been widespread.

80. Ibid., p. 127. This invention was not a new one, as reflected in Woodhull, *Medical Report*, p. 20, which had suggested the use of brass screws, in 1868. It is interesting to note that M1943 U.S. combat boots employed similar fasteners.

81. Billings, *Report on the Hygiene,* pp. l–lii; *QMG, Sec. of War,* 1872, p. 179.

82. *Regulations for the Uniform, 1872,* p. 9.

83. Ashburn, *History of the Medical Department,* p. 115.

CHAPTER 3

1. *ANJ,* June 8, 1878, p. 710.

2. McBarron, "36th Illinois Infantry Regiment." Pack frames are also mentioned in *QMG, Sec. of War,* 1867, p. 542, and in First Lieutenant David B. Taylor, Eleventh Infantry, to Post Adjutant, Fort Richardson, Texas, February 18, 1875, Army Equipment Board, 1878.

3. Todd, *American Military Equipage,* pp. 209–10. Evidence of frontier involvement in these trials is found in Special Orders No. 100, September 25, 1868, Fort Davis, Texas. This order states that the commanding officer of Company E, Forty-first U.S. Infantry, was to issue to his men forty-five sets of Baxter's Patent knapsacks and Buchanan cartridge boxes. The knapsacks were to be packed and worn on all "drills, marches, campaign, etc.," and reported on. Orders and Circulars, 1867–78, Fort Davis National Historic Site, Fort Davis, Texas.

4. The knapsacks selected were patterns of the following types: Penrose, Baxter, Sherlock, Seymour, Clifford, and Mizner. *Ordnance Memoranda No. 11,* August 1, 1870.

5. *QMG, Sec. of War,* 1870, p. 148.

6. Ibid., 1871, p. 126.

7. *A.G.O., S.O. No. 433,* November 6, 1871. The following were named members for this board: Surgeon General Joseph K. Barnes, Assistant Quartermaster General Robert Allen; Colonel Thomas G. Pitcher, First Infantry; Major O. A. Mack, First Infantry; and Major Stephen V. Benet, who would be appointed the chief of ordnance on June 23, 1874.

8. Meigs's recommendation was endorsed by the board and approved by the secretary of war on December 6, 1871. *Ordnance Memoranda No. 13,* pp. 6, 8.

9. Ibid., p. 7.

10. *Directions for Fitting Infantry Equipments,* p. 8.

11. Entry February 27, 1872, Registers of Letters, Telegrams, and Endorsements Received, Watervliet Arsenal, Records of the Office of the Chief of Ordnance, RG 156, NA (hereinafter cited as Reg. of Letters Rec'd, Watervliet Arsenal.) On May 29, 1873, Watervliet Arsenal was given an order for an additional ten thousand sets of infantry equipments, "the flaps [on the valise] to be of seal skin so far as the supply would last," bringing the total initial production to twenty thousand sets. Ibid. A final order for four hundred sets, to be completed from parts of five hundred sets on hand, was made on March 30, 1875. Benet to C. O., Watervliet Arsenal, Letters, Telegrams, and Endorsements Sent Relating to the Manufacture, Procurement, and Repair of Ordnance Supplies and Equipment 1862–94, Records of the Office of the Chief of Ordnance, RG 156, NA (hereinafter cited as Letters Sent, Chief of Ordnance).

12. *Ordnance Memoranda No. 13,* pp. 9–10. It is clear that Hagner had been thinking along these lines since the first meeting. He brought with him to this second board a sample cavalry brace that he had made in the Watervliet shops several weeks before. Benet to C. O., Watervliet Arsenal, January 2, 1872, Letters Sent, Chief of Ordnance.

13. *Ordnance Memoranda No. 13,* pp. 14–15.

14. Entry December 2, 1872, Reg. of Letters Rec'd, Watervliet Arsenal; chief of ordnance's circular quoted in *ANJ,* March 29, 1873, p. 1.

15. Of eight plates examined, only three measured 3¼ inches wide. The largest measured 3⁵⁄₁₆ inches, two were 3³⁄₁₆ inches, and the smallest two measured 3⁵⁄₃₂ inches. Mean width among these examples was 2⅛ inches with a variance of about ¹⁄₃₂ inch, plus or minus.

16. Sergeant John Cox, Company K, First Infantry, recorded that soldiers at Fort Brady, Michigan, once avenged a corporal who had been assaulted by civilian toughs. Carrying weapons into town was prohibited, but the men circumvented this restriction

by wearing their waist belts (an uncommon practice) instead. In the ensuing fight, the soldiers removed their belts and charged the crowd, swinging the heavy U.S. plates like maces. Cox, *Five Years in the Army,* pp. 60–61.

17. *Directions for Fitting Infantry Equipments,* p. 5.

18. In addition to the three primary materials, the Ordnance Department apparently added several variations to this list by mid-1873: "canvas flap, lined; waterproof flap, waterproof flap, lined; and all-canvas, dyed." Just what was meant by a "lined" flap is uncertain. The author has not encountered any examples of these other types. Ordnance Office, *Circular No. 20,* June 10, 1873.

19. *Ordnance Memoranda No. 11,* p. 17. These examples were the following: a pouch and a box, designed by Lieutenant John G. Butler, Ordnance Department; a pouch holding sixty rounds, submitted by Brigadier General Alexander B. Dyer, Ordnance Department; a box by Second Lieutenant Clermont L. Best, First Artillery; a box intended to hold two issue cartons of rifle ammunition, invented by Major Silas Crispin, Ordnance Department; and an altered Pattern 1855 box, contributed by Lieutenant Colonel Benjamin S. Roberts, Third Cavalry.

20. This pouch is further described as having the cover secured by a "turn-buckle" in *Report of the Board,* p. 752.

21. A notation referencing the Hanger No. 2 pouch as the "Tileston modified" is found in the entry for February 27, 1872, Reg. of Letters Rec'd, Watervliet Arsenal.

22. Major Elmer Otis, First Cavalry, Camp Harvey, Oregon to A.G., U.S.A., March 14, 1875, Army Equipment Board, 1878.

23. Ibid.

24. J. E. Emerson patented the steel scabbard body on April 30, 1862. The frog and the belt loop on this scabbard were nearly identical to those for the regulation Pattern 1862 scabbard, except that the rivets pass through from the obverse and are peened on the reverse. The scabbard body was blued and had a small drain hole in the tip, as did its progeny. Twenty thousand were ordered by the government in August 1862. Reilly, *Socket Bayonets,* p. 161.

25. Ibid.

26. Hardin, *The American Bayonet,* p. 44.

27. Entry October 29, 1872, Reg. of Letters Rec'd, Watervliet Arsenal.

28. Federal-contract canteens were produced most often with spouts made of pewter. However, at least one contract was let to a Cincinnati firm in 1863 specifying tin spouts. William G. Phillips to author, February 6, 1993. Although 1858-pattern canteens with tin spouts have commonly been labeled as being of Confederate manufacture, they were rather common among those examined. It is unlikely the regular army would have resorted to converting captured canteens after the war.

29. Captain J. S. Poland, Company A, Sixth Infantry, to Chief of Ordnance, Quarterly Report on Infantry Equipments, Fourth Qtr., 1875, Letters Received, Watervliet Arsenal, 1874–1881 (Box 3), Records of the Office of the Chief of Ordnance, RG 156, NA.

30. This sling is referred to as the Pattern 1870 in *Ordnance Memoranda No. 19,* p. 38. One might question why the production of the lengthened sling was initiated two years after the issue of the new rifle. Frasca and Hill, *.45–70 Springfield,* p. 305, states that the Model 1868 rifle was not manufactured until 1869 and not issued in significant numbers until 1870. Only then did the oversight manifest itself.

31. Ordnance Department records contain orders to the various arsenals beginning in the early 1870s for quantities of "slings lengthened to 63 inches." As late as June 1885, Rock Island Arsenal was ordered to make "10,000 new gun slings—63 inches." Letters Sent, Chief of Ordnance.

32. Todd, *American Military Equipage,* p. 225.

33. *Report of the Board,* p. 751.

34. Meadows, *Military Holsters,* pp. 88–91. The holster originally designed for the 1860 Colt army revolver, the only official cavalry handgun at the beginning of the Civil

War, was too slim to accommodate the somewhat larger-framed 1863 Remington. Thus, a holster of larger capacity was put into production in March 1863. Phillips and Vervloet, *U.S. Single Action*, p. 8.

35. That the board contemplated the design of a new, special device is suggested in the following wording: "Pistol Cartridge Box.—For the present, the infantry cap pouch, to carry twelve pistol cartridges." *Ordnance Memoranda No. 13*, p. 15.

36. Greene, "Bacon or Bullets," p. 28.

37. *Ordnance Memoranda No. 13*, p. 16. This basic pattern, which had been in use since 1839, is described in the ordnance regulations of 1841. Slings were made of white buff leather until superseded by black buff in 1851. Steffen, *Horse Soldier* 1:139, 2:35.

38. *Ordnance Memoranda No. 13*, p. 19.

39. Ibid., p. 16.

40. *Ordnance Memoranda No. 18*, p. 67.

41. *Ordnance Memoranda No. 13*, pp. 12–13.

42. Ibid., p. 14.

43. *Ordnance Manual*, p. 158.

44. The 1859-pattern spurs exhibiting the floral design are not uncommon, although they are encountered less frequently than the plain version. Apparently, both types were produced in large numbers during the Civil War. No information has been found regarding the source of the more decorative style. Presumably, it was simply a contract variation that was allowed to pass government inspection because it did not affect the function or overall appearance of the spurs.

45. Neither *Ordnance Memoranda No. 13* nor *G.O. 60, 1872*, addresses the spur straps, but they are listed in *Ordnance Memoranda No. 18, 1874*, as being among the items of the modified equipments requiring no changes. *Ordnance Memoranda No. 18*, p. 55.

46. The 1863 *Army Regulations* do not authorize the issue of individual mess gear to soldiers. In fact, the only reference to mess gear is found in par. 122, which states, "The only mess furniture of the soldier will be one tin plate, one tin cup, one knife, fork and spoon, to each man, to be carried by himself." The intent of the regulations was to limit the amount of superfluous gear carried by soldiers on campaign, particularly the wartime volunteers, since the regulations make no reference to the Quartermaster Department supplying these items. Further evidence is found in *Ordnance Memoranda No. 19, 1874*, p. 57, wherein the board recommends these items "be furnished by the Ordnance Department and issued as other ordnance stores," thus indicating a change in policy.

47. Only these three items are listed in *Regulations for the Uniform, 1861*, pp. 235–36, as well as in the "Statement of camp and garrison equipage reported on hand at the various clothing depots, June 30, 1867, "found in *QMG, Sec. of War, 1867*, p. 540. An excellent discussion of messing during the Civil War is found in John D. Billings, *Hardtack and Coffee: The Unwritten Story of Army Life*, pp. 127–39.

48. Billings, *Hardtack and Coffee*, p. 125.

49. *Directions for Fitting Infantry Equipments*, p. 7.

50. Paul L. Hedren has done considerable research on late-nineteenth-century army cups. His investigations have revealed numerous variations of this cup, samples of which have been recovered from military fort and camp sites across the West. Although the one described here emerges as the most common pattern, others of similar construction vary from about 4 inches up to 4¾ inches high and from 4⅛ inches to 4⁷⁄₁₆ inches in diameter. Hedren, "Army Tin Cups," pp. 57–60.

51. Ibid.

52. Rarely, a specimen of the tall wire-wrapped cup will bear hand-stamped "U.S." markings on the handle. It is believed these represent Civil War–vintage cups that were retinned, marked, and issued during the Spanish-American War. Such cups are listed in *1911 Francis Bannerman Catalogue*, p. 172.

53. The talma was first issued to the First and Second regiments of cavalry in 1857. Todd, *American Military Equipage*, p. 73; *Regulations for the Uniform, 1861*, p. 474.

54. Quartermaster General, *Specifications for Clothing*, p. 223.

55. Captain Theodore J. Wint, Fourth Cavalry, to Post Adjutant, Fort Richardson, Texas, February 20, 1875, and First Lieutenant Henry Sweeney, Fourth Cavalry, to Post Adjutant, Fort Richardson, Texas, February 16, 1875, both in Army Equipment Board, 1878.

56. *QMG, Sec. of War,* 1870, pp. 197–200, and 1869, p. 340.

57. Ibid., 1893, p. 106.

58. Billings, *Hardtack and Coffee,* p. 42, and Mulford, *Fighting Indians,* p. 27. Mulford was a member of Company M from 1876 until he was discharged on a surgeon's certificate in 1878 for wounds received at the Bear Paws Mountain fight.

59. Small galvanized iron rings have been found at various frontier military sites, including the Little Bighorn Battlefield, suggesting that they may have been used as reinforcements for shelter tent grommets. However, the specifications for shelter tents do not mention these rings, nor has the author seen a specimen exhibiting them. However, the specifications for other tentage, including wall tents, common tents, and tent flies, do list rings of one-half-inch- and five-eighth-inch-diameter to be whipped to the grommets to prevent them from ripping. Virtually all of these items were Civil War surplus. Perhaps it is significant that no such rings were found on the Custer Battlefield, where it can be assumed shelter halves were present in great numbers. Conversely, rings were discovered at the Reno-Benteen Battlefield. Specifically, these have been found in the hospital area, where it is known that Dr. Henry Porter employed tentage, likely tent flies carried by the pack train, to shelter the wounded from the sun. This evidence suggests that grommet stiffeners were not used in the manufacture of shelter tents. *U.S. Army Uniforms,* pp. 206–20, 280; Scott et al., *Archeological Perspectives,* p. 203.

60. It has been questioned whether special shelter tent poles were produced and issued during the Civil War. It may be that few soldiers used them because of the inconvenience in carrying them. Soldiers traditionally discard anything superfluous. However, the fact that poles were a component of the shelter tent from its inception is suggested by the paired holes on the upper corners of each piece. Further evidence is found in *QMG, Sec. of War,* 1867, "Statement of damaged and irregular clothing and equipage ordered to be sold at public auction during the fiscal year ending June 30, 1867," p. 543, wherein "486 1/2 tent poles, shelter, sets" are listed. See also *QMG, Sec. of War,* 1868, p. 337, wherein 139,239 shelter tent "poles and pins, sets" are included in the "Statements of clothing, camp, and garrison equipage on hand at the close of the fiscal year ending June 30, 1868." Evidence for the use of these poles by cavalry in the field during the Indian campaigns is suggested by the recovery of a tin socket from the 1876 Reno-Benteen defense position at the Little Bighorn Battlefield. Scott, et al., *Archeological Perspectives,* p. 97.

61. Specifications for shelter tent poles, pins, and guy ropes are found in *U.S. Army Uniforms,* p. 280.

62. Gaede, "The 'Danish Exchange,'" p. 65.

63. Colonel Frank Wheaton, Second Infantry, Fort Walla Walla, Washington Terr., to A.G., U.S.A., March 15, 1875, Army Equipment Board, 1878.

64. The new specifications were adopted on May 2, 1872, and were included in the 1872 uniform regulations. One of the ways the army used up the old "stock of inferior blankets" was by using them for lining overcoats, per *G.O. No. 9,* 1871, which then led to justification for purchasing new and better blankets. Billings, *Report on the Hygiene,* pp. l, liii; *Regulations for the Uniform, 1872,* p. 18; *QMG, Sec. of War,* 1873, pp. 141–42.

CHAPTER 4

1. The first board was established by G.O. No. 60, August 6, 1869, and the additional examination into small arms and accouterments by *G.O. No. 72,* October 23, 1869. Further elaboration is found in *Sec. of War,* Report of the General of the Army, 1870, p. 32 (hereinafter cited as *Gen. of Army, Sec. of War*).

2. *Ordnance Memoranda No. 11,* p. 15.

3. Selected companies of the Third, Fourth, Fifth, Ninth, Tenth, Eleventh, Twelfth,

Twenty-first, and Twenty-fourth infantry regiments are shown as having small quantities of the "Model 1868 Breech-loading Musket," along with a mixture of Model 1866 Springfields and a few Remingtons, during the last quarter of 1870. Since returns are not available before this date, it is not known just when these arms first reached the troops, but it was certainly not earlier than 1869. No carbines are listed for cavalry during the same period. *Ordnance Returns; Ordnance Memoranda No. 11,* pp. 19–20.

4. *Chief of Ordnance, Sec. of War,* 1870, 1871, pp. 288–89.

5. *Gen. of Army, Sec. of War,* 1870, p. 5.

6. Initially, companies of the Third through Sixth, Ninth through Sixteenth, Eighteenth, and Twenty-third through Twenty-fifth infantry regiments were issued experimental arms. Among the cavalry, experimental arms were issued to portions of the First, Second, Fourth, Sixth, Seventh, Eighth, and Ninth regiments. *Ordnance Returns.*

7. Ibid.

8. *Chief of Ordnance, Sec. of War,* 1872, p. 314.

9. Brevet Major General Alexander B. Dyer to Brevet Colonel T.T.S. Laidley, May 2, 1866, Letters Received, Springfield Armory, Springfield Armory National Historic Site Collections.

10. Frasca and Hill, *.45–70 Springfield,* p. 295.

11. Ibid., p. 5; Fuller, *Breech-Loader in the Service,* pp. 308–10; Waite and Ernst, *Trap-door Springfield,* pp. 16–17.

12. Coffman, *The Old Army,* p. 330.

13. Frasca and Hill, *.45–70 Springfield,* pp. 200–201, and Brophy, *The Krag Rifle,* pp. 5–6.

14. On the Custer and Reno-Benteen battlefields, the total number of .44 Henry cases recovered was 202, as compared with only 14 of the .44–40 cases. Scott et al., *Archeological Perspectives,* pp. 164–65.

15. Target practice at most posts was infrequent. Each soldier was authorized only ten rounds per month for practice. Douglas C. McChristian, *An Army of Marksmen: The Development of United States Army Marksmanship in the Nineteenth Century,* pp. 64–68.

16. Scott et al., *Archeological Perspectives,* pp. 114–115. In fact, allegations against the Springfield are notably absent from contemporary accounts. These came only in later years, when students of the battle, and the army itself, attempted to find excuses for Custer's crushing defeat.

17. Scott, *A Sharp Little Affair,* pp. 79–81.

18. Unsigned note written by Walter M. Camp to himself, June 6, 1925, stating that former Seventh Cavalry Privates Fremont Kipp and Henry Meckling testified that "neither the carbines nor the ammunition of the 7th Cavalry had been inspected from the time they left Ft. A. Lincoln to the day of the battle." Letter No. 11392, Walter M. Camp Collection, Little Bighorn Battlefield National Monument; see also Reneau, *Adventures of Moccasin Joe,* p. 69.

19. One must take into consideration the motives and tactics of the Plains Indians. Fighting as individuals primarily for war honors and booty, by which status was attained in one's tribe, warriors had no particular sense of team cooperation in the manner practiced by white troops. Thus, they were not inclined to develop and launch coordinated attacks against an enemy position such as that found at Reno Hill. Hardly an imposing defensive work by conventional standards, it intimidated the numerically superior Indians, who for the most part were satisfied to remain in protected firing positions some distance from the soldiers. This factor, as much as anything, saved the other seven companies of the Seventh Cavalry from annihilation. Had they been opposed by conventional troops, the soldiers in this vulnerable position would probably have been overrun rather quickly. An excellent firsthand account describing Indian tactics is Marquis, *Wooden Leg,* pp. 256–59.

20. Scott et al., *Archeological Perspectives,* pp. 118–21, 124–26.

21. Shockley, *Trap-Door Springfield,* pp. 6–7.

22. Fuller, *Breech-Loader in the Service,* p. 310.

23. Ibid., p. 311.

24. Frasca and Hill, *.45–70 Springfield*, p. 378.

25. Summary Reports, Infantry Regiments, First through Fourth Quarters, 1874, *Ordnance Returns*.

26. Summary Reports, Cavalry Regiments, Quarter Ending June 30, 1875, *Ordnance Returns*.

27. A statement to this effect is found in Frasca and Hill, *.45–70 Springfield*, p. 305. Although the Model 1868 remained in the hands of militia units for many years, this did not hold true for the regular army.

28. Summary Reports, Cavalry Regiments, Quarter Ending June 1867, *Ordnance Returns*.

29. Captain William Thompson, Seventh Cavalry, to A.A.G., Department of Dakota, March 9, 1874, Miscellaneous Documents, Seventh U.S. Cavalry Records, Little Bighorn Battlefield National Monument (hereinafter cited as Misc. Doc., Seventh Cavalry.)

30. *Proceedings of the Ordnance Board*, p. 24.

31. Parsons, *The Peacemaker*, p. 10.

32. Summary Reports, Cavalry Regiments, Quarters Ending March 31, 1872, Dec. 31, 1872, and June 30, 1873, *Ordnance Returns*.

33. The Martin-primed cartridges loaded initially for the .44 American used the lighter charge, whereas the Frankford Arsenal began loading the 30-grain ammunition in August 1871. *Report of the Board*, p. 746.

34. For reasons unexplained, the Eighth and Tenth regiments did not participate in the field trials. They retained their percussion Remingtons and Colts until the advent of the Model 1873 Colt in 1874. Summary Reports, Cavalry Regiments, Quarter Ending June 30, 1871, *Ordnance Returns*, Roll No. 3; Parsons, *Smith & Wesson Revolvers*, p. 72. A Smith & Wesson No. 3 once owned by Lieutenant James E. Porter, Company I, Seventh Cavalry, is in the collections at Little Bighorn Battlefield National Monument. Both the property marking and the serial number have been filed off this specimen, but the government inspector's marks remain. It is presumed Porter purchased the revolver to use as a personal sidearm, perhaps when the Smith & Wessons were turned in. This could account for the removal of the markings. In any event, this is likely one of the twenty nickel-plated revolvers that were issued to the Seventh Cavalry and were assigned to Porter's company.

35. Summary Reports, Cavalry Regiments, Quarters Ending March 31, June 30, September 30, and December 31, 1872, *Ordnance Returns*.

36. For a detailed account of this exchange, see Graham, Kopec, and Moore, *A Study of the Colt Single Action Army Revolver*, pp. 335–39.

37. *Ordnance Notes*, June 26, 1873.

38. Summary Reports, Quarter Ending March 31, 1874, *Ordnance Returns*.

39. Ibid.

40. Parson, *The Peacemaker*, pp. 33–34.

41. Kopec and Moore, *A Study of the Colt Single Action Army Revolver*, p. 306.

42. King, *Trials of a Staff Officer*, pp. 55–57.

43. Ibid., p. 455.

44. Three theories have been suggested for the change in the breechblock: (1) financial savings realized by less machining; (2) additional strength, though no problem had been voiced previously; and (3) improved gas escape. Frasca and Hill, *.45–70 Springfield*, p. 75.

45. *Report of the Board*, p. 746. Captain Myles W. Keogh, Seventh Cavalry, complained about the 70-grain rifle ammunition used by his company when he wrote, "The ammunition at present issued contain to [*sic*] much powder for the weight of the gun (70 grains gun powder)." Keogh to Adjutant, Seventh Cavalry, March 18, 1874, Misc. Doc., Seventh Cavalry.

46. Marcot, *Spencer Repeating Firearms*, pp. 118–21.

47. McChristian, *Army of Marksmen*, p. 38.

48. Flayderman, *Antique American Firearms,* p. 143, and Parsons, *The Peacemaker,* p. 7.

49. A complete list of serial numbers for U.S. Smith & Wessons is included in Parsons, *Smith & Wesson Revolvers,* pp. 74–75.

50. Ibid., pp. 22, 175.

51. Reilly, *Socket Bayonets,* pp. 168–69, offers the observation that early examples of the 1873-pattern scabbard can be identified by the "U.S." rosette with a period between the letters. He bases this supposition on the existence of a scabbard having a similar escutcheon, which he assumes was produced shortly after the Civil War. Arguing against this is the official photograph of the new infantry equipments, including the angular and trowel bayonet scabbards, taken on November 19, 1874. Close examination of the image clearly reveals no period between the letters on either scabbard. Reilly has no explanation for the origin of the "U.S." rosette. If indeed it was produced some years earlier, its presence on some 1873-pattern scabbards may represent stock left over from the Civil War.

52. *Ordnance Memoranda No. 11,* p. 16.

53. Summary Reports, Quarter Ending June 30, 1871, through Quarter Ending December 31, 1873, *Ordnance Returns.*

54. Hardin, *American Bayonet,* p. 204.

55. Ibid. The chief of ordnance ordered Springfield Armory "to make 10,000 Rice trowels with Chillingworth handles" on December 22, 1873. Letters Sent, Chief of Ordnance.

56. A.G.O. *G.O. 53,* April 19, 1875.

57. *Ordnance Memoranda No. 19,* p. 57.

58. Hardin, *American Bayonet,* p. 205.

59. Summary Reports, Quarters Ending March 31, 1875, through March 31, 1876, *Ordnance Returns.*

60. *ANJ,* December 25, 1875, p. 322.

61. Major Zenas R. Bliss, Twenty-fifth Infantry, in a letter to A.A.G, Dept. of Texas, October 5, 1876, stated, "Intrenching tools . . . are of very little use on the frontier or in the service now required of infantry." Letters Sent, Fort Davis, Texas, Records of U.S. Army Continental Commands, RG 393, NA.

62. Brigadier General S. V. Benet to acting adjutant general, Headquarters of the Army, October 27, 1876, Letters, Telegrams, and Circulars Sent (Misc. Letters) 1812–89, Records of the Office of the Chief of Ordnance, RG 156, NA (hereinafter cited as Misc. Letters Sent, Ordnance Office).

63. Army Equipment Board, 1878, roll 435.

64. Brigadier General S. V. Benet to commanding officer, Springfield Armory: October 22, 1873, ibid.; March 7, 1874, Misc. Letters Sent, Ordnance Office; and March 7, 1874, Letters Received, Records of the Office of the Chief of Ordnance, RG 156, NA (hereinafter cited as Letters Received, Ordnance Office).

65. Letter, Benet to Benton, Springfield Armory, March 4, 1875, Misc. Letters Sent, Ordnance Office.

66. *Report of the Board,* p. 749.

67. A letter from the Commanding Officer, Rock Island Arsenal, to the Chief of Ordnance, dated March 14, 1890, presented in Hardin and Hedden, *Light but Efficient,* p. 11, suggests that some of the scabbards for the ordnance entrenching tool may have had the Varney-type attachment. This consisted of a hinged brass locking device that passed over the waist belt.

68. This order did not apply to noncoms of the regimental and general staff, namely commissary sergeants, ordnance sergeants, and hospital stewards. These senior noncommissioned officers were authorized to wear the sword for dress purposes until the sword was finally phased out at the turn of the century.

69. A suggestion of this is found in Meyers, *Ten Years,* p. 41. Meyers, assigned as a musician in the Second Infantry in 1855, stated that he tripped on his sword because it was still a bit long for his legs.

70. *Regulations for the Uniform, 1872,* p. 12.

71. Hickox, *Collector's Guide,* p. 22.

CHAPTER 5

1. Indicative of the desperate measures taken to dispose of the war surplus, the 1857 dress coats were provided with 1872-style facings on collar, cuffs, and tails and issued at reduced prices. *QMG, Sec. of War,* 1874, pp. 152–53.

2. Ibid., 1873, p. 153; A.G.O., *G.O. 62,* August 4, 1883.

3. Captain Edward G. Bush, Tenth Infantry, Fort Stockton, Texas, to A.G., U.S.A, February 27, 1875, Army Equipment Board, 1878.

4. Chappell, *Brass Spikes,* p. 15.

5. Act. Assist. Surgeon J. Frazer Boughler to Post Adjutant, Fort Craig, New Mexico, March 18, 1875, Army Equipment Board, 1878.

6. A.G.O., *G.O. 67,* June 25, 1873. Since this was the army's first experience with an official campaign hat, soldiers no doubt wore it on occasions for which it was not intended.

7. Colonel George L. Andrews, Twenty-fifth Infantry, Fort Davis, Texas, to A.G., U.S.A., February 25, 1875, Army Equipment Board, 1878.

8. Colonel William B. Hazen, Sixth Infantry, Fort Buford, Dakota Territory, to A.G., U.S.A., March 17, 1875, ibid.

9. *QMG, Sec. of War,* 1877, p. 266.

10. A.G.O., *G.O. 96,* November 19, 1875.

11. Ibid.

12. *ANJ,* December 25, 1875, p. 322.

13. A.G.O., *G.O. 96,* November 19, 1875.

14. A.G.O., *G.O. 21,* March 20, 1876.

15. A.G.O., *G.O. 8,* February 8, 1877.

16. Howell, *United States Army Headgear,* p. 55.

17. First Lieutenant William H. H. Crowell, Sixth Infantry, to Post Adjutant, Fort Buford, D.T., March 14, 1875; Captain Loyd Wheaton, Twentieth Infantry, to A.G., U.S.A., March 10, 1875; and Act. Assist. Surgeon William H. Forwood to Post Adjutant, Fort Richardson, Texas, April 1, 1875, all in Army Equipment Board, 1878.

18. Howell, *United States Army Headgear,* p. 55.

19. In a letter written by Captain George Shorkley, Fifteenth Infantry, to A.G., U.S.A, on March 20, 1875, the captain recorded that his men "often narrow[ed] the brim to moderate the size and make it more convenient." Army Equipment Board, 1878. Some soldiers also resorted to punching ventilation holes in the sides of the hat. One specimen examined had three small holes in each side formed in a triangular pattern.

20. "On our way up the Rosebud to meet Crook a cavalryman's hat was found near the Rosebud. I saw this hat. It was a white wool hat, with brass crossed sabers and a brass letter 'C.' It was passed around among the men to see if any one could identify the owner of it." Interview with George W. Glenn, Walter Camp Field Notes, Folder 109, Brigham Young University, as duplicated in Camp Field Notes, Vol. 7, Hammer Collection, Little Bighorn Battlefield National Monument, Crow Agency, Montana. In a letter to Camp, Glenn described this hat somewhat differently: "Short wore a light hat with the cross sabers drawn on the front of it with the number '7' between the sabers." Hammer, *Custer in '76,* p. 137.

21. Howell, *United States Army Headgear,* p. 56.

22. Lieutenant Colonel George A. Woodward, Fourteenth Infantry, Fort Cameron, Utah, to A.G., U.S.A., March 30, 1875, Army Equipment Board, 1878.

23. First Lieutenant William N. Sage, Company K, Eleventh Infantry, Fort Richardson, Texas, to Post Adjutant, February 19, 1875, ibid.

24. Chief Quartermaster Marshall I. Ludington, Dept. of the Platte, to A.G., Dept. of the Platte, August 4, 1876, Letters and Telegrams Received, Circulars and Orders Fort Fetterman, Wyoming Territory Records, Wyoming State Museum and Archives. This

letter lists clothing supplied to General George Crook's Big Horn Expedition, including 80 Pattern 1874 blouses, 102 pleated blouses, and 1,149 sack coats.

25. A.G.O. *G.O. 86,* October 2, 1875; Innis, "The Fort Buford Diary, pp. 346–47. Sanford's 1874 diary entry suggests that this practice was common even before the general orders were issued.

26. A.G.O., *G.O. 99,* September 21, 1876, and *G.O. 81,* August 25, 1877.

27. Bourke, *On the Border with Crook,* p. 212.

28. King, *Campaigning with Crook,* pp. 81–82.

29. Ibid., p. 120.

30. In Graham, *The Custer Myth,* pp. 345–47, former First Sergeant John Ryan provides a detailed examination of officer garb as he remembered it. For the best photographic record of troops as they appeared in the field during the mid-1870s, see Hedren, *With Crook in the Black Hills.*

31. Billings, *Report on the Hygiene,* p. lii.

32. Colonel Frank Wheaton, Second Infantry, Fort Walla Walla, Washington Territory, to A.G., U.S.A., March 15, 1875; Captain R. F. Bernard, First Cavalry, Fort Bidwell, California, to A.G., U.S.A., March 20, 1875; Lieutenant Colonel George A. Woodward, Fourteenth Infantry, Fort Cameron, Utah, to A.G., U.S.A., March 30, 1875; and Major J. K. Mizner, Fourth Cavalry, Fort Richardson, Texas, to A.G., U.S.A., April 3, 1875, all in Army Equipment Board, 1878.

33. Billings, *Report on the Hygiene,* p. xlviii.

34. *Regulations for the Uniform, 1872,* p. 8; Quartermaster General Montgomery C. Meigs to Adjutant General, U.S. Army, August 6, 1872, Letters Received by the Adjutant General's Office (Main Series) 1871–80, Records of the Adjutant General's Office, RG 94, NA.

35. The quartermaster general instructed the Office of Clothing and Equipage to make and distribute five pairs of 1872-pattern mounted trousers to artillery troops at Fort Adams, Rhode Island, and an additional five pairs of each size to the light batteries at Fort Hamiliton, New York, and Fort McHenry at Baltimore, Maryland. Similar quantities of dismounted trousers were sent out for trial by foot companies stationed at forts near Philadelphia. Meigs to Captain J. D. Bingham, May 31, 1872, and June 14, 1872, Reg. of Letters Rec'd, Clothing Branch, 1870–1872.

36. Ibid., June 25, 1872.

37. Captain J. D. Bingham to Captain Charles Morse, Sixteenth Infantry, January 3, 1874, Book A, 1874, Letters Sent, Records of the Office of the Quartermaster General, RG 92, NA.

38. Colonel Frank Wheaton, Second Infantry, Fort Walla Walla, Washington Territory, to A.G., U.S.A., March 12, 1875, Army Equipment Board, 1878.

39. *QMG, Sec. of War,* 1873, p. 153. The wartime materials continued to be used for the manufacture of some articles as late as 1876. Ibid., 1876, p. 127.

40. Report of Inspection at Fort Randall, Dakota Territory, by Inspector General N. H. Davis, July 25, 1873, Letters Received, Records of the Office of the Inspector General, RG 159, NA.

41. Lieutenant Colonel Joseph N. G. Whistler, Fifth Infantry, Fort Riley, Kansas, to A.G., U.S.A., March 1, 1875, Army Equipment Board, 1878.

42. First Lieutenant John M. Ross, Twenty-first Infantry, Fort Walla Walla, Washington Territory, to Post Adjutant, February 23, 1875, ibid.

43. Capt. Edward G. Bush, Tenth Infantry, Fort Stockton, Texas, to A.G., U.S.A., February 27, 1875, ibid.

44. Act. Assist. Surgeon J. Frazer Boughler, Fort Craig, New Mexico, to Post Adjutant, March 18, 1875, ibid. Regulation suspenders would not be added to the army's clothing table until 1883. *QMG Sec. of War,* 1884, pp. 614, 671.

45. Major James D. Bingham of the Clothing Branch reported, "The stock of dark-blue cloth and light-blue kersey will be so nearly exhausted this year that it will be necessary to purchase a supply next year." *QMG, Sec. of War,* 1873, p. 152. The fact that new supplies were obtained, as well as new standards, is found in Billings, *Report on the Hygiene,* p. lii.

46. Colonel George A. Woodward, Fourteenth Infantry, to A.G., U.S.A., March 30, 1875, Army Equipment Board, 1878.

47. Typical deficiencies of the shirt are cited in letters from Acting Assistant Surgeon E. Alexander, Fort Quitman, Texas, to Captain Charles Bentzoni, Twenty-fifth Infantry, March 15, 1875, Army Equipment Board, 1878. "The shirts are too short for an ordinary sized man and should reach at least six inches lower down," wrote Major Guido Ilges, Seventh Infantry, Fort Benton, Montana, to A.G., U.S.A., March 24, 1875, ibid. And see Woodhull, *Medical Report,* p. 16. Evidence that troops still favored the white flannel shirt as late in the mid-1870s is found in A.A.S. J. Frazer Boughler to Post Adjutant, Fort Craig, New Mexico, March 18, 1875, and First Lieutenant John M. Ross, Twenty-first Infantry, to Post Adjutant, Fort Walla Walla, Washington Territory, February 23, 1875, Army Equipment Board, 1878.

48. Billings, *Report on the Hygiene,* p. lxvii.

49. Captain Loyd Wheaton, Twentieth Infantry, Fort Pembina, Dakota Territory, to A.G., U.S.A., March 10, 1875, Army Equipment Board, 1878.

50. *QMG, Sec. of War,* 1875, p. 231, and 1876, p. 126; Captain Oddment M. Coats, Company C, and Captain Samuel P. Ferris, Company I, Fourth Infantry, Fort Fetterman, Wyoming Territory, July 28, 1875, Endorsements, April 1874–July 1880, Fort Fetterman, Wyoming Territory Records, Wyoming State Museum and Archives.

51. *QMG, Sec. of War,* 1881, p. 303. The coat-style 1881-pattern shirt was disliked by the troops and was quickly abandoned. However, the following year a pullover-style shirt was adopted; it continued in use, with only minor modifications, until the turn of the century. Ibid., 1882, p. 253, and 1883, p. 457.

52. Captain Augustus W. Corliss, Eighth Infantry, Camp McDowell, Arizona Territory, to A.G., U.S.A., March 20, 1875, Army Equipment Board, 1878.

53. Lieutenant Colonel Lewis C. Hunt, Twentieth Infantry, Fort Totten, Dakota Territory, to A.G., U.S.A., March 10, 1875, ibid.

54. Captain John H. Patterson, Twentieth Infantry, Fort Seward, Dakota Territory, to A.G., U.S.A., March 20, 1875, ibid.

55. Kloster, "Uniforms of the Army," p. 6.

56. Acting Assistant Surgeon J. Frazer Boughler, Fort Craig, New Mexico Territory, to Post Adjutant, March 18, 1875, Army Equipment Board, 1878.

57. Woodhull, *Medical Report,* p. 20.

58. *QMG, Sec. of War,* 1876, p. 126. The worsted stockings were not liked by the troops and were therefore dropped the following year. Ibid., 1877, p. 241.

59. First Lieutenant W. N. Sage, Co. K, Eleventh Infantry, to Post Adjutant, February 19, 1875, Army Equipment Board, 1878.

60. Billings, *Report on the Hygiene,* p. liii.

61. Captain John H. Patterson, Twentieth Infantry, to A.G., U.S.A., March 20, 1875, Army Equipment Board, 1878.

62. Bourke, *On the Border with Crook,* pp. 252–53.

63. Greene, "U.S. Army Buffalo Overcoat," p. 73. Buffalo overcoats do not appear on the "Statement of Clothing, Camp and Garrison Equipage, etc. on hand at the close of the fiscal year ending June 30, 1868"; however, twenty-four coats appear on the statement the following year, indicating that they were procured sometime during fiscal year 1869. *QMG, Sec. of War,* 1870, pp. 335, 337.

64. Greene, "U.S. Army Buffalo Overcoat."

65. Miles, *Personal Recollections,* p. 219.

66. Ibid., p. 179.

67. *QMG, Sec. of War,* 1877, p. 194.

68. Entry March 17, 1876, Journal of Private Eugene Geant, Co. H, 7th U.S. Infantry, Special Collections, Little Bighorn Battlefield National Monument, Crow Agency, Montana.

69. Greene, *Yellowstone Command,* p. 180.

70. *QMG, Sec. of War,* 1877, p. 265.

71. Ibid., 1879, p. 274; Howell, *United States Army Headgear*, pp. 58, 59.

72. *QMG, Sec. of War*, 1883, p. 456, and 1884, p. 617.

73. Ibid., 1878, p. 245.

74. A.G.O., *G.O. 96*, November 19, 1875; *QMG, Sec. of War*, 1876, p. 228.

75. "Canton flannel and flannel for blouses will, for the first time since 1865, be purchased during the present fiscal year [1878]." *QMG, Sec. of War*, 1878, p. 193.

76. The regulations noted that "blouses for winter wear" were "to be lined." However, the lined blouse actually was the most common and was worn in all climates, year-round. *Regulations for the Uniform, 1872*, p. 7. Specifications are found in *QMG, Sec. of War*, 1881, p. 399.

77. Captain John F. Rodgers to Colonel L. C. Easton, November 30, 1874, Easton to Meigs, December 2, 1874, and Meigs to Easton, January 4, 1875, Letters Received, Office of the Quartermaster General, Records of the Office of the Quartermaster General, RG 92, NA.

78. "Specifications for Trousers," March 25, 1876, ibid.

79. Specifications identical to those of 1876 were published in *QMG, Sec. of War*, 1881, p. 403.

80. Billings, *Report on the Hygiene*, p. lii.

81. *QMG, Sec. of War*, 1878, pp. 243, 274.

82. Ibid., 1876, pp. 205–6. Formal specifications for this coat were adopted on February 6, 1880, and were published in ibid., 1881, pp. 400–401.

83. The quartermaster's inventory for fiscal year 1877 shows a total of 151,631 overcoats of all patterns on hand. An acquisition of 2,006 coats suggests that some of the new pattern may have been manufactured that year, but no further documentation has been found. Considering the numbers of old overcoats available and the comments contained in the fiscal year 1879 annual report of the quartermaster general, it may be reasonably assumed that none of the new ones reached the troops before 1878. *QMG, Sec. of War*, 1877, p. 246, and 1879, p. 277.

84. *Regulations for the Uniform, 1872*, p. 15 and addenda; Langellier and Woodcock, *Chevrons*, p. 6. Specifications for chevrons are found in *QMG, Sec. of War*, 1881, pp. 399–400. Chevrons were moved to the overcoat cuffs by A.G.O., *G.O. No. 38*, June 6, 1883.

85. *QMG, Sec. of War*, 1877, p. 241.

86. The brass screws did not seem to hurt the feet until the boots and shoes became worn. Assistant Surgeon J.V.D. Middleton to Post Adjutant, Fort Buford, Dakota Territory, March 13, 1875, Army Equipment Board, 1878; Brinckerhoff, *Boots and Shoes*, pp. 15–21.

87. A.G.O., *G.O. 4*, January 27, 1875.

88. A.G.O., *G.O. 73*, July 10, 1873.

89. Colonel John E. Smith, Fourteenth Infantry, Camp Douglas, Utah, to A.G., March 19, 1875, Army Equipment Board, 1878.

90. Typical of the requests for a higher boot was that of Major John K. Mizner, Fourth Cavalry, at Fort Richardson, Texas, in which he recommended a boot four inches higher than the Pattern 1872. Mizner to A.G., U.S.A., April 3, 1875, ibid; Brinckerhoff, *Boots and Shoes*, pp. 12–13; Acting Assistant Surgeon George M. Kober to Post Adjutant, Camp McDermit, Nevada, March 25, 1875, ibid.

91. A question arises as to just which pattern of stockings is pictured in the 1875 QMG photograph of "Uniforms of the Army Prior and Subsequent to 1872." Clearly, the ones shown have white toes, yet the specifications do not mention this feature. The photographs are date-stamped May 18 and May 21, 1875. It may be that the specifications simply did not address the color of the toes or that the specifications dated May 31, 1876, were only then formalized for socks that had been in use since 1875. Kloster, "Uniforms of the Army." Circular No. 8, 1875, contains the cryptic statement, "An improvement of the stockings is contemplated by the Quartermaster-General." Billings, *Report on the Hygiene*, p. xlviii.

92. *U.S. Army Uniforms,* pp. 8–9.

93. *QMG, Sec. of War,* 1878, p. 269.

94. Ibid.

95. Ibid., p. 265. Chintz is a form of printed cotton cloth, usually glazed.

96. Ibid., p. 242.

97. Howell, *United States Army Headgear,* p. 78.

98. *QMG, Sec. of War,* 1881, p. 403.

99. Ibid.

100. Ibid., 1877, p. 268. The specification drawing is found in Greene, *U.S. Army Uniforms,* p. 73.

101. *QMG, Sec. of War,* 1878, p. 241.

CHAPTER 6

1. *Ordnance Memoranda No. 18,* p. 87.

2. Captain Moses Harris, First Cavalry, to Post Adjutant, Fort Walla Walla, Washington Territory, February 22, 1875; Acting Assistant Surgeon George M. Kober to Post Adjutant, Camp McDermit, Nevada, March 25, 1875; and Captain Theodore J. Wint, Fourth Cavalry, to Post Adjutant, Fort Richardson, Texas, February 20, 1875, all in Army Equipment Board, 1878.

3. Captain Alexander B. MacGowan, Twelfth Infantry, Camp Independence, California, to A.G., U.S.A., March 12, 1875; Captain William M'C. Netterville, Company I, Twenty-first Infantry, to Post Adjutant, Fort Walla Walla, Washington Territory, March 1, 1875; and Assistant Surgeon J. W. Williams to Colonel James G. Tilford, Fort Rice, Dakota Territory, March 10, 1875, all in ibid.

4. Lieutenant Colonel Lewis C. Hunt, Twentieth Infantry, Fort Totten, Dakota Territory, to A.G., U.S.A., March 10, 1875, ibid.

5. MacGowan to A.G., March 12, 1875, ibid.

6. Green, "Bacon or Bullets," p. 29.

7. *Ordnance Memoranda No. 18,* pp. 88–89.

8. Lieutenant Matthew Leeper, Company I, Fourth Cavalry, to Post Adjutant, Fort Richardson, Texas, February 19, 1875, Army Equipment Board, 1878.

9. Captain William McC.Netterville, Twenty-first Infantry, to Post Adjutant, Fort Walla Walla, Washington Territory, March 1, 1875, ibid.

10. *Ordnance Memoranda No. 18,* p. 70.

11. Brigadier General Stephen V. Benet to Commanding Officer, Watervliet Arsenal, June 17, 1874, Letters, Telegrams, and Endorsements Sent, Watervliet Arsenal, Vol. 19, Records of the Office of the Chief of Ordnance, RG 156, NA (hereinafter cited as Letters Sent, Watervliet Arsenal).

12. Phillips and Vervloet, *U.S. Single Action Holsters,* p. 15; Meadows, *Military Holsters,* p. 93.

13. Meadows, *Military Holsters,* p. 95.

14. Ibid., pp. 391–93; William G. Phillips, "The Evolution of U.S. Accoutrements 1865–1903," p. 91.

15. Meadows, *Military Holsters,* pp. 392–93.

16. Many contemporary photographs show the eagle plate in use as late as 1888. For a specific case study, see McChristian, "Company C, 3rd Cavalry."

17. *Ordnance Memoranda No. 19,* pp. 11–12.

18. Frasca and Hill, *.45–70 Springfield,* pp. 48–57; *Ordnance Memoranda No. 19,* pp. 46–54.

19. *Ordnance Memoranda No. 19,* pp. 57–58.

20. Documentation is lacking for fixing the initial date of production for the 1874 Type 1 canteen. However, it may be inferred that it began in the months immediately following the secretary of war's approval of the board resolutions in January 1875. That this canteen was considered to be the "official" issue by early in 1876 is confirmed by a description of the canteen as "covered with thick petersham cloth . . . [and with an]

adjustable tongueless buckle (Chambers) . . . and haversack straps," in *Report of the Board,* p. 748. The various exhibit items were received at the exhibition during the spring of 1876 (pp. 11–12). No doubt the actual issue of this pattern, like that of most of the equipment, was irregular and dictated by how soon older patterns could be "worn out in service" and exchanged for the new model.

21. Acting Assistant Surgeon E. Alexander to Captain Charles Bentzoni, Twenty-fifth Infantry, Fort Quitman, Texas, March 15, 1875, Army Equipment Board, 1878.

22. *Ordnance Memoranda No. 19,* pp. 56–57.

23. Hedren, "Army Tin Cups," p. 60.

24. *Ordnance Memoranda No. 19,* p. 60.

25. Brigadier General S. V. Benet to Commanding Officer, Rock Island Arsenal, June 18, 1875, as found in Misc. Letters Sent, Ordnance Office; Benet to C. O., Watervliet Arsenal, July 21, 1875, in ibid. Watervliet received another order for two-thousand sets of infantry equipments on September 23, 1875 (Benet to C.O., Watervliet Arsenal).

26. Brigadier General S. V. Benet to Captain S. P. Farris, Company I, 4th Infantry, Fort Fetterman, Wyoming Territory, December 13, 1876, Misc. Letters Sent, Ordnance Office.

27. Entry January 15, 1875, Reg. of Letters Rec'd, Watervliet Arsenal.

28. Benet ordered Watervliet to make three thousand McKeever boxes and three thousand Dyer pouches on April 20, 1875. Reg. of Letters Rec'd, Watervliet Arsenal. Five thousand more McKeevers were ordered from Rock Island on June 28, 1875. Misc. Letters Sent, Ordnance Office.

29. A letter of December 24, 1875, indicates Hagner was working on a way to adapt the box for holding the screwdriver. Reg. of Letters Rec'd, Watervliet Arsenal. See also February 18, 1876, ibid. Entry for January 25, 1876, notes an order to Springfield Armory for "5,000 shortened screwdrivers for use with the 'new cartridge boxes.'" Reg. of Letters Rec'd, Watervliet Arsenal. Benet to C. O., Watervliet Arsenal, March 27, 1876, directed him to forward a modified box to Rock Island Arsenal. Reg. of Letters Rec'd, Watervliet Arsenal. Entry on June 6, 1876, stated, "All boxes hereafter made will have pocket for screwdriver." Reg. of Letters Rec'd, Watervliet Arsenal.

30. Major Daniel W. Flagler, Rock Island Arsenal, to chief of ordnance, November 29, 1875, and Endorsement, Lieutenant Colonel Julian McAllister, Benicia Arsenal, January 19, 1876, both in Letters Received, Ordnance Office.

31. Ibid., and Endorsement, Brigadier General S. V. Benet, January 31, 1876, Letters Received, Ordnance Office.

32. Benet to C. O., Rock Island Arsenal, Misc. Letters Sent, Ordnance Office, and Benet to C. O.s, Watervliet Arsenal and Benicia Arsenal, January 7, 1876, ibid. San Antonio Arsenal received similar instructions as the result of requisitions from the field for two thousand sets of Pattern 1874 infantry equipments. Benet authorized the canteens and haversacks of that order to be issued, but the boxes were to be supplied from the Hagner pouches on hand, and those were to be converted to .45 caliber. Benet to C. O., San Antonio Arsenal, February 25, 1876, ibid. As late as January 5, 1877, Rock Island Arsenal converted the Hagner pouches of one thousand sets of 1872 infantry brace equipments that had been turned in at the San Antonio Depot. Reg. of Letters Rec'd, Watervliet Arsenal.

33. This is based on figures presented in the "Statements of Ordnance and Ordnance Stores Issued to the Regular Army and to Posts," as found in *Chief of Ordnance, Sec. of War,* 1876–80. An indication that the Ordnance Department intended for troops to make maximum use of the equipments on hand is found in instructions that new McKeever boxes were not to be issued until older patterns were shown to be unserviceable. Index to Letters Sent, Ordnance Office, Records of the Office of the Chief of Ordnance, RG 156, NA (hereinafter cited as Index, Letters Sent, Ordnance Office).

34. Captain O. E. Michaelis to Chief of Ordnance, September 29, 1876, File No. 5475-00-1876, Letters Received, Ordnance Office (hereinafter cited as Michaelis Report).

35. Ibid.

36. Ibid.

37. Entry of August 5, 1876, Diary of Private Richard Flynn, Company D, Fourth U.S. Infantry, Special Collections, Little Bighorn Battlefield National Monument.

38. The field reports of 1873 conveyed a faulty impression to the board because most line units that had received the trial equipments were given little, if any, opportunity to use them. More informed opinions are contained in the responses to G.O. 6, 1875, but these arrived long after the board had adjourned. These documents sat in the Ordnance Office files until the Miles Board convened three years later.

39. Michaelis Report.

40. Hutchins, *Boots and Saddles,* argues that the Seventh Cavalry used the Pattern 1859 equipments exclusively in 1876. Use of the small Civil War–issue saddlebags, therefore, would have necessitated using the Civil War–style haversack. More recent archaeological evidence suggests that the 1874 horse equipments, at least in part, were present at the Little Bighorn. Scott et al., *Archeological Perspectives,* p. 207, and Scott, *Papers on Little Bighorn,* p. 41. The larger 1874 saddlebags negated the need for the haversack.

41. Benet also issued a separate order to Rock Island Arsenal to make "1,000 haversacks conforming in all respects to . . . Ord. Mem. No. 19." Benet to C.O., R.I.A., July 17, 1875, Misc. Letters Sent, Ordnance Office. Another letter referenced in the Indexes to the Letters Sent from the Ordnance Office in 1876 directs "Haversacks—pat. 1874—to be issued to recruits in all branches of the service." This practice is further recorded in General Orders No. 104, October 14, 1876, which stipulated that those clothing bags and haversacks turned in by recruits at their destinations, if not needed there, were to be returned to Watervliet Arsenal for repair and reissue. This left company commanders with the option of keeping the equipment, which many no doubt did. Any imaginative officer or first sergeant would have seen the opportunity to get rid of obsolete patterns in exchange for the new issue. That this was being done is evidenced by a December 12, 1881, letter calling for these items to be stenciled "RECRUIT" to ensure that they were the same ones returned. Register of Letters Received, Watervliet Arsenal. The Michaelis Report clearly indicates that of the ten infantry companies in Crook's command, at least two (both belonging to the Fourteenth) were outfitted completely with the 1874 equipments. The others no doubt had parts of the 1872 gear, whereas others had a mixture of the two.

42. Entry March 17, 1876, Reg. of Letters Rec'd, Watervliet Arsenal. King, in his classic *Campaigning with Crook,* p. 62, includes the haversack as part of the trooper's basic equipment in the Fifth Cavalry in the spring of 1876. Whether or not all men were so equipped is speculative. The *Ordnance Returns* are not clear at all on this point, since they list only "Sets of Cavalry Equipments," which could be either the 1872 or the 1874 pattern. Among the many accounts by Seventh Cavalrymen who participated in Reno's hilltop fight, several mention that rifle pits were scraped out with mess gear. Private Charles Windolph remembered that they dug "shallow holes with our mess kits, our steel knives and forks," suggesting that at least some of the men had haversacks, or else their mess gear would have been in the saddlebags on the horses. Hunt and Hunt, *I Fought with Custer,* p. 103. Another man who served during 1876–77 and wrote his army memoirs shortly after his discharge mentioned the haversack among the items making up the cavalryman's outfit. Mulford, *Fighting Indians,* p. 58. Two of the brass Chambers buckles, unique to the 1874 haversack, and one hook of the type used to adjust the 1872 haversack sling, have been recovered along the route of Major Marcus Reno's retreat on the Little Bighorn Battlefield. Personal communication with Jason Pitsch, Garry Owen, Montana, July 6, 1994.

43. Michaelis Report. To date, National Park Service archaeological projects on the Little Bighorn Battlefield have yet to produce an example of the Chambers buckle, which would indicate the presence of the 1874 haversacks and canteens in that action. However, two uncorroborated finds, one of each type, have been found on the bluffs near the Reno-Benteen position. Weibert, *Custer, Cases, and Cartridges,* p. 107. Whether or not these artifacts are related to the battle cannot be substantiated. It is known that numerous troops visited the site in the years after the battle.

44. Michaelis Report.

45. Use of these straps is first mentioned officially in the Michaelis Report. The

practice is further substantiated in an 1877 report by Captain Clifton Comly, commanding officer at San Antonio Arsenal. Phillips and Carter, "Canteens," p. 70.

46. Brigadier General S. V. Benet to Major D. W. Flagler, March 30, 1877, Letters, Telegrams, and Endorsements Sent to Ordnance Officers and Military Storekeepers, Watervliet Arsenal Series, Vol. 19. For Weir's report, see Weir, "Infantry Equipments," p. 531.

47. Commercial versions of this knife usually had somewhat longer blades with rounded "butterknife" points. One specimen was stamped "Frary Cutlery—1876." Some of these knives were purchased for company messes and found their way to frontier posts, as evidenced by examples excavated from barracks sites at Fort Davis, Texas, as well as on the site of the Valley Fight on the Little Bighorn Battlefield.

48. Apparently, some men were so desperate for prairie belts that they cut pairs of parallel slits horizontally around the leather waist belt to form quasi cartridge loops. Michaelis Report.

49. Michaelis recommended the sergeant for a court-martial because of his impertinence, but higher authorities appreciated the man's honesty and the charges were dropped. *ANJ*, December 9, 1876, p. 282.

50. Colonel Frank Wheaton to A.G., U.S.A., March 12, 1875, Army Equipment Board, 1878. Wheaton stated also that most European nations were enlightened enough to issue canvas gaiters or high-top marching boots to their soldiers.

51. Miles, *Personal Recollections,* pp. 214–15. Miles mentions specifically that bayonets, cartridge boxes, sabres, and caps were among the items discarded by both officers and soldiers at the outset of the campaign.

52. Michaelis Report.

53. Ibid.

54. Ibid.; Entry December 14, 1876, Reg. of Letters Rec'd, Watervliet Arsenal.

55. Colonel Hagner was granted approval to use 29,048 "Cartridge Belts" of grained leather taken from sets of accoutrements (Pattern 1861) to "manufacture leather belts for the insides of Cartridge belts now being made." Entry March 12, 1877, Reg. of Letters Rec'd, Watervliet Arsenal.

56. Phillips, "Cavalry Accoutrements," pp. 99–102.

57. The pistol cartridge pouch, with measured drawings of its components, is shown on Plate 7 of *Ordnance Memoranda No. 18.*

58. One authority who has had the opportunity to inspect a vast array of American militaria has never seen any specimen as described in *Ordnance Memoranda No. 18.* He has, however, encountered a few 1850-pattern knots that have been narrowed in width, which may represent the Ordnance Department's nod to modifying the style during the 1870s. Personal communication from Hayes Otoupalik, January 4, 1992.

59. Two variations of the 1872–74 belt plate have been observed. A specimen in the Arizona Historical Society Collections is pictured and described by Brinckerhoff in *Metal Uniform Insignia.* It measures only 1½ inches high by 3¼ inches wide. Another, now in a private collection, measures 1⅞ inches high by 2⅞ inches wide and has a ³⁄₃₂-inch-wide border. The integrally cast U.S. letters are ¹³⁄₁₆ inch high. Apparently, this plate was made to fit a belt 1⅝ inches wide. The intended application of these variants is unknown, but since there is no evidence of regular army usage, they may have been made for state militia units or they may represent arsenal test samples.

60. A.G.O., *G.O. 104,* October 14, 1876.

61. Colonel P. V. Hagner, Watervliet Arsenal, to chief of ordnance, September 11, 1877, Letters Received, Ordnance Office.

62. An entry in *Report of the Board,* p. 749, states of the clothing bag, "The rubberized flap is being superseded by a layer of rubber between two folds of cloth."

63. Benet to Hagner, February 16, 1876, Reg. of Letters Rec'd, Watervliet Arsenal, directs the manufacture of one hundred sets of infantry equipments using "the lead colored duck." Telegram from Benet to Hagner, October 20, 1876, ordering Watervliet to make, "Clothing bags and Haversacks from material on hand even if not dyed. The

demand is urgent." This was in the wake of the Sioux Campaign. A third reference is found in an authorization from Benet to Hagner on November 15, 1877, for the manufacture of five thousand each haversacks and clothing bags of dyed cotton duck.

64. Entry August 3, 1878, Reg. of Letters Rec'd, Watervliet Arsenal.

65. "Only about 40% of the clothing bags and haversacks sent out with recruits have been returned to Watervliet Arsenal." Company commanders were urged "to enforce the return of those issued, in order that the large demands for same from recruiting depots may be met." Anon., Fort Assiniboine, Montana Territory, June 1879, No. 46, Box 1, Register of Letters Received, Folder 2–1, Montana Historical Society; Fort Assiniboine Records, Entry December 12, 1881, Reg. of Letters Rec'd, Watervliet Arsenal, references the stenciling of clothing bags and haversacks, although the practice may have started earlier.

66. Colonel P. V. Hagner, Watervliet Arsenal, to chief of ordnance, December 21, 1875, Entry 21, Letters Received, Ordnance Office.

67. *Chief of Ordnance, Sec. of War,* "Statement of Ordnance and Ordnance Stores Issued to the Regular Army and to Posts for the Year Ending June 30, 1877," p. 22. Entry February 14, 1876, Reg. of Letters Rec'd, Watervliet Arsenal, refers to the slings being issued with the bags.

68. Phillips and Carter, "Canteens," p. 69.

69. Entry December 3, 1877, Reg. of Letters Rec'd, Watervliet Arsenal.

70. *Ordnance Memoranda No. 29,* p. 18 and plate 14.

71. The 1874-pattern knives and forks also were made with a hardened-lead rim around the handle to form the grip. These are usually, but not always, marked "PAT. DEC. 19. 82" on the handle. Another variant is marked "J. WARD & CO. RIVERSIDE, MASS." The exact origin of the lead-rim variation is unknown, but it points up the evolutionary nature of army equipage of the era.

72. This fork (Cat. No. 20313) was recovered during an archaeological survey conducted by the National Park Service in 1985. The handle measures 3¾ inches, whereas all other examined specimens measure 3⅝ inches. The Little Bighorn specimen also has distinctive bevels between the tines on the reverse side, a feature not noted on other examples.

73. A spoon, presumably having army provenance, was found on the Big Hole Battlefield (August 9, 1877) in Montana. This example measured 8 inches long, with a bowl 1¾ inches wide. Although the general shape of the spoon was very similar to that of the regulation issue, it bore no "U.S." markings. The handle was die-stamped "F," along with a botched attempt to stamp the same letter just below. Cat. No. 528, Big Hole National Battlefield Collections.

74. *Ordnance Memoranda No. 19,* p. 38.

75. Brigadier General S. V. Benet to Capt. O. E. Michaelis, April 13, 1877, Letters Sent, Watervliet Arsenal, Vol. 19.

76. Colonel P. V. Hanger, Watervliet Arsenal to chief of ordnance, March 14, 1877, Letters Received, Ordnance Office.

77. Entry February 13, 1878, Reg. of Letters Rec'd, Watervliet Arsenal.

78. Colonel P. V. Hagner, Watervliet Arsenal, to chief of ordnance, November 26, 1877, bearing the latter's endorsement, Letters Received, Ordnance Office.

79. McChristian, "Model 1876 Cartridge Belt," p. 112. Since this article was published, the author has discovered information revealing that a wider belt, designated herein as the Type 2, was authorized several months before the November 30 date. An order for ten thousand belts of the third type was issued on November 23, 1877, and a second for twenty-five hundred on March 2, 1878. Reg. of Letters Rec'd, Watervliet Arsenal.

CHAPTER 7

1. *ANJ,* April 13, 1878, p. 570.

2. *ANJ,* April 27, 1878, p. 611. Apparently, some companies of the Twenty-first Infantry used the Palmer system, or at least components of it, during the Nez Percé

Campaign. After the Battle of the Clearwater, July 11–12, 1877, one company commander noted that each of the casualties of his unit, "left on the field . . . a Springfield rifle (caliber .45) with gun sling, a trowel bayonet and scabbard, two cartridge boxes, a screwdriver, canteen, haversack, and meat-ration can." Jocelyn, *Mostly Alkali,* p. 237. Jocelyn was a captain in the Twenty-first Infantry.

3. *ANJ,* April 13, 1878, p. 570.

4. A.G.O., *G.O. 76,* July 23, 1879, pp. 11–12.

5. *ANJ,* December 9, 1876, p. 282.

6. *ANJ,* April 13, 1878, p. 509.

7. *ANJ,* April 20, 1878, p. 595.

8. A.G.O., *G.O. 76,* July 23, 1879.

9. Colonel P. V. Hagner to chief of ordnance, April 13, 1878, Register of Letters in Ordnance Office Files, Army Equipment Board, 1878.

10. Entries July 8, 1878, and January 24, 1880, Reg. of Letters Rec'd, Watervliet Arsenal. The first document refers to the manufacture of "10,000 cartridge belts with ring for carrying bayonet scabbard," and the second describes more specifically belts made like those ordered on May 9, 1878, "provided with the three (3) rings for its [bayonet] attachment."

11. Dorsey, *American Military Belts,* p. 75.

12. *Chief of Ordnance, Sec. of War,* 1882, Appendix 15, "Report of Principal Operations for the Year Ending June 30, 1882—Fort Abraham Lincoln Ordnance Depot," p. 121; Douglas McChristian, "The Mills Cartridge Belt: Fort Lincoln Depot Modification," *Military Collector and Historian* (forthcoming).

13. Entry of January 24, 1880, refers to a subsequent order for two hundred sets of blanket bag equipments "same as ordered May 9, 1878." Reg. of Letters Rec'd, Watervliet Arsenal. Further reference to this order is found in Phillips and Carter, "Canteens," p. 71. Notification of the new equipment's availability for issue is documented in a register of letters relating to equipment excerpted from the letters of the Office of the Chief of Ordnance and included in Army Equipment Board, 1878. No evidence was found to indicate that Pattern 1874 equipments, except waist belts, were ordered to be made later than the summer of 1878, though the component parts—haversacks, canteens, and clothing bags—were issued well into the 1880s.

14. The "Reports of Ordnance and Ordnance Stores Issued to the Regular Army and to Posts" for fiscal years 1879, 1880, and 1881 list the numbers of blanket bags as 1,001, 940, and 2,795, respectively, indicating official adoption of the knapsack and its accompanying items. *Chief of Ordnance, Sec. of War,* 1879, 1880, and 1881.

15. A special blanket roll support was developed in 1892 by Lieutenant Charles Dodge, Jr., Twenty-fourth Infantry. Some five hundred of these were made and issued for field trial in 1894, but the invention proved to be a miserable failure. Hutchins, "Dodge Blanket Roll." The army briefly sanctioned the blanket roll, failing everything else, during the period 1903–10.

16. The first contract for Mills belts was let on November 9, 1880, and an order for forty thousand was issued to the Gilbert Loom Company on March 15, 1881. Phillips, "The Woven Cartridge Belt," p. 66.

17. Phillips and Vervloet, *U.S. Single Action,* pp. 19–21.

18. Chappell, *Summer Helmets,* p. 10.

19. A.G.O., *G.O. 76,* July 23, 1879, p. 17.

20. Ibid., p. 19.

21. Chappell, *Summer Helmets,* p. 7.

22. Ibid., p. 11.

23. Ibid.

24. *QMG, Sec. of War,* 1878, p. 243; A.G.O., *G.O. 76,* July 23, 1879, pp. 14–15.

25. Greene, *Yellowstone Command,* p. 179.

26. *QMG, Sec. of War,* 1881, p. 281, and 1884, p. 610. A complete history of the buffalo and canvas overcoats is provided in Greene, "U.S. Army Buffalo Overcoat."

27. *QMG, Sec. of War,* 1878, p. 331.

28. Ibid., p. 262.

29. A coat-style dark-blue flannel shirt with piped collar and cuffs, five small regulation eagle buttons, and no pockets was adopted per A.G.O., *G.O. 4,* January 7, 1881.

30. A.G.O., *G.O. 76,* July 23, 1879, pp. 2–3.

31. Steffen, *Horse Soldier* 4:76.

32. Mills submitted samples of his belts to each of the postwar equipment boards. He sent no less than ten belts of his design to the 1870 St. Louis Board. None of the belts met with success until the Miles Board of 1878–79. Mills, *My Story,* p. 310; *Ordnance Memoranda No. 11,* p. 7. A fine synopsis of the pocket belt is found in Phillips, "Pocket-Type Rifle Cartridge Belt."

33. Early specimens have plain pressed-tin buttons and exhibit a distinctive block-lettering style with very thick solid letters and no stencil gaps. Later examples with cross-hatched buttons bear "U.S." markings in Roman letters 1½ inches high.

34. Similar buttons, having four holes for attachment by sewing, were adopted by the Quartermaster Department in 1885 for use on clothing. It is assumed that the Ordnance Department followed suit with a button adapted for rivet attachment. *QMG, Sec. of War,* 1885, p. 603.

35. Entry of October 28, 1878, Reg. of Letters Rec'd, Watervliet Arsenal.

36. Entry of November 21, 1878, ibid.

37. Benet informed Hagner that General Sherman thought that "the belts should be made single—each belt to be provided with plate—and each with eyelets and lacings, so that in an emergency two belts could be laced together. As a rule the belts will be worn single." Entry of August 5, 1880, ibid.

38. *Chief of Ordnance, Sec. of War,* 1880, p. 10.

39. Dorsey, *American Military Belts,* pp. 73–74.

40. Entry of November 21, 1878, Reg. of Letters Rec'd, Watervliet Arsenal. Although it is not clear in the sketchy notation, Hampson may have advocated turning the sheath in the frog, per Hagner's plan, so as to rotate the bayonet socket away from the body. This is a simple modification of the 1873 scabbard, and by so doing, one places the socket in a more convenient position for withdrawing ammunition from the belt.

41. *Chief of Ordnance, Sec. of War,* 1881, pp. 271–73.

42. *QMG, Sec. of War,* 1881, p. 398.

43. Ibid., 1878, p. 331.

44. Ibid., 1881, p. 402.

45. Ibid., p. 404.

46. Ibid., 1882, p. 301.

EPILOGUE

1. *QMG, Sec. of War,* 1885, p. 601.

2. Ibid., 1879, p. 229.

3. Ibid., 1880, p. 331.

4. *ANJ,* August 23, 1884, p. 60.

5. Leggings were authorized for the cavalry on February 20, 1894. Steffen, *Horse Soldier* 3:64.

APPENDIX I

1. *Ordnance Memoranda No. 11,* Board of Officers at St. Louis, Mo., June 10, 1870, p. 17.

2. Letters Received, File No. 1738, Records of the Office of the Chief of Ordnance, RG 156, NA.

BIBLIOGRAPHY

MANUSCRIPT MATERIALS

Fort Davis National Historic Site. Fort Davis, Texas. Orders and Circulars, 1867–78.

Little Bighorn Battlefield National Monument, Crow Agency, Montana.

    Diary of Private Richard Flynn, Company D, Fourth U.S. Infantry. Special Collections.

    Journal of Private Eugene Geant, Co. H, Seventh U.S. Infantry. Special Collections.

    Miscellaneous Documents, Seventh U.S. Cavalry Records. Walter M. Camp Collection.

    Walter Camp Field Notes. Hammer Collection.

Montana Historical Society. Helena, Montana. Fort Assiniboine Records.

National Archives, Washington, D.C.

    Record Group 92. Records of the Office of the Quartermaster General.

    Record Group 94. Records of the Adjutant General's Office.

    Record Group 156. Records of the Office of the Chief of Ordnance.

    Record Group 159. Records of the Office of the Inspector General.

    Record Group 393. Records of U.S. Army Continental Commands.

Phillips, William G. "The Evolution of U.S. Accoutrements 1865–1903." Master's thesis, University of Wisconsin, Greenbay, 1984.

Springfield Armory National Historic Site Collections, Springfield, Massachusetts. Letters Received, Springfield Armory.

Wyoming Room, Sheridan Public Library, Sheridan, Wyoming. Fort Phil Kearney Records. Hagen Collection.

Wyoming State Museum and Archives. Cheyenne, Wyoming. Wyoming Territory Records.

    Circulars and Orders, Fort Fetterman.

    Endorsements, April 1874–July 1880, Fort Fetterman.

GOVERNMENT PUBLICATIONS

Adjutant General's Office. *General Orders.* 1866–80.

Annual Reports of the Chief of Ordnance to the Secretary of War. 1869–82.

Annual Reports of the Quartermaster General to the Secretary of War. 1867–91.

Billings, John S. *Report on the Hygiene of the United States Army with Descriptions of Military Posts.* Circular No. 8. Washington, D.C.: Government Printing Office, 1875. Reprint. New York: Sol Lewis, 1974.

Directions for Fitting Infantry Equipments, U.S. Army. Springfield, Mass.: National Armory, 1872.

Heitman, Francis B., comp. *Historical Register and Dictionary of the United States Army, from*

Its Organization, September 29, 1789, to March 2, 1903. 2 vols. Washington, D.C.: Government Printing Office, 1903. Reprint. Urbana: University of Illinois Press, 1965.

Metallic Cartridges, as Manufactured and Tested at the Frankford Arsenal, Philadelphia, PA. Washington, D.C.: Government Printing Office, 1873.

Ordnance Manual for the Use of the Officers of the United States Army. Philadelphia: J. B. Lippincott and Co., 1861.

Ordnance Memoranda No. 11, Report upon the Subject of Small Arms, Accouterments, and Equipments for the Use of the Army of the United States. Washington, D.C.: Ordnance Office, 1870.

Ordnance Memoranda No. 13, Infantry Equipments, Cavalry Equipments, Knapsacks, Haversacks, Canteens, Etc., Horse Equipments, Tools, and Materials of Cavalry. Washington, D.C.: Ordnance Office, 1872.

Ordnance Memoranda No. 18, Proceedings of the Board of Officers Convened under Special Orders Nos. 238 and 253, A.G.O., 1873, on Horse Equipments, Cavalry Equipments, and Accouterments, Saddlers' and Smiths' Tools and Materials, and Standard Supply-Table of Ordnance Stores for Cavalry Service. Washington, D.C.: Government Printing Office, 1874.

Ordnance Memoranda No. 19, Proceedings of the Board of Officers Convened under Special Orders No. 120, A.G.O., 1874, on Infantry Equipments, and Materials and Supplies Necessary for Efficient Outfit of Infantry-Troops in Field and Garrison. Washington, D.C.: Government Printing Office, 1875.

Ordnance Memoranda No. 29, Horse Equipments and Cavalry Accoutrements as Prescribed by G.O. 73, A.G.O., 1885. Washington, D.C.: Government Printing Office, 1891.

Ordnance Notes. Washington, D.C.: Government Printing Office, 1873.

Ordnance Office. Circulars. Series of 1873. Washington, D.C.: Government Printing Office, 1873.

Price List of Ordnance and Ordnance Stores. Washington, D.C.: Government Printing Office, 1877.

Proceedings of the Ordnance Board at Its Sessions from January 4 to February 11, 1868. Washington, D.C.: Government Printing Office, 1868.

Quartermaster General. *Specifications for Clothing, Camp, and Garrison Equipage and Clothing and Equipage Materials*. Philadelphia: Quartermaster General of the Army, 1889.

Regulations for the Uniform and Dress of the Army of the United States, 1861. Washington, D.C.: George W. Bowman, 1861. Reprint. Staten Island, N.Y.: Jacques Noel Jacobsen, Jr., 1978.

Regulations for the Uniform and Dress of the Army of the United States, July, 1872. Washington, D.C.: Government Printing Office, 1872. Reprint. Staten Island, N.Y.: Jacques Noel Jacobsen, Jr., 1972.

Report of the Board on Behalf of the United States Executive Departments at the International Exhibition, Held at Philadelphia, PA., 1876. Vol. 1, Washington, D.C.: Government Printing Office, 1884.

Report of the General of the Army to the Secretary of War. Washington, D.C.: Government Printing Office, 1870.

Revised United States Army Regulations of 1861. Washington, D.C.: Government Printing Office, 1863.

Risch, Erna. *Quartermaster Support of the Army: A History of the Corps, 1775–1939*. Washington, D.C.: Office of the Quartermaster General, 1962.

Uniform of the Army of the United States, 1882. Washington, D.C.: Office of the Quartermaster General, 1882. Reprint. Staten Island, N.Y.: Jacques Noel Jacobsen, Jr., 1971.

Upton, Bvt. Major General Emory. *Infantry Tactics—Double And Single Rank Adapted to American Topography and Improved Firearms*. New York: D. Appleton and Co., 1874.

Weir, Lieutenant W. B. "Infantry Equipments." *Ordnance Notes* 67 (June 1, 1877).

Woodhull, Alfred A. *A Medical Report upon the Uniform and Clothing of the Soldiers of the U.S. Army.* Washington, D.C.: Surgeon General's Office, 1868.

BOOKS

Ashburn, P. M. *A History of the Medical Department of the United States Army.* Cambridge, Mass.: Houghton Mifflin Co., 1929.

Billings, John D. *Hardtack and Coffee: The Unwritten Story of Army Life.* Chicago: Lakeside Press, 1960.

Bourke, Captain John G. *On the Border with Crook.* Lincoln: University of Nebraska Press, 1971.

Brinckerhoff, Sidney B. *Metal Uniform Insignia of the Frontier U.S. Army, 1846–1902.* Museum Monograph No. 3. Tucson: Arizona Historical Society, 1972.

Brinckerhoff, Sidney B. *Boots and Shoes of the Frontier Soldier, 1865–1893.* Museum Monograph No. 7. Tucson: Arizona Historical Society, 1976.

Brophy, Lieutenant Colonel William S. *The Krag Rifle.* Highland Park, N.J.: Gun Room Press, 1986.

Butler, David F. *United States Firearms: The First Century, 1776–1875.* New York: Winchester Press, 1971.

Chappell, Gordon. *Brass Spikes and Horsehair Plumes: A Study Of U.S. Army Dress Helmets, 1872–1903.* Museum Monograph No. 4. Tucson: Arizona Pioneers Historical Society, 1966.

_____. *The Search for the Well-Dressed Soldier, 1865–1890: Development and Innovation in United States Army Uniforms on the Western Frontier.* Tucson: Arizona Historical Society, 1972.

_____. *Summer Helmets of the U.S. Army, 1875–1910.* Wyoming Museum Monograph No. 1. Cheyenne: Wyoming State Archives and Historical Department, 1976.

Coffman, Edward M. *The Old Army: A Portrait of the American Army in Peacetime, 1784–1898.* New York: Oxford University Press, 1986.

Cox, Rev. John E. *Five Years in the Army.* New York: Sol Lewis, 1973.

De Trobriand, Philippe Regis. *Military Life in Dakota: The Journal of Philippe Regis De Trobriand.* Translated and edited by Lucile M. Kane. St. Paul: Alvord Memorial Commission, 1951.

Dorsey, R. Stephen. *American Military Belts and Related Equipment.* Union City, Tenn.: Pioneer Press, 1984.

Emerson, Lieutenant Colonel William K. *Chevrons: Illustrated History and Catalog of U.S. Army Insignia.* Washington, D.C.: Smithsonian Institution Press, 1983.

Flayderman, Norm. *Flayderman's Guide to Antique American Firearms and Their Values.* Chicago: Follett Publishing Co., 1980.

Frasca, Albert J., and Hill, Robert H. *The .45/70 Springfield.* Northridge, Calif.: Springfield Publishing Co., 1980.

Fuller, Claude E. *The Rifled Musket.* Harrisburg, Pa.: Stackpole Co., 1958.

_____. *The Breech-Loader in the Service, 1816–1917.* New Milford, Conn.: N. Flayderman and Co., 1965.

Ganoe, William Addeman. *The History of the United States Army.* New York: D. Appleton and Co., 1924.

Garavaglia, Louis A., and Worman, Charles G. *Firearms of the American West, 1866–1894.* Albuquerque: University of New Mexico Press, 1985.

Giese, Dale F., ed. *My Life with the Army in the West: The Memoirs of James E. Farmer, 1858–1898.* Santa Fe, N.M.: Stagecoach Press, 1967.

Gluckman, Major Arcadi. *United States Martial Pistols and Revolvers.* Buffalo, N.Y.: Ken Worthy Press, 1939.

Graham, Ron; Kopec, John; and Moore, C. Kenneth. *A Study of the Colt Single Action Army Revolver.* Dallas: Taylor Publishing Co., 1976.

Graham, W. A. *The Custer Myth: A Source Book of Custeriana.* New York: Bonanza Books, 1953.

BIBLIOGRAPHY

Greene, Jerome A. *Yellowstone Command: Colonel Nelson A. Miles and the Great Sioux War, 1876–1877*. Lincoln: University of Nebraska Press, 1991.

Hammer, Kenneth, ed. *Custer in '76: Walter Camp's Notes on the Custer Fight*. Provo, Utah: Brigham Young University Press, 1976.

Hardin, Albert N., Jr. *The American Bayonet, 1776–1964*. Pennsauken, N.J.: Albert N. Hardin, Jr., 1964.

Hardin, Albert N., and Hedden, Robert W. *Light but Efficient: A Study of the M1880 Hunting and M1890 Intrenching Knives and Scabbards*. Dallas: Taylor Publishing Co., 1973.

Hardorff, Richard G. *The Custer Battle Casualties: Burials, Exhumations, and Reinterments*. El Segundo, Calif.: Upton and Sons, Publishers, 1989.

Hebard, Grace Raymond, and Brininstool, E. A. *The Bozeman Trail: Historical Accounts of Blazing of the Overland Routes into the Northwest, and Fights with Red Cloud's Warriors*. Glendale, Calif.: Arthur Clark Co., 1960.

Hedren, Paul L. *With Crook in the Black Hills: Stanley J. Morrow's 1876 Photographic Legacy*. Boulder, Colo.: Pruett Publishing Co., 1985.

Hicks, Major James E. *U.S. Military Firearms, 1776–1956*. La Canada, Calif.: James E. Hicks and Son, 1962.

Hickox, Ron G. *Collector's Guide to Ames U.S. Contract Military Edged Weapons: 1832–1906*. 1992.

Howell, Edgar M. *United States Army Headgear, 1855–1902: Catalog of United States Army Uniforms in the Collections of the Smithsonian Institution*, vol. 2. Washington, D.C.: Smithsonian Institution, 1975.

Howell, Edgar M., and Kloster, Donald E. *United States Army Headgear to 1854: Catalog of United States Army Uniforms in the Collections of the Smithsonian Institution*, vol. 1. (Washington, D.C.: Smithsonian Institution Press, 1969).

Hunt, Frazier, and Hunt, Robert, eds. *I Fought with Custer: The Story of Sergeant Windolph, Last Survivor of the Battle of the Little Big Horn*. New York: Charles Scribner's Sons, 1947.

Hutchins, James S. *Boots and Saddles at the Little Big Horn: Weapons, Dress, Uniforms, Equipment, Horses, and Flags Of General Custer's Seventh U.S. Cavalry in 1876*. Fort Collins, Colo.: Old Army Press, 1976.

Jacobsen, Jacques, Jr., ed. *Regulations and Notes for the Uniform of the Army of the United States, 1861*. Reprint. Staten Island, N.Y.: Manor Publishing, 1978.

————. *Regulations and Notes for the Uniform of the Army of the United States, 1872*. Reprint. Staten Island, N.Y.: Manor Publishing, 1972.

————. *Regulations and Notes for the Uniform of the Army of the United States, 1882*. Reprint. Staten Island, N.Y.: Manor Publishing, 1971.

Jocelyn, Stephen Perry. *Mostly Alkali*. Caldwell, Idaho: Caxton Printers, 1953.

Katcher, Philip. *U.S. Infantry Equipments, 1775–1910*. London: Osprey Publishing, 1989.

Kautz, Brigadier General August V. *Customs of Service for Non-Commissioned Officers and Soldiers*. Philadelphia: J. B. Lippincott and Co., 1864.

Keenan, Jerry. *The Wagon Box Fight*. Sheridan, Wyo.: Fort Phil Kearny/Bozeman Trail Association, 1990.

King, Captain Charles. *Campaigning with Crook and Stories of Army Life*. New York: Harper and Brothers, 1890.

————, *Trials of a Staff Officer*. Philadelphia: J. B. Lippincott Co., 1895.

Langellier, John Phillip. *They Continually Wear the Blue: U.S. Army Enlisted Dress Uniforms, 1865–1902*. San Francisco: Barnes-McGee Historical Military Publications, 1974.

Langellier, J. Phillip, and Woodcock, Michael L. *Chevrons of the United States Army, 1861–1897*. Vol. 1, San Rafael, Calif.: American Military Tradition, n.d.

Lewis, Berkeley R. *Small Arms and Ammunition in the United States Service*. Washington, D.C.: Smithsonian Institution, 1956.

McChristian, Douglas C. *An Army of Marksmen: The Development of United States Army Marksmanship in the Nineteenth Century*. Fort Collins: Old Army Press, 1981.

McConnell, H. H. *Five Years a Cavalryman; Or, Sketches of Regular Army Life on the Texas Frontier Twenty Odd Years Ago.* Freeport, N.Y.: Books for Libraries Press, 1970.

Marcot, Roy M. *Spencer Repeating Firearms.* Edited by Charles R. Suydam and Gerald Denning. Irvine, Calif.: Northwood Heritage Press, 1983.

Marquis, Thomas B., interpreter. *Wooden Leg: A Warrior Who Fought Custer.* Lincoln: University of Nebraska Press.

Meadows, Edward Scott. *U.S. Military Holsters and Pistol Cartridge Boxes.* Dallas: Taylor Publishing Co., 1987.

Meyers, Augustus. *Ten Years in the Ranks, U.S. Army.* New York: Stirling Press, 1914. Reprint. New York: Arno Press, 1979.

Miles, Nelson A. *Personal Recollections and Observations of General Nelson A. Miles.* Chicago: Werner Co., 1896.

Mills, Anson. *My Story.* Edited by C. H. Claudy. Washington, D.C.: Byron S. Adams Press, 1921.

Mulford, Ami Frank. *Fighting Indians in the Seventh United States Cavalry.* Reprint. Bellevue, Nebr.: Old Army Press, 1970.

1911 Francis Bannerman Catalogue. New York, 1911.

Norton, Charles B. *American Breech-Loading Small Arms: A Description of Late Inventions, Including the Gatling Gun and a Chapter on Cartridges, 1872.* Reprint. Arvada, Colo.: Frontier Press, 1974.

Ostrander, Major Alson B. *An Army Boy of the Sixties: A Story of the Plains.* New York: World Book Co., 1924.

Parsons, John E. *The Peacemaker and Its Rivals: An Account of the Single Action Colt.* New York: William Morrow and Co., 1950.

_____. *Smith & Wesson Revolvers: The Pioneer Single Action Models.* New York: William Morrow and Co., 1957.

Peterson, Harold L. *The American Sword, 1775–1945.* Philadelphia: Ray Riling Books Co., 1965.

Phillips, William G., and Vervloet, John P. *U.S. Single Action Cartridge Handgun Holsters, 1870–1910.* Alexandria, Va.: Museum Restoration Service, 1987.

Railsback, Thomas C., and Langellier, John P. *The Drums Would Roll: A Pictorial History of U.S. Army Bands on the American Frontier, 1866–1900.* Poole, Eng.: Arms and Armour Press, 1987.

Reedstrom, Ernest L. *Bugles, Banners, and War Bonnets.* Caldwell, Idaho: Caxton Printers, 1977.

Regulations of the Army of the United States, 1857. New York: Harper and Brothers, Publishers, 1857.

Reilly, Robert M. *American Socket Bayonets and Scabbards.* Lincoln, R.I.: Andrew Mowbray, 1990.

Reneau, Susan C. *The Adventures of Moccasin Joe: The True Life Story of Sgt. George S. Howard.* Missoula, Mont.: Blue Mountain Publishing, 1994.

Rickey, Don, Jr. *Forty Miles a Day on Beans and Hay: The Enlisted Soldier Fighting the Indian Wars.* Norman: University of Oklahoma Press, 1966.

Ryan, John. *Ten Years with General Custer among the American Indians.* Edited by John M. Carroll. Bryan, Tex.: J. M. Carroll, 1980.

Scott, Douglas D. *A Sharp Little Affair: The Archeology of the Big Hole Battlefield.* Reprints in Anthropology Volume 45. Lincoln, Nebr.: J & L Reprints, 1994.

_____, ed. *Papers on Little Bighorn Archeology: The Equipment Dump, Marker 7, and the Reno Crossing.* Reprints in Anthropology Volume 42. Lincoln, Nebr.: J & L Reprint Co., 1991.

Scott, Douglas D.; Fox, Richard A., Jr.; Connor, Melissa; and Harmon, Dick. *Archeological Perspectives on the Battle of the Little Bighorn.* Norman: University of Oklahoma Press, 1989.

Shockley, Colonel Philip M. *The Trap-Door Springfield in the Service.* Aledo, Ill.: World Wide Gun Report, 1958.

Steffen, Randy. *The Horse Soldier, 1776–1943, the United States Cavalryman: His Uniforms, Arms, Accoutrements, and Equipments.* 4 vols., Norman: University of Oklahoma Press, 1979.

Sutherland, R. Q., and Wilson, R. L. *The Book of Colt Firearms.* Kansas City, Mo.: Robert Q. Sutherland, 1971.

Sylvia, Stephen W., and O'Donnell, Michael J. *Civil War Canteens.* Orange, Va.: Moss Publications, 1983.

Todd, Frederick P. *American Military Equipage, 1851–1872.* Providence, R.I.: Company of Military Historians, 1974.

Uniform Regulations for the Army of the United States, 1861. Reprint. Washington, D.C.: Smithsonian Institution, 1961.

Upton, Brevet Major General Emory. *A New System of Infantry Tactics Double and Single Rank Adapted to American Topography and Improved Firearms.* New York: D. Appleton and Co., 1867.

U.S. Army Uniforms and Equipment, 1889: Specifications for Clothing, Camp, and Garrison Equipage, and Clothing and Equipage Materials. Reprint. Lincoln: University of Nebraska Press, 1986.

Waite, M. D., and Ernst, B. D. *Trapdoor Springfield: The United States Springfield Single-Shot Rifle, 1865–1893.* North Hollywood, Calif.: Beinfeld Publishing, 1980.

Weibert, Don. *Custer, Cases, and Cartridges.* Billings, Mont.: Don Weibert, 1989.

ARTICLES AND PERIODICALS

Army and Navy Journal. New York, 1866–80.

Cordy, Anne E., and Yeh, Kwan-nan. "Investigation of Thread Colour Change in United States Civil War Uniforms." *Textile History* 17, no. 1 (1986): 91–98.

Gaede, Frederick C. "The 'Danish Exchange' US Army Blanket." *Military Collector and Historian* 36, no. 2 (Summer 1984): 64–66.

Green, J. Edward. "Notes on the 1874 McKeever." *Military Collector and Historian* 29, no. 1 (Spring 1977): 40–41, 43.

————. "Bacon or Bullets: A Study of the Dyer Cartridge Pouch." *Man at Arms* 3, no. 5 (September/October 1981): 28–30.

Greene, Jerome A. "The U.S. Army Buffalo Overcoat and M1883 Canvas Blanket-Lined Overcoat on the Northern Plains Frontier, 1876–1891." *Military Collector and Historian* 44, no. 2 (Summer 1992): 73–79.

Hedren, Paul L. "Army Tin Cups on the Western Frontier." *Military Collector and Historian* 44, no. 2 (Summer 1992): 57–63.

Hill, Michael D., and Innis, Ben, eds. "The Fort Buford Diary of Private Sanford, 1876–1877." *North Dakota History* 52, no. 3 (Summer 1985).

Hutchins, James S. "The Cavalry Campaign Outfit at the Little Big Horn." *Military Collector and Historian* 7, no. 4 (Winter 1956): 91–101.

————. "The Army Campaign Hat of 1872." *Military Collector and Historian* 16, no. 3, (Fall 1964): 65–73.

————. "The Dodge Blanket Roll Support." *Military Collector and Historian* 20, no. 3 (Fall 1968): 92–95.

————, ed. "Captain Michaelis Reports on Army Weapons and Equipment on the Northern Plains." *Man at Arms* 10, no. 1 (January–February 1988): 27–37.

Innis, Ben, ed. "The Fort Buford Diary of Pvt. Sanford." *North Dakota History* 33, no. 4 (Fall 1966): 335–78.

Johnson, Paul D. "Identifying Civil War Cavalry Carbine Cartridge Boxes." *Military Collector and Historian* 40, no. 1 (Spring 1988): 109–19.

Kloster, Donald E. "Uniforms of the Army Prior and Subsequent to 1872." Parts 1, 2. *Military Collector and Historian* 14, no. 4 (Winter 1962): 103–12; 15, no. 1 (Spring 1963): 6–14.

Langellier, J. Phillip. "Digging In: Early U.S. Army Entrenching Tools, 1865–1895." *Man at Arms* 6, no. 1, (January/February 1984): 40–45.

Lord, Francis. "Mann's Accouterments of the Civil War." *Military Collector and Historian* 27, no. 1 (Spring 1975): 20–22.

McBarron, H. Charles. "36th Illinois Infantry Regiment, 1863." *Military Collector and Historian* 9, no. 2 (Spring 1957): 39–41.

McChristian, Douglas C. "The Model 1876 Cartridge Belt." *Military Collector and Historian* 34, no. 3 (Fall 1982): 109–16.

————. "Company C, 3rd Cavalry: Equipment Analysis." *Military Images Magazine* 4, no. 5 (March–April 1983): 4–6.

Perry, Milton F. "Lieutenant Metcalfe's Detachable Magazine." *Military Collector and Historian,* 11, no. 2 (Summer 1959): 40–44.

Phillips, William G. "Emerson Steel Bayonet Scabbard 1862." *Military Collector and Historian* 21, no. 3 (Fall 1969): 97–98.

————. "The Evolution of the Pocket-Type Rifle Cartridge Belt in the United States Service." *Military Collector and Historian* 22, no. 1 (Spring 1970): 1–10.

————. "Cavalry Accoutrements, 1874: The Rare Pieces." *Military Collector and Historian* 44, no. 2 (Summer 1992): 98–102.

————. "The Woven Cartridge Belt, 1879–1903." *Military Collector and Historian* 44, no. 2 (Summer 1992).

Phillips, William G., and Carter, Rila. "Oblate Spheroid Canteens, 1858–1916: A Standard Pattern Recognition Guide." *Military Collector and Historian* 41, no. 2 (Summer 1989): 66–78.

Sword, Wiley. "Custer's Seventh Cavalry Firearms." Parts 1, 2. *Arms Gazette* 1, no. 10 (June 1974): 33–33, 52–53; 1, no. 12 (August 1974): 34–38.

Index